History of Maryland

You are holding a reproduction of an original work that is in the public domain in the United States of America, and possibly other countries.You may freely copy and distribute this work as no entity (individual or corporate) has a copyright on the body of the work.This book may contain prior copyright references, and library stamps (as most of these works were scanned from library copies).These have been scanned and retained as part of the historical artifact.

This book may have occasional imperfections such as missing or blurred pages, poor pictures, errant marks, etc. that were either part of the original artifact, or were introduced by the scanning process. We believe this work is culturally important, and despite the imperfections, have elected to bring it back into print as part of our continuing commitment to the preservation of printed works worldwide. We appreciate your understanding of the imperfections in the preservation process, and hope you enjoy this valuable book.

The Landing of The Pilgrims of Maryland.

HISTORY OF MARYLAND,

BY

JAMES McSHERRY.

EDITED AND CONTINUED BY

BARTLETT B. JAMES, PH D (Johns Hopkins)
WESTERN MARYLAND COLLEGE.

Author of "The Labadist Colony in Maryland," "History of The Women of Great Britain," "The Colonization of New England"

BALTIMORE
THE BALTIMORE BOOK CO
1904.

WITHDRAWN

Copyright
BY
THE BALTIMORE BOOK COMPANY
1904

AUTHOR'S PREFACE

The editor of the work which it is the purpose of these brief preliminary words to present to the public for its sufferance and, it is hoped, a measure of satisfaction, has held in mind during his labors certain facts which he conceived to be fundamental in his undertaking

Conformity of style and literary usage was regarded as important. Following the line of least resistance, he undertook to adapt the style of Mr McSherry to that of his own rather than to affect a manner of writing which to him would have been forced and unnatural, and certainly to the reader clumsy and unrewarding Numerous verbal changes have therefore been made throughout the text A certain fulsomeness which appears especially in the eulogies in the work has been corrected These and similar literary changes embrace the greater part of the exercise of the editorial function up to the chapter which relates to the close of the Revolutionary War From that period to the end of the work the story was too meager to have linked to it the great subsequent events of Maryland's history It thus became necessary to rewrite the work from that point, although in so doing everything of the author's has found incorporation, although not always *in situ* A comparison with the original work will show the large extent of the amplification which was found to be necessary

The part of the book for which the writer is wholly responsible he would prefer to submit without a word other than one of acknowledgment of indebtedness to the authors to whom he makes reference in his foot notes, especially those who have illuminated particular facts of Maryland's history by scholarly monographs

To Mr William Morse Keener, LL B, he makes grateful acknowledgment for services in the reading of proof and otherwise relieving him of irksome features of his task

If the complete history of Maryland herewith offered to the reader shall be found a fairly satisfactory treatment of its subject and shall fill a mission of usefulness in enlarging popular knowledge of the State's great past and shall serve to inculcate patriotic sentiments in the rising generation he shall feel that he has not worked in vain

BARTLETT BURLEIGH JAMES.

Baltimore, April 20. 1904

HISTORY OF MARYLAND.

INTRODUCTORY CHAPTER

THE discovery of America in 1492, by Christopher Columbus, at a time when the chivalry of Spain was in its brightest and latest glory, threw open to the brave spirits fresh from the conquest of Granada, and the victorious battle fields of Italy, a new world, full of wild adventures, of novel wonders, and teeming, in their fancies, with measureless riches. The graceful forms of a strange race, whose complexions were tinted with the hues of the sun, the gorgeous specimens of their wealth and their works of art, displayed before the admiring court of Ferdinand and Isabella, turned all hearts towards this El Dorado of the west; and the discovery of the beautiful isles of the great gulf, was followed by the conquest of Mexico and of Peru by the exploration through the swamps of Florida and the plains of Louisiana in quest of the fabled waters of perpetual life — expeditions wilder than any ever sketched out before in the fancy of the novelist, or the song of the minstrel, sometimes crowned with success, ofttimes disastrous in the extreme.

The rich mines of the south, its fertile soil spontaneously producing alike the necessaries and luxuries of life, its beautiful sky and its balmy air, similar to, but surpassing their own, allured the Spaniard and the Portugese, who never once turned their steps to the colder climate and the temperate skies of a more northern latitude, a century passed before another race, from a congenial land, shaped their course towards that people, excelling in wealth, in freedom, in the arts, the dwellers in the more enervating countries of the south.

But the one was fostered and cherished by the blasting kindness of a royal hand — the other grew up, untended and unheeded, breasting the storms, providing for its own safety, protecting itself and gaining from use the strength of manhood, even in its early infancy. The Spaniards cast their lot amongst a semi-civilized race, whom they subdued, and with whom they intermingled their blood, and became a royal government over a conquered people. The English came to build up their empire in a wild, uncultivated forest, with a savage foe around them. Thus it was that the mingled race of the north, composed, as in time it came to be, of many different peoples, gathered the best features from each. The colonists of Spain, carefully nursed by the crown, and swaddled into weakness and effeminacy, deteriorated by commingling with an inferior race.

Scarcely had the report of the wonderful discoveries of Columbus reached the court of Henry the Seventh, of England, before the spirit of adventure awoke in that kingdom, and an expedition was planned by a citizen of Venice, domiciled in England, Giovanni Caboto — or John Cabot, as he is usually called — for the purpose of exploring a more convenient route to the Indies, a portion of which the recent Spanish acquisitions were supposed to be. Many delays occurred from the want of sufficient aid to undertake the voyage, and it was not until a short time before the death of John Cabot that the king consented to further the enterprise, by issuing his license, dated on the 3d of February, 1498, authorizing him " to seize upon six English ships in any port or ports of the realm of England, of 200 tons burthen or under, with their requisite apparatus, &c "* Upon the death of his father, Sebastian Cabot applied to the king for assistance to carry out the design. He was furnished with one ship at the royal expense, while three or four more were fitted out by the merchants of Bristol. In May, 1498, the fleet weighed anchor, and after several weeks sailing due west, discovered land, which they

---
* Bozman's Maryland, vol 1, p 12

called Newfoundland. A few days after, they made another island, which they named St John. Still pursuing a western course, Cabot reached the main land, just in season to contest with the Spanish navigators the honor of having first touched the Continent of America. He coasted along the newly discovered shores as far south as the thirty-eighth degree of north latitude, when his provisions falling short, and a mutiny breaking out among the sailors, he was compelled to put about and steer for England, where he arrived in safety It is highly probable that Cabot, in this voyage, discovered and touched upon the Atlantic coast of Maryland, which lies within the thirty-eighth and thirty-ninth degrees The eastern shore of Worcester county was, therefore, the last portion of the continent which he visited. Several abortive attempts were made to follow up the discoveries of Cabot, but during the remainder of the reign, the spirit of enterprise appeared to have died away, or turned to other objects In the meanwhile, the French, Spanish and Portugese prosecuted their discoveries with unabated zeal and complete success Giovanni Verazzini, a Florentine, in the service of France, made three voyages of discovery along the coast of North America, the second of which, in 1524, afterwards became famous, as the foundation of much of the French claims to their extensive possessions in the New World. But the only interest which these explorations have to the student of Maryland history, lies in the fact that the Florentine was the second navigator who passed along the shores of that state, and the first to cross the mouth of the Chesapeake The bay itself was discovered in 1585 by Governor Lane of the first colony of Virginia. Yet this vast inlet was not traversed for some years It is said that Captain Bartholomew Gilbert, in 1603, was the first to enter and explore it

Somewhat more than a century passed, from the discovery of North America by Cabot, before any successful attempt was made by the English to colonize it. These enterprises are, to a certain extent, connected with the history of Maryland, and therefore need to be touched on here In the year 1606 the London and Plymouth Companies were formed and, by letters patent issued on the tenth day of April in that year, the portion of the Continent lying between the thirty-fourth and forty-fifth degrees north latitude, was granted to them in nearly equal shares,— the territory from the first-mentioned degree to the forty-first being assigned to the London, and from the thirty-eighth to the forty-fifth to the Plymouth Company; and, as by this provision there was a territory of three degrees in extent which was common to both, it was further specified, that the party who first settled within this region, thus overlapped by the two grants, should possess the coast fifty miles each way from the point of settlement, and one hundred miles to the interior, while no settlement was to be made by the other company within one hundred miles thereof.

The London Company immediately began their preparations, which, although they were completed somewhat later than those of the Plymouth Company, were productive of greater results The fleet consisting of a vessel of one hundred tons, one of forty and one of twenty, with one hundred and five colonists on board, set sail from Blackwall, on the Thames, on the 19th of December, 1606, under the command of Capt. Christopher Newport * He carried sealed instructions which were not to be opened until his arrival in Virginia After encountering many difficulties and delays, the ships had nearly reached their destination at Roanoke, when on the 26th of April, they were driven by a violent storm into the Chesapeake Here Captain Newport opened his instructions, which provided for a council of seven for the government of the colony In the early part of May they began to explore the James river, and having received a beautiful peninsula from an Indian chief, they laid the foundation of Jamestown on the 13th of May, 1607.

The new colonists suffered much from scarcity of provisions, frequent attacks of the savages, and internal dissen-

---

* Bozman, vol i. p 99

sions; and, but for the prudence and energy of Capt. John Smith, would very probably have met with the same evil fate which befell former settlements. At length, however, the arrival of two ships from England laden with supplies, relieved their present necessities and increased their numbers by seasonable reinforcements But instead of seeking in the cultivation of the soil the true wealth of the earth, the Virginians turned their whole attention to gathering cargoes of glittering sands for the returning ships. In vain Smith remonstrated; the discovery of this imaginary gold had intoxicated them, and they scorned the humbler but surer resources of agriculture The consequences were soon felt in a growing scarcity of food

Smith was not idle Turning his eyes towards that vast inland sea near whose mouth they were situated, he judged rightly that an exploration of its shores would open extensive resources to the colonists, by means of trade with the Indians On the 2d of June, 1608, in an open boat, accompanied by a physician, Dr. Russel, six gentlemen and seven soldiers, he departed from the fort at Jamestown on this daring expedition. They boldly struck across the bay, and having discovered Smith's Islands, made the eastern shore, and were directed by two Indians whom they found there, to the habitation of the Werowance, or chief of their tribe, at Accomac. Departing thence, they examined many creeks and harbors, discovered some islands, which they named Russel's — now known as Watts' Islands, and after naming several points, at length reached the river Wighcocomo or Wighco, supposed to be the Pocomoke, whose mouth afterwards became the southern point of boundary in the charter of the province of Maryland. After suffering from lack of water, and being driven about by storms, they entered the Nanticoke river, called by the Indians Cuskarawaock, where the natives assembled in large numbers to oppose their landing. A few shots proved sufficient to disperse them. In the course of several days, however, a good understanding was established and the Indians vied with each other in supplying the wants of the strangers, considering a few beads an ample remuneration for all they could bestow. Not satisfied with the appearance of the eastern shore, they passed out through Hooper's straits, or the Straits of Limbo, as they named them, and stood directly for the cliffs on the western coast, along which they sailed thirty leagues northward, finding no inhabitants. They were now some distance above the Patapsco, which river they described as navigable for ships, and named Bolus, supposing the red and white earth upon the banks to be *bole armoniack* They had already been in their open boat fourteen days, and their provisions were much damaged by water, and the men themselves, worn out with laboring at the oars, besought their captain to return He succeeded in persuading them to continue the exploration three or four days; at the end of which time several of the men falling sick, and the complaints of the remainder becoming louder, Smith, after having reached as far north as Poole's Island, steered towards the south. On the 16th of June they discovered the Potowmac, or *Patawomek*, up which they sailed about thirty miles, where after meeting with a hostile reception, they landed on the Virginia shore. From this place, about Nominy Bay, they continued up the river, touching at various points, until they had passed the present site of Washington, "having gone as high as they could in their boat" Here they were met by savages in canoes, loaded with the flesh of deer, bears and other animals, of which they obtained a portion. After many adventures, they reached Jamestown in safety, on the 21st of July, one month and nineteen days from the date of their departure.

Not satisfied with the results of his expedition, the indefatigable Smith fitted out another, being accompanied by most of those who had been with him on the first They set out on the 24th of July, 1608, and made directly towards the mouth of the Patapsco Thence they proceeded to the head of the bay and explored the entrances of the Susquehanna, Northeast, Elk, and Sassafras rivers. The banks of the Susquehanna and the Sassafras or as Smith called it the Toghwogh, they found inhabited On the bay they met seven or eight canoes of Massawomek Indians who prepared to assault them, they, however, by signs, obtained an amicable conference. They sailed up the Sassafras, where the natives received them with the greatest kindness, danced before them, and offered them fruits and furs There they learned that the Susquehannas, residing on the river of the same name, were considered to be the most warlike and powerful tribe of that region Having fully explored the head of the bay, and the Susquehanna as far as they could penetrate, which was to the point called Smith's Falls, they returned to Virginia after an absence of three months * In 1620, the bay was again explored by Mr. John Pory, who visited several towns belonging to the savages inhabiting its shores †

The Virginia Company, having become dissatisfied with their charter, petitioned the king for a new one, which was accordingly issued on the 23d of May, A. D. 1609 By it the king granted and confirmed to them " all those lands, countries and territories, situate, lying and being in that part of America, from Point Comfort all along the sea coast northward two hundred miles," and to the same extent southward, " and all that space and circuit of land lying from the sea coast of the precinct aforesaid, up into the land throughout, from sea to sea, west and north-west, and all the islands lying within one hundred miles along the coast of both seas of the precinct aforesaid."

Three years after, in 1612, finding new powers necessary, the Company applied for a third charter, which was issued to them on the 12th of March, 1611-12 and was confirmatory of the second charter Disputes having arisen in the Company, the crown became hostile to its continuance, and a writ of quo warranto was issued against it in November, 1623. In May, 1624, judgment was given against the Company in King's Bench, and its charters forfeited. The administration of its affairs was taken under the immediate control of the

---
* Smith in Bozman—the notes of Bozman upon him, vol 1, pp 105 to 133
† Ibid, p. 148

crown, the settlement reduced to a royal government, and a commission issued by the king to a provisional council for the direction of its affairs Thus the extensive territory, heretofore granted to the late London Company, reverted to the crown and became the subject of grants for the erection of new provinces.

Among those who had become interested in the London or Virginia Company, under its second charter, in 1609, was Sir George Calvert He had been educated at Trinity College, Oxford, where he took his degree of Bachelor of Arts in 1597 and finished his education by a tour on the Continent On his return he obtained an office at the court, under Sir Robert Cecil, one of the principal secretaries of state In 1617 he was knighted by the king, having been appointed one of the clerks of the privy council. In 1619 he became one of the secretaries of state, an office which he filled with honor to himself and great profit to his sovereign, whose high estimate of his services was proved by the grant of a pension of one thousand pounds a year, which he bestowed upon him in 1620 In the warm debates in the House of Commons, where he represented. first Yorkshire, in 1620, and, subsequently, the University of Oxford he always maintained the rights and protected the interests of the king, and that monarch, afterwards, did not fail to prove his grateful recollection of his loyalty Sir George Calvert had early engaged in the schemes of colonization of that period, and upon the dissolution of the Virginia Company, of which he had been a member, he was named by the king one of the royal commissioners to whom the government of that colony was confided

Up to this time he had been a Protestant. but in 1624, having become unsettled in his religious convictions, he renounced the Church of England, and embraced the faith of the Catholic church Moved by conscientious scruples, he determined no longer to hold the office of secretary of state, which would make him, in a manner, the instrument of persecution against those whose faith he had adopted, and tendered his resignation to the king, informing him that "he was now become a Roman Catholic, so that he must be wanting in his trust or violate his conscience in discharging his office." The king was moved by his honest avowal, and while he accepted his resignation, continued him as a member of his privy council for life, and soon after created him Lord Baltimore, of Baltimore in Ireland.

The laws against the Catholics in England were particularly severe, and rendered it impossible for such persons to practice their religion in quiet and safety. Sir George Calvert, although he was assured of protection from the gratitude and affection of the king, determined to seek another land and to found a new state, where conscience should be free and every man might worship God in peace and perfect security.* It was a grand and noble design, and he set about perfecting it. At first he fixed his eyes on Newfoundland, in the settlement of which he had been interested. Having purchased a ship, he sailed with his family to that island in which, a few years before, he had obtained a grant of a province under the name of Avalon.** Here he only resided two years, when finding the climate and soil unsuited for the establishment of a flourishing community, he determined to seek a more genial country in the south. Accordingly, in 1628, he sailed to Virginia,† with the intention of settling within the limits of that colony, or more probably to explore the uninhabited country on its borders, in order to secure a grant of it from the king Upon his arrival within the jurisdiction of the colony, the authorities tendered him the oaths of allegiance and supremacy, to which, as then framed, he could not conscientiously subscribe Lord Baltimore refused to take them, but prepared a form of oath of allegiance which he and all his followers were willing to accept. His proposal was rejected, and being compelled to leave their waters, he explored the Chesapeake

---

* McMahon, 193
** A D. 1623, Bozman, vol 1, p 240
† McMahon, 193

above the settlements ‡ He was pleased with the beautiful and well-wooded country, which surrounded the noble inlets of the great bay, and determined there to found his principality, assured that he had selected a territory possessing all the elements of future prosperity — fertile in soil, traversed by majestic rivers, and enjoying a climate unsurpassed upon the continent He returned to England to obtain a grant from Charles I, who had succeeded his father, James I Remembering his services to his house, Charles directed the patent to be issued. It was prepared by Lord Baltimore himself, but before it was finally executed, that great and good man died, and the patent was delivered to his son Cecilius, who succeeded as well to his noble designs, as to his titles and estates

The charter was issued on the 20th of June, 1632, and the new province, in honor of Queen Henrietta Maria, was named *Terra Mariæ* — MARYLAND.

The charter was a grant from the king to Lord Baltimore, and his heirs and assigns, of all the territory lying within the limits set forth, with extensive jurisdiction and powers of government over it. The rights of the settler were fully provided for in this instrument The power of making laws was jointly vested in the people or their representatives, and the lord Proprietary — the title conferred upon Lord Baltimore — although extraordinary power was reserved to the latter, or his governor, in cases of sudden emergency, when the people or their delegates could not be well assembled The province was forever exempted from taxation by the crown, except with its own consent, and many other important privileges were secured The eclesiastical laws of England with regard to churches and chapels, in so far as they related to the matters of consecration and presentation were extended to the colony, but the question of state religion was left untouched, and therefore within the legislative power of the colonists themselves. The king reserved to himself one-fifth of the gold and silver which might be found in the province, and the yearly

‡ Bozman, vol I, pp 255-258, McMahon, 9

HISTORY OF MARYLAND 15

tribute of two Indian arrows. Having thus a noble territory, with his rights and the prosperity of his future state secured by a liberal charter, Lord Baltimore prepared to establish his first settlement in Maryland He fitted out two vessels, which he named the *"Ark"* and the *"Dove,"* and collected a body of two hundred emigrants, nearly all of whom were Catholics and gentlemen of fortune and respectability, who desired, like himself, as had his father, to flee from the spirit of intolerance which pervaded England, and to rear their altars in freedom in the wilderness * The colonists were accompanied by two Jesuit priests, Fathers Andrew White and John Altham, and were placed under the command of Leonard Calvert, whom his brother, the Lord Proprietary, had appointed Governor of Maryland, intending to remain in England for the present to superintend in person the interests of the settlement in its infancy, and to send out additional emigrants.

---

* Burnap, Bozman, McMahon
† Relatio Itineris in Marylandiam—Bozman, vol 2, p 26

CHAPTER I.

THE FIRST SETTLEMENT OF MARYLAND.

"On the 22d day of November, 1633, being St. Cecilia's day, the 'Ark' and the 'Dove' weighed anchor from Cowes, in the Isle of Wight." The pious pilgrims " placed their ships under the protection of God, imploring the intercession of the Blessed Virgin, of St. Ignatius, and all the guardian angels of Maryland,"* for the success of the great enterprise which they had undertaken. They left behind them the homes, in which they had been born, their friends and relatives, to face the dangers of the sea, and the perils and hardships of a wilderness, in order to plant the seed of freedom and religious liberty, to secure to themselves and their chilrden the inestimable privilege of worshiping God according to the dictates of their consciences. It was a mighty undertaking; standing out, in history, as an era in the progress of mankind

The pilgrims narrowly escaped the Needles, a series of breakers at the extremity of the Isle of Wight, but, relying on the protection of God, they drove boldly out to sea under a strong and steady breeze. No sooner had they escaped this peril, than the fear of capture by the Turks, whose cruisers were then a terror to all Christian nations, kept them in constant alarm for the safety of the "Dove," which was neither so good a sailer, nor so well manned and armed as the "Ark." After a time they were joined by a London merchantman, the "*Dragon,*" well armed, and bound for Angola, and, thus being relieved by the strength of their fleet from all fear of danger, they continued their voyage in high spirits, " making the air and sky resound with the clangor of trumpets"

---

* Relatio Itin, &c Father White's manuscript is the authority for this whole chapter.

On the evening of the 25th of November, the wind veered around to the north, and a violent storm arose. The crew of the Dragon, fearing to encounter its full fury, changed their course and steered for England, while the company on board the Dove, dreading the effect of the furious tempest upon their little bark, yet unwilling to abandon the enterprize, notified the officers of the larger vessel that if they were in danger of shipwreck, they would hang out a light from the mast head. The captain of the Ark, knowing the strength of his vessel, bore steadily on his course. In the middle of the night the storm increased in violence, and the crew of the larger vessel, beheld with dismay two lights suspended from the mast head of the pinnace. But they were unable to afford their comrades any assistance; and, in a few moments, these lights disappeared, and with sorrowful hearts they gave up the little Dove, and her gallant crew, as lost. When morning at length broke over their long and dreary night, there was no sign or vestige of the Dove upon the waters. The storm still raged with somewhat diminished fury, and during the three succeeding days, Tuesday, Wednesday and Thursday, the Ark was tossed about by contrary winds, making little headway. At length, on the night of the third day, the rain began to descend in torrents, and a sudden blast of the tempest split the mainsail from top to bottom. The vessel, having unshipped her rudder, was driven about at the mercy of the waves. The minds of the bravest were filled with fear, for the Ark seemed about to be engulfed in the raging billows. The pilgrims betook themselves to prayer, and many strove, by the sacrament of penance, to prepare themselves to meet the fate which now seemed inevitable. But the violence of the storm began to abate. At length the sea became calm, and the remainder of the voyage, which extended through a period of three months, was pleasant and prosperous.*

After passing the Madeira Islands, the pilgrims became alarmed at the appearance of three supicious looking vessels, which were bearing down towards them. The captain imme-

---

* Narratio Itineris, &c

diately cleared his ship for action, but the supposed pirates soon changed their course and disappeared They continued on their voyage, and touched at the Fortunate, or as they are now called, the Canary Islands The governor consulted with the principal officers and gentlemen as to the best mode of loading the ship with a return cargo, so as to repay part of the expenses of the expedition, which had been borne entirely by Lord Baltimore At first they determined to steer for St Christopher's, then changed their destination towards Bonavista, one of the Cape de Verde Islands, and a great mart for salt; but after sailing two hundred miles, fearing their provisions would fall short, they altered their course for the Barbadoes, where they arrived on the 5th of January, 1634, O. S Their reception was cold and inhospitable, and the people demanded extravagant prices for the provisions which they desired to purchase. They now learned that a Spanish fleet way lying at Bonavista, and that, had they persisted in their original intention, their capture would have been certain At the Barbadoes, too, a conspiracy amongst the slaves to massacre their masters, and to seize the first ship which should touch at the island, had just been discovered Theirs being the first, would have fallen a sacrifice but for the timely discovery of this plot

There was yet one dark cloud hanging over their prosperity — the disappearance of the pinnace. Imagine, then, their joy when she bore in sight after a separation of six weeks. On the night of the terrific storm which parted them, the Dove, after having shown her signal, no longer able to breast the storm, had changed her course and taken refuge in the Scilly Islands, whence, the ship Dragon bearing her company as far as the Bay of Biscay, she sailed in pursuit of the Ark, and at length overtook her at the Antilles.

On the night of the 24th of January they weighed anchor and departed from the Barbadoes The next day they passed St. Lucia, and in the evening arived at Matalina, where they saw several canoes of cannibals, who they were told had lately eaten some English interpreters. The day after, they reached

Montserrat. They were kindly entertained at St. Christopher's by the governor and two captains, and were also treated with great hospitality by the governor of the French colony in the same island. At length, on the 24th of February, they came in sight of Point Comfort in Virginia. They were now approaching the end of their wanderings. Yet this joyful prospect was somewhat clouded by the fear of hostility on the part of the Virginians, who were resolutely opposed to Lord Baltimore's design. But the royal letters, which they bore with them, secured them a favorable reception from the governor, and, after spending eight or nine days in that colony, they again set sail on the 3d of March, steering for the mouth of the Potomac, to which they gave the name of St. Gregory. They had now arrived in the land of their adoption, and they were delighted with the wide expanse of the noble bay, and the majestic river, upon whose shores they were about to rear an empire. On the banks of the Potomac they found mighty forests stretching as far as the eye could reach, a soil rich and fertile. The air was sweet and balmy, although it was now in the month of March. They returned thanks to God for the beautiful land which he had given them.

On the beach they beheld, during the day, groups of armed natives prepared to resist their landing, and at night they saw innumerable alarm fires kindled throughout the country as signals to the savage tribes, while messengers passed from one to the other far into the interior, carrying the strange tidings "that canoes, as big as an island, had brought as many men as there were trees in the forest." In spite of these demonstrations of apparent hostility, they succeeded in establishing confidence in the breasts of the natives, and having satisfied them that their intentions were peaceful, purchased from them the territory which they required. Maryland's settlement was not marked by the shedding of the blood of the natives.

The ships now approached the Heron Islands, on one of which, St. Clements — thought to be Blackstone's Island — the colonists determined to land, and, although the island was too small for a settlement, to build a strong fort for their protection in case of any outbreak On the feast of "the Annunciation of the Blessed Virgin," being the 25th of March, in the year 1634, they took solemn possession of the soil of Maryland and offered up the holy sacrifice for the first time within its borders Mass was celebrated and the pilgrims formed in procession, led by Governor Leonard Calvert, the secretary, and the other officers, carrying on their shoulders a huge cross, hewn from a tree, which they erected with religious exercises. Under such auspices was begun the founding of Maryland

The chief of the Piscataways was the most powerful in that region, and had many sachems and tribes subject to him. The governor, Leonard Calvert, therefore determined to visit him and secure his friendship. With the Dove and another small pinnace, which he had purchased in Virginia, he set out with a portion of his men, accompanied by Father Altham, leaving the ship at anchor at St. Clements As they advanced up the river, the Indians fled towards the interior. At length they reached a village on the Virginia side, named Potomac, after the river, and governed by Archihu, uncle of the king, yet a youth. Father Altham preached to the people and their chiefs They listened with attention and replied to him through his interpreter He told them that the pale faces had come neither to make war upon them nor to do them any wrong, but to instruct them in Christianity, to make them acquainted with the arts of civilized life, and to live with them like brothers. "You are welcome," replied the chief Then Father Altham informed him that, as he had not the time to enter upon further discourse, he would return to visit him again "It is good," said Archihu, "we will use one table —my people shall hunt for my brother, and all things shall be in common between us"

Having parted with this hospitable chief, Leonard Calvert ascended to Piscataway, where he found the natives armed, and assembled upon the shore to the number of five hundred, ready to dispute his landing. By means of signs, he contrived to make them understand that he came for peace and not for war, and at length, the chief or emperor ventured on board the pinnace. Satisfied of the peaceful intentions of the pilgrims, and pleased to have such skilful and powerful people for his allies, the chief granted them permission to settle within his territories

The savages about St Clements soon became more familiar with the colonists, who were now busily engaged in putting together a brigantine, the planks and timbers of which they had brought out from England

The governor had brought with him, from Virginia, Captain Henry Fleet,* who was well acquainted with the Indian tribes and spoke their language This man now directed them to a spot suitable for the site of a town, and, weighing anchor, the whole colony sailed from St Clements. They entered the mouth of the St Marys river, on the left bank of which was the village of King Yaocomico. On the right shore, about a thousand paces from the river, they selected a site, and having purchased from the Indians, in exchange for hatchets, axes, hoes and cloth, about thirty miles of territory, which they called "Augusta Caroline," now the county of St Marys, they landed and began the founding of the city of St Marys.

The men on shore fired salutes in honor of the occasion, while salvos of artillery from the ships filled the hearts of the savages with wonder and dismay. Thus with ceremonial the pilgrims took possession of the soil, which they had purchased from its native owners This important event took place on the 27th of March, 1634,† and may be considered as the date of the actual settlement of the state, although it would seem, from the solemnities on the island of St Clement, that the pilgrims intended on that day, being the feast of the Annunciation, to take formal possession of the province of Maryland.

---

* The author of the " Relation " says Governor Calvert found him at Piscataway
† Bozman, vol 2, p 30

Although the colonists had used every means to conciliate the Indians, they were aware of the danger of relying too implicitly on their variable natures, and their first work was to erect a guard house and store house. For the present the settlers found refuge in the rude huts of the Indians, who the more readily received them and sold them their villages and corn grounds, and their other territory, because, in order to escape the incursion of the Susquehannahs, they had determined to remove their habitations to another region secure from their terrible enemy. Providence, says Father White, had prepared the way for the pilgrims, and the Indians began already to depart, giving up to them their huts and cultivated fields. The colonists had brought a large supply of provisions with them from England, at the Barbadoes they had increased their stores, and they were now put in possession of arable land just in season to plant their corn for the coming crop. They immediately set about this necessary work, and the ensuing fall gathered so plentiful a crop that they were enabled, after providing for their own subsistence, to send ten thousand bushels to New England in exchange for salt fish and other provisions * The woods abounded with game which the Indians taught them how to hunt, and the rivers and bay were full of fish and oysters. God had indeed bestowed upon the founders of Maryland a beautiful land, flowing with milk

---

* Bozman, vol 2, p 32 The author of "A Relation of Maryland," says, they bought so much corn from the Indians, that they sent 1,000 bushels of it to New England Winthrop says, that the "Dove," a pinnace of fifty tons from Maryland, brought corn to trade with the people of Plymouth colony, with letters from the governor, and the commissioners of Maryland, proposing to open trade between the colonies It seems that quarrels broke out, between the crew of the Dove and the Puritans, and "the merchant" of the Dove (who afterwards died before the pinnace left Plymouth) was taken into custody to secure the appearance of the sailors, who were charged with profanity, &c, and summoned by the governor, on the advice of the ministers, to answer these accusations The proof against them, however, was insufficient, and they were discharged, with a reprimand to their captain —THE AUTHOR

and honey, and had surrounded their path with blessings and
promises of future prosperity and happiness

The huts of the Indians were of an oblong, oval form,
nine or ten feet high, lighted by a hole in the roof, which also
served as a vent for the smoke. They made their fire in the
centre, and slept around it at night. The tents of the chiefs
were larger and contained several apartments, and were supplied with beds, made by poles laid across four stakes, which
were driven in the ground — the whole covered with leaves
or skins. One of these huts was given to Fathers White and
Altham, and was fitted up by them to serve as the first church
in Maryland. The Indians of the neighborhood were tall and
comely, but disfigured themselves with paint. Their dress
was a mantle of deer or other skins, falling from the shoulder,
and an apron about the waist. Around their necks they wore
strings of beads, and upon their foreheads the figure of a fish
worked in copper. Their hair was gathered into one lock, tied
with a fillet and ornamented with feathers. Their weapons
were bows, and arrows barbed with horn or sharpened pieces
of flint stone — heavy clubs of knotted wood hardened in the
fire, spears pointed with flint stone heads, and stone axes with
hickory branches twisted round them for handles. These
spear and arrow heads, and axes, were worked smooth and
to a sharp edge, and sometimes polished like marble. They
were very skilful in the use of their arms, and the bow and
arrow were in their hands no mean weapons. Their principal
food was Indian corn, which they prepared in several ways —
hominy and pone when the corn was ripe and succotash and
roasted ears when young and tender. Each of these modes
the colonists borrowed with some little improvements. To
these preparations they added fish, game and oysters, besides,
they had in proper season strawberries in immense quantities
and nuts of every kind. Thus they lived in the midst of a
simple abundance. They were of a noble disposition, grave,
yet cheerful and kind, generous with what they possessed,
frugal, avoiding intoxicating drinks, chaste in their lives, considerate in forming resolutions, but firm in maintaining them
when formed

They worshiped one God, but they also propitiated the evil spirit whom they called *Okee* Corn and fire were adored as deities in the following manner. The people gathered from the different villages and formed a circle round a great fire, the younger persons in the inner row They then cast a piece of deer's fat into the flame and, with uplifted hands, cried *"Taho! Taho!"* After this they cleared a space and a bag containing a pipe and a powder called *"Potu,"** was produced This bag was carried around the fire, the boys and girls singing in the meanwhile " Taho! Taho!" The pipe and powder were then taken out and each one smoked a short time, breathing the vapor over his limbs to sanctify them Father White says they seemed to have some faint tradition of the flood

Such were the peaceful and gentle Indians, who welcomed the early settlers of Maryland into their midst; alike conferring and receiving favors. For if they sold the pilgrims their territory, taught them how to hunt the deer, to plant maize and prepare it for the table, and shared their huts and their daily food with their white brethren, the colonists explained to them the arts of civilized life, their priests unfolded to them the inestimable privileges of Christianity, and instructed and received many of them into the fold of Christ †

---

* Tobacco?

---

† The above account is taken principally from Father White's Journal, found in Rome by the Rev Wm McSherry, S J, a manuscript copy of which was kindly furnished me from Georgetown College The author of "A Relation" differs from Father White in some particulars, his account is sufficiently interesting, to be inserted here somewhat at large. He says, they sailed from Point Comfort, in Virginia, on the 3d of March, 1634, and two days after reached the Potomac, twenty-four leagues from Point Comfort; and then sailed fourteen leagues up the river, " and came to anchor under an island, which they called St Clement's" Possibly, then, the Maryland Pilgrims *first* landed in their future home on the 6th of March, 1634

After describing the governor's visit to Piscataway, the author proceeds —" While the governor was abroad, the neighboring Indians, where the ships lay, began to cast off fear, and to come to their court of guard, which they kept night and day upon St Clement's isle, partly to defend their barge, which was brought in pieces out of England, and there made up, and partly to defend their men, which were employed in felling trees and cleaving pales for a palizado,— and at last they ventured to come aboard the ship The governor finding it not fit for many reasons to seat himself as yet so high up the river, resolved to return back again and take a more exact view of the lower parts;— so, leaving the ship and pinnaces there, he took his barge, .(as most fit to search the creeks and small rivers) and was conducted by Capt Henry Fleett, who knew well the country, to a river on the north side of Potomac river, within four or five leagues of the mouth thereof, which they called St. George's river They went up this river about four leagues, and anchored at the town of Yaocomico — from whence the Indians of the country are called Yaocomicos At their coming to this place, the governor went on shore, and treated friendly with the Werowance there, and acquainted him with the intent of his coming thither, to which he made little answer, (as it is their manner to any new and sudden question) but entertained him and his company, that night, in his house, and gave him his own bed to lie on (which is a mat laid on boards) and the next day went to show him the country; and that day being spent in viewing the places about that towne, and the fresh waters, which there are very plentiful and excellent good (but the main rivers are salt) the governor determined to make the first colony there, and so gave orders for the ship and pinnaces to come thither

" To make his entry peaceable and just, he thought fit to present the Werowance and the Wizoes of the towne, with some English cloth, (such as is used in trade with the Indians) axes, houes (hoes) and knives, which they accepted very kindly, and freely gave *consent* that he and his company should dwell in one part of their towne, and reserved the other for themselves; and those Indians that dwelt in that part of the towne which was allotted to the English, freely left them their houses and some corne that they had begun to plant It was also agreed between them, that, at the end of harvest, they should leave the whole towne, which they did accordingly And they made mutual promises to each other to live friendly and peaceably together, and if any injury should happen to be done on any part, that satisfaction should be made for the same, and thus upon the *27th day of March,* Anno Domini 1634, the governor took possession of the place and named the towne St Maries

" Three days after their coming to Yaocomico the Arke with the two pinnaces arrived there. The Indians much wondered to see such ships and at the thundering of the ordnance when they came to anchor The next day they began to prepare for their houses, and first of all a court of guard, and a store house; in the mean time they laid aboard the ships" (Then follows Governor Harvy's visit, as related in the text)

"After they had finished the store house and unladed the ship, the governor thought fit to bring the colony on shore, which were attended by all the gentlemen and the rest of the servants in armes — who received the colony with a volley of shot, which was answered by the ordnance from the ship At this ceremony were present the Weiowances of Patuxent and Yaocomico with many other Indians"

(They buy one thousand bushels of corn and send to New England)

"Finding ground cleared they planted corne although late in the year, and made gardens which they sowed with English seeds of all sorts and they prospered exceeding well

"They procured from Virginia, hogges, poultry, cowes and some neat cattle The hogges and poultry are already (1635) increased in Maryland, to a great stock, sufficient to serve the colony very plentifully "—THE AUTHOR

CHAPTER II.

THE PROTESTANT REVOLUTION

SHORTLY after the new settlement had been planted at St Marys it was visited by Governor Harvey of Virginia Governor Calvert received him with great ceremony, and for the purpose of conciliating the neighboring chiefs, gave him a banquet on board his ship to which he also invited them The king of Patuxent was particularly friendly to the whites, and to do him honor, he was seated between the two governors at the table. An Indian, one of his subjects, coming into the cabin of the ship and perceiving his prince thus seated, was seized with the suspicion that some evil design was meditated against him, nothing but the repeated assurances of the chief himself could prevent him from leaping overboard to carry the alarm to shore, which might have been productive of the most fatal consequences However, when the feast was over and the king about to depart, he addressed the surrounding Indians and said: "I love the English so well, that if they should go about to kill me, and I had so much breath as to speak, I would command the people not to avenge my death; for I know they would do no such thing, except it were through my own fault."

Nothing could prove more plainly than this little incident how firmly knit was the friendship between the two races, and how different was the conduct of the settlers of Maryland towards the natives from that which characterized the people of many other colonies Meanwhile the settlement continued to prosper, when suddenly a coolness became observable on the part of the natives in their immediate vicinity. This was the earliest evidence of the beginning of Claiborne's first rebellion.

Prior to the issuing of its charter, Maryland being included in the limits of the royal government of Virginia, Captain William Claiborne obtained from the governor and council of that province a license to trade with the Indians on the Chesapeake He accordingly established a trading post upon Kent Island, and some time after, another at the mouth of the Susquehanna. Perhaps he had entertained a hope of enlarging his temporary occupation, and of securing a grant of it as proprietor. At all events, the charter to Lord Baltimore would destroy his trade, and he determined to resist it No sooner had the settlers landed at St. Marys, than Claiborne, having received notice from Governor Calvert that if he remained he would be deemed a subject of the colony, applied to the council of Virginia, of which he was a member, for instructions how to proceed.* This body, which had always opposed the grant to Lord Baltimore, and was secretly determined to support the claims of Claiborne, replied that they saw no reason why he should give up any territories which he held of them; and, taking this for his pretext, he prepared to maintain his possessions. His first effort was to destroy the colony by means of the hostility of the Indians. For this purpose he began to insinuate suspicions into their minds, through the instrumentality of Fleet, the interpreter, whom he had seduced into his schemes, telling them that the Maryland settlers were Spaniards, and his and their secret enemies †

Scarcely had the colony been planted a month at St. Marys when these insidious measures produced their effect in the jealousy which appeared in the conduct of the natives Immediately all other works were suspended, and the settlers turned their whole attention to finishing a block-house for their protection in case of necessity, at the same time carefully regulating their conduct to the savages so as to dissipate their coldness and reawaken the old feelings of confidence and intimacy In six weeks the block-house was completed But in the meanwhile their unchanging friendliness to the Indians

---
* Bozman, 27-32, &c
† Ibid, 32

had convinced them of the sincerity of their conduct and the falseness of the insinuations against them, and they gradually renewed the kindly relations which had formerly existed, and which were never again broken The colonists once more returned to the work of building up their new city, and devoted the time from the finishing of their block-house to the ripening and gathering of their corn in erecting houses to replace the temporary huts of the Indians which they yet occupied.

Claiborne, foiled in his first attempt, became desperate and resolved on open measures of hostility His schemes were so far perfected that early in the year of 1635 he fitted out an armed pinnace with a crew of fourteen men under one of his adherents, Lieutenant Warren, to cruise against the colonists. Governor Calvert and his people met the crisis without hesitation, and two pinnaces were immediately armed and manned, and sent against the freebooters under the command of Captain Cornwallis. They came within sight of Warren's galley in the Pocomoke River on the eastern shore, and prepared for action, awaiting however the fire of the enemy. As they approached, the insurgents opened fire upon them and killed one of their men. But the fire was immediately returned with great effect and the galley was captured with the loss of three of her crew, one of whom was her commander, Lieutenant Warren. The survivors were carried prisoners to St Marys Claiborne, who was not in the engagement, finding his armament destroyed, fled into Virginia, where he expected to find protection from those who had secretly supported him But, determined to vindicate his authority and establish the rights of his brother, the Lord Proprietary, Governor Calvert despatched commissioners to Virginia to demand his person as a rebel and a traitor. His friends could only aid him so far as to have him sent to England by the governor, with the witnesses against him, that he might be tried there for the offence he had committed.*

Under the charter the power of legislation was vested in Lord Baltimore and a majority of the colonists or their depu-

---

* Bozman, vol. 2, p 35

ties, who were to be assembled by the governor Accordingly, in the beginning of the year 1635, the freemen of the colony were convened together at St. Marys Of their proceedings there is little known, as the greater portion of the public records were subsequently destroyed But it may be presumed that as yet they were more busily engaged in perfecting and strengthening their town than with legislative cares.

The Indians, in compliance with the conditions of their sale to the settlers, had as soon as their own crop of corn was gathered, departed from the town, and delivered it up entirely to the whites; who, for the present, beset as they were by the intrigues of Claiborne, and fearful of trusting too implicitly to the faith of their allies, restricted their settlements to its immediate vicinity. Within the city, lots of five and ten acres were granted to all who might apply for them, and tracts in the interior, ranging from one hundred to three thousand acres, in proportion to the number of settlers the person applying for them introduced into the colony: reserving thereon, however, a quit rent of twenty shillings for every thousand acres.* By these means, men of wealth and standing were induced to assist the growth of the province by bringing numerous emigrants from the mother country.

Lord Baltimore still remained in England, superintending the interests of the colony and fostering emigration, when he received notice that the assembly of the freemen had passed certain laws which were sent to him for his approval. Believing that the right of framing laws was vested in himself by the charter, he rejected them and set about preparing a com-

---

*The first conditions were, in 1633, for every five persons between the ages of fifteen and sixty, two thousand acres of land, at a rent of four hundred pounds of wheat;— for less than five persons, at the rate of one hundred acres for each man, one hundred for his wife and each servant, and fifty acres for each child under sixteen, at a rent of ten pounds of wheat for every fifty acres In 1635, for every five men brought in, a grant was made of one thousand acres, at a rent of twenty shillings Grants of one, two, and three thousand acres were erected into manors, with the right, to their owners, of holding courts leet and courts baron "—THE AUTHOR

plete system for the government of the province, at the same time directing the assembly to be called together on the 25th of January, 1638, to have his dissent announced to them.† In the meanwhile, the inhabitants of Kent Island, to a certain extent, had submitted to the government of Maryland, and early in 1637 a court was established there, in the name of the province for the trial of civil and criminal causes In December following, the better to secure its tranquillity, Captain George Evelin was appointed commander of the island. Many of the factious adherents of Claiborne still looked forward to a successful establishment of his pretensions, and continued to excite a resistance to the processes of the civil courts This spirit of oppositon at length grew to such a height, that governor Calvert himself was compelled, in the following year, to make an expedition to the island at the head of a military force to bring it to complete subjection to his authority * In the settlement at St Marys, the plantations had already extended to the west side of St Georges river, and, there being large accessions of emigrants in this year from the mother country, it was found necessary to erect a new hundred, a division similar to our election districts.

Early in 1638, the Assembly, directed to be convened by Lord Baltimore, was summoned by the governor, and met at the little capital of St Marys The constitution of these early legislatures was so different from those of the present day as to require a more particular notice By the charter, every free man was entitled to share in making the laws which were to govern him, either in person or by his deputy. In the youth of the colony, when the inhabitants were still few in number, and could be easily assembled, the whole body of freemen were required to attend, and those who found it inconvenient to be present, were permitted to cast their votes by proxy. Thus in the present assembly, its secretary, Mr. Lewger, held and voted twelve proxies But as in a new country, with savage neighbors, where a man's presence at his plantation was always

---

† Bozman, Bacon
* Burnap's Life of Calvert — 112, Bozman, 44

necessary, it would be sometimes difficult to get a full assemblage, the governor was invested with the power of summoning, by special writ, those whose presence he particularly desired. As every one, at that period, possessed the right of being present, this summons must have been simply obligatory in its nature, and intended to compel the attendance of those who were especially qualified to advise and assist as legislators, and yet were unwilling to perform the onerous duty required of them To suppose the power was aristocratical, and originally intended to secure the governor the control of the house, is absurd, as no matter how many of his adherents he might call together, every other freeman in the colony could claim and take his seat in the house with equal powers and privileges. Subsequently, when the number of hundreds increased, two burgesses were elected from each; yet, even then, any one who had not voted at their election might come forward and claim a seat in the legislature. At a still later period, this right was taken away by the general assembly itself, and, then, this body was composed of the delegates from the several hundreds, the council, and those who might be summoned by special writ. With this strange power in his hands, a governor could at any moment obtain the control of a house thus constituted and limited, by adding to it a sufficient number of his own friends At first there was but one house—the governor's council and the delegates sitting together—but in process of time they were divided into the upper and lower houses; the council appointed by the Lord Proprietary forming the upper, and the delegates of the people the lower.

The legislature which now assembled, composed of the people themselves, secured some of the most important rights of the colonists Upon the guarantees of their charter they began to lay the sure foundations of the broader liberties of Maryland

Lord Baltimore now caused the system of laws which he had digested, to be presented to them in place of those passed by the legislature of 1635, which he had negatived because they were not framed by himself. But the people, fully convinced that the initiative was in them, and that the charter only intended to confer upon the Proprietary a veto power, vindicated their rights by immediately rejecting the whole system, and set about framing such bills as they thought proper for their situation. The controversy which arose on this point, was not of long duration. After having vetoed the forty-one bills adopted at this long session, and insisted for a time upon his claim, the Lord Proprietary determined to abandon it, preferring the welfare and prosperity of the colony, which must suffer from want of laws during the existence of the controversy, to his own individual privileges, and sensible that the power of negativing any bill of which he disapproved, was quite sufficient to protect his rights and authority in the province.*

The insurgents captured in the engagement with Lieutenant Warren by Captain Cornwallis, had not yet been tried, for, hitherto, there had been no competent tribunal Now, however, Thomas Smith, the second in command to Warren in his piratical and rebellious expedition, was brought to trial for the murder of William Ashmore, who had been killed by the fire of the pinnace at the opening of the skirmish.† After a full examination of the testimony, he was found guilty and sentenced to death, though it is not certain that he was executed. Claiborne, the leader of the rebellion, was attainted and his property confiscated to the use of the province These proceedings were, probably, the cause of the renewed disturbances in Kent, which required the governor's presence in that island, as has already been related. The house adjourned from time to time, until his return from the expedition in the month of March.

Claiborne himself was still in England, and as active in his hostility as ever Secret intrigue and open violence had failed in the new world, and now he endeavored to reach his object through the known avarice and unscrupulousness of the royal court. It would seem that he was never brought to trial for his rebellion; for he boldly laid claim to the Isle of

---
* Bozman, vol 2, p. 92.
† Ibid, p 64

Kent and its dependencies, and charged the Proprietary's officers with having violently assailed his pinnaces and slaughtered his men He presented a petition to the king setting forth his supposed grievances, and offering to pay to the crown the yearly rent of two hundred pounds sterling for the grant of the Isle of Kent, his station at the mouth of the Susquehanna, and thirty-six miles width of territory, on each side of that river, from the bay to the Canada lakes, which would have proved a very large and valuable territory. The matter was referred to the lords commissioners of the council for the plantations, who reported after a full investigation, that "the lands in question (between Claiborne and the Proprietary) belonged absolutely to Lord Baltimore, and that no trade with the Indians could be carried on there without his consent, and that, with regard to the violences complained of, no cause for any relief appeared, but that both parties should be left to the ordinary course of justice."* Thus again baffled, Claiborne returned to Virginia to carry on his old schemes of annoyance; but the legislature of that colony interfered and compelled him to desist. Then, assuming the attitude of a supplicant, he despatched an agent to Maryland praying the restoration of his property which had been confiscated by the government His prayer was rejected, and, despairing of success, he abandoned his efforts until a more favorable period should arrive.† During the first four years of the settlement, the colony was circumscribed within narrow limits, although the Indians in the immediate vicinity persevered in their friendly relations with the whites. To these natives alone, therefore, the labors of the two missionaries were devoted in part, for their presence was also required in the settlements; and the governor, doubtful of the disposition of the savages in the interior, had forbidden them to penetrate thither, lest, by their loss, the people should be deprived of the consolation of their services The Indians of Patuxent received them most favorably, and bestowed upon them a plantation, called

---
* Bozman, vol 2, p 72, etc
† Burnap, 115

Mettapaunien, or "St. Mattapany," on the river Patuxent, where a missionary station and storehouse were at once established to serve as the starting point for their labors in the wilderness

It was impossible that such zeal and energy should not produce abundant fruits In five years from the date of the settlement, they had extended themselves throughout a large portion of the province; they had visited many tribes and made numerous converts; they had possessed four permanent stations, the most distant of which was one hundred and twenty miles from St. Marys, the seat of the colony—one at the settlement, one at Mattapany, one at Kent island, and one at Kittamaquindi, the capital of Tayac. They were the pioneers of the colonists; and, thus having possession of the shores of the great bay, and command of its rivers, they penetrated from these stations, in every direction, to the tribes of the interior, preaching Christianity to the savage, and, by their gentle influence maintaining the peace and quiet of the settlements more firmly and securely than could have been done by the whole militia of the province. But of their works the most important in its results was the baptism of Tayac

The Piscataways, or Pascatoways* as they are called in Father White's Journal, were the most extensive and powerful tribe in Maryland. Their domain was bounded on one side by the region of the Patuxents, and on the other by the country of the Susquehannas, and covered a territory one hundred and thirty miles in extent, perhaps including the fairest and richest portion of Maryland The chief of these Indians was called Tayac, a title of honor and station; his name was Ciltomachen.

---

* The precise situation of these people is disputed. Burnap supposes they were the Patapsco tribe, and that Kittamaquindi, their capital, was near the present site of Baltimore B. U Campbell, Esq, thinks, and with more probability, that they were the Pscataways—and that Kittamaquindi was situated about fifteen miles below the present city of Washington See Burnap's Life of Leonard Calvert, 87-88, and Campbell's Memoir on the Early Missions of Maryland, in the proceedings of the Maryland Historical Society, 8th January, 1846
—The Author

He had obtained his power in the tribe by putting his brother, the former chief, to death. The mode of his conversion was singular. The king of the Patuxents who had professed so much affection for the English, and had listened with great docility to the missionaries, suddenly changed his whole demeanor, and became cold and indifferent towards them. Fearing treachery on the part of the chief, Father White, by the advice of the governor, withdrew from St Mattapany and removed to the Piscataways, where he was received with great kindness. The chief soon became attached to him, and made him share his simple hospitality. Tayac, so he informed Father White, had been warned in dreams of the approach of missionaries, who loved him and his people, and would confer great blessings upon them.

Shortly after the arrival of Father White, the Indian chief fell sick, and forty conjurers, or medicine men, in vain tried every remedy within their power, when the missionary, by permission of the sick chief himself, administered some medicine to him, and caused him to be bled. The treatment was skilful and judicious, the invalid began to recover, and was soon restored to perfect health. Then he determined to be baptized together with his wife and daughter, and was carefully and diligently instructed by Father White, in order that he might be prepared to receive that sacrament with proper dispositions. He laid aside the dress of skins, which he had heretofore worn, assumed that of the English, and commenced to learn their language. He delighted in religious conversation, and when the governor once dilated to him on the great advantages his people would derive from the trade of the settlers, he replied—"Verily, I consider these as trifling, when compared with this one benefit, that, by their aid, I have arrived at the true knowledge of the one God, the most important of all knowledge."

Being convinced himself, he sought to bring his people to the same faith. In an assembly of the chiefs of his empire, he told them, "that the superstitions, which they had formerly believed, ought to be abolished and Christianity adopted; that there was hope only in one true God, and that stones and herbs, which they had heretofore worshiped, were merely the humblest of his works" Then, placing a stone upon his foot, he tossed it to a great distance, thus showing his contempt for that, which he had before received as a deity. The people, already prepared by the preaching of the missionary, loudly applauded the speech and action of the king; and thenceforth the idols began to fall into disrepute. The good dispositions of Tayac were strengthened by a visit which he made to St Marys, in company with Father White. He was much impressed by the conduct of an Indian, who was executed there for murder. The missionaries endeavored to prepare the criminal to meet his fate, and Tayac himself acted as their interpreter The Indian was baptized and suffered with such calmness and resignation that the king, moved by the spectacle, expressed a desire to be baptized But, in order that the ceremony might be performed with becoming preparation, it was deferred

On the fifth of July, 1640 (O. S), in the presence of the governor, Leonard Calvert, the secretary, Mr. Lewger, and many other of the principal inhabitants of the province, Tayac, his queen, their little son—and many of the chief men of his council, had administered to them the rites of baptism The king assumed the name of Charles, in honor of the English sovereign, his queen that of Mary In the afternoon, the king and queen were married according to Christian usage

Much was hoped from the conversion of Tayac, but, in less than a year, he died His young daughter now became queen of the Piscataways, not long after was baptized at St. Marys, having already learned the English language The example of Tayac and his family was followed by many other natives. The inhabitants of the town of Potopaco, now Port Tobacco, to the number of one hundred and thirty, together with their queen, were baptized—the chiefs and principal men of Potomac town, on the Virginia shore, and the chiefs of several neighboring villages were converted While Anacoston, sachem of a tribe adjoining the Piscataways, became so firmly attached to the whites, that he wished to take up his residence among them, as a citizen of the colony

Thus guarded and protected by a circle of Christian Indians, bound to them by the ties of gratitude and religion, it is not surprising that Maryland suffered but little from the hostility of the natives — yet even it was disturbed by a few troubles, which were dignified by the title of the Indian wars

It was natural that a feeling of jealousy should spring up in the breasts of the natives, as they beheld the rapid increase of the colonists, and the extension of their settlements, swallowing up their hunting grounds and occupying the graves of their forefathers Yet no cause of offence was given them by the colonists, and their affection for the missionaries suppressed every feeling of discontent in the minds of the Christian Indians. The Susquehannahs were the most hostile and warlike of the tribes of Maryland, but their country lay far north and west of the settlements, while, between, stretched the land of the friendly Tayac The Nanticokes, who also appeared inimical to the whites, inhabited the eastern shore. The waters of the bay served as a barrier to their incursions, until the settlements spread across it, and then the colony had become too powerful to dread any, or all the tribes united together The Nanticokes were composed of several tribes, and called, in their own language, "Nentego," and, in the Delaware, "Unechtgo," or "Seashore Settlers," and their territory stretched along both sides of the Nanticoke river, in Somerset and Dorchester county. The other principal tribes on that shore, in common with the Nanticokes, of the Lenape, or Delaware race, were the Ozinies, on the Chester river, the Toghwochs, on the Sassafras; the Atquinachunks, on the Delaware; the Wycomeses, and the Choptanks. On the western shore, after the Susquehannas, the Patuxents and the Piscataways were the most important

These numerous tribes, united together, would have proved very formidable to the settlers; yet there never was any combination of a serious nature attempted The Indian wars of Maryland never rose beyond petty expeditions to chastise some hostile tribe or to capture and punish particular individuals, who had committed aggressions upon the persons or property of the colonists Only once did the savages make a successful inroad of any consequence, and that was against a missionary station which they destroyed, killing the inhabitants and carrying off a considerable booty. But speedy retribution overtook them, for they were severely punished by the military force of the province.

The dread of attack from these powerful and warlike savages, rendered it necessary that some general system of defence should be adopted. The people were obliged by law to keep a sufficient quantity of arms and ammunition in their houses so as to be ready at a moment's warning, and every male, capable of bearing arms, was enrolled in the militia, and made subject to be called out for the common defence. In 1642, when the fear of an invasion by the Susquehannas was very prevalent, new precautions were adopted, no man being allowed to fire three shots in a quarter of an hour, except to give an alarm, and every one who heard three shots within that space of time was directed to repeat the signal. The women and children were then to betake themselves for safety to the blockhouses, of which there was one in each hundred, while the men armed and rallied to meet the foe A garrison was placed in the fort of St. Inigoes, near the capital,* as a main stronghold; and to provide for any sudden outbreak; when the inhabitants left their homes for religious worship they carried their arms with them.†

In 1639 an expedition was sent against some Indians of the Eastern shore, who had given cause of offence, and also against the Susquehannahs, who had been molesting the friendly tribes of Patuxent and Piscataway The armament consisted of two pinnaces and a skiff, manned with thirty marksmen, whose service was compulsory, and several volunteers To equip and victual this force, the governor was under the necessity of sending a shallop to Virginia, to procure a

---
* Bozman, 212, Bacon
† Burnap

supply of arms, ammunition and food * At the same time, the militia of the province was put upon a better footing, drilled and exercised. In 1642, the Ozinies became hostile, and as they could muster sixty warriors, created considerable uneasiness in Kent Island. To prevent an outbreak a proclamation was issued forbidding their appearance on the island, and authorizing the inhabitants to put to death any who should disobey the prohibition The disaffection, however, continued to spread among the tribes, and the Susquehannas, Wycomeses and Nanticokes were, in the ensuing year, declared enemies of the province It was at this period that the Susquehannas struck a heavy blow in the destruction of the mission station to which reference has already been made—and, while they were ravaging the western and northern frontier, the Nanticokes, on the Eastern Shore, threatened the colonists with invasion across the bay. Governor Calvert determined to anticipate their attack Having assisted the Governor of Virginia, upon a similar occasion, in punishing the Indians of the eastern shore for an outrage upon the settlements of that colony, he wrote to him, proposing to undertake a joint expedition with two hundred men, to be raised equally by the two provinces, to chastise the enemy At home, he directed all the frontier settlers to be drawn into the forts and blockhouses, proclaimed martial law, and authorized the commanders to call out every third man capable of bearing arms. A proclamation, similar to that for the protection of Kent Island, was issued, by which every Indian, under penalty of death, was prohibited from passing within a line drawn from the Patuxent to the Potomac The promptness of his measures produced the desired effect, for, though the colony suffered occasionally from a hostile inroad, nothing of importance occurred, and in a short time a truce was concluded with the Nanticokes

While occupied with these Indian affairs, new troubles sprung up in a different quarter The limits of the charter extended to the north beyond the Schuylkill, and, as that region presented many advantages, a party of Maryland colonists

---

* Bozman, vol 2, p 162

settled there, and began to reclaim and recultivate the wilderness.* Lower down, in the Delaware Bay, the Swedes had already built a fort. The Dutch of New York laid claim to the whole territory, and fitted out an expedition of two armed sloops to take possession of it, and to drive away its occupants. The province was too much engaged with more pressing affairs at home to afford assistance to the settlers on the Schuylkill These probably abandoned that region, for which the restless New Englanders now also contended, as included in their grants.

In the meanwhile, the colonists, in spite of external enemies and internal malcontents, had gone on improving and strengthening their settlements, and extending their legislation Lord Baltimore, having in August, 1638, granted to the people the right of originating laws, authorized his brother, in his name, to agree to such bills as seemed proper and necessary, until he himself should express his disapproval under his seal. A new Assembly was therefore summoned This body met at St. Marys, on the 25th of February, 1639, O. S, and adopted many useful measures The most important was an act establishing general laws for the government of the province By it were secured the rights and franchises of the church, the prerogatives of the lord Proprietary, and the liberties of the people, according to the magna charta. Its subsequent sections provided for the administration of justice, the maintenance of civil rights, and the punishment of criminal offences. A county court was established at St. Marys, which was still the only county of the province, although there were many subdivisions of hundreds, besides the several settlements upon Kent Island, now incorporated into a separate hundred A court of chancery was erected, the jurisdiction of justices of the peace extended and defined, the duties of the present orphans' court vested in the secretary, a short insolvent system, framed, and oaths of office prescribed. In addition to these, the planting of Indian corn and tobacco was regulated, weights and measures ascertained, the custom or duty on the exporta-

---

* Bozman, vol 2, 205; McMahon, 23

tion of tobacco fixed, and military discipline provided for.*

Heretofore, every free man who had not voted at the election for burgesses, was entitled to take his seat in the house, it was now enacted, that only the lieutenant governor, his secretary, such gentlemen as he specially summoned, and the elected representatives of the different hundreds, should henceforth constitute the General Assembly The privileges, thus given to the governor, might have been of dangerous consequence—but Leonard Calvert's long and virtuous administration fully justified the confidence which the people then placed in his honor and integrity. A bill, passed at this session, displays forcibly the condition of the infant province A water mill, for the use of the people, was of the utmost importance, and the governor and council were authorized to contract for its erection provided the cost should not exceed twenty thousand pounds of tobacco, the early currency of Maryland, equal, according to the rates of a later period, to the sum of three hundred and thirty-three dollars and thirty-three and one-third cents, which was to be raised by general taxation in two years† A similar provision was made for

---

* Bacon

† Bozman, vol 2, p 156 The author of "A Relation of Maryland" says, "Th have also set up a water mill for the grinding of corne adjoi. g to the towne —1635" Unless this attempt failed, wherefore the necessity of setting up one by taxation?

This author gives the names of some of "the gentlemen adventurers" who accompanied the first colony

Leonard Calvert, the governor, } his lordship's brothers
George Calvert,

Thomas Cornwallis, Esq, } commissioners
Jerome Hawley, Esq,

Richard Gerard, son of Sir Thomas Gerard, K B

Edward Wintour, } sons of the Lady Anne Wintour
Frederick Wintour,

Henry Wiseman, son of Sir Thomas Wiseman, Bart

John Saunders,   Thomas Dorrel,
Edward Cranfield,   Captain John Hill,
Henry Green,   John Medcalf,
Nicholas Fairfax,   William Saire
John Baxter,   See also Bozman, vol 2 p 26.

building a "towne house " Both these laws, while they display the past weakness of the colony, also prove its growing extent and population, which rendered such improvements necessary Heretofore, hand mills had sufficed to grind the Indian corn in sufficient quantities for the sparse settlements—and the house of the governor had been large enough to accommodate their delegates. With the necessity came the improvement, and the erection of the first water mill and the first Statehouse, may be considered an epoch in the history of Maryland

CHAPTER III

THE PURITANS IN THE PROVINCE

WHILE the little colony was thus steadily progressing, in spite of the difficulties which surrounded it, the horizon, in the far east, began to darken The contest between the king and the parliament had broken out in England, and it seemed that the latter was about to become victorious The government of Maryland had sprung from a royal grant, its Proprietary was an adherent of the king, and the storm, which was hurling the king from his throne, could scarcely pass by, leaving the Proprietary and his province unscathed The spirit of disaffection already began to appear in the settlements; brought there by a colony of Puritans, who had been driven out of Virginia, which tolerated neither Catholic nor Dissenter, and received with open arms in Maryland, to repay liberality with dissension and kindness with civil war As the success of parliament increased, their party grew in strength. Governor Calvert, uncertain what course to pursue, and anxious to view, in person, the tendency of affairs in the mother country, determined to return to England to consult with his brother, Lord Baltimore. To provide for the government of the province, he appointed Mr Giles Brent " lieutenant general, admiral, chief captain, magistrate, and commander," and set sail for England in the early part of the year 1643 During his absence, the spirit of disaffection increased and at length broke out in Claiborne's and Ingle's rebellion

The Indians, either urged on by their malcontents, or perceiving the internal dissensions of the settlers, were again in motion Even prior to the departure of Leonard Calvert, the

Susquehannahs assumed a threatening attitude, and the governor appointed Captain Cornwallis, a man of great skill and courage, exceedingly popular, and possessing the full confidence of the militia, to take command of an expedition to be raised by draft But as that experienced officer preferred willing services to the compulsory aid of pressed men, the design was changed, and he was authorized to assemble and organize a body of volunteers The Susquehannahs had now become more formidable, having been furnished with fire arms and instructed in their use by the Swedes and Dutch of New York and the Delaware, who carried on a wholesale traffic in arms and ammunition with the Indians bordering on the English and French colonies, to the manifest danger of their settlements and contrary to the law of nations.* While these warlike Indians were threatening the colony on the north, Captain Richard Ingle, an associate of Claiborne, and a pirate and a rebel, was discovered hovering about the settlement with an armed ship, holding communications with, and endeavoring to strengthen the numbers of, the disaffected. Governor Brent immediately issued a proclamation ordering his arrest and the seizure of his ship Ingle was taken, but soon succeeded in making his escape, and joined Claiborne to concoct fresh designs against the peace of the province

At length, in 1644, Leonard Calvert returned to Maryland, bearing new commissions from his brother, Lord Baltimore, for the more firm establishment of the government. He found the province in great disorder, the public officers at variance with one another, the encroachments of the Indians continuing, the pirate Ingle at large, his untiring enemy, Claiborne, up in arms and once more in possession of Kent Island A reconnoitering party of eight men, under Mark Pheypo and John Genalles, was immediately despatched across the bay, in a light shallop, to watch the movements of the insurgents, and preparations were made to dislodge them. They were proclaimed public enemies.† But the efforts of Governor Cal-

---
* Bozman, vol 2, p. 273
† January, 1645, O S

vert to obtain possession of Kent Island failed; and the two rebels, emboldened by their success and certain of assistance from their friends, invaded the western shore, and, after a short struggle, obtained complete possession of the province. Governor Calvert was compelled to fly to Virginia, and the conquerors immediately commenced a system of outrage and oppression upon those who had adhered to his fortunes and supported the laws of the colony Many were robbed of all their possessions, and banished from the province, and those who were permitted to remain, were so despoiled as almost to become destitute of the means of subsistence † Even the missionaries were seized, their stations plundered and broken up, and they themselves, with the venerable Father White, the apostle of Maryland, among the number, sent in chains to England, where long imprisonment awaited them ‡ They took possession of the provincial records, which they so mutilated and destroyed, that it is almost impossible to obtain an accurate account of their proceedings, or of the struggle which preceded their success *

In England, the parliament had at length utterly overthrown the power of the king, who was now a captive in their hands; and the last stronghold of his partizans had been surrendered to the arms of their successful generals. Claiborne and Ingle acted in the name of the parliament, and their success, in these circumstances, seemed a death blow to the supremacy of Lord Baltimore, in the province. He felt this, and accordingly, in 1646, directed his brother, the late governor, and Mr. Lewger, the secretary, to collect and take charge of such of his private property as might be saved from the wreck of his fortunes, apparently abandoning forever the hope of recovering his Proprietary rights. But Leonard Calvert would not so easily submit to the overthrow of his just authority, and the destruction of their common prospects The inhabitants of Virginia had remained loyal to the crown,

---

* Bozman, 290; Burnap, 218
† Bozman; Burnap
‡ Campbell

and, perhaps, the majority of the people of Maryland were at least firmly attached to the mild and parental government of the Calverts In Virginia, therefore, Governor Calvert found a safe refuge, and soon began to collect the means for a final effort to subdue the rebels; in Maryland, the systematic outrages, the oppression, and the misrule of the usurpers, before long prepared the people to sustain him in his attempt. At length, having completed his preparations, and believing the time propitious for his undertaking, about the close of the year 1646, at the head of the military force which he had levied, he crossed the Potomac, surprised the enemy, and, having gained an almost bloodless victory, re-entered St. Marys in triumph, and once more took possession of the government.

Captain Hill, who had acted as governor under a commission from the council, submitted and retired to Virginia, without attempting to maintain his power; and in a short time the whole western shore, after having been under the dominion of the rebels for nearly two years, joyfully renewed its allegiance to Lord Baltimore Banished from England, Father White again ventured back into the kingdom, in defiance of the laws, to pursue his duties as a priest, and was again imprisoned. He died in London, on the 27th of December, 1656, in the seventy-eighth year of his age.

Kent Island, however, the stronghold of the malcontents, did not submit so easily as the rest of the province; and it was found necessary to declare martial law, to cut off all communication from without, and to send an expedition, under the governor himself, into the island, before the rebels could be reduced once more under the authority of the Lord Proprietary Proper measures were immediately adopted to secure the tranquillity of the island, or county as it was now called. Desirous of healing old differences and of subduing the hostility of the disaffected by kindness and generosity, the governor granted an amnesty to most of the offenders, and returned to St Marys.*

---

* Bozman

Order was restored once more to the colony; renewed prosperity, the necessary result of its internal resources and its re-established tranquillity, already commenced to dawn upon the inhabitants, when a fresh, and almost irreparable, misfortune befell them, in the death of their amiable yet enterprizing governor. At St Marys, surrounded by his family and friends, on the 9th of June, 1647, Leonard Calvert breathed his last, having, in virtue of the power vested in him by his brother, named Thomas Greene his successor as governor of Maryland † During the space of fourteen years, he had guided the colony through the storms which darkened around its infancy—he had devoted his whole life and energies to its permanent establishment—with a disinterested self-devotion, he had striven, in the wilderness, for its glory and its prosperity, and it seemed as if, through a special providence of heaven, to reward his labors, a beam of sunshine and tranquillity had broken over the province as he was about to die, at peace with all, triumphant over the enemies of Maryland, full of honor, and enriched with the blessings of a rescued people. His character, public and private, was without stain, his abilities were unquestioned, his government kind and parental, and his memory was long cherished by the colonists with grateful recollection He was, indeed, a great and good man

Governor Greene immediately entered upon the duties of his office, and his first effort was to prevent any attempt to disturb the peace of the colony, on the part of Captain Hill or his adherents, who had taken refuge across the Potomac, As the session of the provincial court was approaching, he issued a proclamation, prohibiting any of the refugees from claiming the assistance or judgment of the court, in any case, in their favor, until they had taken the oath of fealty, therein prescribed, to the government But a difficulty now sprung up from another source During the past commotions, the colonists had neglected, or been unable, to plant a sufficient quantity of corn, and a scarcity of food began to be apparent.

---
† Burnap

The troops which Governor Calvert had enlisted in Virginia, were not yet paid or discharged, and it was found difficult to furnish them with subsistence. They had been denied the privilege of plundering the rebels, and the poverty of the province rendered it very difficult, after the late disorder, to raise their arrears of pay. To satisfy their present demands, Governor Greene issued a proclamation, directing a seizure of all the corn which the people might have, over and above a sufficiency for their own use, to be paid for out of his lordship's estate at the rate of one hundred and twenty pounds of tobacco per barrel, or to be replaced, provided enough should be imported into the colony.* Mrs Margaret Brent, a relative and the administratrix of the deceased governor, a woman of great spirit and energy, had already exhausted all the resources of his estate to meet the crisis, and the legislature, which met shortly after, confirmed the measures of the governor, allowing each family to retain two barrels of corn per head, excepting infants, and fixing the rate of compensation for the quantity pressed for the public service, at one hundred and fifty pounds of tobacco per barrel. The governor had considered it prudent, in the deranged state of affairs, to prohibit the exportation of corn or horses from the province until the scarcity should be remedied; this measure was also approved of, and continued. At the close of the session, to heal up all existing differences, a general pardon was proclaimed for those rebels who might embrace its terms, except Captain Richard Ingle. Thus ended the rebellion, which had been boldly conceived, and energetically executed, which was successful for a time, but was overthrown through the excesses of its leaders and the loyalty of the people to the Calverts. Its lingering consequence was longest felt in the threatening attitude of the Indians, who still continued so hostile, that the governor found it necessary to adjourn the county court, lest the absence of jurymen, parties, and witnesses from the frontier districts in attendance

---

* Bozman, 309, 313, 315

upon it should weaken those exposed portions of the settlements and subject them to outrage

Mingling in the political causes which brought on this rebellion, was a feeling of religious intolerance in the Puritan faction, which wreaked itself upon the offending missionaries and first infringed on the rights of liberty of conscience in Maryland

Lord Baltimore now perceived that, while concessions to the Puritans might be necessary to maintain his province, new safeguards were required to prevent the growing feeling of bigotry from destroying the sanctuary which he had erected at the cost of so much care and treasure Therefore, in 1648, he appointed William Stone governor of the province, and prescribed that famous oath of office which secured the continuance of liberty of conscience and full toleration to all persons who professed to believe in Jesus Christ.* Governor Stone had undertaken to transport into the province five hundred settlers, who were probably Protestants like himself, the new secretary and the greater portion of the council Heretofore, the most of those appointed to office by the lord Proprietary had been Catholics, but now, the Puritans being triumphant at home, he hoped by this measure to propitiate them, at the same time that, by an oath of office, he secured to all Christians the full toleration which had hitherto most scrupulously been observed Governor Stone entered upon his duties towards the close of the year 1648, or the opening of the ensuing year. On April 2, 1649, the General Assembly was convened at St Mary's, and, to give additional security to the safeguards which Lord Baltimore had already provided, passed an act that must forever render memorable the founders and people of Maryland After enacting severe punishments for the crime of blasphemy, and declaring that certain penalties should be inflicted upon any one who should call another a sectarian name of reproach, it proceeds with the sublime declaration · "and whereas the enforcing of conscience, in matters of religion, hath frequently fallen out to

---

* Bozman, vol 2, p 335; McMahon, 226

be of dangerous consequence, in those commonwealths where it has been practised, and for the more quiet and peaceable government of this province, and the better to preserve mutual love and unity amongst the inhabitants, &c, no person or persons whatsoever, within this province or the islands, ports, harbors, creeks or havens thereunto belonging, professing to believe in Jesus Christ, shall from henceforth be any ways troubled, or molested, or discountenanced for or in respect of his or her religion, nor in the free exercise thereof, within this province or the islands thereunto belonging, nor any way compelled to the belief or exercise of any other religion, against his or her consent.*

The passage of this act is one of the proud boasts of Maryland, and its exact execution until the government was overthrown by the Puritans, and, from its restoration, until the Protestant revolution, forms one of her greatest glories In the north, the Puritans drove the Episcopalian from their borders and bound the peaceful Friend to the whipping-post, bored his tongue, slit his ears, or condemned him to die upon the gallows In Virginia, the Catholic and the Puritan were alike disfranchised and banished, by the Episcopalians; and even Rhode Island, founded by the mild and gentle Roger Williams, denied to Catholics a participation in the political rights that were enjoyed in that community by all others.† Only in Maryland, was there true toleration and liberty of conscience The Catholic and the Protestant, the Puritan, the Episcopalian, the Presbyterian and the Friend, there joined hands in peace and fellowship, worshiping God according to the dictates of their conscience — for there was none to "molest or discountenance them Whoever dared to stigmatize his fellow man as "heretic, schismatic, idolater, Puritan, Independent, Presbyterian, Popish Priest, Jesuit, Jesuited Papist, Lutheran, Calvinist, Anabaptist, Brownist, Antinomian, Barrowist, Roundhead, Separatists, or any other name or term,

---

* Bacon's Laws
† Grahame, vol 2, p 23, note

in a reproachful manner, relating to matter of religion,"* was subject to a fine of ten shillings sterling, one half to be paid to the party insulted, and in default thereof, to be publicly whipped and imprisoned until he should make ample satisfaction to the party offended, by asking and receiving his forgiveness, publicly, and in the presence of the chief officer of the place where the offence had been committed

That the Catholics were still in the majority is evident; it was their only refuge from persecution, and hither, therefore, every emigrant turned his steps Germans, French and Italians sought a home within the borders of Maryland. With the tide of emigration thus in their favor, with the large body of Catholic settlers who had come over in the first five or ten years, to increase the numbers of the early pilgrims, it is not probable that they should have been already outnumbered by the refugees, who, driven from other colonies, sought asylum in Maryland.† Indeed, Gov Sharp says, in 1758, writing to Lord Baltimore, that up to the date of the Protestant revolution in 1689, the Catholics were the majority of the people‡ The law, as is evident from the second section, was framed by a Catholic assembly, while it was assented to by a Protestant governor and council; so that a portion of the honor is due to both. All the people of Maryland may claim this glory of their forefathers, as their equal and common heritage, while all must equally regret the penalties, which its first section announces, but which do not appear to have ever been enforced. But this act, in its best provisions, was

---

* See Bacon's Laws for the act

† Burnaby, an English Episcopal clergyman, who visited Maryland in 1760, 114 years after this time, when this toleration had been destroyed, and the number of Catholics decreased by oppressive and restraining laws, says, that there were still "as many Catholics as Protestants," alluding to the Established Church, and meaning "Episcopalians —who were probably more numerous than any other Protestant denomination It is not credible, therefore, that they were in the minority in 1649, or even long after
—THE AUTHOR

‡ See his letter in Annals of Annapolis

only the solemn recording of that principle, which had heretofore governed the province and which had been laid down by its Catholic founders, and proclaimed from its first settlement. And yet the greatest misfortunes of the province sprang out of the most important exercise of this liberality.

The Puritans had established a conventicle in Virginia, and three ministers were sent from Boston to convert the "ungodly Virginians," but as their numbers began to increase, the government determined to break it up, and, in 1642, the members were dispersed and driven from the province.* Many of them, with Richard Bennett at their head, sought refuge in Maryland, were kindly received, and settled at a place they called Providence, near the present city of Annapolis, in Anne Arundel. They were no sooner seated in their new habitation than they refused to take the oath of fealty to the province, which the law required from all emigrants upon obtaining patents for their lands. They declined this oath, "because it was an oath," says one of their defenders, "to support a government which upheld antichrist," that is secured freedom of conscience to Catholics and Episcopalians, as well as to themselves. They formed themselves into a community, governed by their own congregational church system, occupied the lands without any formal grants, and had no recognised connection with the colony, until in July, 1650, when their settlement was erected into a county, and a commander and justices of the peace appointed, as in Kent and St. Marys.

Events in England had now taken such a course as to affect materially the condition of Maryland. The king, who had been seized by the republicans, was brought to trial before a tribunal, sentenced to death, and publicly executed on the 30th of January, 1650. The parliament, to forever destroy royalty in England, issued a decree declaring it treason for any one to acknowledge his son Charles as king. In spite of this prohibition, he was immediately and formally proclaimed by the authorities of Maryland and, to commemorate his accession, a general pardon for all offences was published by the

---

* Bozman, vol 2, p 370

governor. This daring act of loyalty aroused the adherents of the parliament and led to the reduction of Maryland

The Puritans had gradually grown in strength, since their first admission into Maryland Besides the colony brought over by Governor Stone, another had lately arrived from England, under Richard Brooke, and settled in the county of Charles, which was erected for them, and of which their leader was made commander. When the assembly was called, consisting of fourteen delegates, it was found that the partisans of the commonwealth were in the majority.

At first, however, the Puritans of Providence had refused to send representatives and it was not until the governor visited them in person to persuade them to do so that they consented. At the same time, they began to give currency to a report, doubtless derived from their friends in England, that Lord Baltimore's government was about to be overthrown, and the province "reduced" under the control of the commissioners of parliament The authorities made an effort to put a stop to these rumors, but it was soon discovered that they were not without foundation Parliament had passed an ordinance for the reduction of the Barbadoes and Virginia, which, however, was not put in execution until the year following, when a commission was issued to sundry persons, among whom were William Claiborne, whose intriguing appears throughout the whole transaction, and Richard Bennett, heretofore so hospitably received into the province when exiled from Virginia The appointment of these two men boded ill for Maryland With a fleet of several armed vessels, and a force of seven hundred men, the commissioners, who were in England, set sail for the colonies After a short struggle they obtained possession of the Barbadoes, and proceeded to Virginia, where they were joined by Bennett and Claiborne The governor of Virginia made his submission and received favorable terms Although the duties of the commissioners had now been performed, the opportunity of revenging fancied wrongs, and gratifying ancient hostility was too favorable for Claiborne to permit it to pass unimproved Bennett joined eagerly in the scheme, and, although the province of

Maryland, after having been included in the commission, was exempted from it, under color of some general terms, they resolved to extend their authority over it. Towards the close of March, 1652, they arived at St Marys, and requied that the colony should conform to the laws and submit to the authority of the commonwealth, saving Lord Baltimore's rights. To this Governor Stone consented. But when they insisted that the name of the Proprietary should be erased from all writs and processes, and that of the commonwealth used in its stead he felt himself compelled to resist. They then demanded an inspection of his commission, and when he produced it, violently seized upon it and removed him and his subordinates from office. They next appointed a council, of which Robert Brooke was made president and acting governor, took possession of the records and entirely abolished the authority of the Proprietary in the province. The commissioners then departed to Virginia, and declared Richard Bennett governor, and Claiborne secretary of that province; and having made some further regulations for its government, revisited St. Marys to arrange that of Maryland on a similar basis. They reinstated Governor Stone in his office, upon somewhat modified conditions, delivered over to Claiborne Kent island and Palmer's island at the mouth of the Susquehanna, and returned again to Virginia. Thus, Claiborne was once more successful, and the power of Lord Baltimore overthrown.*

A treaty was now entered into with the Susquehannahs, by which they ceded to the colony all their territory from Palmer's island to the Patuxent, and a large tract on the eastern shore. No sooner had this powerful tribe thus buried the hatchet, than the Nanticokes broke in upon the eastern shore settlers, burning, killing and ravaging. Terror prevailed among the inhabitants and an earnest effort was made by the governor to raise a force and protect the frontiers. Every seventh man capable of bearing arms was ordered to muster into service, to be fitted out at the expense of the remaining six. Boats were pressed into service and the whole

* Bozman, vol 2, p 448

expedition ordered to rendezvous at St. Mattapany, under the command of Captain Fuller. The Puritans of Anne Arundel, however, refused to make their levies, offering as their excuse, the hardship of the season, December and January Delays thus arose, and, perhaps the note of preparation causing a cessation of outrage, the soldiers already levied were discharged to their homes and the expedition abandoned.†

For several years, the inhabitants had devoted themselves very extensively to the culture of tobacco, somewhat to the neglect of corn, which, during the late commotions, had been still less attended to; a second season of scarcity was the consequence Tobacco and corn were from the earliest period the staples of Maryland commerce The first crop of Indian corn gathered by the pilgrims at St Marys afforded them a surplus with which as we have seen they opened a coasting trade with New England, and also later, with New Amsterdam Subsequently, when the culture of tobacco and corn grew extensive, this trade increased Indeed, the greater portion of their tobacco passed through the hands of the Dutch, who were then monopolizing the carrying trade of the world In 1640 all commerce with foreign countries was prohibited to the colonies by the British parliament By the famous navigation act, the carrying trade, which the Dutch still enjoyed between England and the colonies was entirely cut off Thus the colony was deprived of the privilege of free trade, and suffered greatly from the consequent diminution of its commerce in tobacco, which increased the distress due to the scarcity of corn.

The Lord Proprietary, thus dispossessed of his province, did not rest quietly under the manifest wrong and injustice done him He immediately took steps to call the commissioners to account for their illegal proceedings in Maryland, while their agents presented a petition, in their behalf to the parliament. This was dismissed Cromwell having in the meantime seized the reins of government and the Dutch war being then at its height, no further notice was taken of the

---
† Bozman

matter. Lord Baltimore, perhaps relying upon the growing tendency of Cromwell to monarchical power, determined to right himself in spite of the republicans, and directed Governor Stone to require all persons to take the oath of fidelity, and to re-establish the proprietary government, which was acordingly done in 1654.

No sooner had Claiborne and Bennett, in Virginia, heard of these proceedings, than they hastened to Providence to restore the old order of things. Both parties began to arm; but the commissioners, having gathered the Puritans in strength on the northern boundaries of the loyal districts, threatened them on the south with an invasion by a strong force from Virginia, and Governor Stone, timid or disaffected, again submitted. They took possession of the province, and issued a commission for its government in the name of Cromwell. whom Stone had already proclaimed. At its head they placed Captain William Fuller Their next step was to disfranchise the Catholics. An Assembly was called, and it was especially prohibited for any Catholic or royalist to vote for or to sit therein as a delegate.* As soon as this body, thus constituted, and representing but a minority of the people, assembled, it proceeded to pass a law enacting that no persons professing the faith of the Catholic church "would be protected in the province, but that they ought be restrained from the exercise thereof." At the same time they denounced "prelacy," as they denominated the church of England Thus was placed the first stain upon the fair name of Maryland, by the act of ungrateful refugees from the north By the same Assembly an act was passed to prevent the taking of the oath of fidelity to the Lord Proprietary

When Lord Baltimore was apprized of these proceedings, he despatched a special messenger, William Eltonhead, to the colony, with a severe rebuke to Governor Stone for thus yielding his authority without a blow and instructions to resume it immediately. Accordingly. in the opening of the year 1655, Stone issued commissions to his friends and began to make

---

* Bacon

levies among the people of St Marys, who had remained faithful to the Proprietary. In a short time he found himself at the head of two hundred men Believing himself strong enough to strike, he despatched a party of twenty men under William Eltonhead and Josias Fendall, to recover the records of the province, which the commissioners had seized and removed to the house of Richard Preston on the Patuxent, and to capture a magazine of arms and ammunition gathered there by the Puritans. The party was completely successful, and the records, together with the magazines, were once more restored to St. Marys. Then, having pressed into his service ten or twelve vessels, lying in the harbor, Governor Stone embarked part of his force and set out against the people of Providence On his way he was met by messengers from Captain Fuller and his council, remonstrating against his proceedings, desiring to know by what authority he acted, and protesting, "that by the help of God, they were resolved to commit themselves into the hands of God, and rather die like men, than live like slaves." Governor Stone returned no answer to the message and detained the messengers in the hope of taking his enemies by surprise. Three of them, however, made their escape to Providence, and the Puritans put upon their guard, began preparations for defence.

There was an armed merchantman, the "Golden Lyon," commanded by Captain Heamans, at anchor in the harbor. This vessel with its crew, they succeeded in winning to their cause With this aid, and their own people collected and armed, and with the certainty of reinforcements from Claiborne's men upon the Isle of Kent, which lay plainly in sight across the noble expanse of water, they felt themselves strong enough to bid defiance to their opponents. In the meanwhile, Governor Stone despatched envoys to the Puritans to demand an unconditional submission. As this had no effect, he immediately entered the mouth of the harbor with his twelve transports. As he was about to effect a landing, the Golden Lyon fired a gun at his little fleet, and sent a second shot close to the boats. He demanded the reason for this conduct, but the merchantman persisted in taking sides with the Puritans, and, his own small craft having no gun to oppose her, he assumed during the night a position higher up the creek. Early next morning, the Golden Lyon and some other vessels, with two pieces of cannon, were moored across the mouth of the creek so as to blockade the fleet. As soon as the governor drew out his little force in line upon the shore, they opened their batteries upon them, killing one of his men and compelling him to withdraw. While affairs were thus progressing, Captain Fuller, at the head of one hundred and twenty men, embarked in boats from Providence, and, having gone some distance up the river, landed, and made a circuit round the creek to the place where lay the forces of Governor Stone. As soon as their approach was discovered, the two parties, shouting their respective battle cries "*In the name of God fall on—God is our strength!*" and, "*Hey for St. Marys!*" rushed to the conflict. For a time the fight was well sustained; but at length the undisciplined levies of the yeomen of St. Marys, began to yield before the charge of the Puritans, whose captain, with many of his men, had been inured to battle in the wars of England under the victorious banner of Cromwell. Defended by a fallen tree, a portion of the Marylanders continued to maintain the action long after the main body had been defeated. Of the whole force only four or five escaped. Fifty killed or wounded attested the obstinacy of the conflict. The rest were taken prisoners. Among the slain was Thomas Hatton, secretary of the province, while Governor Stone, Col. Price, Major Chandler, and Captains Gerard, Lewis, Fendall and Guither (the governor and several others being also wounded) were among the prisoners. The vessel, arms and ammunition fell into the hands of the conquerors. The Puritans were completely victorious, their loss was only two killed and several wounded (two of whom died soon after the conflict. This battle so disastrous to the fortunes of Lord Baltimore was fought on the 25th of March, 1655.

The Puritans immediately stained their victory by an act as cruel and bloody as it was unnecessary The governor and several of his council and others to the number of ten were condemned to death, although they had surrendered themselves upon the pledge of quarter, and four of them, William Eltonhead, Lord Baltimore's special messenger; his servant, Lieutenant Lewis, and Mr. Leggatt, were actually shot in cold blood The rest only escaped at the stern intercession of the victorious soldiery themselves, and in response to the prayers of the ladies of the settlement Nothing in the history of the colony can compare with this cold blooded and nefarious outrage The governor and his council were detained prisoners for some time, and were prohibited from communicating with their friends. Governor Stone was not allowed even to write to his wife at St Marys, without first submitting his letters to the inspection of his keepers. The lady was at length permitted to visit her husband, and to nurse him Before leaving St Marys for this purpose, she wrote a detailed account of these unfortunate occurrences to Lord Baltimore Being thus undisputed masters of the colony the Puritans proceeded to confiscate the property of all who had taken up arms to resist their encroachments *

Both parties now appealed to Cromwell; Bennett, who had hastened to England, on the part of the Puritans, and Lord Baltimore in his own behalf. After various proceedings, the protector referred the matter to the lords commissioners, Whitelock and Widrington, who, it appears, reported in favor of the Proprietary's right to the government, but owing to the pre-occupation of the protector and his council with more pressing matters the report remained unconfirmed. Claiborne and Bennett renewed their petitions and representations, while Lord Baltimore without waiting for further approval, determined to make another effort to restore his authority On the 10th of July, 1656, he appointed Capt Josias Fendall, governor of the province, but, before he could take any effective steps, the new governor was arrested by the

---

* Bozman, vol. 2, pp 501-520, McMahon, 207

Puritans "upon suspicion," and brought before the provincial court to answer the charge "of dangerousness to the public peace." He denied the power of the court to try him and was ordered to be imprisoned until Cromwell should settle the disputed affairs of the colony. A month later, having grown weary of confinement, he made his submission, took an oath not to disturb the peace of the commonwealth, and obtained his release.

In the meantime, the controversy had been referred to the "commissioners of trade," in England. That body reported in favor of the Lord Proprietary, who therefore renewed his instructions to Governor Fendall, directing that the act for freedom of conscience should be duly observed in Maryland, commanding him to reward with grants of lands those who had been active in his behalf and to take especial care of the widows of those, who had been killed in his service,— particularly Mrs. Hatton, Mrs Lewis and Mrs Eltonhead — and tendering them the assurance that his lordship would endeavor to obtain justice upon their husbands' murderers.[*] He appointed his brother, Philip Calvert, secretary of the province, and sent him thither early in the spring of 1657. The new governor and secretary obtained possession of the capital without difficulty, and soon succeeded in extending their authority over St Marys county. Their success did not immediately extend beyond this. Maryland was now under a divided rule. The Puritans — Captain Fuller and his council — governed in the north, at Providence, destined hereafter under the name of Annapolis to become the capital of the colony and the state, while Governor Barber (whom Fendall, being compelled to visit England on the affairs of the province, had appointed by virtue of his commission to act in his absence), and the friends of the Lord Proprietary, held possession of the ancient city of St. Marys. The Puritans, determined to consider their authority as still undisputed and probably having possession of the records and public seals, summoned an Assembly, which convened

---

[*] Bozman, vol 2, p 698

at Patuxent on the 24th of September, 1657, and proceeded to confirm the authority of the party. They also levied a poll tax to pay the public expenses and appointed commissioners to collect the fines imposed upon the adherents of the Proprietary.† But their power was near its end.

Cromwell had grown weary of republicanism. He had rejected the title of king for the power of dictator and had sought to gather about him the old nobility of England. The republicanism of the Puritans was therefore no longer a recommendation, and the prospects of the Proprietary began to brighten daily. Bennett, the agent of the Puritans, soon perceived the turn of affairs and, despairing of maintaining their supremacy, hastened to make an agreement with Lord Baltimore in their name by which the whole province was to be surrendered to its rightful owner, leaving the disputes which had arisen and the offences which had been committed during the troubles to the adjudication of the protector. It was also agreed that patents for their lands, under the condition of plantation, should be issued to them and all persons desirous of quitting the province should have the privilege of doing so without hindrance. Lord Baltimore further pledged himself never to consent to the repeal of the law in favor of freedom of conscience which the Puritans now desired to be enforced as a protection to themselves.* This agreement Governor Fendall brought with him on his return from England in 1658, together with instructions relative to grants of lands, ordering, among others, a grant of ten thousand acres to Edward Eltonhead. The agreement placed restrictions upon the governor's powers and subjected him in their exercise to the advice and consent of Philip Calvert, or, in case of the latter's death, of Thomas Cornwallis, the early hero of the colony, its leader, and the steady friend at once of Proprietary and people. Barber surendered his powers into the hands of Governor Fendall, the articles of agreement were publicly read and a day appointed for the meeting of the rival authorities at St.

† Bacon.
* Bozman, vol 2, p 554

Leonard's Creek On the 22d of March both parties assembled at the place designated, but the Puritans objected to a clause in the oath of fidelity, demanded a mutual indemnity for all past transactions, and requested that they might not be disarmed and left defenceless at the mercy of the Indians. Upon consideration, so far as regarded persons already in the province, the oath was modified and the remaining demands conceded by the governor and council and, two days after, the amended agreement was solemnly adopted, Fendall's commission as governor of Maryland read and proclaimed and writs issued for a General Assembly to be held at St Leonards on the 27th of April following.[*]

Thus ended the ascendency of the Puritans in Maryland and the colony was once more peacefully restored to the government of the Lord Proprietary after nearly six years of successful rebellion No sooner had Governor Fendall overthrown the power of the Puritans, however, than he set about undermining that of the Lord Proprietary. At the session of 1659, the House of Delegates, doubtless by his contrivance, demanded that the governor and council should no longer sit as an upper house, as they had done since the year 1649, and claimed for itself the rights of supreme judicial and legislative power For a time Fendall made a show of resistance, but soon he yielded, and, with two of his council, took his seat in the lower house [†] The upper house was then declared dissolved, and Fendall, having resigned his commission from the Lord Proprietary into the hands of the Assembly, accepted from that body a new one in their own name and by their own authority. To secure obedience to this new and almost republican government an act was passed declaring it to be felony to disturb the existing order of things and the people were commanded by proclamation to acknowledge no authority except that which came immediately from the assembly or from the king, who had now been restored to the throne

---

[*] Bozman, vol 2, 562
[†] McMahon

of England.* But the power of this new rebel was of short duration. The people were tired of intestine commotions and looked back with regret to the mild government of Leonard Calvert. They, therefore, readily submitted to Philip Calvert, whom Lord Baltimore appointed governor upon receiving the intelligence of Fendall's rebellion, and who now appeared among them armed only with the proclamation of the king, which commanded all his faithful subjects to yield him obedience. Fendall gave himself up, and contrary to the express orders of Lord Baltimore, was respited by the governor from the punishment which he had merited. He made use of his clemency only to excite new troubles in after days.

Of the precise object of Fendall's designs it is now difficult to form an estimate. That they tended almost to republicanism there can be no doubt; possibly he hoped by the overthrow of the power of Lord Baltimore to secure to the legislature of the colony a virtual supremacy with only a nominal subjection to the king. His chief associates were Mr Robert Slye, Speaker of the House and Mr. Gerard and Col Nathaniel Utye, two members of his council. It is not improbable that the idea of colonial independence had already entered their minds.

Of Claiborne, the arch-disturber of the peace of Maryland, little further is known. After this last overthrow of his persistent schemes against the province of Maryland he abandoned all hope of a successful struggle with the power of his ancient enemies, and retired into Virginia where he settled in New Kent county, probably named by himself in remembrance of that beautiful island in the Chesapeake in which the hopes of his turbulent and ambitious life had been centered and for which he had contended so untiringly. He still continued a man of distinction and in 1666 represented New Kent in the Virginia House of Delegates.†

---

* Bacon, 1658
† Burke, 140

CHAPTER IV.

THE PROTESTANT REVOLUTION.

After the storm, a calm succeeded. For a long time the government remained fixed and the colony increased in numbers, in products and commerce, and enjoyed all those blessings which flow from peace and prosperity

For a period of thirty years the steady stream of quiet advancement flowed on in Maryland, which makes this portion of its records less fruitful of notable events than that which preceded it. At no time in the early history of the State were there great wars, civil or foreign, or extensive combinations among its Indian foes. Its civil wars were almost bloodless; its Indian enemies were not more difficult to subdue than a mere band of robbers Their depredations seldom exceeded a petty theft or occasional murder and a single company of men were generally sufficient to repel them In the course of ten years of civil commotion the largest force ever brought into the field was not more than one-sixth of the enrolled men of the province. It is not in martial prowess that the most interesting portion of Maryland's early history must be sought.

The people of the colony, under a brother of its founder, having proclaimed Charles II king, set about legislating* to remedy the consequences of the late troubles and to increase their prosperity A mint was established for coining shillings, port duties were laid and regulations for masters of ships adopted, a tax of eighteen pounds of tobacco per head was imposed for the proper maintenance of the government

---
* 1660 — See Bacon

and special provision was made for soldiers wounded or disabled in the service of the colony The mode of payment of port duties is worthy of notice as indicating the needs of the times. Every vessel having a flush deck fore and aft coming to trade in the province was required to pay one half pound of powder and three pounds of shot for every ton burden. To insure the circulation of the new coinage, every householder was compelled to take from the mint ten shillings for each taxable person in his family, for which he was to deposit tobacco, at the rate of two pence per pound. For nearly two years the affairs of the province were prosperously conducted by Philip Calvert In 1662, he was superseded by his nephew, the Hon Charles Calvert, son of the Lord Proprietary and heir of the province. When in 1660 Philip Calvert had assumed the government of the colony its inhabitants numbered twelve thousand Nothing evidences more strongly the excellence of his administration and that of his nephew, than the rapid increase in population. In the space of five years it had swollen to sixteen thousand souls — an increase of one-third, and in 1671 to twenty thousand As the population increased, it had been found necessary to enlarge the number of counties, of which there were already seven—St Marys, founded in 1634; Kent, in 1650; Anne Arundel, 1650, Calvert, 1654, Charles, 1658, Baltimore, 1659; and Talbot, 1660-61.† As yet there were few towns, and these never reached extensive growth. St Marys contained but little more than fifty or sixty houses and Providence, or Annapolis, was still smaller. The people were planters and farmers; such occupations are not favorable to the growth of towns. They obtained all their supplies of manufactured articles from the mother country, which monopolized their trade The principal planters found it convenient to make importations of large quantities of goods, which they stored away and which served, not only to supply their own demands, but also those of their neighbors. Thus, to a great extent, was the internal trade provided for through

---

†McMahon, Bacon

St. Marys There was no manufacturing business to build up towns and even the mechanics whose trades were in most demand were generally drawn by the convenience of their customers from the towns into the clusters of settlements in the interior There was no influence, therefore, calculated to foster and build up the city but that of its being the seat of government, and it was this alone that sustained St. Marys.

The first Assembly, which was convened by Charles Calvert, continued the spirit of improvement which had characterized the administration of the late governor. It declared the laws of England to be in force in the province, and made appropriation for a statehouse and prison. The publication of marriages was provided for and an inducement held out to farmers to raise English grain. A levy of twenty-five pounds of tobacco on each taxable person was devoted to the use of Gov. Charles Calvert * At the next session, in 1663-4, the Assembly was still busied about the administration of internal affairs and laying the foundations of much of the present systems of laws.

It passed laws for the regulation of the duties of sheriffs, the conveyance of land, the quitting of title, the preservation of orphan estates, the general administration of justice, the appointment of a public notary, the making of ferries, the erection of a magazine and the improvement of harbors. It also passed laws governing the relation of master and slave.† There could be no better picture of the condition of the settlement, the tendencies of its rulers, and the necessities of its people, than the simple enumeration of the laws which they found it convenient and proper to adopt. Indeed, during this long and peaceful period the history of the province is scarcely more than the recital of its domestic legislation. The law relating to masters and slaves is worthy of further notice as the first evidence of the existence of slavery in Maryland.

---

* Bacon, 1662
† Bacon, 1663-4

The introduction of negro slavery into the colony was at a very early period Slaves made their first appearance in Virginia in 1620 when a Dutch ship touched at that colony with a cargo of slaves, of whom twenty were bought by the Virginians. When the Indians "first beheld these black people they thought them a breed of devils" and for a long time called them "*Manitto*"— a word signifying either God or devil. "When the whites first came," said an old Indian long afterwards, "our fathers believed they were surely gods, but the appearance in their midst of this new and, to them, hideous race completely astonished them and confused their preconceived ideas of things"* In 1663, for the first time, distinct mention of *negro* slaves is made in the laws of the colony and it is evident that there were already many in the province. Throughout the laws of Maryland a strong distinction is constantly drawn between the terms "servant" and "slave" Prior to the act of 1663 many laws were passed relating to the condition of servants and apprentices, but the only use of the word "slave," is in the act of 1638 "for the liberties of the people," which describes "the people," as consisting of all Christian inhabitants, "*slaves* only excepted"† — a term which is never, elsewhere, applied to any but negroes. As slavery existed in Virginia prior to the settlement of Maryland it is probable that it was introduced gradually, with the increasing wealth of the settlers of the new colony.

There was another species of servant in the colony, however. of whom frequent mention is made These in time came to make up a large portion of the population. White emigrants, who were unable to bear the expenses of a voyage to the new world, or to maintain themselves upon their arrival, bound themselves to serve for a limited number of years any one who would advance the necessary funds. In time this practice became extensive Indentures were made to the captain of the ship or some other person, and, upon their arrival in the colony, the unexpired time of the servant

---

* Kalm's Travels in North America, 1748
† Bacon, 1638, Holmes' Annals, vol 1, p. 256

was sold to the highest bidder In the early stage of the colony they were called indented apprentices, afterwards the general term of " redemptioners " was applied to them Upon the expiration of their term of service they became useful citizens and enjoyed the same franchises as their former masters.

The very industry of the planters and the fertility of the soil now brought unexpected difficulties not only on Maryland, but also on her sister colonies of Virginia and Carolina At first the high price of tobacco led the greater portion of the people to devote their attention to its cultivation and a greatly increased production was the consequence A fall in the price ensued, and a deterioration in the quality of the article, due to careless culture, reduced its value so low that the year's produce would scarcely supply clothes to the planters. A scarcity of corn was also frequently felt through the neglect to put out sufficient crops and the Assembly of Maryland often found it necessary to direct the attention of the planters to this subject and to compel them, under severe penalties, to raise at least a certain porportion of corn in addition to their tobacco

In 1663 the evil had become so great that the king himself urged remedial action upon the consideration of the colonies. There were only two remedies — a diminution of the quantity raised or a cessation for a time of its cultivation. For either purpose joint action of the three colonies was required, and accordingly commissioners from Maryland and Virginia met at Wicomocomico to arrange a basis for the necessary treaty. It was determined at this meeting, that after the twentieth of June of the succeeding year, no tobacco should be planted in either colony, that the Assembly of Maryland should be called to ratify the agreement — and that the governors and councils of both colonies should solemnly swear to use their utmost efforts to have the laws passed in pursuance of the agreement and carried into effect.* This

---

* Burke's History of Virginia, vol. 2, p 134

scheme, however, was not perfected until 1666 when the Assembly of Maryland passed an act † prohibiting the planting of tobacco throughout the province for one year from the 1st of February, 1666, to the 1st of February, 1667 Formal notice of this act, together with a copy of the governor's proclamation, was forwarded to Virginia by the chancellor and the legislature of that colony declared in force a similar measure, provisionally adopted by them at the preceding session. The Lord Proprietary disapproved of the act of the Maryland Assembly but his "disassent" was not signified until the November following, when the law had already produced the desired effect.

The fame of the liberty enjoyed in Maryland had already gone abroad and persons of different nationalities sought an asylum within her borders and were admitted to the rights of citizenship. Thus, in 1666, an act was passed for the naturalization of several families from France, Spain, and Bohemia Similar acts constantly recur in the proceedings of subsequent legislatures.‡

In England, in Virginia, in Massachusetts and the north, the pillory and the whipping post awaited members of the Society of Friends; everywhere, save in Maryland, they were proscribed There, only, was their religious worship "held publicly and without interruption "§ "In Maryland," says Burke,|| "where the governor and a majority of the people were papists and royalists, a religion and government whose spirit is thought to be hostile to liberty, and averse to toleration, they were immediately hailed as brothers and admitted to all the rights of freemen" The members of the colonial legislature and the council, many persons of quality and justices of the peace, came together to listen to the preaching of George Fox, the zealous leader of the Quakers, while he tar-

---

† Bacon
‡ Ibid
§ Bancroft, vol 2, p 237.
|| History of Virginia, vol 2, p 131

ried in Maryland.* The emperor of the Nanticokes and his subject kings and their subordinate chiefs, gathered around him to hear his words. The heir of the province was present at one of these assemblies For a time, however, the Friends were involved in difficulties with the government from their refusal to perform military duty and their rejection of oaths; but at a later period they were relieved from these trammels

From the date of the treaty with the Susquehannahs, in 1652, the frontiers of the settlements had been but little molested. The Susquehannahs, once so powerful, had begun to give place to the Senecas, a portion of the Five Nations, who penetrated through the province of Pennsylvania, conquering and driving before them the Indian inhabitants and molesting the white settlers. Occasional bodies of these daring marauders approached the frontiers of Maryland, and it was found necessary, for a time, to maintain a body of rangers, under Captain John Allen, for their protection In the summer of 1675, a number of murders and outrages had been committed on the people of Virginia and Maryland residing along the Potomac, by a band of savages and suspicion fell upon the Susquehannahs A joint expedition was sent by the two provinces to chastise them. The Virginia forces were under the command of Colonel Washington — those of Maryland under Major Trueman On Monday, the 25th of September, the Maryland troops appeared before a fort of the Piscataways held by the Susquehannahs, and were met by a deputation of chiefs who laid the blame of the inroad upon the Senecas, who, they stated, were by that time at the head of the Patapsco river on their return.

The next morning, Colonel Washington, Colonel Mason and Major Adderton of the Virginia troops joined Major

---

* 1666 Bancroft NOTE.—During his stay in Maryland, Fox, with his companions, Barclay and Keith, paid a visit to the Labadists, a religious community established on Bohemia Manor, whose practices had much in common with those of the Friends, and endeavored to effect a union with them —James, the Labadist Colony in Maryland, p 29

Trueman and were visited by the same deputation. They charged these Indians with the murders which had been committed. Thereupon Major Trueman, yielding to the advice of his associates, caused five of the chiefs to be bound and put to death. They continued to affirm their innocence, and in the vain hope of securing their safety, displayed a silver medal and some papers which had been given them by former governors of Maryland in token of amity and protection. This severe proceeding attracted the indignation of the House of Delegates and an inquiry was set on foot. Major Trueman was impeached before the upper house for the murder of the five Indian chiefs, who had come into his camp in the guise of envoys. He pleaded guilty, and a bill of attainder was brought in against him. Such extenuating circumstances were adduced by the defendant that the House refused to pass sentence of death upon him and, a dispute arising between the two houses, as to their respective powers as well as the guilt of the accused, he escaped punishment.* The importance given to the affair proves, at least, the strict justice of the people of Maryland in their intercourse with the natives, and the horror with which a breach of faith towards them was viewed.

Charles Calvert continued to act as governor until the death of his father on the 30th of November, 1675, by which event he became himself the lord Proprietary. Intending to return to England as soon as possible, he convened an Assembly for the purpose of reducing to some system the laws of the colony, to many of which his father had not given his assent. "A general revision took place and those laws which were thought proper to be continued were definitely ascertained."† During his administration as governor the Assembly had effected many improvements. Roads had been built, courthouses and jails erected, coroners appointed in all the counties, and the publication of the laws within the province by proclamtion of the sheriff in the county courts provided

---
* Annals of Annapolis, pp 66-82
† McMahon, p 215

for. In 1671 the Assembly granted to Lord Baltimore a duty of two shillings per hundred weight on all tobacco exported from Maryland One half of the proceeds were to be applied to the defence of the province, the other to his own use as partial compensation for his great expenditure in establishing the colony, which was estimated to have exceeded forty thousand pounds sterling in the two first years Out of this grant great difficulties afterwards arose.

Having reformed the system of laws and believing his presence no longer necessary in the province, the lord Proprietary appointed Thomas Notely, Esq, deputy governor, during his absence, to act in the name of his infant son, Cecil Calvert, as nominal governor, and returned to England in the year 1676 Upon his arrival, he found that complaints had been made against his government by certain Episcopal clergymen, who represented the province as in a frightful condition, and proposed, as a remedy, that a support should be provided for them by law * They inveighed against him, because the Catholic priests held landed estates in the colony. In rebuttal, Lord Baltimore pointed to the laws of toleration in force in the province, and to the conditions under which these lands had been acquired He was advised by the committee of trade and the plantations, to whom the matter was referred, to provide a public support for the clergy of the church of England † This he declined to do and so thus ended the first effort to establish the Episcopal church by law in Maryland The authorities of Virginia had charged his government with not assisting in the defence of the frontiers. This complaint was also declared to be groundless In 1680 Lord Baltimore returned to Maryland and once more assumed the personal direction of its government During his absence a singular case had been brought before the General Assembly. A physician named Edward Husbands was charged with attempting to poison the governor and the members of the two houses He met the charge with great warmth, cursing the

---
* McMahon, 216
† Bancroft, vol 2, p. 242

Assembly, for which he was sentenced to be forever barred from practising as a surgeon, and to receive twenty lashes on the bare back. He was bound over to appear before the provincial court to answer the charge of attempting to poison. It is probable that Lord Baltimore on his return stayed these arbitrary proceedings, as he dissented † from every act passed during that year, and no further mention is made of Husbands or his alleged offence

In the following year, Fendall, still revolving his restless projects, attempted, in conjunction with an Episcopal clergyman named Coode, to excite a rebellion among the people. They failed, were arrested, tried and convicted; but escaped with their lives, to further disturb the peace of the province. For four years the Proprietary continued to govern the colony in person. In 1684, the complexion of affairs in England seeming to demand his presence there, he appointed a council of nine deputies, with William Joseph president, to direct the affairs of the province, under the nominal governorship of his infant son, Benedict Leonard Calvert, and departed from the colony, little imagining that he was bidding it adieu forever When he reached England, he found James II on the throne, and his province in greater peril than it had been under his father, Charles II, who had threatened him with the issuance of a writ of quo warranto Danger impended alike from the king and from the enemies of the king At length, in April, 1687, the writ of quo warranto was issued, requiring Lord Baltimore to show cause why the charter should not be forfeited But before the proceedings could be brought to a termination the king was deposed and driven out of England by the revolution of 1688 While the charter was saved, the authority of the Lord Proprietary was overthrown by an uprising of the people. Events in Maryland were bringing to a close the long period of repose and toleration enjoyed under the mild administration of the second Lord Proprietary, for dissensions, excited by the troubles in the mother country at length broke out into open revolution

---

† Bacon, 1674

For thirty years religious freedom had prevailed in Maryland. Until the last few years, no distinction had been made in the matter of religious creeds, and then, only because Lord Baltimore was compelled by order of the king to select his officers entirely from the Protestant inhabitants of the colony The feeling which caused the revolution in England extended its effects to Maryland. The Lord Proprietary, upon the success of the revolution in England, announced his adherence to William and Mary and transmitted orders to his deputies to have their accession to the throne proclaimed in the province Unfortunately these instructions were delayed, and, even after the new sovereigns had been acknowledged in the surrounding colonies, the authorities awaited directions from the Lord Proprietary The ill-will of the people had already been excited against the deputies by an attempt to infringe upon the rights of the Assembly, and every measure which they now adopted, being viewed through the eyes of prejudice tended only to strengthen suspicion and confirm opposition. The settlements were filled with disturbing rumors. The deputies in vain sought to stop their circulation The public arms were collected, in apprehension of a general outbreak The unfortunate delay in proclaiming William and Mary brought matters to a crisis.

In April, 1689, *"An association in arms for the defence of the Protestant religion, and for asserting the rights of King William and Queen Mary to the province of Maryland, and all the English dominions,"* was formed; at its head was John Coode who had once before been found guilty of treason and rebellion. The deputies were driven for protection to the garrison of Mattapany, which was besieged and compelled to surrender in the following August, leaving the associators in undisputed possession of the province. Coode was a man of loose morals and desperate habits. Although a minister of the church of England, he was presented for atheism and blasphemy by the grand jury, under the very government which he was now foremost in establishing. To escape trial he fled into Virginia, whence he frequently came back in secret to the province, declaring that as he had overthrown one government, he would pull down another. His attempts however failed and he was at last taken, tried and convicted, but pardoned in consideration of the services he had rendered during the revolution of 1689.*

The first act of the associators was to call a convention of the people, which met at St Marys on the 23d of August, 1689. They drew up and forwarded to the king an account of their proceedings which was filled with accusations against Lord Baltimore and his government. The king sustained the acts of a revolution which was only a continuation of that which had placed him upon the throne and the province for a time continued under the administration of the convention. Anxious, however, to secure the domination of their party under the name of the king they requested him to take the government of the colony into his own hands, and, accordingly, in 1691, he appointed Sir Lionel Copley governor.

Sir Lionel arrived in Maryland in the ensuing year, and, on the 9th of April, dissolved the convention and summoned a General Assembly, which met on the 10th of May, 1692, at the city of St Marys. Its first act was the recognition of William and Mary, its next the establishment of the Episcopal as the State Church of Maryland. Every county was divided into parishes and taxes were levied upon the people without distinction for the support of the ministers and the repair of the old and the building of new churches.† "Thus," says McMahon, "was introduced, for the first time in Maryland, a church establishment, sustained by law, and fed by general taxation."‡ But matters did not rest here, persecution followed disfranchisement. The Catholics had already been deprived of the right of holding offices, and the new government did not wait long before it proceeded to severer measures. In 1704 an act was passed "to prevent the growth of popery," by which it was made a penal offence for a bishop or priest of the Catholic church to say mass or to perform any of their

---
* McMahon, 239
† Bacon, 1688
‡ Page 243

offices or for any Catholic to teach school. But the harshness of these measures was not fully sustained by public opinion; and, by subsequent legislation Catholic priests were permitted to exercise their functions in private houses. Out of this privilege grew a custom of erecting chapels, under the same roof, and connected with the dwelling of some Catholic family, where Catholics might gather to enjoy the exercise of their religion. But the intolerance of the established church did not spend its zeal upon Catholics alone. It had no sympathy with Protestantism that differed from itself. Dissenters, as they were called by the Episcopalians, were deprived of the equal rights and privileges which they had formerly enjoyed under the rule of the Proprietary. Quakers were treated with indignity and their meetings for silent prayer and meditation declared unlawful assemblages. In 1702, however, the provisions of the English toleration act for "Dissenters" were extended to Maryland, and in 1706 relief was granted to the Quakers. "And thus, in a colony which was established by Catholics, and grew up to power and happiness under the government of a Catholic, the Catholic inhabitant was the only victim of religious intolerance."* The supremacy of the "law church" over all others was still, however, maintained.

Having endeavored to prevent the increase of Catholics at home, they determined to cut off all accessions to their numbers from abroad. Laws, restraining their emigration into the colony were passed and frequently re-enacted down to the revolution of 1776. These restrictions and oppressions produced their effect — and the Catholic population continued to decrease, until, in 1758, seventy years after the Protestant revolution, according to the statement of Governor Sharpe, they numbered only one-thirteenth of the population.

The Assembly next endeavored to deprive the Proprietary of his rights in the province. He was still entitled to all the unsettled lands, with the right of making grants of them and to the quit rents and certain duties or imposts not connected with the government. Among these was the port duty

---

* McMahon, 246.

and the duty of two shillings per hundred on all tobacco exported from the colony. The king, being appealed to by Lord Baltimore, issued a royal letter authorizing him to collect his revenues in the province, but the convention refused to submit. They threw his agents into prison. Sir Lionel Copley had been directed by the king to protect the rights of Lord Baltimore and ensure the collection of his dues. Darnall, the receiver-general of the Proprietary, however, still met with opposition, and it was not until the matter was expressly decided by the king and council in favor of Lord Baltimore, that the Assembly yielded up to him his port and tonnage duties, and entered into a compromise in relation to the issuing of land patents.*

The people of St. Marys and the surrounding country had adhered to the Proprietary in all his struggles and the Assembly determined to punish them by removing the seat of government. But a more sufficient reason was found in the fact that the settlements had extended far into the interior and along the shores of the bay, and St. Marys was thus on the verge of the colony and difficult of access to the members of the legislature and those who had business before that body and the courts In vain St Marys prayed and protested; her existence depended upon the possession of the seat of government and her authorities offered to provide a public conveyance to run from Patuxent daily during the sessions of the Assembly and the courts and weekly for the rest of the year The Assembly rejected their prayers and the seat of government was removed to "the townland at Proctor's," or Providence, which was thenceforth called Annapolis. St. Marys dwindled into practical extinction and "in the very State to which it gave birth, and the land it redeemed from the wilderness, it now stands a solitary spot dedicated to God, and a fit memento of perishable man."† No effort was spared to secure the growth of the new town; a portion of the population of the old followed the government to Annapolis, which,

---
* McMahon, 247
† McMahon, 253-5

in 1708, was raised to the rank of a city Four or five years later it contained about forty houses, a statehouse and free school of brick and a brick church were soon after erected.

A controversy arising about the incorporation of Annapolis, the Assembly displayed its usual firmness Governor Seymour, having failed to obtain a charter for the new city, in 1708 granted one in his own name, claiming power to do so under the charter of Maryland, which, however, could not be interpreted to convey that right to a royal governor who ruled in opposition to the charter rights of the Proprietary An election was held in the new city for two delegates to represent it in the approaching Assembly. At the opening of the session, these deputies attempted to take their seats, but were refused admission on the ground that the charter had been illegally granted The lower house was summoned before the upper by the governor, who endeavored to conciliate them. But they were inflexible, whereupon the governor dissolved them A new Assembly was called; but its first act was to demand whether the governor had received any authority from the queen, other than his commission, to erect a city and the production of such authorization if he possessed it At length a compromise was effected and the Assembly passed an act to confirm the charter with certain specified restrictions *

In 1691, Sir Lionel Copley was succeeded by Francis Nicholson, who was principally active in securing the success of the established church and promoting the cause of education. He was first commissioned in 1691, but being then absent in England, the government was assumed by Sir Edmond Andros, upon the death of Copley, and exercised by him until the arrival of Nicholson in 1694.

The French war had already broken out on the frontiers of the northern colonies and the growth and strength of Maryland and Virginia induced the royal governors to seek their assistance. This led to the famous scheme of "crown requisitions," by which each colony was required to furnish certain proportions of men and money to aid in the defence of New

---
* McMahon, 255, Annals

York, the chief point of assault. The people of Maryland generally disregarded or disobeyed these demands. Sometimes they furnished the assistance required — on one occasion, being unable to raise £133, the sum demanded, it was advanced by Governor Nicholson himself. Thomas Tasker, the treasurer of the State, was subsequently despatched with another sum to New York with instructions to represent the difficulty with which the money had been raised, the inability of the people to meet further demands upon them, and the necessity of providing for the defence of their own border. Yet, in the next century, this system continued for a long time and was productive of great good. It taught the colonists to rely on their own resources, to know their extent, how to husband them, and their great power when they acted unitedly. During the government of Nicholson, several improvements were effected. In 1695 a public post was established, the route extending from the Potomac, by way of Annapolis, to Philadelphia. A number of offices were designated on the route which the postman was required to traverse eight times a year,— to carry all public messages and to deliver letters and packages for the inhabitants, for which services he received the salary of fifty pounds sterling a year. This rude system was sustained only three years. In 1710 the English government found it necessary to establish a general post throughout the colonies. In 1696 the Assembly passed an act for the establishment of an academy at Annapolis, to be called King William's School, and in the succeeding year, through the efforts of the governor, a portion of the royal revenues were set apart for the purchase of books and the foundation of a public library for the institution.*

In 1704 the Statehouse was destroyed by fire and the legislature appropriated the sum of one thousand pounds sterling for the erection of a new one, holding their sessions in the meanwhile in a house rented at twenty pounds a year, from Col. Edward Dorsey. The new building was of brick, and was finished in 1706. In the conflagration, many of the records

---

* Annals of Annapolis, 90, etc.

of Anne Arundel county were destroyed, and a special commission was appointed to hear and determine all disputes concerning land, in order to remedy the loss. Their decisions upon all matters brought before them were recorded, and form a portion of the land records of the county.*

During the twenty-five years of royal dominion in Maryland there is little remarkable in its history beyond boundary disputes and the encroachments which the crown was already beginning to make upon the liberties of the people. While the colony was poor and weak it was permitted to struggle on, neglected by the crown, but no sooner had it grown rich and populous than the cupidity of England was aroused. In 1701, a bill was introduced into parliament for the destruction of the charters of Massachusetts, New Hampshire, Rhode Island, Connecticut, the Jerseys, Pennsylvania, Maryland, and the Bahama islands, and to sustain it, an effort was made to obtain evidence from the colonies against their present systems. An order was addressed to the governor of Maryland to collect testimony concerning the abuses of the lord Proprietary's government, but the insignificance of the charges which were gathered, proved the justice of his administration and the opposition of the people to the proposed change. They, however, did not hesitate to allege that their neighbor, Pennsylvania, was a mere receptacle of runaway slaves, and Jersey, the resort of pirates. The agents of the several colonies were heard against the measure before parliament, and, so successful was their defence, that, although it was favored by the crown, it could not be carried through. The ministry, however, did not despair. In 1715, when the government was surrendered once more to Lord Baltimore, another effort was made against the charters. Again the colonies united in remonstrating against the injustice; and again their united energies preserved for them the constitutions which they loved.† In these petty struggles, is found the germ of liberty which led to the independence of the nation.

---

* Bacon, 1705, ch 3
† McMahon, 272

The royal government tended to restrain the internal progress of the colony. In 1671, its population had already risen to nearly twenty thousand; at the close of the royal domination, forty-four years later, it had only reached thirty thousand, a large portion of which increase must be set down to the period before the revolution of 1688-9. After that event, the same inducements for emigration no longer existed—the Catholic—instead of toleration found oppression, and the "dissenter" met with no encouragement to cast his lot within the borders of Maryland. Lands were no longer given as a bounty and the fluctuations of the tobacco trade and the distress occasioned by the neglect of other agricultural pursuits not only discouraged immigration, but induced the departure of many of the old inhabitants to seek homes elsewhere. To add to these misfortunes in 1694-5 an unusual scarcity prevailed and a destructive disease made its appearance among the livestock of the farmers and planters. In these two years 25,429 cattle and 62,375 hogs died. This was a heavy blow to the colony. But their misfortunes did not stop here—two years later a violent epidemic made its appearance among the people of Charles county, resulting in great loss of life.

Heretofore the colonists had been without home manufactures, relying entirely upon the mother country for their supplies. But in 1697, urged by the difficulty in procuring goods from England, an effort was set on foot in Somerset and Dorchester counties to make woollen and linen cloths. Every attempt of this kind was closely watched and quickly suppressed by the British government, which wished to compel the colonies to consume goods of English manufacture, as a source of profit and a means of securing their dependence upon them. Therefore, these efforts to supply a domestic manufacture either signally failed or languished and died.

The era of the royal governors of Maryland was one of inaction, during which the limits of the settlements were but little advanced, the population but feebly increased and the amount of foreign trade and domestic resources, if not diminished, at best only remained stationary. The brotherly spirit of the law of 1649 had departed. Strife and controversy had awakened the bitterest feelings of hostility between Protestants and Catholics "At one time, they (the Catholics) were not permitted to walk in front of the courthouse, and were actually obliged to wear swords for their personal protection."* But the cause of the royal dominion was about to be removed. Charles, Lord Baltimore, having reached the age of eighty-four years, expired on the 20th of February, 1714, full of years and honors

---

* McMahon.

CHAPTER V.

THE RESTORATION OF THE PROVINCE

Upon the decease of the lord Proprietary, his title and his province descended to his son, Benedict Leonard Calvert. He had abandoned the faith of his father and become a Protestant, but only lived long enough to be acknowledged lord Proprietary. By his death, on the 16th of April, 1715, the title to the province devolved upon his infant heir, Charles Calvert, who, with his brothers and sisters, was reared a Protestant. There being no longer any obstacle on the score of religion, the government of the province was restored and a commission was issued in his name by Lord Guilford, his guardian to Hart, the last royal governor, continuing him as the representative of the Proprietary. The restoration produced but little change in the province. Scarcely, however, had it been consummated before a second attempt against the charters of the several colonies was made in parliament. A petition was presented, in the name of the youthful Lord Baltimore, stating that he and his brothers and sisters were Protestants, and that they depended for their support upon their revenues from Maryland and praying that the province might be spared. The other colonies resisted also, and the project was abandoned. The first legislature which assembled under the new Proprietary passed a body of laws still further strengthening the groundwork of their liberties. But there was one act of a contrary tendency, which the great Revolution abrogated. It introduced into Maryland all the test oaths and disabilities which were in force in England.

For a period of forty years the colony enjoyed almost undisturbed tranquillity. Its chief incidents were contests between the governor and council and the delegates of the people in the lower house. Its only warlike measures consisted of grants of men occasionally sent to the assistance of the northern colonies. The first controversy arose about the extension of the laws of England to the colony. The Proprietary desired to limit their introduction as interfering with his own legislatve rights as well as those of the people, while the people themselves demanded the adoption of all such laws as might be beneficial to them or which might tend in any way to extend or secure their rights. A war of petitions and protests, resolutions, dissents, addresses and proclamations ensued. For ten years the struggle continued and the sturdy commoners did not cease their efforts, until, in 1732 they had achieved the substance of their demands. The next advance in the path of freedom related to the revenues of the Proprietary.

In 1739, the Assembly resolved that the duties levied by the Proprietary were unjust and oppressive and protested against the settling of officers' fees by proclamation by the governor and the creation of new offices with new fees without the consent of the Assembly. They passed a bill for the appointment of an agent in London to carry their grievances before the crown. It was rejected by the upper house. Determined not to be silenced, the lower house selected a committee of their own body to perform the same duty, at the same time authorizing them to employ an agent in London, thus avoiding the possible interference of the upper house. But the governor's party fell upon a scheme to counteract this design. The Assembly was prorogued and it was immediately contended that the power of the committee ceased with the existence of the body from which it was derived and of which the committee itself was part. Baffled for the time, the popular party did not cease their exertions, and at the opening of the next session in 1740, they renewed their opposition. They were successful in a measure and obtained the right of full access to the records which had been before denied them appointed their agent and sent him full instructions and testimony to sustain his applications.* Some of their demands were granted, but the tonnage and tobacco duties continued a standing subject of complaint and resistance until the Revolutionary War closed all controversies and removed all grievances.

From the earliest period the government of the colony had pursued the peaceful and just policy of extinguishing by purchase the title of the Indians to the lands within the limits of the province. Where the affection of the natives for the graves of their fathers proved stronger than the inducement of material advantage they were permitted to remain, and were protected in the unmolested enjoyment of their hunting grounds. Thus, in 1698, an act was passed, and renewed in 1704, to assure to Panquash and Annotoughquan two kings of the Nanticokes, and their subjects, the possession of their lands in Dorchester county, "it being most just," says this equitable law, "that the Indians, the ancient inhabitants of this province, should have a convenient dwelling place in this their native country, free from the encroachments and oppressions of the English, especially the Nanticoke Indians, in Dorchester county, who for these many years have lived in peace and concord with the English, and, in all matters, in obedience to the government of this province."† As an acknowledgment of the authority of Lord Baltimore, the were required to pay him, annually, the nominal tribute of a single beaver skin Thus it appears that even the warlike Nanticokes had yielded to the colonial government and become peaceful dwellers under its protection. By degrees they began to remove, and in 1748, the great body of them departed from the eastern shore to Wyoming and Chemenk, carrying with them the disinhumed bones of their fathers to deposit them in other graves in their new settlements.‡ Before their final departure, however, their friendly relations with the whites became disturbed Instigated by the Senecas, they entered into a conspiracy with them

---

* McMahon, 283
† Bacon, 1704, ch 58
‡ Holmes' Annals, vol 2, p 37 — note

to rise and massacre the settlers. The attempt arose out of the dissatisfaction of the Senecas at the failure of a claim which the Six Nations asserted to the lands west of the Susquehanna, in Pennsylvania and Maryland. It was discovered by the governor of Pennsylvania, and by him communicated to the authorites of Maryland, who promptly placed the frontiers in a state of defence ‡ The alarm which had been excited in the colony by this unexpected, and probably exaggerated affair, soon subsided, but it served to warn the government to adhere to its early policy

The tribes of the Six Nations were the most powerful confederacy of Indians on the continent, and, to prevent any further difficulty with them, it was determined to extinguish their claims to territory in Maryland by purchase. At the session of 1742 the governor recommended this subject for the consideration of the Assembly. They concurred in his views, but a contest arose as to the power of appointing commissioners to effect the proposed arrangement. The Assembly asserted their right to select a portion and named Dr Robert King and Charles Carroll to act in conjunction with the appointees of the governor, and laid down certain instructions for the guidance of their conduct Governor Bladen considered this as an usurpation of his power and refused to confirm their proceedings The House remained firm and the negotiation was suspended. Having failed to bring his opponents to subjection, in 1744 Governor Bladen on his own responsibility appointed commissioners who, in conjunction with the representatives of Virginia and Pennsylvania, met at Lancaster, Pa , and concluded a treaty with the Six Nations, whereby, in consideration of the payment of three hundred pounds current money, they agreed to relinquish all claim to any territory within the boundaries of Maryland.

The planting of towns and cities was encouraged by early Maryland legislation and a number of acts were passed establishing towns,* though few of them ever grew to any impor-

---
‡ Burke, vol 3, p 106
* Bacon, 1683, ch 5, 1684, ch 2; 1688,, 1716, ch 14, etc

tance. In 1729 Baltimore was laid out in sixty lots on the lands of Charles Carroll, by commissioners appointed by the legislature, and in 1732, it was increased by an addition of ten acres, on the land of Edward Fell The advantages which it possessed from a commercial point of view soon began to draw population and attract enterprize, and, while the numerous other towns erected by the legislature either remained unsettled or soon died away, Baltimore grew and flourished For a time Elkridge Landing was a great tobacco market and vied with it for the commerce of the northern part of the colony. But the superior advantages of Baltimore soon enabled it to surpass its rival. In the meanwhile, Annapolis had continued to grow, and being the seat of a rich and aristocratic government, drew around it the wealth and fashion of the province. There the fine arts found patronage and literature began to spring up As a testimony of its advancement it could boast in 1745 the earliest and for a long time the only newspaper printed in the colony. The first number of the "Maryland Gazette" was issued on the 27th of January, 1745, by Jonas Green, who had been appointed printer to the province in 1740. This paper continued to be published by the descendants of its founder until 1839, in which year it was discontinued A printing press, however, had been established in the colony as early as 1726 for the purpose of printing the laws and public documents, which, prior to that date, had been printed at Philadelphia by William Bradford * Annapolis bore worthily the title of "the Athens of America "†

After Baltimore, the most important of the new towns because of its subsequent growth, was Frederick, the county town of Frederick county, situated in the rich and fertile valley watered by the Monocacy river It was laid out in September, 1745, by Mr Patrick Dulany. In 1748, on the formation of the new county of Frederick it was made the county town and is now the second city in Maryland Georgetown, now in the District of Columbia, was laid out under an act

---
* Holmes Annals vol I, p 539
† Annals, McMahon

of Assembly in 1751, in eighty lots, comprising sixty acres of land * An inspection house for tobacco already existed there, and the new town at the head of navigation on the Potomac possessed advantages which soon gave it strength and life.

The requisitions which had heretofore been made upon Maryland by the crown had been confined to assistance to the northern colonies, but a great expedition was contemplated in 1740 against the Spanish dominions in the new world To meet the expense of raising and equipping five hundred volunteers, Maryland's quota, the legislature appropriated the sum of twenty-five hundred and sixty-two pounds But this being found insufficient in a subsequent session of the same year five thousand pounds was voted and an indemnity from the prescribed penalties granted to the owners and captains of the vessels which might transport the troops to the place of rendezvous in the islands, should there be indentured apprentices among them ‡ Every colony north of Carolina was called on for its quota and all responded.§ At Jamaica the place of rendezvous, in the beginning of the year 741 were assembled twenty-nine ships of the line, and eighty smaller vessels. They were manned by fifteen thousand sailors and bore an army of twelve thousand soldiers completely armed and equipped— the most considerable up to that time ever gathered in those waters The land force was under command of Wentworth, the naval under Vernon. They attacked Carthagena, one of the strongest of the Spanish towns, and captured several forts, but were finally repulsed with terrible destruction Sickness raged throughout the fleet and camp; men died in crowds, and were cast into the sea What share the Maryland forces bore in the expedition is not known, but it is said that nine out of ten of the colonial levies perished. The fleet returned to Jamaica in November after an absence of nine months, during

---

* Bacon
‡ Ibid.
§ Bancroft

which it is computed twenty thousand men lost their lives.* Yet the colonists seem not to have been dispirited by the disastrous result of this powerful armament, and, on the 26th of June, 1746, the Assembly voted another supply of four thousand five hundred pounds, to raise a body of men to aid in an expedition against Canada.† The requisition was met with promptness, and before the summer had passed, three companies raised in the province by Captains Campbell, Croft and Jordan sailed from Annapolis, " with cheerful hearts, in high spirits and all well clothed and accoutred, to join the main body of the forces ".‡ In November of the same year, a further appropriation of eleven hundred pounds was made to pay the additional expenses of this volunteer force.

In 1751 Charles, Lord Baltimore died, having ruled his province, in person or by his governors, for the space of thirty-six years. His was an era marked by general internal peace, and increasing prosperity, but replete with acts testifying to the unyielding spirit of the people in the maintainance of their rights, and their zeal for their extension. During this period seven governors presided over the province. John Hart was commissioned in 1715—Charles Calvert succeeded him in 1727. Benedict Leonard Calvert, brother of the Lord Proprietary, was appointed in 1727, but, being compelled by ill health to return to England, Samuel Ogle was named to replace him. In 1733, Lord Baltimore himself, finding his presence necessary in the colony because of the acute nature of the boundary disputes with Pennsylvania, arrived in Maryland and assumed the government in person. Upon his return to England, two years later, he appointed Mr. Ogle his representative. In 1742, Thomas Bladen was commissioned and continued to rule the province until 1747, when Mr. Ogle was for the third time appointed. He continued in office two years after the death of Lord Baltimore.

---

* Bancroft
† Bacon
‡ Annals of Annapolis

In this period the colony increased more rapidly than during the royal administration. Since 1660, seven new counties had been laid out. Many of the counties formed in these early times were later changed in their limits and extent by subdivision or alteration by subsequent legislation. Somerset was erected by the governor's order of the 22d of August, 1666, Dorchester by the legislature, in 1669, Cecil in 1674, by the proclamation of Governor Charles Calvert; Prince George's by act of Assembly, in 1695, Queen Anne's, in 1706; Worcester in 1742, although a county of that name had been formed as early as 1672. But the whole of its territory, lying within the present limits of Delaware, was lost to Maryland when the boundary of that province was adjusted. Frederick county was erected in 1748 out of portions of Prince George's, Anne Arundel and Baltimore counties, and originally included the whole territory north and west of these counties. Two other counties, Harford and Caroline, were laid out by acts of the Assembly at the session of 1773.* Montgomery and Washington counties were carved out of Frederick by the Convention of 1776. Alleghany was erected out of part of Washington, in 1789 and in 1836, Carroll cut off a large tract from Frederick and Baltimore counties.

The population of the province in 1748 was estimated at 130,000 souls, of whom 94,000 were whites and 36,000 blacks. In 1756, five years after the death of Charles Lord Baltimore, the population was 154,188, of whom 107,963 were whites and 46,225 black, being an increase of 24,188 in eight years.† Along with this extension of population the internal resources of the province had developed. The people had always been anxious to develop the richness of their soil and were keenly appreciative of its agricultural and mineral resources. They also had sought to develop manufactures. Linen and woollen manufactories were established in Dorchester, but even prior to this nearly every family produced a sufficiency of homespun articles for its common use and for the clothing of the ser-

---
* McMahon
† Holmes makes it in 1755, 108,000

vants and slaves; but the jealousy of England discouraged domestic manufactories. The legislature, however, ventured to impose a duty upon the exportation of raw hides, leather and old iron, for the protection of tanners, shoemakers and smiths. Grants of lands were made to those who undertook to erect water mills, to encourage the making of flour for exportation. Abundance of iron ore was found in the province which could be worked to advantage, but the English government, to insure the preference to its own iron, offered the payment of a bounty upon the importation of the metal into the colony. The legislature, to counteract the effect of this measure, in 1719, ordered that a grant of one hundred acres of land should be made to every one who would erect a furnace or forge. The good effect of this step was evident in the erection of a number of works, of which there were already, in 1749, eight furnaces and nine forges. Large quantities of woodland, in addition to the bounty grants, were taken by their owners. As early as 1742 copper works were in operation in the colony, and in that year the Assembly, to encourage their proprietor, relieved all the laborers employed at his works from levy for seven years, and from the duty of working upon the public roads and bridges, and attending at musters.* The making of wine was attempted with indifferent commercial success. Wheat and Indian corn were largely exported, but the great staple of Maryland trade was tobacco, which had grown to such importance that in 1736 one hundred and thirty ships were engaged and in 1747 fifty thousand hogsheads were exported. The average exportation, however, was about thirty thousand hogsheads †

In each county, free schools were established, supported by general taxation. There were between forty and fifty parishes in the colony, and the clergy of the established church were well provided for by law; a tax of thirty pounds of tobacco per head was levied on all titheables of the parish for their support the proceeds of which, in not a few parishes,

---

* Bacon
† Burnaby

amounted at that day to three hundred pounds sterling, or about fifteen hundred dollars per annum. They were presented to their livings by the governor, and were under the jurisdiction of the Episcopal bishop of London,† who governed them through a commissary, appointed by himself and resident in the province This system was first introduced in 1692, and Thomas Bray, the commissary, then inspected and arranged the church affairs of the colony At that period, the parishes were only thirty in number, and but sixteen of these were supplied with clergymen Dr. Bray procured the erection of several additional chapels, and supplied the people of the different parishes with books of Common Prayer and practical devotion.‡

During this period the currency was in great disorder The sudden depression of the prices of tobacco frequently sapped the specie of the colony to pay for the manufactures, which were imported in large quantities; and even the bounty offered by the government for the introduction of gold and silver failed to remedy the evil An issue of paper money, or government bills of credit, was resorted to, but this became depreciated at one period to half its nominal value Yet this financial policy was persisted in, in spite of the experience of its efficiency, and by a single law in 1733, an issue of ninety thousand pounds was authorized A portion of this large sum was ordered to be expended in the erection of a governor's house and of county jails; the rest was thrown into circulation by loans and otherwise To redeem these bills a tax of one shilling and three pence was laid upon every hogshead of tobacco exported; the proceeds of this impost, together with the interest received by the trustees on the loans, were placed in the hands of trustees in England to be invested in stock of the Bank of England. They were made redeemable in thirty-one years It was an experiment to supply by means of a government bank paper the drain of specie from the province. The bills were made legal tender in the payment of all debts

---

† Ibid
‡ Holmes, vol I. p 443

and fees, "clergy's dues and tobacco for building and repairing churches excepted."* To remedy the embarrassments to the internal trade from the fluctuation of the value of bills of credit, in 1732 the legislature made tobacco a legal tender at one penny per pound, and Indian corn at twenty pence per bushel†—a striking evidence of the distress, to which the deranged condition of the currency had reduced the province. In addition to the difficulties which this condition of internal affairs entailed upon them, the government of the colony was deeply occupied throughout all this period with boundary disputes.

In the charter of no colony were the boundaries more distinctly laid down than in that of Maryland, and yet no colony has been subjected to greater difficulties about limits or been robbed of larger or more valuable territory. Its extent was marked out in the charter by five lines,—beginning at a point on the Chesapeake, called Watkins' Point, near the river Wighco and running east to the ocean,—then, by the Delaware Bay, to that portion of the bay under the 40th degree,—then, by that degree, due west, until it reached the meridian of the first fountain of the Potomac,—then, by that meridian, to the first fountain, and lastly by the southern shore of that river to the bay, and across to Watkins' Point. The first controversy was natural enough. It arose with Virginia, as to the actual position of Watkins' Point. This colony had, from the first, denied the validity of the charter of Maryland and claimed the whole territory included in it as her own. But she abandoned her pretensions by the treaty of 1658. She, however, continued to encroach upon the limits of that charter, by her location of them. She had commenced settlements upon the tongue of land now forming Accomac and Northampton counties. To secure the footing of Maryland, Governor Calvert, in 1661, issued a commission to Edmond Scarborough, John Elzey, and Randall Revel, to make settlements and grant lands on the Eastern shore in the name

---
* Bacon, 1733, ch. 6
† Holmes vol 1, p 553

of the province The terms offered were favorable, and, within a year, the number of titheables at Manokin and Annamessex, reached fifty They succeeded in forming a treaty of friendship with the emperor of the Nanticokes The Virginians however, soon became restless and Scarborough, who was the surveyor general of that colony, demanded that the new settlers should submit to their authority. Meeting with opposition from Elzey, he caused him to be arrested in Accomac. Having extracted an equivocal promise of obedience from his prisoner he released him, and, entering the settlements in a hostile manner, succeeded in compelling a partial submission. Elzey immediately placed the affair before the Governor Calvert and demanded aid to enable him to repel the outrage; but that peaceful officer preferred representing the transaction to Governor Berkeley of Virginia, who promptly disavowed the whole proceeding The negotiations which followed, terminated in the appointment of a commissioner by each government to ascertain the true position of Watkins' Point, and to mark the boundary between the possessions of the two colonies on the eastern shore Philip Calvert was named on the part of Maryland, and Edmond Scarborough on the part of Virginia. They finally adjusted the dispute on the 25th of June, 1668, and the line was distinctly indicated, and exists as the present boundary of the two States.*

The next dispute in order of settlement, was that by which the province of Delaware was lost to Maryland. The English having made the first discoveries on this portion of the North American continent, claimed the whole territory. In despite of the right which they had thus obtained by the laws of civilized nations, the Dutch began settlements at New York, in 1828-9,—and, together with the Swedes, at a later period, commenced colonies on the Delaware, principally on the eastern side A controversy immediately sprung up between these two nations, which resulted in the final subjection of the Swedes, in 1655. In the meanwhile, however, the charter of Maryland was granted, and the settlement at St.

---

* McMahon

Marys made and, if there were any virtue in grants at all, Lord Baltimore was clearly entitled to the possession of Delaware, which the Swedes and Dutch had occupied in disregard of the rights of England In 1642, a small colony of Marylanders attempted to make good these rights, by settling on the Schuylkill, but were compelled to abandon the country by their opponents Too much engaged at home to give due attention to this distant border, the colonial government took no steps to assert their claims until the reduction of the Swedes by the Dutch and the union of both into one colony. Then, Col Nathaniel Utye was despatched, in 1659, to the Delaware settlements to notify the inhabitants that they were seated in his lordship's territory, without permission and to deliver their authorities a written command from the governor of Maryland, to depart from the limits of the province. He was at the same ordered to inform the settlers that favorable terms would be granted to them, upon submission to the lord Proprietary

The demand was not only refused but the governor of New York, Peter Stuyvesant, at the close of the year despatched two commissioners to Maryland, with instructions to insist upon the rights of the Dutch to the settlements upon the Delaware. Arguments on both sides were used in vain, and the envoys having received and rejected a new demand for submission, closed the negotiation and returned home without having effected any thing. Entertaining doubt as to whether the Dutch were really trenching on their limits, and having no hope of assistance from the other colonies, in case of open hostilities, the Maryland government deferred further action until the advice of the lord Proprietary should be obtained, and it should be definitely ascertained whether the settlements at Newcastle were within the 40th degree. An agent was despatched to Holland to represent the case to the States General, which directed that the settlers should be withdrawn from about Cape Henlopen, but refused to abandon the more northern posts. The Dutch, however, were about to be supplanted by more dangerous adversaries They had commenced to infringe on the New England provinces, and it was determined to reduce them to subjection to the British government. In 1664, Charles II granted to his brother, James, Duke of York, all the territory lying between Connecticut and the eastern shore of the Delaware; and an expedition was fitted out to enforce the grant In September, New York surrendered to Governor Nichols, while the settlements on the Delaware submitted to Sir Robert Carr, and the inhabitants of both were admitted to the rights of English colonists New Jersey was granted, by the Duke of York, to the lords Berkeley and Carteret.

William Penn soon after became interested in this province, and, in the course of his connection with it, learning the richness of the country west of the Delaware, determined to make application to the king for a grant. The petition was laid before the Duke of York's secretary and the agents of Lord Baltimore, at their request, the grant was so made as not to infringe upon Maryland. The lines were marked out by lord Chief Justice North That bordering Maryland, was "a circle nine miles around Newcastle to the beginning of the 40th degree of latitude," and then, by the 40th degree, westward. To ascertain this degree, Markham, the agent of Penn, went to the province, and was met by Lord Baltimore at Upland, now called Chester, where, upon actual observation, it was discovered that the 40th degree, instead of being in the vicinity of Newcastle, extended near to the Schuylkill, making the boundary described impossible. The conference was therefore fruitless, and Penn set about obtaining from the Duke of York a grant of the Delaware settlements which his agents, in conquering the possessions of the Dutch, had seized upon and continued to hold in spite of the claims of Lord Baltimore. At length, the duke, in 1682, conveyed to him the town of Newcastle and the territory twelve miles around it, and extending even to Cape Henlopen—an act equally dishonest and disgraceful to both—the one giving that which he knew was the property of another,—the other accepting a gift from him who, he knew, could not rightfully bestow it.

Penn, having thus strengthened his position, obtained an interview with Lord Baltimore in Maryland some time in December, 1682, and presented a letter from the king directing the Lord Proprietary to fix his northern boundary one hundred and twenty miles from his southern limit. Lord Baltimore declined obedience, relying upon his charter which secured to him the territory to the 40th degree. Thus this second conference ended without results, as did also a third, held at Newcastle in May, 1683. As Lord Baltimore, now acting with energy, was endeavoring to extend his settlements into, and had made a formal demand for the delivery of the disputed territory, Penn hastened to England to attack the charter of Maryland, on the ground that Delaware was settled, at the time when the charter was issued, and that instrument only included unsettled territory. His former patron, the Duke of York, had now ascended to the throne as James II, and Penn succeeded so far as to obtain, in 1685, a decree from the commissioners of plantations that the territory between the two bays should be divided by a straight line into two equal portions as far as Cape Henlopen, and that portion, now constituting the Delaware, be given up to Penn. Fearing the destruction of his patent, the Lord Proprietary was compelled to submit, and, although the king was soon dethroned, this decision formed the groundwork of the subsequent final settlement. However, until 1732, the line continued to be disputed, and many outrages were committed by both parties in endeavoring to sustain their pretensions. In that year an agreement was entered into by the Proprietary to adopt the border fixed by the decree of 1685 on the east, and and on the north a line drawn due west, fifteen miles south of Philadelphia.

When Lord Baltimore perceived the full extent of his agreement, he endeavored to set it aside; however, in 1750, a decree in chancery, for its performance, was obtained against him by the Penns. Upon his death, his son, Frederick, Lord Baltimore continued to resist its execution, and proceedings were commenced against him by Thomas and Richard Penn, the surviving Proprietaries. Finding by representations from Maryland, that the condition of the border was frightful and lawless, he at length, on the 4th of July, 1760, agreed to an amicable arrangement The lines already indicated were adopted and commissioners appointed to mark them out * The commissioners—in the execution of their duty, on the northern line, or " Mason and Dixon's," as it is called, after the scientific gentlemen who laid it out—set up at the end of every mile a stone with the letter P. and the arms of the Penns engraved on the north, and "M" and the escutcheon of Lord Baltimore on the south side. Some of these stones are still to be found upon the line. They were, however, prevented by fears of hostile Indians from proceeding further than Sideling Hill—a distance of one hundred and thirty miles from the place of beginning. Similar land marks were placed on the Delaware boundary and thus, after a struggle of more than a century, a large and fertile territory was forever lost to Maryland.

The charter of Maryland defined the western boundary by the meridian of the first fountain of the Potomac, and the question arose whether the north or south branch of the Potomac was the main head of that river. The decision involved a large territory, as the south branch extended far to the south and west of the north branch, and the meridian of its first springs would necessarily throw the western boundary farther back than that of the north branch, and include the fine country between the two streams. During his exile, the unhappy Charles II granted to several of his followers that portion of Virginia lying between and bounded by the heads of the Potomac and Rappahannock After the restoration the grant was re-issued to Lord Culpeper, who, by assignments from the other lords, had become sole proprietor, and the title descended from him to his daughter, the wife of Lord Fairfax. This grant in terms did not interfere with that of Maryland. But the question then arose, which was the true head of the Potomac, the north or south branch. It is very clear that the south branch is the principal stream being at least sixty miles

---

* McMahon. 44-5

longer than the north. Lord Fairfax began to make grants, and, in 1748, formally opened a land office in "the Neck," as his territory was called. In that year he entered into an agreement with the authorities of Virginia by which they adopted the northern branch of the Potomac as the common boundary without regard to the claims of Lord Baltimore, who, in consequence, in 1753, directed Gov. Sharpe, to investigate the matter and maintain his rights Accordingly, the governor, having ascertained by the testimony of Col. Thos Cresap that the south branch was the true head, wrote to Lord Fairfax, protesting against any such arrangement, and claiming the boundary on the south branch. In 1771, Cresap, under the direction of the Proprietary, surveyed both branches, and, in 1774, the Maryland commissioners for the Proprietary began to grant lands in the disputed territory on the west. The revolution only changed the parties to the controversy Upon the adoption of its constitution in 1776, Virginia expressly recognized all the rights of Maryland to the territory contained within the charter, yet when commissioners were subsequently appointed to mark off the disputed territory it restricted its agents to the boundary assumed by Lord Fairfax The representatives of Maryland refused to treat with persons having no power to discuss and adjust the subject of dispute.

CHAPTER VI

THE FRENCH AND INDIAN WAR

In 1751, Frederick, last of the Lords Baltimore, while yet a minor became by the death of his father, Proprietary of Maryland. The French war had just been brought to a close, it was one, however, in which Maryland had borne little part. The province was not immediately concerned in its dangers, and contented itself with furnishing occasional supplies of men and money to assist the northern colonies. But a new contest was approaching in which it was deeply interested, and which poured the horrors of Indian invasion across its border. It was the last war between the English and French for dominion in the new world, and terminated in the overthrow of the latter, in the conquest of their possessions, and eventually led to the humiliation of the former in the independence of the United States.

The governor of Canada, having conceived the bold idea of connecting that colony with the French possessions in Louisiana, immediately began to construct a chain of forts along the Mississippi and Ohio rivers, passing through a territory to which the English laid claim. As early as 1749, a grant of lands west of the Alleghanies had been made to an association called the Ohio Company, which, principally for the purposes of traffic with the natives, erected posts extending as far as the Ohio river. These movements led the French governor to the formation and execution of his design. Several of the company's trading posts were taken and pillaged, the traders made captives. Strong positions were selected, fortified and garrisoned, to maintain open communication from New Orleans to Quebec, along the course of the Alleghany, Ohio, and

Mississippi. Virginia was principally interested in the controversy and its governor immediately despatched Colonel Washington on an embassy to the French commandant to protest against his proceedings and to demand an evacuation of the territory. Marching through a hostile Indian country, Washington performed his difficult and dangerous mission with that courage, zeal and perseverance. The demands of Virginia were rejected and nothing was left but recourse to hostilities. In the war which ensued, Maryland became involved simply in self-defence and for the assistance of sister colonies, but Virginia and Pennsylvania were contending for the acquisition of a large and fertile territory. At the beginning of the war, therefore, the legislature of Maryland stood aloof, in spite of the commands of the crown, the remonstrances of the governor and the entreaties of Virginia, declaring to each their determination to resist any and every foreign invasion and to contribute their assistance to the neighboring colonies, when they conceived their necessity required it.

They, however, consented to send Charles Carroll and Benjamin Tasker, as commissioners, to the general convention which the English government had directed to assemble at Albany, and also appropriated the sum of five hundred pounds to purchase presents, with which to secure the good will of the Indians. When the convention met, they entered into designs very different from those entertained by Maryland and beyond the power granted to its delegates. They resolved that a general union among the colonies was necessary for their preservation, and a plan of confederacy, submitted by Dr. Franklin, was adopted. Ever jealous of their colonial independence, proud of their charter, and fearful of the invasion of their rights of internal sovereignty, the people of Maryland had constantly resisted every attempt to effect a union of the colonies under one government. Nor did they now yield. The plan was submitted to the General Assembly and was unanimously disapproved of by the lower house as "tending to the destruction of the rights and liberties of His Majesty's subjects in the province." The time had arrived, however, when they could no longer avoid taking part in the war Colonel Washington's forces had been captured at Great Meadows by the French and Indians, who, from Fort Duquesne—occupying the present site of Pittsburg—poured their savage and plundering bands upon the unprotected frontiers of Pennsylvania, Maryland and Virginia It became necessary, therefore, to reduce this French stronghold. The General Assembly convened at Annapolis, on the 17th of July, 1754, and voted a supply of six thousand pounds, to be applied to the aid of Virginia and for the needs of the friendly Southern Indians, whose wives and children had to be supported during the expedition

Although legislative action was thus long delayed, the people of the province had taken part in the war from its commencement They organized companies of rangers and frontier guards for the protection of the border settlements. A fort had been erected at Cumberland—far beyond the settlements—which served as the resting place in the expeditions undertaken against the French on the Ohio. In some of these, the people of Maryland bore a part. In September, 1753, two companies, under Captain Dagworthy, Lieutenants Bacon and Forty had marched from Annapolis to the western frontier In the ensuing year the government of Virginia contemplated an expedition against Fort Duquesne, or the erection of a stronghold to restrain its garrison, and its force having been joined by several companies from Maryland and North Carolina, in August was ordered to commence its march But when it was found that the number of troops did not exceed half that of the enemy and that no sufficient provision had been made by the legislature for their supply, the enterprize was abandoned. It was, however, re-undertaken with vigor in the ensuing campaign after extensive preparations had been made to insure its success

The command of all the forces engaged against the French on the Ohio, by a royal commission was conferred upon Gov. Sharpe of Maryland, the actual command in the field devolving upon Colonel Fitzhugh Colonel Washington, displeased at the treatment accorded him by Governor Dinwiddie, resigned his commission and retired from the service. Justly appreciating his talents and qualifications for the peculiar duty before him, Governor Sharpe was desirous of retaining them for the common cause, and requested Colonel Fitzhugh to address a letter to Washington urging him to join them, offering him the rank of captain But Washington refused, declaring that he could not consent to accept the commission of captain when he had already held that of colonel*

On the 24th of December the General Assembly of Maryland was again convened and passed a law for the levying of troops for the ensuing campaign and, as an inducement to men to enlist, provided that if any citizen of the province should be so maimed in the service as to be incapable of maintaining himself, he should be supported at the public expense. In the ensuing session, February, 1755, they regulated the rates of transportation of military material and the mode of quartering soldiers in the province and prohibited by severe penalties any inhabitant from supplying the French or their Indian allies with stores, ammunition or provisions. All these measures were preparatory to that expedition which ended so disastrously for the whole country

Early in the year General Braddock, at the head of a strong body of troops, embarked at Cork for the colonies, and, on his arrival at Alexandria with his fleet of transports,† a council of the colonial governors was summoned to meet him at Annapolis On April 3 General Braddock, Governor Dinwiddie, and Commodore Keppel arrived at Annapolis and were joined on the 11th and 12th by Governors Shirley of Massachusetts, De Launcey of New York, and Morris of Pennsylvania But the place of meeting having been changed, these gentlemen in company with Governor Sharpe of Maryland, proceeded to the general's headquarters at Alexandria. Three expeditions were determined on the first against Fort Duquesne, conducted by Braddock, reinforced by the Maryland and Virginia

---
* Sparks, vol 2, p 64-5
† Green's Gazette

levies, the second, against Niagara and Fort Frontignac, and the third, against Crown Point The council having completed its plans, and the different governors proceeded to their respective stations

On the 17th Governor Sharpe returned to Annapolis and in a few days after went to Frederick, where a portion of the army was already quartered in order to expedite the necessary preparations for transporting the supplies. He was soon met by General Braddock, who began his march to that place from Alexandria with Dunbar's regiment immediately after the conclusion of the council, intending to remain until his stores should be forwarded to Fort Cumberland, his ultimate point of rendezvous During his stay at Frederick, he was joined by Colonel Washington, whom he had invited to serve as his aid-de-camp through the campaign, and to whose skill and courage the army was afterwards essentially indebted [*] After the departure of the general and his forces from Frederick to Winchester, Va, on the 7th of May, the forces of Maryland, in large numbers, marched from the different counties to defend the frontiers and to replace the garrisons of the outposts; while with commendable public spirit, money, clothing, and provisions for the volunteers were advanced by gentlemen of the province [†]

The impressment of wagons, horses, and teamsters was carried on with great activity, especially in Frederick. To such an extent, indeed, had this been carried that the contractors for erecting a new courthouse in that town found it impossible to obtain horses to transport the materials to the site of the building.[‡] Benjamin Franklin, then postmaster-general for the colonies, had met Braddock at Frederick to concert a plan for forwarding despatches, and, learning the scarcity of wagons, undertook to furnish them from Pennsylvania He succeeded in hiring one hundred and fifty in York and Lancaster counties by giving his own bond to the owners

---

[*] Sparks
[†] Recital in rejected Bill of 1762, Sec 44
[‡] Frederick county records

for their indemnification, a responsibility which involved him in great difficulty after the defeat at the Monongahela.* Yet withal such was the scarcity of means of transportation that Braddock was unable to begin his march from Fort Cumberland until the middle of June. A further delay was caused by the necessity of cutting a road for the troops through rough and mountainous country. Fearing that the French would collect a strong force at Fort Duquesne, the general selected a body of twelve hundred men, and, leaving the remainder of the army to advance with the heavy stores hurried forward to surprise the enemy.

On the 8th of July he reached the Monongahela; and, expecting to begin the investment of the fort on the following morning, arranged his forces for the attack. Three hundred British regulars, grenadiers and light infantry, under Lieutenant Colonel Gage, formed the van, followed at some distance by the artillery and the main body of the army which was divided into small columns. The provincial officers, accustomed to the wiles of an Indian enemy, repeatedly warned Braddock of the danger of an ambuscade, but their admonitions were derided. Twice the army crossed the river in its march. No sooner had it passed over the second time than it was enveloped in a heavy fire as the advance entered a narrow defile. The regulars were instantly thrown into confusion. The volleys of an unseen foe mowed down their ranks, and their own random fire added to the slaughter. At length panic seized them and they broke and fled in wild disorder. In vain did their officers attempt to rally them. In vain did they charge upon the foe when deserted by their men. Wherever an epaulette appeared it became the mark of the unerring Indian. Colonel Washington, alone unwounded of all the aids-de-camp, brought up the provincials, who, adopting the Indian tactics, gallantly covered the retreat of the frantic British regulars. The persistent Braddock maintained the action until he received a mortal wound. The rout then became general †

---

* Sparks
† Marshall, Sparks, Bancroft's Life of Washington, pp 19-22

Sixty-four out of eighty-five officers, and about one-half the rank and file were killed or wounded The victorious force of the enemy consisted only of thirty Frenchmen and three or four hundred Indians — of whom seven Indians and four Frenchmen were killed — while that of the defeated army was twelve hundred regulars and provincials

The defeat must be attributed to the rashness of General Braddock, who, however, displayed great coolness and bravery upon the field and had five horses killed under him before he received his fatal wound Colonel Washington had two horses shot under him, and his uniform was riddled with balls He was the only mounted officer who escaped unhurt Providence had reserved him for greater things The rout did not cease until the fugitives had reached the camp of the main body, forty miles from the scene of action There Braddock breathed his last. Colonel Dunbar became infected with the panic, destroyed his baggage and stores, and placing the wounded in the wagons which had been used in their transportation, retreated hastily to Fort Cumberland Utterly desponding, he soon after marched to Philadelphia, where, although it was yet the month of August, he went into winter quarters, abandoning the defenceless frontiers to the fury of the savage

A period of terror and desolation ensued. The settlements were attacked and broken up and the borders of Pennsylvania, Maryland and Virginia became the extended field of petty raids, marked by murder and devastation. Some of the smaller posts were captured and their garrisons massacred and Frederick, Winchester, and Carlisle became the frontiers of the colonies† Fort Cumberland, under Colonel Dagworthy, still held out, but that isolated fortress could afford no protection against the roving bands of savages who passed around it to seek their prey in the settlements beyond The feeling of panic left by the flying British troops spread even to the bay shore. Many of the inhabitants from the interior fled to Bal-

---

* McMahon
† Marshall

timore, and there preparations were made by the citizens of that town to embark their women and children on board the vessels in the harbor preparatory to a flight to Virginia. If the news of the defeat excited terror in some, it also nerved others to preparation for the coming danger. The people in the west gathered at Colonel Cresap's and strengthened his blockhouse for defence. Others sought protection at Fort Cumberland. Even before the defeat, as if in anticipation of it, a party of Indians had made their way into the settlements and committed many ravages. On the 3d of July, they attacked the house of Mr Williams, in Frederick county, and massacred twelve members of his household.[*] After the defeat, a party of inhabitants flying to Fort Cumberland were waylaid and fifteen killed. Three only escaped, one of whom, a boy, had been scalped and left for dead, but revived and succeeded in making his way to that fort.

As soon as the intelligence of Braddock's disastrous defeat reached Annapolis Governor Sharpe set out for Frederick, and on the 17th of July marched to the west at the head of a body of troops which he had hastily assembled. Private subscriptions were opened to defray the expenses. Annapolis and the surrounding country alone raised one thousand pounds. The militia were called into service, and in October, were relieved by a force of volunteers, raised to meet the emergency. But the country people still continued to come in as new inroads were constantly taking place and many families had been cut off.

Such was the effect of the panic on the militia that when Major Prather endeavored to assemble those of the frontier for the purpose of pursuing one of the hostile bands, he found it impossible to do so. Each man dreaded to leave his own house unprotected, lest in his absence, his family should fall a prey to the enemy. But, from the lower part of Frederick county, which was secure from depredations, volunteers under Colonel Ridgely and Captain Alexander Beall, with some companies from Prince George's county and several from Fredrick-

---
[*] Green's Gazette

town itself, hastened to the scene of desolation. They arrived too late to punish the savages and could only remain to protect the survivors from further depredations. In this disastrous year more than twenty plantations were laid waste and their occupants massacred or carried into a dreadful captivity. So great had grown the fear of the Indians that the most improbable rumors found credence In November it was reported that a body of French and Indians were within thirty miles of Baltimore, and two thousand men were quickly assembled to oppose their advance *

The people of Annapolis, far removed as they were from the frontier, caught the infection of fear and began to fortify their town. Serious apprehensions for a time were entertained that a body of the savages might penetrate the intermediate country, surprise the town and massacre the inhabitants However the excitement was allayed by the return of several volunteers from the west who reported affairs in a better condition.†

In the midst of this panic the effectiveness of the troops on the frontier was weakened by disputes and dissensions between the leaders. Captain Dagworthy, who now commanded the Maryland levies, had been an officer in the Canada expedition during the last war, and held the king's commission. Upon entering the Maryland service he still laid claim to precedence of rank under his old commission, which, emanating from the king, was considered to confer a superiority over all colonial commissions Dagworthy asserted his right of precedence over the other colonial officers at Cumberland. He was supported by Governor Sharpe, who claimed the post as a Maryland fort, and subject to his jurisdiction. and properly under the command of a Maryland officer; while Dinwiddie of Virginia contended that it was the king's fort and that Dagworthy could not outrank the field officers of the Virginia regiment The affair was laid before Braddock, who decided in favor of Dagworthy After the death of that general the dispute was revived and Lieutenant Colonel Stephen of the

---
* Green's Gazette
† Annals of Annapolis.

Virginia forces, was ordered by his government to see that none of the provisions sent thither by Virginia should be distributed to the Maryland or Carolina companies. But Dagworthy refused to permit any interference in his command, claiming to outrank Colonel Washington himself. That officer, however, having obtained leave of absence, laid the matter in person before General Shirley, the commander-in-chief, then at Boston, and in March, 1756, procured an order settling definitely the relative rank of the different claimants.* Dagworthy was reduced to the position of provincial captain, as holding a commission from the governor of Maryland, thus subjecting him to all colonial field officers, and the command of Fort Cumberland was conferred upon Washington himself. Thus ended this vexatious dispute, which, by dividing the forces at the fort had rendered them of little service to the colonies.

The legislature assembled in February and took into consideration the state of the province. The act prohibiting trade with the enemy was revived. On the 22d of March, 1756, a bill was passed providing for raising a sum of forty thousand pounds, of which eleven thousand were to be applied to the erection of a fort and several blockhouses in the western frontier, and for levying, arming, paying and maintaining a body of troops, not exceeding two hundred men, to garrison these posts. Three thousand pounds were placed in the hands of two commissioners, Colonel Benjamin Tasker and Charles Carroll, to engage the services of the southern Indians, one thousand pounds were directed to be distributed in bounties of ten pounds for each scalp of an hostile Indian, or for each prisoner brought in by any inhabitant of the province and twenty-five thousand was reserved for the joint expedition in contemplation against Fort Duquesne. Messrs William Murdock, James Dick and Daniel Wolstenholme, were appointed agents to pay out these several sums, with a commission of two and one-half per cent on all disbursements. Thir-

---

* Spark's Life and Writings of Washington, vol 2, where the letters relating to this dispute are collected.

ty-four thousand pounds of this sum were raised by bills of credit, a system already in full operation in the colony, but the legislature taught by recent difficulties, wisely provided at once a sufficient sinking fund, by imposing new duties and laying additional internal taxes. Some of the features of the bill mark the spirit of the time—a double tax was laid upon the lands of Catholics; and, as if to make atonement for the oppression of one class, they asserted the liability of all to their own legislative supremacy, and subjected even the manors and lands of the Lord Proprietary to the common burdens Another, in the list of twenty-two subjects of taxation on which the Assembly thought proper to levy, is singular enough to justify notice· "On all bachelors, of twenty-five years of age and upwards, worth one hundred pounds and less than three hundred, a duty of five shillings per annum was laid; and, if worth over three hundred pounds—twenty shillings per annum," and, to heighten its effect, this subject of taxation was significantly placed in the list of luxuries, and between the duties on "wines and liquors," and "the billiard table "*

Fort Cumberland, lying nearly sixty miles beyond the frontier, was found to afford no protection from the savages, so that the people had been compelled to erect stockades and blockhouses on the verge of the settlements, as places of immediate resort and security in sudden danger Under the act which had just been passed Governor Sharpe, to remedy this defect, selected a site for a new fort near the present town of Hancock, to be called Fort Frederick He purchased one hundred and fifty acres of land, and began at once under his personal inspection the erection of a large and durable fortress of stone, capable of containing a garrison of three hundred men. By the middle of August the fortifications were far enough advanced to afford accommodation to the troops, and were immediately garrisoned by a force of two hundred men under the command of Colonel Dagworthy In the meantime

---

* Bacon. From April, 1762, to November, 1763, this tax produced £904 1s 2d

the Indians had been active. Secretly by night, small parties penetrated into the country, struck a fatal blow, and then retired, generally before successful pursuit could be made Their audacity increased with their success, and a party made way even to the neighborhood of Emmitsburg, somewhat more than sixteen miles from Frederick, assailed the settlement, and, after shooting a man named Alexander McKeasy in his own door, escaped without loss But they were not always so fortunate, the desultory war had raised up a number of partizan Indian fighters, the most successful and unsparing of whom was Col Thomas Cresap, a man of undaunted courage. On the 20th of May, 1756, at the head of one hundred men—his "red caps'—he overtook a party of Indians, and completely routed them, killing a number On the 30th of June he came suddenly upon another roaming band whom he also defeated * Yet such was the effect produced upon the out settlers by these destructive inroads, which it was equally impossible to foresee or to prevent, that they continued to desert their cabins and clearings and poured in towards the lower country "The whole settlement of Conococheague in Maryland is fled," writes Colonel Washington, in August, 1756, "and there now remains only two families from thence to Fredericktown That the Maryland settlements are all abandoned is certainly a fact, as I have had the accounts transmitted to me by several hands and confirmed yesterday (28th) by Henry Brinker, who left Monocacy the day before, and who also affirms that three hundred and fifty wagons had passed that place to avoid the enemy, within the space of three days."†

The neighboring colonies having failed to coöperate with Maryland in the proposed expedition and the season having passed for any such attempt, the legislature was again convened in September and devoted the sum of twenty-five thousand pounds, laid aside for the purpose, to other and more pressing objects of service Five thousand pounds were appropriated to raising and maintaining three hundred men for

---
* Green's Gazette
† Sparks, vol 2, p 183

the royal American regiment and to furnish a supply of wheat for Lord Loudon's troops at New York, three thousand pounds for bounties for scalps or prisoners taken by persons not in the pay of the province, and three thousand five hundred pounds for forming a company of one hundred men, to be incorporated with the battalion already under the command of Colonel Dagworthy, at Fort Frederick. One-third of this force was required to be constantly on duty on the frontiers as rangers for the protection of the inhabitants and to increase their activity, in addition to their pay, each soldier who, while on such duty took a scalp or a prisoner, was allowed a bounty of thirty pounds. Additional appropriations were made toward completing Fort Frederick, for purchasing arms and ammunition and erecting a magazine, and, to reimburse the governor the expense of maintaining the rangers whom he had employed on the frontier, during the preceding spring.*

Provision having thus been made for defense, the confidence of the people to the westward was somewhat restored, although the settlements were not fully reoccupied until the close of the war. Even in 1761, several years after the reduction of Fort Duquesne, the people of the western portion of Frederick county when desirous of building a bridge on the road from Conococheague to Pittsburg at a cost of only forty pounds, were compelled to have recourse to the county court for assistance from the general assessment, assignment as their reason that the country was thinned of its inhabitants, that the settlers who had removed on account of the war had not yet returned to their dwellings, and that the few who remained were unable to bear the charge; while the work was absolutely required by the public service, being on the route by which supplies were carried to the royal troops at Fort Pitt.† Indeed, it was impossible to form a complete cordon of defence across the frontier, for small parties of the enemy would easily make their way into the settlements, strike a successful blow and retreat in safety before the rangers could come to the rescue

---
* Bacon
† Jud Rec L L, p 840 — Fred Co

The inhabitants at the breaking out of hostilities were to a great extent unpracticed in Indian warfare, and, therefore, fell an easy prey to their vigilant and unsparing enemy. Elated by their bloody victory on the Monongahela, in which they had almost annihilated a force of three times their number, composed of chosen troops under a British general, they boasted that at length they were about to drive the invaders from the graves of their forefathers and recover their ancient hunting grounds From the Miami, the Ohio, and the borders of the lakes, their war parties concentrated at Fort Duquesne, to pour out upon the extended frontiers, sometimes in parties strong enough to take the smaller fortresses by storm, but generally numbering but two or three, striking unexpectedly into the settlements, burning the farm houses, killing or capturing the inhabitants thus taken by surprise, and hurrying away as rapidly with their booty.* But the borderers soon began to learn their mode of warfare and to prepare for it; and aided by the rangers and garrisons of the forts, and protected by their own rude blockhouses, made successful defence against their inroads.

In the ensuing April the Assembly was convened at Baltimore, and further provisions were made for the security of the frontiers. A portion of the first appropriation being still unexpended, and the sum of three thousand pounds, intended to secure the services of the southern Indians yet unapplied, the whole, amounting to more than ten thousand pounds, was devoted to increasing the forces in the west to five hundred men. To promote the recruiting service, those who enlisted were exempted from levy and other charges for three years, and the maimed and disabled were promised an annual pension for their support † Finding that every effort at a combined expedition had failed the year before, the government now sought only to defend its own frontier; and, during the season, succeeded in securing the services of a band of Cherokee Indians to aid in that object

---

* Narrative of Col James Smith
† Bacon

The enemy were not long in recommencing their assaults. In June it was reported that a large body of French and Indians, with heavy cannon, were marching against Fort Cumberland to besiege it. Governor Sharpe instantly set out for Frederick, accompanied by a number of volunteers, to gather troops and relieve the menaced post. There, however, a subsequent express informed him that it was only a small party of about three hundred men, without artillery, and, fully confident in the ability of the troops already on the frontier, aided by the Cherokees, to prevent their ravages, he returned to Annapolis after a week's absence. The enemy, however, had no design upon the fort; they separated into small parties, as was their wont, and broke into the settlements—principally of Virginia. A few attempted to ravage Maryland, but were overtaken and several of them killed by the friendly Cherokees, who rendered important services to the colony. In addition to the troops already on the frontier, Captains Butler, Middagh, and Luckett's companies of militia were ordered to relieve the garrison of Fort Frederick then under the command of Captain Beale. During their tour of duty, they acted with spirit, and prevented the ravages of three different parties of the enemy. Besides furnishing this garrison for Fort Frederick, the people of Frederick county raised two hundred men, who, in August, marched under Governor Sharpe to strengthen that fortress and to garrison Fort Cumberland, where in the ensuing month they were joined by a company of volunteers from Cecil county, under Captain Jesse Hollingsworth.*

Fort Cumberland, so long the subject of dispute between the governors of Maryland and Virginia, and maintained by the latter against the strong wishes of Colonel Washington, was now finally given up to Maryland, by the order of Lord Loudon, and was destined henceforth to be garrisoned by Maryland troops. It soon became a source of discord in another quarter.* In October, Governor Sharpe applied to the legislature for means to support the garrison which he had

---
* Green's Gazette
* Sparks

placed there. The Assembly, averse to maintaining a force too far beyond the frontiers to protect the inhabitants, replied with warmth that they had been stationed there contrary to the intention of the act by which they had been raised and if evil consequences arose from want of supplies the blame must rest upon the heads of those who had taken the responsibility of placing them there without warrant of law As the step had been taken by order of Lord Loudon, they denied his authority to control the forces raised and paid by the colony without their consent; whereupon that nobleman wrote to Governor Sharpe, protesting against this doctrine as without precedent, and peculiar to Maryland alone. Governor Dinwiddie likewise pronounced it ' inconsistent and unmannerly, in the Maryland Assembly, to make any hesitation, or to dispute his lordship's power " But the Assembly had been too long accustomed to a sturdy maintenance of their rights to yield to the protests or abuse of British royal governors.

But this limited and petty warfare of posts and defensive expeditions, while it exhausted the force of the colony could produce no permanent results. The neighboring provinces of Virginia and Pennsylvania, with far more extensive borders to protect, had suffered more severely than Maryland; and the governments of the three colonies at length became fully convinced that the readiest and most effectual mode of protecting their frontiers was the expulsion of the enemy from his stronghold. Early in 1758, another expedition against Fort Duquesne was determined on

Lord Loudon having returned to England at the close of the last campaign, the command of the British forces in the middle and southern colonies, was committed to General Forbes, and it was hoped by the colonies that active and energetic measures would now be taken Virginia, which was principally interested, had already one regiment in the field, and had directed the formation of another The forces of Maryland, amounting to five hundred men under Colonel Dagworthy, held its frontier from Fort Frederick, aided by their

Indian allies. In the Assembly, which met at Annapolis in March, 1758, an effort was made to bring a still larger force into the field. But Maryland was once more to a certain extent secure. The old controversies between the upper and lower houses recommenced and the delegates once more asserted and sturdily adhered to the demands, which during the perils of the three preceding years they had allowed to slumber. In April the House framed a bill for the supplies required to raise one thousand men and among other property imposed taxes upon the Proprietary's quit rents and estates, on the salaries and emoluments of public officers and the usual double tax upon the lands of Catholics and those who refused to take the test oath of supremacy,* and also claimed the sole right of originating and amending money bills. The upper house protested against these taxes as unjust and contended that the claim of the lower house was arbitrary and unconstitutional But the delegates were immovable. Rather than submit, the government abandoned all hopes of further supplies and Colonel Dagworthy and his troops were ordered to join the expedition as the quota of Maryland. To supply garrisons for the fortresses thus left vacant by the departure of Dagworthy, Governor Sharpe called out the western militia and marched at their head to Fort Cumberland, of which post he took command as soon as Colonel Washington with his regiment joined the main army at Raystown. During the continuance of the governor at the fort, the army suffered a serious loss of ammunition from the blowing up of the magazine.

Although it was desirable that the campaign should open early in the season, the Virginia troops did not reach Fort Cumberland, their place of rendezvous, till July. They were then occupied in cutting a road from that post to Raystown, where the advance of the army was stationed under Colonel Bouquet—General Forbes being detained by sickness at Carlisle. As if to increase these delays and render the expedition abortive, the English officers, in spite of the remonstrances of Colonel Washington, determined to make a new road to

---
* Bacon. 1716, ch 5

Fort Duquesne, instead of taking the route of General Braddock. It was already late in the season, the enemy were daily strengthening their forces, and it was feared that winter would overtake the army in the mountains. The worst results were foreboded.

In September an advanced body had reached Loyal Hanning, about ten miles beyond Laurel Hill, and, towards the close of the month, Major Grant was detached to reconnoitre, with a select corps of more than eight hundred men, consisting of three hundred and thirty Highlanders, one hundred and fourteen royal Americans, one hundred and seventy-six Virginians, ninety-five Marylanders, one hundred and twelve Pennsylvanians and thirteen Carolinian troops * In the night he took post upon a hill, about eighty rods from Fort Duquesne, unobserved by the French, and in the morning, by way of bravado, beat the reveille and sounded the bagpipes in several places. As soon as the English were discovered, the Indians sallied from the fort, and, having under cover of the river banks, reached a height that overlooked Grant's position, surrounded him and commenced the attack † The Highlanders, drawn up in close formation, were slaughtered almost unresistingly, by the deadly fire of the enemy, and at length gave way, while the Maryland troops, to whom were joined the Carolinians, took cover in bushes and behind trees and keeping the enemy at bay, sustained the action. The Pennsylvanians broke at the first fire. The Virginians, under Major Lewis of Colonel Washington's regiment, had been detached two miles to the rear to guard the baggage; as soon as the action began, they hastened up to the assistance of Grant, but were unable to maintain their ground ‡ The English were defeated with a loss of two hundred and seventy-three killed and forty-two wounded; Majors Grant and Lewis, and many of their men were taken prisoners. The Marylanders behaved with great gallantry, and, although they suffered severely, succeeded

---
* Green's Gazette.
† Smith's Narrative.
‡ Green's Gazette

in covering the retreat of the remainder of the troops. Out of ninety-five men they lost twenty-three privates and one officer, Lieutenant Duncan McRae, killed and missing, and seventeen wounded—nearly one-half their whole force. Captain Ware, Lieutenant Riley and Ensign Harrison, with fifty privates made good their retreat ‡ The loss of the enemy was trifling.

This defeat, so similar to the disaster of Braddock, induced the Indians to believe that the remainder of Forbes' army would retreat, as the force under Colonel Dunbar had done on the like occasion. A large portion of them, accordingly left the fort and returned to their hunting grounds, with their prisoners and plunder, in spite of the solicitations of the French to remain.§ This was a fortunate circumstance for the success of the expedition. Forbes' army was still toiling on its way, liable to be taken at disadvantage by a strong force, and did not reach the post at Loyal Hanning until the fifth of November, nearly a month after the battle. Here the recent defeat, and the lateness of the season, had nearly produced the results expected by the Indians. A council of war was held which determined that it was unadvisable to proceed farther during the present campaign. In the meanwhile, the enemy, who had carefully watched the march of the army, thinking it a favorable moment to make another fortunate blow and complete their victory, detached a body of troops with the Indians yet remaining at the fort, to the number of one thousand men, and attacked Colonel Bouquet with great spirit at Loyal Hanning, on the 12th of October. After four hours of hard fighting they were repulsed but during the whole ensuing night kept up an occasional fire upon the works. Before day, however, they retreated, carrying with them their killed and wounded, thus concealing their loss in the action. The loss of the English was sixty-seven rank and file killed and wounded. In this affair the Maryland troops had one officer, Lieutenant Prather, and two privates killed, Ensign Bell and six privates wounded and eleven missing

‡ Ibid
§ Smith's Narrative

Still the savages hovered around the army. On the 12th of November, near Loyal Hanning, Colonel Washington, with a scouting party, fell in with a detachment of the enemy and a skirmish ensued. A second party of Virginians coming to their assistance in the heavy mist were mistaken for a body of the foe and a fire opened upon them and returned before the unfortunate error was discovered Capt Evan Shelby, of Frederick county, who commanded a company of Maryland volunteers in this skirmish, killed with his own hand one of the leading chiefs of the enemy.[*] After these disastrous actions, the hostile Indians abandoned their allies and left the fort, saying that it was an easy matter to deal with the regulars, but impossible to withstand the provincials

Reanimated by success and learning the desertion of the Indians from a prisoner taken by Captain Ware of the Maryland troops, the English determined to prosecute their attempt At length, taught by experience the inefficiency of regulars in such a service, they threw Colonel Washington in advance and succeeded on the 22d of November after a painful march in reaching Fort Duquesne which the French, hopeless of maintaining with their diminished garrison, after setting it on fire, had abandoned the night before. The works were immediately repaired the place renamed Fort Pitt, and a garrison of two hundred men, drawn from the Pennsylvania, Maryland and Virginia troops, assigned for its defence.[†]

The capture of this fortress, the centre from which so many predatory expeditions had gone forth, filled the colonies with joy. Governor Sharpe by proclamation appointed a day for public thanksgiving and praise and the Assembly, to testify its gratitude to the brave men who had served in their forces, appropriated fifteen hundred pounds to be distributed as a gratuity among them Lieutenant Colonel Dagworthy received £30, each captain £16, lieutenant £12, ensign £9, and non-commissioned officer £6 The remainder was devoted to the purchase of clothing and suitable necessaries for the privates.

---

[*] Green's Gazette; Bacon
[†] Green's Gazette

From this time forth, Maryland had little concern in the war, although its rangers, numbering two hundred and thirty men, were engaged in the expedition against the Shawanese towns, the only affair of moment after the capture of Fort Duquesne. Occasional bands of Indians passed Fort Pitt and committed depredations upon the frontiers, but the hardy settlers were now fully able to protect themselves The principal features of its late history are of a pacific and legislative character. Yet that legislative history is full of interest, for it led eventually to the revolution It was a continuous struggle for the rights of the commons

CHAPTER VII.

THE DAYS BEFORE THE REVOLUTION

FROM the earliest period a contest had been waged in Maryland between the two principles contained in the charter. The result of that contest, in every stage had been a further and broader development of the democratic and a diminution of the aristocratic features The germs of both were fully contained in that instrument, but the spirit of the people and the necessities of the times tended constantly to the vigorous growth of the one and the utter destruction of the other This contest was now rapidly verging to its final issue

The representatives of the people who sat in the lower house insisted upon an exclusive right to frame and amend bills for raising money, the upper house, which was simply the council of the governor and with him represented the Proprietary, by whom they were appointed, claimed for themselves a share in the imposition of taxes. While immediate danger impended over the colony in 1756, the commons had permitted their claim to slumber that the public safety might be secured; but now that the war had been removed from their borders, they planted themselves firmly upon their old position Remonstrance and petition from the friends of the Proprietary and commands from the crown were alike disregarded. Fully concurring in the necessity of conquering Canada in order to secure peace to the colonies, at each session they passed bills to afford aid and assistance to the royal arms, but in every instance, from their unwavering adherence to their position the bills failed to become laws. Nine times in succession did they thus adopt a bill similar to that rejected in 1758 and as often was it negatived by the upper house. The opinion of His Majesty's attorney general, Pratt, was in vain brought before them to induce them to yield. They claimed that they were the sole representatives of the people and that "the people could only be taxed by their own consent." It was impossible to subdue their firmness The other colonies murmured and the English government became indignant at the repeated refusals of Maryland to aid the royal arms. The statesmen of England, satisfied at length that it was impossible to compel the colonies to tax themselves by means of royal requisitions, determined to have recourse to indirect taxation.

Peace was declared in 1763 and the French colonies were ceded to England. She possessed the whole northern continent, but to counterbalance this acquisition she found herself laboring under a heavy debt contracted during the war She had already encroached upon the rights of the colonies by compelling them to furnish requisitions, resisted by Maryland alone, and, finding these insufficient to meet her wants, she prepared to advance one step further in their complete subjugation. They were rich and populous and firmly attached to liberty. Freedom on the one part and supremacy on the other were prizes worth struggling for

The condition of Maryland was prosperous in spite of the ravages it had suffered during the war. Its population in 1761 amounted to 164,007 persons, of whom 114,332 were whites and 49,675 blacks, principally slaves. It possessed few manufactures. Even then, however, 2,500 tons of pig-iron and 500 tons of bar iron were annually produced and the greatness of its recources was undisputed. Its people were frugal and industrious, they had spread themselves almost to the utmost limits of the province Peculiarly fitted for commerce and navigation, with most of its territory within thirty miles of streams navigable for boats, its soil rich and exuberantly productive to the labor of the husbandman and planter, it needed only the acquisition of independence to make it a powerful, flourishing and sovereign state Such was the spectacle that met the eyes of England. The result of its scrutiny was the passage of the stamp act

Under pretence that the government had assumed large burdens in their defence and the apparent obligation on their part to bear a portion of those obligations Lord Grenville in 1763 notified the agents of the colonies in London that at the ensuing session of parliament he intended to propose a duty on stamps for the purpose of raising a revenue from the provinces, at the same time giving them the privilege of suggesting as a substitute any other mode of parliamentary taxation that would be more agreeable to them In the session which followed a resolution to the same effect was adopted, but the ministry did not yet venture to take the final step They were preparing the way The restrictions on colonial trade were tightened and the lucrative commerce with the Spanish and French islands was entirely cut off The indignation of the people was aroused; they saw at once that England designed to deprive them of their liberties and to make them the mere subjects of the British parliament. "Assemblies remonstrated, public meetings denounced and agents petitioned. The measure was resolved upon and, on the 22d of March, 1765, the Stamp Act was finally imposed "[*] The interval of two years, which had been intended as a preparation of the minds of the people for submission, only enabled them to gather their energies for universal resistance, in the open manifestation of which, it is true, Massachusetts and Virginia took the lead, from the advanage of opportunity, though, in unanimity, firmness and success, Maryland surpassed them all It is its proud boast that its soil was never polluted by the obnoxious stamps. Everywhere the utmost indignation was excited, the columns of the Maryland Gazette teemed with articles assailing the measure Pamphlets were issued, public appeals were made, and the minds of the whole people of the province were firmly arrayed against it. The other colonies expressed their opposition by remonstrances and protests

---

[*] McMahon, 332

through their legislative bodies, if Maryland did not at once speak through the same channel, it was because the Assembly was prorogued from 1763 until September, 1765, and it could only have recourse to the pen, the press, or open violence. But at the session of September, 1765, the Assembly solemnly protested against the measure and indignantly complained that thus for two years they had been deprived of the power of publicly declaring their lasting opposition Ere that period arrived, however, the people of the colony had already vindicated their rights in a more summary manner

Zachariah Hood, a native of Maryland and a merchant at Annapolis, was appointed in the summer of 1765 stamp distributor for the province He brought with him from England a cargo of goods, together with the obnoxious stamps When he arrived in the harbor of Annapolis, the ferment reached its height The people gathered in crowds at the dock, determined to prevent his landing, an outbreak ensued, in which one of their number, Thomas McNeir, had his thigh broken, and Hood, at the very seat of government, was compelled to draw off from the shore and effect a landing, clandestinely, at another time and place. No sooner had the tidings of his arrival spread through the country, than the people gathered into the city and prepared to show their utter detestation of the man who could consent to become the instrument of foreign tyranny The effigy of the stamp distributor was mounted on a one-horse cart with sheets of paper in its hands and paraded through the streets amidst the execrations of the crowds, while the bells tolled a solemn knell The paraders marched to the hill, tied the effigy to the whipping-post and bestowed upon it nine-and-thirty lashes, which the crowd humorously styled giving "the Mosaic law" to the stamp distributor. It was then swung from a gibbet, over a tar barrel and set on fire. Similar exhibitions of popular feeling occurred in Baltimore, Frederick, Elkridge and other towns.*

---

* Annals of Annapolis, 90, etc.

Hood offered for sale at reduced prices the large stock of goods which he had imported, but the people not only refused to purchase them, but carried their resentment to the extent of tearing down a house which he was preparing for the reception of his merchandise. They also threatened him with personal violence. In fear of his life Hood fled from the province and sought refuge in New York under the guns of fort St George. But Hood found no safety even under the guns of a British fortress. Determined to vindicate the honor of their native province and to punish a son who had taken part against her a number of daring patriots followed* him to Long Island, seized him in the midst of his fancied security and gave him the alternative of resigning his office and renouncing and abjuring, under oath, its exercise forever, or of being conducted back to Maryland and delivered up to the just indignation of the people. Hood prayed, protested and sought compromise. but the patriots were inexorable. His abjuration was fully made out and sworn to before a justice of the peace at Jamaica and he was set at large.

Thus when the Assembly met in September they found the work of resistance accomplished. It only remained for them solemnly to declare their rights which had thus been vindicated by the people. No deliberation was needed, for there was no difference of opinion. Many of the delegates indeed acted under instructions from their constitutents. They took favorable action upon a proposition which Massachusetts, assuming the initiative, addressed to the colonies, for a meeting of colonial deputies, and appointed as Maryland's representatives Col. Edward Tilghman, William Murdock and Thomas Ringgold. These gentlemen were expressly directed to take care that any representation or petition, prepared by the congress to be presented to the English government, should contain an assertion of the absolute right of the colonies to be free from taxation "save by their own consent. or by that of their representatives, freely chosen and appointed."†

---
* Grahame, vol I, 397
† Votes and Proceedings, 1765, p 7

And now, in behalf of the people of Maryland, they proceeded to make a solemn declaration, which was emphatic even in that day of protests and resolutions, and placed the rights of the province upon broad and incontrovertible grounds. On the last day of that short but glorious session of only five days, they unanimously resolved that the early settlers of Maryland had brought with them all the rights of British subjects and could not be taxed but by their own consent; that their rights had been fully secured to them by their charter in which express renunciation was made of the power of the crown to tax the people of the province; that the trial by jury was their birthright, and, finally, that the people of Maryland had always enjoyed the right of being governed by laws to which they themselves gave assent Not being represented in the British parliament they asserted the legislature alone had the power to impose taxes, and, therefore, that taxes laid under color of any other authority were unconstitutional and an infringement of their rights * Having thus rendered this session sacred to the cause of liberty, they entered into no other business. Refusing to give the governor advice he asked concerning the disposition of the stamp paper which was daily expected to arrive in the province, they were prorogued to meet in November following.

The Proprietary government yielded slight assistance to the ministry in putting the Stamp Act in operation in the colony Governor Sharpe, after the delegates had refused to interfere, upon the recommendation of the upper house who represented that if the stamps were landed they would certainly be destroyed, determined to deposit them until further orders should be received from England, in one of the royal cruisers stationed on the Virginia coast In the meanwhile, the war of words went on Daniel Dulany, a man eminent for learning and ability and distinguished as a lawyer, published a pamphlet, which was universally acknowledged to be one of the best defences of the rights of the people which appeared during

---

* Votes and Proceedings, H D, September, 1765, p. 10

the controversy In this work he reviewed the whole ground and concluded with an appeal to the people to produce manufactures for themselves and compel their antagonists to yield by striking at their interests Yet while he thus defended the cause, he disapproved of the proceedings of "the sons of liberty," in which some of the most active and distinguished men of Maryland had taken part The course of Daniel Dulany upon this subject is a strong testimony of the secret hostility to the measure of the Proprietary party of which he was an adherent, when, however, the question was made of the rights of the Proprietary against the people and finally of independence, which must destroy their rights entirely, Daniel Dulany was found in the ranks of those who vainly attempted to stay the torrent of popular progress and to sustain the tottering power of Proprietary and crown.

The colonial Congress met at New York on the first Tuesday of October, 1765, all the representatives of Maryland were present at this body, which proceeded to prepare an address to the crown, a petition to parliament and a declaration of the rights and grievances of the people. Their proceedings were submitted to the Assembly of Maryland at its next session in November and were unanimously approved by the House, which passed a vote of thanks to the commissioners for the able manner in which they had performed their duty, and at their May session, 1766, caused the Journal of the Congress to be printed with their own. Fearful lest an insidious attempt should be made to bind the consciences of the judges, magistrates and other provincial officers, the House, immediately on the opening of the November session, upon adopting the usual rules for their government, directed that the committee on grievances should likewise act as a committee on courts of justice: and instructed the members to "observe the nature of all the commissions to the several courts of judicature within the province, and, especially to observe any alterations that may at any time happen by accidental omission, or otherwise, therein, and particularly relating to such words therein, as require the several judges and justices to hear, try and determine, according to the laws, statutes, ordinances, and reasonable customs of *England* and of these provinces" —and instantly to report the same to the Assembly The committee was also directed to examine the oaths of office taken by the magistrates, and the House declared, as a necessary portion of these oaths, the following clause "To do equal law and right to all the king's subjects, rich or poor, and not to delay any person of common right, for the letters of the king, the lord Proprietary, *or for any other cause,* but if any such letters come to them, they shall proceed to do the law, the same letters notwithstanding"* These provisions were, to a certain extent, aimed against the enforcement of the stamp act

America had been compared to a conquered country; the House declared that Maryland could not be so considered, that the inhabitants had planted themselves there, with the permission of the crown. and had become prosperous, with the blessing of God, by their own labor, and unanimously resolved. that those who asserted that they had forfeited any part of their English liberties, were not well wishers to their country and mistook its constitution They, likewise, declared that the "province hath always, hitherto had the common law and such general statutes of England as are securative of the rights and liberties of the subject, and such acts of Assembly as were made in the province to suit its particular constitution, as the rule and standard of its government and judicature " and intimated that by these alone should the judges, and magistrates and other officers be guided. These resolutions, the unanimous expression of the representatives of the people, afford a distinct indication of the popular feeling. They, however, fall short of its depth and excitability, which was evidenced on the slightest opposition on the part of the upper house and governor to the acts of the lower house †

Many of the debts incurred during the late war, still remained unpaid, and not a few unascertained, some of which

---

* Votes and Proceedings, H D, 1765, November session
† Votes and Proceedings

were claims for money advanced to fit out or supply their companies by the different officers, among whom were Capt. Evan Shelby, to whose services the House bore ample testimony; Captains Ware and Price, afterwards officers of Smallwood's battalion, Capt. Joshua Beall, and Lieut. Rezin Beall, afterwards brigadier general of the Maryland troops of the flying camp. At November session, a resolution was passed for the payment of such claims as had been adjusted together with the journal of accounts The upper house rejected the resolution on the ground that there were some equally deserving whose demands had not been included and suggested certain allowances for the clerks of council and others. The lower house agreed to all these items save those claimed for the clerks of the council and refused to separate the journal of accounts from the list of debts. A warm controversy ensued between the two houses, in the meanwhile the claims of all concerned being postponed

The people of the west were principally interested, and there the deepest feeling was aroused—excited, according to the assertions of Governor Sharpe, by the efforts of Colonel Thomas Cresap, a member from Frederick county, who was reported to have said that nothing would be done unless the people took it in hands They gathered in force at Frederick to the number of three or four hundred men, armed with rifles and tomahawks, proceeded to elect officers and declared their intention to march by companies to Annapolis and settle the disputes between the two houses The inhabitants of Elkridge pursued a similar course and despatched two magistrates to Annapolis with the significant threat that according to the tenor of the express they should receive from the capital, a number of men would or would not be in sight of that place in two days time. These ominous facts were communicated to the House by Governor Sharpe with the recommendation to consider seriously the bad effect of large bodies of people assembling to overawe either branch of the legislature. The House replied with assurances that every proper step should be taken to prevent such an occurrence, at the same time de-

HISTORY OF MARYLAND 131

fending Colonel Cresap, until evidence should be brought against him. The session lasted but ten days longer, and these were spent in disputes which had no result but that of postponing the question to the ensuing session

The associators, for the armed men who had thus assembled had bound themselves together by written pledges in a petition prepared for presentation to the lower house, declared "their satisfaction at the conduct of that body in opposing the stamp act," declared their set purpose to oppose future attempts of the sort to invade their liberties, and requested that they might be informed if the upper house persisted in its unjust pretensions "in order that the signers might come down and cause justice to take place" Their zeal, however, seems to have been restrained by the more prudent element of the popular party, and the session passed off without further demonstration The controversy was not settled until December, 1766, when a committee of conference was appointed and a compromise effected

The Stamp paper having at length arrived at Newcastle on the Delaware, in October, 1765, on board His Majesty's ship Sardome, commanded by Captain Hawker, the governor, unwilling to enforce the obnoxious law and desiring to screen himself behind the lower house again demanded some expression of opinion on their part as to its disposal. They persisted in their refusal to do so By the advice of the council, he directed Captain Hawker to retain it on board his ship. To the commands of the English secretary to execute the law at all hazards, he replied that it was impossible without the aid of a strong military force and that the peace of the colony had hitherto only been preserved by the cautious measures he had adopted. Knowing that a considerable time must elapse before further orders could arrive, or troops be sent, the governor hoped to weather the storm without exciting the hostility of either party. But a new difficulty arose and he was constrained to extend his conciliating policy still further.

The law had made stamps necessary in many transactions, for a time therefore a partial cessation of business ensued.

But the obstacle was soon overcome and the Frederick county court had the high honor of first deciding the unconstitutionality of the stamp act.* This decision was received with joy and the people hastened to celebrate so important and significant an event. The festival took place in Frederick on the 30th of November, 1765. "The sons of liberty" marched in funeral procession through the streets, bearing a coffin on which was inscribed "THE STAMP ACT, *expired of a mortal stab received from the Genius of Liberty, in Frederick county court, 23d November, 1765, aged 22 days.*". Zachariah Hood, the late unfortunate stamp distributor, was represented as the chief mourner and the whole affair ended merrily in a ball. In the public offices, at Annapolis, however, business still continued to be interrupted for the want of stamps, the time-serving officers hesitating to treat the law as a nullity and fearing to attempt its enforcement This inconvenience the people determined to remedy and in February, 1766, the inhabitants of Baltimore and the adjoining country formed themselves into an association of "the Sons of Liberty"—a society for the maintenance of the rights of the people, and adjourned to meet at the capital to put an end to this abuse. The public officers were very politely notified of their coming and requested to be in readiness to receive them. On the first of March they assembled according to adjournment and presented a petition requesting the resumption of business by the 31st of March The timid officials temporized and the sons of liberty adjourned to meet again, having called on their brethren in the counties to assemble with them. On the 3d of April they came together in great strength and again laid their petition before the general court At first they met with a refusal. They again "earnestly insisted and demanded with united hearts and voices" in terms to which resistance was no longer possible Then the court yielded, perhaps not unwillingly, and the public officers followed their example Business was again resumed as if the British parliament had never thrown an obstacle in its way and the stamp act, the offspring

---

* McMahon, 359

of its power, though still unrepealed, had ceased to exist even indirectly in Maryland

Its fate in the province foreshadowed its downfall in England The opposition, hoping to gain strength in their party contests, united with the friends of the colonies in assailing and overthrowing the administration that had obtained its passage. Pitt brought his eloquence to their assistance in parliament. and on the 18th of March, 1766, the obnoxious act was repealed. But while performing this act of simple justice, the parliament did not fail to censure the recalcitrance of the colonies and to renew its claim to the power of imposing taxes upon them The repeal of the obnoxious measure was received with acclamation in Maryland Everywhere the people manifested their joy by festivities and illuminations. In the midst of their rejoicings they did not forget the debt of gratitude which they owed to the distinguished and enlightened statesmen of England, who had proved themselves friends of the colonies in the long struggle In November, 1766, the House of Delegates, "taking into their most serious consideration, the noble and spirited conduct of the Right Honorable William Pitt, now Earl of Chatham, and the Right Honorable Charles Pratt, Lord Camden, late lord chief justice of the common pleas, and now lord high chancellor of England, in defending and supporting the rights and liberties of their fellow-subjects in general," "to transmit to posterity their grateful sentiments of the inflexible integrity, and conspicuous abilities of these shining ornaments of their country, and as a monument of their virtue" and "a lasting testimony of the gratitude of the freemen of Maryland," unanimously decreed that a marble statue of Chatham should be erected in the city of Annapolis, and a portrait of Lord Camden, by some eminent hand, placed in the provincial court—a refinement of compliment worthy of the eminent men who led the proceedings in that day They also directed their agent in London, Mr. Garth, to tender their most sincere acknowledgments to the Earl of Chesterfield, Lord Shelburne, Secretary Conway, General Howard, Colonel Barrè, Sir George Saville, Alderman Beckford, and all other members of the lords or commons who had "acted the like glorious part of defending, through principle, the just rights of the colonists."* Messrs. Ringgold, T. Johnson, Wolstenholme, Hall, Grahame, Hanson, Murdock and Chase were directed to draw up and report a bill making the resolution effective. It passed the lower house; but, as like every act of that unyielding body, it assumed that the right of originating money bills was vested in the delegates alone, the governor and council withheld their approval. The act of gratitude, therefore, failed, but its failure even was honorable to the sturdy independence of the House. Thus the stamp act ended in victory for the people, tending to unite them more firmly together and proving their strength, thus united, aginst the schemes of oppression. It prepared them to resist the next invasion of their rights with even greater energy.†

The English government, even in the moment of defeat, still clung to the idea of raising a revenue from the colonies. It goaded their pride to yield, yet they determined to proceed hereafter in a more cautious manner. Townshend declared, in parliament, in 1767, that, *"he* knew how to raise a revenue from the colonies without giving them offence;" and his opponents, who had originated the stamp act, replied with a taunt "You dare not tax America." But the tax was determined on. On July 2, 1767, an act was passed by parliament, laying a duty upon tea, paints, glass and paper imported into the colonies, under the specious pretence of regulating commerce. But Townshend was not more fortunate than Grenville. The old spirit of resistance again broke out, the press teemed with appeals to the public, and the colonists were soon prepared to meet this as they had met the stamp tax. Massachusetts again took the lead, and having framed a petition to the crown, addressed a second circular to the sister colonies advising them to adopt similar measures.

The legislature of Maryland did not assemble until the 24th of May, 1768, but public opinion had already settled their

---

* Votes and Proceedings, November, 1766, p 136
† McMahon, 320-364

course. The British government finding that the spirit of resistance was aroused, had ordered the various governors to prorogue the Assemblies of their provinces, if they manifested any disposition to unite in measures of opposition, hoping thereby to disable the patriots and reduce their strength. But the Assembly of Maryland was too wary to be thus circumvented. The patriots prepared their measures in advance. They then took into consideration the Massachusetts circular and appointed a committee to draft a petition to the king. Immediately the message of the governor was presented and they were warned that they would be prorogued if they persisted. Without reply or delay, they instantly adopted the petition and passed a series of resolutions, which they had already framed, and, having successfully taken every step the occasion demanded, drew up a sharp reply to the governor, stating their readiness to be prorogued. This message was borne to the governor by Robert Lloyd, the speaker of the House, attended by all the members in procession. They were accordingly dissolved.*

This spirited body contained among its members many of those distinguished patriots who bore honorable share in the revolution in the council chamber or the battle field. Thomas Johnson, Wiliam Paca, Samuel Chase, Matthew Tilghman, Thomas Cockey Dye, Francis Ware and William Smallwood sat in the House, besides many others of less note. A special committee was appointed to inspect the state arms. Their report displays the poverty of the magazine: there were 785 muskets, old and new, 420 bayonets, 262 swords, 35 pistols, 47 pikes, 2 halberts, 97 kegs of shot and musket ball, 80½ barrels of powder, and 15 pieces of cannon.†

The colonists were not yet prepared for an appeal to arms. It was necessary that every peaceful means of redress should be exhausted, and, having tried petition and remonstrance, they determined to resort again to "Non-importation" which had been introduced in the days of the stamp act. This policy

---
* Votes and Proceedings, 1768
† Votes and Proceedings, 1768

was first revived in Boston, but was not generally adopted until all hope of redress from parliament was abandoned. At an early period of the struggle county associations had been formed in Maryland for the purpose of united action and it was now deemed expedient to bring them together. On the 9th of May, 1769, upon solicitation by the people of the counties several merchants of Annapolis addressed a circular to the people calling a general meeting at that city for the purpose of consulting on the most effectual means of lessening the future importation of goods from Great Britain. On the 20th of June the people assembled at beat of drum and entered into articles of non-importation of British superfluities, as well as for promoting frugality and the use of American manufactures. They unanimously pledged themselves to these purposes, and also to hunt out and punish all infractions of the pledge. To extend the operations of the association, twelve printed copies of the resolutions were sent to each county, that they might be signed by the whole people.

In the beginning of the ensuing year, the spirit of the associators was put to the test. "The Good Intent," a British bark, arrived in the harbor of Annapolis with a cargo of the obnoxious articles. A meeting of the associators was called and a committee of three appointed to examine into the case; and upon their report it was resolved that the goods should not be landed. Accordingly the brig was compelled to return to London with her whole cargo.* Nor was this the only or most striking instance of resistance to the tax upon tea. Long before the destruction of tea in Boston harbor by disguised men the patriots of Maryland calmly, openly, and in the presence of the governor and the provincial officers discussed and set at defiance this obnoxious act and effectually prevented its execution. When other measures were required they were not found wanting. Their calm but determined opposition brought the English merchants to their senses; and they resolved to send no more prohibited goods to Maryland.

---

* Annals of Annapolis

While Maryland was thus firmly vindicating its rights, the other colonies began to fall away from their duty

The English ministry, alarmed at the unbroken front of the opposition, promised, in an address to the colonies, the repeal of the duty on all articles except tea which accordingly was done on the 17th of April, 1770, New York and Philadelphia did not hold to their agreement and several merchants of Baltimore also resolved that they would import the articles, now released from duty, and requested the general convention of the associators of Maryland to consider the matter. Delegates from all the counties met at Annapolis, but far from yielding their assent to the proposition, denounced it and its authors, and declared that they would hold no communication with them if they persisted in their intention. Thus while the people of the cities proved recreant, those of the counties remained firm They had already proclaimed the merchants of New York and Philadelphia faithless to their pledge and traitors to the cause, they would not yield to the solicitations of those of Baltimore At last Boston gave up the system, and the societies of Maryland began to despond Yet they did not abandon their pledge, and if for a time they seemed to do so, it was because more absorbing and more direct questions arose

The public officers of the province had always been compensated by fees for each service performed, instead of regular salaries. These fees were fixed by the legislature from year to year, and were rated in tobacco, payable either in that article, or in money, at a fixed valuation per pound The profits of some officers had become enormous. Mr McMahon estimates the annual receipts of the secretary of the colony at $4,376, of the judges of the land office at $6,876; and of the commissary's office, at $3,923 * It is not strange that the people became restless at these exactions But there was another burden which now no longer exists, the clergy of the Episcopal church were supported by tithes. But the act of 1702, passed at an Assembly, which as it was now contended, was improp-

---
* McMahon, 382

erly convened, the rate had been fixed at forty pounds of tobacco per head, subsequently, by the act of 1763, it was lowered to thirty pounds, and yet, even then, so large were the proceeds that as an example, the income of the parish of All Saints in Frederick amounted to one thousand pounds sterling or nearly five thousand dollars a year These fees and tithes were collected by the sheriff by process of execution, if not voluntarily paid *

In the general spirit of opposition to unjust burdens and abuses which had arisen, these two did not escape, and the legislature, in 1770, when the acts authorizing these impositions had expired, took up the question and endeavored to diminish the amount of the fees and obtain other reforms But the persons most directly interested and holding the most profitable offices—Daniel Dulany, secretary, Walter Dulany, commissary general. Calvert and Stewart of the land office, sat in the council or upper house. and resisted every attempt to infringe upon their profits From this moment Daniel Dulany and his compeers became arrayed against the patriots. Interest proved stronger than public spirit and the popular champion during the stamp tax struggle became the defender of Proprietary rights and royal privileges during the subsequent contests After an ineffectual attempt to arrange the affair, the House after having ordered the arrest of the clerk of the land office for taking illegal fees, was prorogued by Governor Eden. There was now no law in existence for the collection of officers' fees, and that for the rating of tithes had also expired For the clergy it was contended that the act of 1702 was revived by the expiration of that of 1763, and they proceeded to collect their tithes, at the rate of 40 pounds of tobacco instead of thirty, while for the protection of the officers, who, with the established clergy, formed the mainstay of the royalist party, the governor on the 26th of November issued a proclamation fixing the old rates of fees and requiring

---

* McMahon, 398

the officers to receive the amount of money if tendered.*

The people of Maryland had never yet submitted to an arbitrary exercise of power, and the proclamation at once revived the fire of the Sons of Liberty Parties were formed. The officers and the established clergy and their adherents rallied around the governor, against the body of the people, headed by the almost unbroken front of the lawyers of Maryland, including the eminent jurist, Daniel Dulany. As in former controversies, public opinion was appealed to in every way by popular addresses, pamphlets, and discussions in the columns of the Maryland Gazette.

Charles Carroll of Carrollton was descended from a family which had settled in the province before the Protestant revolution. He was born in 1737, at the city of Annapolis, and at eight years of age sent to France to be educated At the age of twenty he commenced the study of law in London. He returned to Maryland in 1764, just in time to aid in the struggle which his countrymen were waging against tyranny. He had opposed the stamp tax, he took part again in the contest against parliament. Daniel Dulany was his foremost adversary and the controversy was the most marked of that day. It was carried on under the names of the *"First Citizen"* and *"Antilon."* The articles were able and eloquent. The cause Charles Carroll represented prevailed, for he fought on the side of popular rights. Yet this noble patriot "was a disfranchised man and could not even vote at an election,† and had heaped upon him epithets of bigotry and of hate He triumphed with the people, lived to see them free and great and prosperous, and survived as the last of the noble band of signers of the Declaration of Independence.

The elections coming in the midst of the controversy, turned upon its issues. They resulted in the complete success of the popular party. In recogniton of the brilliant leadership of Charles Carroll, the people assembled at public meetings

---

* McMahon, 399
† Ibid, 391

instructed their delegates to convey him a vote of thanks, which was done

The last Assembly, in 1771, had petitioned against the arbitrary exercise of power. Now, the people determined to give additional weight to the proceedings of the new house. Upon the closing of the polls at Annapolis the popular candidates, Messrs Paca and Hammond, were declared elected, and the people set about celebrating their victory. They marched in procession to the gallows, preceded by two flags, on one of which was inscribed *"Liberty,"* and on the other, *"no proclamation,"* with the representatives elect between them; then followed a sexton and a clerk, a coffin containing a copy of the proclamation cut out of one of Mr Dulany's articles in its defence,—and muffled drums and fifes, playing the dead march, and a large concourse of people from town and country, with six pieces of cannon bringing up the rear. The coffin with its contents, the obnoxious proclamation, was suspended from the gallows, then cut down and buried, amid loud shouts and discharges of minute guns, whose sound swept ominously to the government house and its defeated adherents. On the coffin was inscribed the following significant words:

"The proclamation, the child of folly and oppression, born the 26th of November, 1770, departed this life 14th of May, 1773, and buried on the same day, by the Freemen of Annapolis"[*]

Similar feeling was evinced throughout the state when the result of the elections was announced. It might have warned a government not devoted to ruin. The clergy of the established church still insisted upon their arbitrary claims and they had recourse to the courts to sustain their exactions. But the lower courts in many instances decided against them. The controversy had now lasted three years, and thrown the colony into commotion, unsettling the course of its laws and interrupting public business. The whole tobacco inspection system was destroyed and affairs could no longer remain in

---

[*] McMahon, 396-7

such a condition. At length a compromise of several of the subjects of dispute was effected and the rest were merged and forgotten in a new and more exciting contest.

The tax upon tea had not yet been repealed and although the non-importation societies for a time declined in their vigor, so constant was the opposition of the people and so obnoxious had the use of that article become, that it ceased to be imported and large quantities accumulated in the warehouses of the East India Company in England. The British government determined to make a last effort to subdue the colonies and to enlist the interests of the company in their project, offered it a drawback of the amount paid in duty. Thus the price of tea in the colonies would not be increased by the duty and, in that aspect, the submission to it would have been merely nominal. But a principal was at issue and the people would not submit. The East India Company, however, eagerly accepted the offer and vessels loaded with *"the detestable weed,"* as the colonists termed it, were sent to Charleston, Philadelphia, New York and Boston. At Charleston the tea was landed, but the agents dared not expose it for sale, the vessels destined for New York and Philadelphia were compelled to return to England without landing their cargoes. At Boston a more determined effort was made; and, sustained by a strong body of troops, the royal governor resolved to carry the measure into effect. But the patriots, by a bold and sudden stroke were victorious Disguised as Indians, a party entered the ships, broke open the chests and threw the tea overboard. This spirited measure called down upon Boston the vengeance of the government and in March, 1774, she was deprived of her privileges as a port of entry and discharge, and steps were taken to further strip the people of Massachusetts of their liberties. The only effect of these measures was more completely to arouse the colonies.

The people of Maryland were not wanting in this crisis, a general convention was called for, public meetings were at once held in all the counties and delegates chosen, who met at Annapolis on the 22d of June, 1774. The resolutions of this distinguished body breathed a spirit of the most determined opposition to the tyranny of England They proposed an absolute cessation of intercourse with the mother country, directed subscriptions to be made for the relief of the Bostonians, and having named Matthew Tilghman, Thomas Johnson, Robert Goldsborough, William Paca and Samuel Chase, delegates to the general congress, declared that the province would break off all trade or dealing with any colony, province or town that refused to come into the common league

Nor was it long before the firmness of the non-importation associators was tried, and if the tea party of Boston has been thought worthy of renown, the tea burning at Annapolis, open and undisguised, surpassing the former in every respect, should not be forgotten

In August, 1774, the brigantine "Mary and Jane," Capt. George Chapman, master, arrived in the St. Marys river with several packages of tea on board, consigned to merchants in Georgetown and Bladensburg. The committee of Charles county immediately summoned the master before them, and desired Mr Findlay, one of the consignees, to also appear. The explanations and submission of these gentlemen were declared satisfactory and, as the duty had not been paid, they were discharged upon the pledge that the teas should not be landed but should be sent back in the brig to London. The committee of Frederick county pursued a similar course with the consignees at Georgetown * But a more serious infringement of the rules of the "association" soon occupied public attention

On the 14th of October, the brig Peggy Stewart arrived at Annapolis, having in its cargo a few packages of tea consigned to Thomas Williams & Company. The duty was paid by Mr Anthony Stewart, the owner of the vessel This submission to the oppressive enactment of parliament, called forth the deepest feeling A public meeting was held at which the owner of the vessel and the Messrs. Williams, the consignees,

---
* American Archives, 4th series, vol, 1, pp 703-5.

in the most humble manner apologized for their offence and consented to the burning of the tea But the people were determined to exact a more signal vindication of their rights, the easy compliance of Mr Stewart with the act had aroused their anger and threats were poured out against his vessel and himself. Alarmed at the impending danger, Mr. Stewart, by the advice of Charles Carroll of Carrollton, to soothe the violence of the people and make amends for his fault, offered to destroy the vessel with his own hand. The proposition was accepted and while the people gathered in crowds upon the shore to witness its consummation, Mr. Stewart, accompanied by the consignees, went on board the brig, ran her aground on Windmill Point and set fire to her in presence of the multitude. Two months later the people of that portion of Frederick, which is now embraced in Washington county, having met at Hagerstown, compelled one John Parks to walk bareheaded, holding lighted torches in his hands, and set fire to a chest of tea which he had delivered up and "which was consumed amid the acclamations of a numerous body of people." The committee voted that no intercourse should be held with Parks and the people, to complete his punishment for having concealed "the detestable weed," assailed and sacked his dwelling. Similar evidences of popular determination were manifested throughout the colony, and while they tended to exasperate the royalists, their success gave new spirit to the patriots.*

The anxiously expected congress assembled on the fifth of September, 1774. It issued a manifesto setting forth the rights and grievances of the colonies, and proposing as a measure of retaliation a very extensive scheme of non-importation of British goods On its adjournment, the Maryland Convention was again assembled on the 21st of November and having unanimously approved of the proceedings of the congress, adjourned over to the 8th of December, to give time to the counties not yet represented to send in their delegates. With

---
* Annals of Annapolis, 158-165

their organization on that day, closed forever in fact the power and dominion of the last Proprietary of Maryland

The people of the colony had always loved and revered the family of the founder of the province and under the government of his descendants had enjoyed a large liberty and a constantly increasing prosperity It seemed as if Providence, when the great struggle for liberty and independence was approaching, had interposed to sever that link, which might have bound them to England and served to lessen their ardor in the common cause In 1758 Frederick, last of the lords Baltimore, became a widower and never married again, but, after having led a dissolute life, died in Italy in 1771, at the age of forty. Having no legitimate children, he devised the province to his natural son, Henry Harford, Esq The title of Lord Baltimore could not descend to him, and thus the name of the founders of the colony passed from their descendants just as their rule over it was about to cease Although the people might have clung with affection to the memory of the old lords Baltimore, a Proprietary who was not only an alien, but of illegitimate birth, could only increase their discontent and make them seek more eagerly for independence As Henry Harford was the last Proprietary his representative, Robert Eden, was the last English governor of Maryland. He remained in the colony long after his authority had passed from him to the people In the month of June, 1776, by permission of the committee of safety, he embarked on board the British sloop of war, Fowey, and joined Lord Dunmore, the late governor of Virginia, in the bay. On reaching England he was knighted for his services After the close of the war, the late Proprietary and his governor returned together into the State, where the latter died not long after near the city of Annapolis

A period of one hundred and forty years had passed since the two hundred colonists under Leonard Calvert landed on the wild shores of the little river-island at the southern extreme of the province. Their descendants had already extended to its northern boundary, covered its eastern shore with wealth and civilization, crossed the Blue Ridge, filling its rich valleys with a bold and hardy population, and planted themselves upon the sides of the Alleghanies On its bays and rivers floated the fleets of a growing commerce, while some of its towns were growing into populous cities Although devoted to agriculture the people turned their attention to the mineral wealth of their soil, and the forge and the furnace were already actively at work, while other manufactures needed only a fostering hand to be successfully established

In 1774 the power of the lord Proprietary, with that of the British crown, was verging to its fall and the province was governed by a sovereign convention of the people. Many struggles, and not a few revolutions had aided in bringing about this change, and in all there were elements of progress. Until the year 1649 there were no restrictions, no penalties upon any Christian belief. When religious dissensions began to creep into Maryland the act of 1649 was passed, reflecting the intolerant spirit of the times. While the men of that day, Protestants and Catholics, were desirous of assuring to all "professing to believe in Jesus Christ" full and equal rights; they did not dream of extending them to those who denied the articles which all denominations agreed in considering the requisites and the common ground of Christianity. "Blasphemy against God, *denying* our Savior Jesus Christ to be the son of God, or *denying* the Holy Trinity, or the godhead of any of the three persons" thereof, they considered great crimes, for which they prescribed "the punishment of death and the confiscation of lands and goods to the lord Proprietary. Blasphemy is even now deemed an offence against the laws To all Christians equal rights and privileges were extended by the Proprietary government, and this, measured by the sentiments of that age, is no slight glory. In the revolution of '89, this toleration was overthrown, as it had been suspended during the days of the commonwealth, but its gradual extension to all dissenters from the established church, as the political excitement of that period passed away, prepared the people for the equality which dawned like a brilliant morn upon the opening revolution of 1776. Yet the Jew remained enthralled until a much later period.*

---

* 1824-5.

CHAPTER VIII.

THE REVOLUTION

WITH one accord the patriots of Maryland at the call of the convention, hastened to bury all private animosities, all local differences, all religious disputes, and to equalize all rights and "in the name of God, their country and posterity, to unite in defence of the common rights and liberties "* The dominion of the British crown and the rule of intolerance in Maryland sunk under the same blows and perished together, never more to be revived.

On the 8th of December, 1774, the convention again assembled and proceeded to make preparations for an armed resistance to the power of England. And now was presented the singular spectacle of two governments over the same people, the old, silent and powerless, and yet possessing all the machinery of power and the will to exert it; the new, exercising an irresistible authority throughout the colony, peacefully and without direct contravention of law controlling even the business of the people, overlaying and rendering useless the old, and, by common consent, exercising supremacy. The convention itself was the general legislative and executive body and its resolves and recommendations were received by the people as laws, being carried into effect through the county committees of safety, vigilance and correspondence. All who refused to submit to these decrees were summoned before them and the judgment of the committees upon them published and from that moment the offenders became the mark of public scorn and contempt. The connection of the province with

---
* Maryland Conventions, p 10

other colonies was preserved through the delegates sent to the national congress and through the general corresponding committee. This simple machinery was rendered effective by public opinion. It formed the first transition step from the old establishment to the present system.

Having thus provided for the exercise of their authority, the convention proceeded to resolve that if the crown attempted to carry out by force the measures against Massachusetts, Maryland would assist her to the last extremity. To give earnest of their sincerity, they ordered that all the men in the colony from sixteen to fifty years of age should be enrolled and organized into companies and armed, equipped and drilled, ready for instant service, and that an assessment of ten thousand pounds * should be levied on the counties, in proportion to their population, to be expended in the purchase of arms and ammunition, under the charge of the county committees. Matthew Tilghman, John Hall, Samuel Chase, Thomas Johnson, Jr. Charles Carroll of Carrollton, Charles Carroll, barrister, and William Paca were appointed corresponding committee for the colony, and Messrs. Tilghman, Johnson, Robert Goldsborough, Paca, Chase, Hall and Thomas Stone, delegates to congress. Then, having called on their sister colonies to prepare for the general defence and besought all men to enter with united hearts and hands into the approaching struggle, the convention adjourned on the 12th of December to meet again at Annapolis on the 24th of April, 1775 †

The resolves of the convention were immediately carried out, old and young enrolled with the greatest enthusiasm,

---

* The proportion assigned to the counties is a matter of interest, as showing their relative wealth and population at that period

St Mary's	£600	Baltimore,	£933	Talbot,	£400
Charles,	800	Harford,	466	Queen Anne's	533
Calvert,	366	Worcester,	533	Kent,	566
Prince George's,	833	Somerset,	533	Cecil,	400
Anne Arundel,	866	Dorchester,	480		
Frederick,	1,333	Caroline,	358		£10,000

† Conventions of Maryland

and money, arms and ammunition were everywhere collected to meet the approaching crisis. Maryland was girding herself for the struggle. It broke out in open conflict just before the meeting of the convention.

The 19th of April, 1775, the first blood was shed in the revolutionary war on the field of Lexington, and the result of the contest between provincial valor and patriotism and British skill and discipline served only to rouse the whole people. The British government, finding every attempt to compel submission to their arbitrary enactments had failed, in the fall and winter of the preceding year, gathered a strong force at Boston and cut off all communication between that city and the country. This step only hastened the preparations of the patriots, instead of overawing them. Magazines of arms and ammunition were collected, and minute men enrolled, and the country put in such a state of defence that at a moment's warning the militia swarmed together in thousands.

In the midst of this excitement General Gage, who commanded the British troops, sent a detchment to destroy the provincial magazines at Concord and Lexington. At Lexington, warned in spite of the precautions of the enemy, about seventy minute men hurriedly assembled to make resistance. As the British approached, Major Pitcairn, who led their van, galloped up, calling out, "disperse, rebels!" The soldiers at the same time charged, firing a volley upon their half-armed opponents, and the militia dispersed, leaving on the ground eight men killed and wounded. Immediately the news spread abroad, and before the British had finished their work of execution at Concord, their advance parties were driven in. From Concord to Lexington a continuous fire poured upon them from every fence and cover. Worn and exhausted, they reached Lexington where they were joined by strong reinforcements with cannon. But no sooner had the march been recommenced than the galling fire of the provincials again opened upon them. The route of the retreating column was marked with their slain. At length they found security under the guns of their ships near Bunker Hill, on the evening of the 19th of April, having lost in killed, wounded and prisoners two hundred and seventy-three men. The loss of the Americans did not exceed ninety At each point where the skirmishing took place the British gave the first fire, the provincials remaining upon the defensive, desirous not to violate the letter of the law.

The first blood shed in the cause of liberty aroused the land.* North and south went the news upon the wings of the wind; day and night hurried expresses from town to town, from committee to committee to arouse the country. A full account reached New York on the 25th of April at two p. m., Baltimore at ten p. m., and Annapolis next morning at half past nine o'clock † Onward thence the news went southward from town to town, endorsed by each committee, with the time of its receipt and its departure, and the solemn order "night and day to be forwarded." Speedily it penetrated the farthest recesses of the colonies. From Massachusetts, through Rhode Island and Connecticut. through New York, New Jersey and Pennsylvania, through Maryland, Virginia, North Carolina and South Carolina, to Charleston, it went in twenty days, from April 20 to May 10, over the rough and difficult roads of that period. Each committee on the main route made and retained copies of the despatches and sent off others by express throughout the interior. By this admirable arrangement, the whole land was bound together, intelligence conveyed, and a common system of action preserved

The war had now commenced and nearly twenty thousand volunteers immediately assembled about Boston. The British troops were themselves besieged.

The convention of Maryland after a session of four days in which it reappointed delegates to congress had just adjourned when the news of these successful battles reached Annapolis. The province was too far from the scene of conflict to take an immediate part in the struggle. and upon its

---

* The first rumors of the battle reached New York on the morning of the 23d and were forwarded south
† American Archives, 1775, vol 2, p 366, etc

own soil not a single hostile foot was pressed, nor an enemy's sword unsheathed The note of preparation went on busily. The enrollments were hastened, minute men were raised, there was no hesitation on the part of the great body of the people. New York, by reason of its large Tory population, remained impassive and it was found necessary to march a body of Connecticut troops within striking distance to overawe the Tory tendencies of many of the people, but Maryland had long since prepared for resort to arms.

On the seventh of June the memorable battle of Bunker Hill was fought Hesitation ceased, and doubt everywhere gave place to certainty Congress determined to carry on an offensive war Boston was ordered to be invested, and General Washington, nominated before that body by Thomas Johnson of Maryland on the 15th of June, 1775, was chosen commander in chief of the American forces.*

In the midst of these exciting events, on the 26th of July the convention of Maryland again assembled, and their first step was to adopt the famous "Association of Freemen of Maryland," which was subscribed to by all the patriots, and became the written constitution of the province until the new system was framed in 1776. It approved of the war measures of congress, called on the people to sustain them by raising forty companies of minute men and provided a complete military system It vested the executive power during the recess of the convention in a committee of safety, eight of whom were selected from the eastern and eight from the western shore, and directed a large issue of paper money to defray all necessary expenses It also required the voters of the counties to elect a committee of observation who were to exercise a superintending power in their respective counties.

To redeem their pledges to the common cause the convention and committees set about the formation of a regular force to be composed of a battalion under the command of Colonel Smallwood, and seven independent companies be-

---

* Sparks, vol 3, p 480

sides two companies of artillery and one of marines.* By a resolution of congress passed on June 14, 1775 two companies of riflemen were called for from Maryland, which, with two from Virginia and six from Pennsylvania, were to be formed into a battalion and marched by companies as soon as enlisted, to the camp around Boston. The two Maryland companies were assigned to Frederick county and the committee of that county on the 21st of June appointed Michael Cresap captain, Thomas Warren, Joseph Cresap, Jr, and Richard Davis lieutenants of the first company, and Thomas Price, captain, Otho Holland Williams and John Ross Key lieutenants of the second.† These companies were soon filled with the hardy pioneers of western Maryland, and before the close of July took up their march for the camp where they arrived in August.‡ By a subsequent resolve of Congress, in 1776 six more companies were ordered to be raised, four from Virginia and two from Maryland, which were to be incorporated with the four companies previously enlisted into a regiment under the command of Colonel Stevenson of Virginia, Lieutenant Colonel Moses Rawlings, and Major Otho H. Williams of Maryland

Yet impatient of the necessary delay in organizing these troops, numbers of young men hastened at their own expense to join the camp before Boston The non-importation system had rendered the colonies destitute of the necessaries of either peace or war and it was now found almost impossible to provide the hastily collected troops with ammunition or clothing. Throughout the war the scarcity of these articles and of the necessary hospital stores, crippled the patriots and caused greater loss of life than the sword of the enemy. The arsenal at Annapolis was almost devoid of supplies, and the statesmen of Maryland perceived the necessity of at once providing for a permanent supply of military stores. A sum of money was set apart by the convention for the manufacture of salt-

---
* Convention Journals
† American Archives, 4th S., vol 2, p. 1046
‡ Ibid, 3d vol, p 2

petre for the public use And to encourage a general production of this indispensable material, a bounty of two pence was offered for every pound of the rough article made in private factories Powder mills were also erected; the manufacture of wool, flax, and hemp encouraged and the making of gun barrels and all the munitions of war undertaken But the Colonial troops were still very deficient in artillery and it was thought that this want too could be supplied at home A citizen of the state contracted to supply the province with cannon

As yet Maryland had not been threatened with hostilities But a period of real danger was approaching. Dunmore, the late royal governor of Virginia having been driven from that colony took refuge on board a man of war in those waters and commenced a series of depredations upon the counties bordering on the bay. At the same time he kept up his communications with the royalists in that colony and endeavored to extend his influence to Maryland In July, 1775, John Conolly of Lancaster Co, Pennsylvania, presented to his lordship a plan for raising an army in the western parts and cutting off all communication between the northern and southern provinces The scheme, as set forth in the records of the Frederick county committee of safety certainly displayed no small degree of talent and skill in its projector. The disaffected on the western borders were to be enrolled by the aid of large bounties The Indians were to be called in to their assistance, and the troops stationed at Detroit with all the artillery and munitions of war from the line of fortresses on the northwest were to form the nucleus of the army, which was to march quickly on the defenceless frontier, cut its way to Alexandria, and being joined there by Lord Dunmore, fortify itself under the guns of his fleet. It was thus expected to overawe the patriots, strengthen and confirm the royalists, and effectually cut off all communication between the north and south Lord Dunmore approving the plan despatched Conolly to Boston with letters of introduction to General Gage, who having given his proposals a favorable consideration, sent him back to Virginia with instructions In pursuance of these Dunmore issued to him "a commission as Lieutenant Colonel commandant of the forces to be raised in the back parts and Canada with power to nominate his subordinate officers." Accompanied by Dr. John Smith of St. Marys county and Allen Cameron of Virginia, both natives of Scotland, he succeeded in effecting passage through the most dangerous portion of his route with safety, disseminating his evil principles on the way and preparing for the accomplishment of his purpose.

But just as he was about to emerge from the hostile settlements to prosecute the remainder of his journey in supposed security he was arrested with his companions and sent under guard to Frederick where he was examined by the committee of safety A copy of his plan, a letter from Lord Dunmore to White Eyes, a Delaware chief, to secure his cooperation and a treasonable letter to a citizen of Virginia were discovered upon his person. Finding further disguise useless he admitted the charge against him and with his companions was put in close confinement to await the action of the convention and congress, who were forthwith notified of the affair by Mr Hanson, the chairman of the committee. In December, congress directed the prisoners to be forwarded to Philadelphia Dr. Smith succeeded in escaping during the night, but was retaken* and the prisoners were delivered safely in Philadelphia Conolly was afterwards exchanged, and reappeared at a later period in the prosecution of his old scheme †

While thus endeavoring to organize a force on the west, Dunmore was actively at work disseminating the seeds of disaffection through his agents on the eastern shore. He was partially successful and raised several companies of men pledged to support the royal cause if arms, ammunition and a small additional force should be furnished them. They even became so bold as openly to tear off the black cockade which the patriots wore at their militia trainings to replace it with the red cockade and to parade under officers of their own selection. A party under one of their leaders in November

---
* Sparks, vol. 3, pp 126-212-271.
† Proceedings of the committee of safety of Frederick

seized on a small craft and sailed secretly to obtain the necessary supplies of ammunition, but before the malcontents could mature their plans the committee of safety of the eastern shore, aided by the committees of Somerset and Worcester counties assembled a body of a thousand militia, crushed the attempt and secured the principal conspirators.

Although defeated in these attempts, Dunmore did not desist from his efforts In January, 1776, he invaded Accomac and Northampton, the Virginia counties on the eastern shore. As soon, however, as the fact was known by the convention which was then in session, three companies of minute men were called out for two months' service from Kent, Queen Anne's and Dorchester under orders to march to the assistance of the inhabitants Two of these only were in a condition to march; the third, from Dorchester, possessed only ten guns fit for service and was unable to procure a supply. The two companies that marched to Northampton numbered one hundred and sixty-six men and were generally well armed but many of Captain Kent's men were even without shoes They were received by the people with public demonstrations of joy and continued on the station long after their orders had expired, in order to afford protection to the people *

While Dunmore with his detachments was thus threatening the eastern shore he attacked Norfolk with the heavy vessels of his fleet. For the protection of the harbors of Maryland batteries were erected near Baltimore and Annapolis and several merchant vessels were manned and armed as ships of war. In addition to the batteries, the entrance of the basin at Baltimore was obstructed by three heavy chains of wrought iron stretched across its mouth, and by vessels sunk in the channel The public records were removed for safe keeping from Annapolis to Upper Marlborough. These preparations were not useless Early in March, 1776, the Otter, British sloop of war made her appearance in the bay with two tenders and captured several small vessels After hovering about Annapolis it anchored a few miles below Baltimore with the in-

---

* American Archives, 4th S., vol 4—Conventions of Maryland, p 40

tention of destroying the State ship Defence, then nearly completed in that harbor. Captain Nicholson, who commanded the Defence, determined to retake the prizes and having hastily got his vessel ready, and shipped a number of volunteers with a portion of Captain Smith's company as marines, bore down upon the enemy. He was accompanied by several smaller vessels crowded with men. The morning was hazy and the British were taken completely by surprise. The tenders escaped with difficulty and all the prizes were recaptured manned and cleared for action.

The Otter, intimidated by the prompt action and formidable appearance of Nicholson's squadron bore away for Annapolis But finding this place equally well fortified and a strong body of the newly organized regulars, as well as militia, assembled to protect the town and shipping, she, with her tenders dropped down the bay without having won either booty or success * The militia and independent companies which had been put under marching orders upon the first appearance of the enemy in the waters of Maryland, now followed them down the bay shores as fast as possible Having plundered a small island on the Eastern Shore they made their appearance off Chariton creek in Northampton county, where Maryland minute men were stationed The tender entered the creek for the purpose of cutting out several schooners, however, they stranded During the night Captains Kent and Henry threw up a small breastwork opposite the schooner to prevent the captors from carrying her off, early the next morning the tender attempted to dislodge them. After a heavy fire lasting an hour, the tender was compelled to sheer off without her prize. The enemy having withdrawn, Captains Kent and Henry were ordered by the Maryland committee of safety to return to the province

Congress found it necessary to establish a continental navy against these maritime depredations so as not to leave the defence of the shipping and the coast towns to the few and scattered ships of the different colonies which were incapable

---

* Annals of Annapolis, American Archives

of concentrated effort and were therefore useless as a means of cooperation with the army. On the 5th of June the gallant Nicholson received a commission in the new navy and took command of the continental frigate Virginia Many other Marylanders entered into the service, among whom none were more distinguished than Captain William Halleck and Joshua Barney who had shared in the attack on New Providence Early in the year the first continental fleet sailed from Philadelphia, under Commodore Hopkins The stars and stripes were hoisted off that city amid the acclamations of thousands. The fleet consisted of five ships, fitted out at Philadelphia At the Capes they were joined by the Hornet and the Wasp, from Baltimore

In spite of this state of actual hostilities, Mr Eden remained in the province as its ostensible governor, while the real supremacy was in the hands of the convention His easy and affable manners, the politic course he had adopted towards the patriots, and, more than all else, his utter want of power to hurt had as yet preserved him from the exile which had been the fate of other provincial governors. Heretofore, too, he had held a neutral position in the contest. But certain letters from Lord Germaine, of the English ministry sent through Lord Dunmore in approval of his conduct and commanding him to hold himself in readiness to assist the crown when occasion should present, were intercepted by a Maryland cruiser, and it was no longer deemed prudent to permit him to remain in the colony General Charles Lee, then at Charlestown, into whose hands the letters were placed, immediately wrote to the committee of safety at Baltimore, advising that the person and papers of Mr Eden should be at once secured. Mr Purviance applied to Major Gist, who commanded the newly raised regulars of the Maryland line then at Baltimore, and Captain Samuel Smith's company was detached for that purpose. The committee of safety of Maryland, resenting this proceeding on the part of the military, summoned Captain Smith before them, and after reprimanding him ordered him to return to Baltimore At the same time, however, considering the presence of Governor Eden no longer consistent with the safety of the colony, they gave him notice to depart which he did on the 24th of June, on board the *Fowey*, which Lord Dunmore despatched to receive him. This nobleman, who had already ravaged Virginia, now made his appearance in the Potomac and threatened Maryland. The convention found it necessary to order the militia to the coast to cut off his communication with the disaffected element and to protect the inhabitants from plunder. At the same time they earnestly set about organizing their portion of the flying camp which congress had called for from the middle colonies. The quota to be furnished by Maryland was three thousand four hundred and five men, to serve until December, unless sooner discharged by congress, under whose control they were placed. But all minor notes of preparation were absorbed in that great and final step, the Declaration of Independence.

For a time the people had continued to look forward to reconciliation and an adjustment of their rights. But their feelings toward Great Britain had rapidly undergone a change. The war, which had been commenced against the measures of the ministry, arrayed itself against the claims of the crown. The tyranny of the king absolved the allegiance of the people. The battles fought during the past year, the victories obtained, and the sufferings so patiently endured, taught the patriots their own strength. England's persistance in pouring new troops into this country to conquer, rather than to conciliate, aroused a spirit of hostility which rendered compromise or submission impossible. The colonists had gone too far to recede had they so desired. The great idea of nationality swelled within the breasts of the patriots, the chains of habitual dependence loosened.

As early as May, congress, looking to a long contest, recommended the colonies to adopt permanent governments. And on the 7th of June, Richard Henry Lee introduced his famous resolution, "that the united colonies are, and of right ought to be, FREE AND INDEPENDENT STATES, and that all political connexion between them and the state of Great Britain is, and ought to be, totally dissolved " This resolution was debated from time to time and the conventions of the several colonies, except Pennsylvania and Maryland, directed their delegates to vote in its favor The convention of Maryland had instructed their representatives in the preceding December and had renewed that instruction in May, to endeavor to heal the differences with the mother country, if at the same time they could secure the full and complete liberties of the colonists under the British constitution. At all events, they were not to vote for the severance of existing relations, or an alliance with any foreign power without the previous advice and consent of the convention Before the convention assembled again on the 21st of June, a change had been wrought in public feeling, and the first question which was agitated in that body was the all absorbing one of independence. The delegates to congress were ordered to obtain permission to attend the convention and to have the national question postponed until their return with the final resolve of Maryland

On the 28th it was unanimously ordered that the delegates to congress should unite on behalf of the province in declaring the colonies free and independent, reserving to the State, however, complete internal sovereignty.* Principally instrumental in obtaining the passage of this resolution was Charles Carroll of Carrollton As a reward for his labors in behalf of the measure in convention he was, on the 4th of July, chosen a delegate to congress in conjunction with Matthew Tilghman, Thomas Johnson, Jr., William Paca, Samuel Chase, Thomas Stone and Robert Alexander.

On the 2d of July Lee's resolution was passed, and the Declaration of Independence, which had already been prepared, was introduced, discussed and amended. On the 4th it was adopted, and was signed by the delegates in congress assembled. "There go some millions," exclaimed a member as Charles Carroll added his name to the great instrument, in allusion to his known wealth "Nay, there are several

---

* Convention Proceedings

Charles Carrolls, he cannot be identified," said another in his hearing; and immediately the subject of these remarks added to his signature, "of Carrollton," the name of his estate, and used to designate him particularly. Having been chosen a delegate after the resolution had been passed, Carroll might, in fact, have avoided signing the declaration at all

The Declaration of Independence, solemnly attested and signed by the delegates in congress and approved by the colonies, was everywhere received with the most enthusiastic feelings. It was read at the head of the armies of the new republic and proclaimed with the applause of a people determined to maintain it with their blood On the 22d of July it was publicly read at Baltimore, at the head of the independent companies and the militia, accompanied with salvos of artillery and "universal acclamations, for the prosperity of the United States " At night, the town was illuminated, and an effigy of the king of England paraded through the streets and burned in derision of his forfeited authority.

This step having been taken it was necessary to frame a permanent government for the new State. The convention accordingly ordered elections to be held for delegates to a convention to form a constitution. Then having confided the supreme power into the hands of the committee of safety until that body should be assembled it adjourned on Saturday, the 6th of July One of its last acts was to place the State troops at the disposal of congress The battalion under Colonel Smallwood and the independent companies in Talbot, Kent, Queen Anne's and St. Mary's counties attached to his command, were ordered to proceed to Philadelphia and report themselves to the chief continental officer stationed there, and be marshalled into the national service By another resolution passed in obedience to a requisition of congress, they directed the raising of two companies of riflemen and four of Germans, consisting each of ninety officers and men: one of rifles from Harford, two of Germans from Baltimore and one of rifles and two of Germans from Frederick county. The different county committees were required to despatch the companies of the flying camp as fast as they were organized, and the State committee of safety, to superintend the immediate march of the regulars under Smallwood.

CHAPTER IX.

THE BATTLES OF THE OLD MARYLAND LINE

After evacuating Boston, General Howe retired to Halifax to wait for reinforcements. But conceiving the design of seizing New York, whose inhabitants were favorable to British supremacy, and cutting off the northern from the middle states, he embarked for that port and arrived off Long Island towards the close of June. There were but a few American troops on the island, placed there for the purpose of carrying off the cattle, and he landed without opposition. He was received with the greatest demonstrations of joy by a portion of the inhabitants of Long Island, New York and New Jersey, many of whom took the oaths of allegiance, and embodied themselves into a corps under the command of Tryon, the last royal governor of New York. In the early part of July Admiral Lord Howe joined his brother with a fleet of 150 sail and a reinforcement of 20,000 men, swelling his force to 30,000. The American army under Washington, after being reinforced by several bodies of militia, amounted only to 17,000 men, of whom nearly one fifth were sick or unfit for duty.

It was at this dark hour that the Maryland Line entered the field and bore the first shock of battle. No sooner was the approach of Howe known in Maryland, than Smallwood's regiment took up its route for the seat of war. On the 10th of July six companies from Annapolis under Smallwood himself, and three from Baltimore, embarked for the head of Elk river,* whence they marched to New York and were incorporated into Lord Stirling's brigade. Well-appointed and

---

* Annals of Annapolis

organized, composed of young and spirited men who had already acquired the skill and precision of drilled soldiers, and coming at a time when the army was lamentably deficient in discipline, they immediately won the confidence of the commander-in-chief; and, from the moment of their arrival, were thrown upon the advanced posts and disposed as covering parties On the 20th of August the four independent companies remaining in Maryland were ordered by the convention to join Colonel Smallwood and place themselves under his command, thus incorporating the whole force of 1444 men in one body. The brigadier general of the Maryland flying camp now rapidly organizing, was also ordered to be subject to Colonel Smallwood's command, and the county committees were urged to hasten the enrollments and forward the men to the camp as fast as possible

From the 21st to the 27th of August the British were occupied in landing their forces on Long Island On the 20th the Maryland troops, together with those of Delaware, were ordered to the scene of the approaching conflict Colonel Smallwood and Lieutenant Colonel Ware were detained in New York, on a court martial they applied in vain to General Washington to permit them to accompany their men, and the battalion marched under the command of Major Gist The American army under Putnam was drawn out to occupy the passes and defend the heights between Flatbush and Brooklyn. During the night of the 26th, General Clinton, with the van of the British army, silently seized one of the passes and made his way about day-break into the open country in the rear of the Americans He was immediately followed by another column under Lord Percy To divert the attention of the Americans from their left, another division under Grant, marched slowly along the coast, skirmishing with the light parties on the road.

Putnam fell into the trap and Stirling was ordered with two regiments, one of which was the Maryland, to meet the enemy on the route to the narrows About break of day he took his position advantageously upon the summit of the hills and was joined by the troops driven in by the advancing columns of the enemy. For several hours a severe cannonade was kept up on both sides and Stirling was repeatedly attacked by the brigades under Cornwallis and Grant, who were as often gallantly repulsed. At length the left wing of the American force having been completely turned by Clinton and the centre under Sullivan broken at the first attack of General De Heister, the position of Stirling's brigade on the right became perilous in the extreme. The passes to the American lines at Brooklyn were in the possession of an overpowering British force; two strong brigades were assailing him in front, and in his rear lay an extensive marsh traversed by a deep and dangerous creek, eighty yards in width at its mouth. Nearer its head, at the Yellow Mills, the only bridge which might have afforded the brigade a safe retreat had been burned down by a New England regiment under Colonel Ward in its very hasty retreat, although it was covered by the American batteries. The only hope of safety therefore for the gallant troops who still maintained the battle and held the enemy at bay was to surrender, or else to cross the dangerous marsh and creek at its mouth where no one had ever been known to cross before.*

Colonel Smallwood, having arrived from New York, and learned the perilous situation of his battalion, applied to General Washington for some regiments to cover their retreat. After a moment's hesitation, as to the prudence of risking more troops upon a lost battle, unwilling to abandon these brave men to their fate he detached him with Captain Thomas' independent company from New England which had just arrived from New York, and two field pieces, to take a position on the banks of the stream and protect the remnant of the brigade in the attempt to cross it.

The scene of the conflict was within a mile of the American lines, and while Smallwood was hastening to their aid, Stirling prepared to make a last effort to check the advance of the enemy and give time to a portion of his command to

---

* Colonel Smallwood's letter to convention, Annals of Annapolis.

make good its retreat For this purpose he selected four hundred men from the Maryland battalion, under Major Gist, placed himself at their head, and having ordered all the other troops to make the best of their way through the creek, advanced against Cornwallis' brigade. As they drew out between the two bodies of the enemy it was thought by the lookers on from the camp that they were about to surrender, but as with fixed bayonets they rushed to the charge upon the overwhelming force opposed to them, fear and sorrow filled every heart, and Washington himself wrung his hands, exclaiming, "Good God! what brave fellows I must this day lose" Five times this little band charged upon the powerful forces of Cornwallis Each time it was driven back only to gather energies for a fiercer assault, until upon the sixth attempt the heavy column of the British, reeling under the repeated shocks, gave way in confusion †

But in the very moment that victory seemed within their grasp, Grant's brigade assailed them in the rear, and the Hessians of De Heister, fresh troops, came to the aid of Cornwallis in front Already outnumbered more than ten to one, with their ranks thinned by the terrific slaughter, and worn down by long fighting, these devoted men could no longer make head against their foes A portion, with Lord Stirling at their head, surrendered themselves prisoners of war, while three companies, animated by the most determined valor, cut their way through the crowded ranks of the enemy and maintained their order until they reached the marsh, where, from the nature of the ground, they were compelled to break and escape as quick as possible to the edge of the creek. This desperate conflict gave time to the remainder of the brigade to make good its retreat across the marsh and swim the water, carrying with them twenty-eight prisoners. A heavy cannonade from four field pieces was kept up by the enemy upon the retreating troops, and a strong column of Hessians advanced to attack them in the marsh, where, as their guns were already wet and muddy, they must have all been cut off but for the unlooked-

---

† Lord Stirling's letter, Sparks, vol 4, p 516

for fire of the reinforcements under Smallwood, which, placed on the opposite shore, drove the pursuers back to the mainland where they formed some six hundred yards distant while the remnant of the Marylanders swam the creek. Several of them, and some of the Pennsylvanians and Delawarians were drowned in the attempt or perished in the marsh. Captain Thomas' men aided materially in bringing over the exhausted survivors.

The loss of the Maryland troops in this long contested battle was most severe From sunrise until the last gun was fired upon the field they were hotly engaged: and, when the rest of the army had been routed or had fled, maintained the battle unaided against two brigades of the enemy. "They were distinguished in the field," says a letter-writer of that day, "by the most intrepid courage, the most regular use of the musket, and the judicious movements of the body" Nearly half of their force was annihilated. Their loss in killed and wounded was 256 officers and men. Captain Veazy and Lieutenant Butler were slain, and among the prisoners were Captain Daniel Bowie, also wounded; Lieutenant William Steret, William Ridgely, Hatch Dent, Walter Muse, Samuel Wright, Joseph Butler (wounded), Edward Praul, Edward Decourcy, and Ensigns James Fernandes and William Courts The people of Long Island point out to strangers the spot where half of the Maryland battalion stemmed the advance of the whole left wing of the British army when no other troops were left upon the field.

The position of the American army at Brooklyn had now become precarious The British invested their works in form, and it was determined to retreat to New York before the ferry should be occupied by the enemy's fleet. On the night of the 29th, this masterly movement was effected Although the Maryland troops had enjoyed but one day's rest since their bloody defence at "the Yellow Mills," they were ordered on duty at the advance post of Fort Putnam, within two hundred and fifty yards of the enemy's lines, and with two Pennsylvania regiments on the left, were to protect the retreat of of the army. Under cover of a foggy night and morning the movement was successfully effected in spite of the disorder of the eastern troops, it was not discovered by the enemy until the last detachment of the Marylanders and Pennsylvanians was half way across East River and out of reach. Drawn off within ear shot of the enemy, yet so silently as not to give the slightest intimation of their departure to his sentinels, the Maryland troops again displayed their steadiness and discipline. Two days after this event Colonel Smallwood's regiment was ordered to Harlem opposite to Montresore's and Buchanan's Islands, of which the enemy soon took possession; so that a barrier of only two hundred yards of shallow water separated the two forces, across which the men easily conversed with one another.

As the British were now throwing forward their forces to surround the Americans on York Island, and, it was found impracticable to defend the city because of the disorganized condition of the troops, a council of war resolved that the army should be withdrawn into the lines below Fort Washington. The more portable military stores had already been removed, when on the 15th of September the enemy effected a landing without opposition, in the face of two brigades of Connecticut militia, who fled disgracefully at the first fire from sixty of the British light infantry,* and although "from the brigadier down to the private sentinel they were caned and whipped by Generals Washington, Putnam and Mifflin," they could not be brought "to stand one shot."† Disgusted with such cowardice, General Washington immediately sent an express for the Maryland regiment, drew it from its brigade, and ordered it down towards New York to cover the retreat of the army, knowing that he could rely upon its maintaining its position against all odds Smallwood posted his regiment upon an advantageous eminence on the main road near the enemy, where they remained under arms the best part of the day until the last troops had passed. Then the British, dividing

---

* Sparks, vol 4, Marshall.
† Colonel Smallwood's letter to the Maryland convention

their main body into two columns, endeavored to outflank and surround him Having maintained his position as long as it was necessary, and having received notice to retreat, he retired in good order and reached the lines about dusk

On the next day a body of British about three hundred strong made their appearance in the plains below the American position and the commander-in-chief, to accustom his troops to meeting the enemy, detached Colonel Knowlton with a corps of New England rangers, and Major Leitch with three companies of the 3d Virginia regiment which had just arrived in camp, with orders to attack them. The assault was judiciously made. Early in the action, however, Colonel Knowlton fell, and Major Leitch was mortally wounded But the captains of the companies still maintained their positions. A reinforcement of seven hundred men being received by the British, General Washington ordered up Major Price, with three of the Maryland independent companies, and Richardson's and Griffith's regiments of the Maryland flying camp, which had joined the army on the 8th of September These troops attacked the enemy with the bayonet, drove them from their position and were pursuing them towards their lines when the commander-in-chief ordered their recall The loss of the Americans was about fifty killed and wounded, that of the enemy more than double that number *

Determined to force Washington from his position or to surround and cut off his communications, General Howe landed a strong body of forces at Frog's Neck, about nine miles above Harlem The Maryland troops were immediately marched to King's Bridge, to reinforce the detachments already there, and to watch the advance of the enemy. At the same time it was determined by a council of war to evacuate York Island. posting however, a sufficient garrison to maintain Fort Washington. Accordingly, leaving the force at King's Bridge to cover the rear and to secure the removal of the heavy stores and baggage, the army began at once to retire

---

* Sparks, vol 4, p 98

On the 18th of October, having been reinforced, Howe commenced the pursuit, and after several skirmishes with Glover's brigade took post on the 21st at New Rochelle, where he was joined by another strong body of troops. Both armies now moved towards White Plains where an entrenched camp had been marked out, and already occupied by a body of militia. As the enemy approached, General Washington concentrated his forces, and prepared to give him battle. On the right of the army, and about one mile from the camp, on the road from the North river, was a hill of which General McDougal, with sixteen hundred men, including the Maryland battalion under Smallwood, was ordered to take possession. On the 28th the enemy advanced in two columns to dislodge him. Colonel Rahl, with a brigade of Hessians, made a circuit to fall upon the rear of McDougal, while Brigadier General Leslie, with the 2d brigade of British troops, the Hessian grenadiers under Count Donop, and a Hessian battalion, assailed him in front. At the opening of the cannonade the militia took to flight and the artillery fell into confusion and retired. Smallwood's Maryland regiment was immediately advanced to the foot of the hill to meet the enemy and a long and severe contest ensued. It sustained itself gallantly under the fire of fifteen pieces of the British artillery; but at length, overpowered by numbers, it was compelled to give ground. The enemy moved with great resolution upon the remaining forces, who made but a show of resistance by keeping up an irregular fire in their retreat. Putnam, with Beall's brigade of the Maryland flying camp, now came up to reinforce McDougal, but, finding the foe already in possession of the hill, he deemed it imprudent to attempt to regain it, and drew off his men.* The loss of the Americans was between three and four hundred killed, wounded and taken.

The Maryland line suffered severely and Colonel Smallwood himself was among the wounded. The regulars of that gallant corps, worn down by the hard service they had endured, and the effects of their wounds, aggravated by the want of

---
* Sparks, vol. 4, p. 528, Marshall.

proper medical attendance and hospital supplies, had been much weakened as an effective force On the 12th of October there were three hundred officers and men on the sick list—many of them incapacitated for duty—Majors Price and Gist and Captain Stone were lying ill in New Jersey and Colonel Smallwood and Lieutenant Colonel Ware even prior to the battle, were scarcely able to command their troops.* Yet under all these trying circumstances, almost without field officers, the Maryland line displayed its wonted valor at White Plains, and by its sustained resistance to an overpowering force won new honor for its State. Its loss in this hard fought battle was over one hundred men, which shows how obstinate was its defence. It had fought three battles in three months, it had been the first of the revolutionary troops to use the bayonet against the British regulars and had used it freely and with effect in each fierce conflict.

General Washington continued to fortify his position, and Howe, satisfied of its strength and the courage of the troops who defended it, determined to await the arrival of six more battalions which joined him two days after Washington, having now removed his stores and heavy baggage to a much stronger ground in his rear, unwilling to risk a battle with Howe's present force, withdrew during the night to North Castle, about five miles from White Plains, and stationed General Beall's brigade of Maryland militia at the bridge over Croton river Abandoning the hope of a successful assault upon his new position, General Howe broke up his camp and retired slowly down the river, towards King's Bridge, determined to obtain possession of Forts Washington and Lee. As soon as the American commander learned from his scouts that Howe's march southward was not a feint, suspecting that he designed striking through the Jerseys to Philadelphia, he divided his army and leaving three thousand men at Peekskill, crossed the Hudson with the troops raised south and west of that river

---

* Smallwood's letter in "Annals."

Anxious to preserve his little army, he had directed, upon the approach of the enemy, the evacuation of Fort Washington, but having been assured of the spirit and resolution of the garrison, he determined to risk its defence. On the 16th of November General Howe prepared to assail it. It was defended by some of the best troops in the American service, under the command of Colonel Magaw, a brave and experienced officer. He had posted his men in three divisions. Colonel Cadwallader of Pennsylvania, commanded within the lines; Colonel Rawlings of Maryland with his regiment of riflemen, was stationed on a hill to the north of the lines, while Magaw himself remained within the fort. Howe arranged his forces into four columns of attack, and about ten o'clock moved them to the assault. The first division of five thousand Hessians and Waldeckers, under General Knyphausen, advanced against Colonel Rawlings on the north, while the fourth division moved against Cadwallader, and the second and third crossed the East river in boats and landed within the lines. The attack of the first and fourth divisions was received with great steadiness and spirit by the Maryland and Pennsylvania troops at their respective positions, but the detachment stationed on the East river soon gave way, and Colonel Cadwallader was compelled to draw off a portion of his men to their assistance. Thus weakened, his main body was soon overpowered and began to retire.

Rawlings still maintained his ground with undiminished spirit although not protected by entrenchments. Posted among the trees, his riflemen poured in upon the advancing column a murderous fire which they in vain endeavored to sustain. The Hessians broke and retired. Again they were brought to the attack and again repulsed with dreadful slaughter. The Maryland riflemen remembered the destruction of their brethren of the battalion by the Hessians at Yellow Mills and did not forget to avenge it. But what could a single battalion of riflemen, even of such matchless skill and courage, effect when opposed to five thousand men armed with the bayonet? Had every other post been defended as theirs was, victory would have crowned the American arms that day.* But all the other troops were already in full retreat The three divisions of the enemy were about to fall upon their rear while they contended with a force in front of them far greater than their own At length, by sheer fighting and power of numbers, the Hessians reached the summit of the hill. Rawlings, perceiving the danger to his rear and learning the retreat of the Pennsylvanians, abandoned his position, as no longer tenable, and retired under the guns of the fort Being again summoned, Colonel Magaw, finding it impossible to maintain the post, as his ammunition was nearly exhausted, surrendered the garrison prisoners of war. Two thousand six hundred men, of whom two thousand were regulars were taken prisoners, which was a severe loss to the American army. Among the captives were Major Otho H. Williams, Lieutenants Luckett, Lingan, Davis and Evans, and others of the rifles Some few of the Marylanders escaped across the river † The loss of the enemy was nearly twelve hundred killed and wounded, more than half of which was sustained by the Germans in their assault upon Rawlings' Maryland and Virginia riflemen

Immediately after this disaster, Fort Lee was evacuated, and Washington, greatly weakened by the loss of men, retreated on the Jerseys. The term for which most of his troops were engaged was about to expire and they began already to leave the camp in great numbers Every effort to raise the militia of New Jersey and Pennsylvania to supply their place proved ineffectual, and the American general commenced his famous retreat towards the Delaware He reached the Raritan on the 1st of December, the day on which the term of the Maryland and Delaware flying camp expired, and there was compelled to discharge the greater portion of these troops in the face of the enemy. Some few remained as volunteers and many of the Marylanders re-enlisted in the new regiments then forming by the State. With an army reduced to less than

---

* Marshall, Sparks, and Wilkinson's Memoirs
† Sketch of the life of Everheart.

four thousand men Washington retired slowly before the immense force of the enemy, the bare feet of his destitute soldiers leaving their foot prints marked with blood upon the frozen ground On the eighth of December he crossed the Delaware, secured all the boats so as to prevent the further advance of the British, and placed his diminished forces in positions best calculated to defend the passage of the river. After a futile effort to obtain the means of transporting his troops across the Delaware, Howe distributed his men in winter quarters on the Jersey shore, calmly awaiting the freezing over of the Delaware in order to march into Philadelphia, and expecting daily the dispersion of the shattered American army.

The critical situation of Philadelphia, the seat of the federal government, the reduced condition of his army and the despondency of the whole country, required at the hands of the American leader a bold and vigorous stroke and he prepared to make it With the continental regiments of Maryland, Virginia, Pennsylvania and New York, Rawlings' and Hand's rifles and the German battalions, he opened the campaign in the midst of winter. In the dead of night he crossed the Delaware, at McKonkey's Ferry, with twenty-four hundred continentals, and dividing this small force, threw one column towards Trenton by the river road and led the other in person to the same point, by the Pennington road At eight o'clock he drove in the outposts and assailed the town. At the same time the fire of the second division was heard in the opposite direction The British under Colonel Rahl, taken by surprise, attempted to form, but losing their commander in the very opening of the action, they were thrown into confusion and endeavored to make their escape by the Princeton road. A detachment, however, cut off their retreat, and the whole body threw down their arms and surrendered. Twenty were killed and one thousand taken prisoners. The American loss was only two killed, two frozen, and five or six wounded The victory was complete and almost bloodless. Yet one portion of Washington's extensive design was not carried into effect. General Irvine had been ordered to cross with his force and attack the enemy at Burlington, and General Cadwallader to come up on the rear of the enemy at Trenton. The former could not get his artillery over, because of the rapid current and the floating ice, while the latter was unable to effect a passage with any portion of his troops Thus that part of the comprehensive scheme which aimed at sweeping the enemy from the Delaware remained unexecuted Owing to this failure, a body of five hundred of the British stationed in the lower part of Trenton, finding the road open, escaped to Burlington. With his prisoners and the captured stores, General Washington immediately recrossed the Delaware to his former position

The victory at Trenton raised the spirit of the country The new levies came in with more rapidity and the American leader, in order to follow up his success, recrossed the river and took up his position at Trenton with five thousand men Immediately a strong column of the enemy moved against him and he retired beyond the Assumpink, which runs through the town. Finding all the passes guarded the British encamped and lit their watch fires for the night intending to begin the assault at break of day. During the darkness, having heaped up his camp fires with fuel to deceive the enemy, Washington drew off his army and marched silently upon Princeton, where a smaller British force was stationed. As they neared the town General Mercer was despatched with his brigade, composed of the remnants of the Maryland regiment under Captain Stone,* the Delaware regiment and some militia, numbering in all three hundred and fifty men, to destroy the bridge over Stonybrook, by which Lord Cornwallis must march if he came to the relief of the force at Princeton. One of the regiments stationed at Princeton under Mawhood had already commenced its march to join Cornwallis At daybreak this detachment and Mercer's brigade came upon each other near the bridge. Mercer's brigade rapidly pressed on to the summit of a hill upon the road and assumed an advantageous position behind a

---

* Washington, in several of his letters, says that Smallwood's regiment was now reduced to a mere handful of men.

hedge near Clark's house. Mawhood attempted to dislodge him. At the first fire Mercer's horse was disabled and one of his colonels mortally wounded and carried to the rear This caused a slight confusion, which was augmented by the death of Captain Neal, who commanded the artillery, and Mercer himself, while endeavoring to rally his men, received a bayonet wound which proved mortal Many of his troops were only armed with rifles and, unable to withstand the bayonet, they broke after the third fire.* At this moment Washington ordered up the main body of the army and throwing himself into the midst of the fire of the enemy led them in person to the charge He rallied Mercer's men under a heavy cannonade from the enemy, and the Pennsylvanian and the Virginian regiments coming rapidly up, the whole body rushed forward with a loud cheer The struggle was short and decisive The British were broken and routed. The regiments in Princeton made but a moment's stand, and the Americans entered the town in triumph One hundred of the enemy were killed on the spot and three hundred taken prisoners; the loss of the Americans was about one hundred killed and wounded, among whom were many valuable officers At break of day Cornwallis discovered that the American army had disappeared; and suspecting the plan of Washington, hastily retraced his steps towards Brunswick to protect his magazines and heavy stores. His advance entered Princeton just as the rear of the American army abandoned it, on its way to assume a position at Morristown to recruit the men from the fatigues and hardship which they had endured.

The good results of these victories were immediately felt, confidence was restored, and the hopes of the people became brighter They effectually recovered New Jersey from the British, against whom the Americans, constantly reinforced by militia from Maryland and the adjoining states, in spite of the severity of the season, maintained an uninterrupted partizan warfare, cutting off their foraging parties, attacking their outposts, reducing them to great suffering for want of

---

* Wilkinson's Memoirs, vol I, p 142

provisions, and yet always avoiding any decisive action The British soon found themselves under the necessity of contracting their cantonments, and, yielding to the masterly skill of their great opponent, abandoned most of their conquests. Thus closed the campaign of 1776, a dark and bloody one, yet full of glory to the Maryland line, which, a powerful regiment at the opening in the month of August, was now reduced to a mere handful of men under the command of a captain. Indeed the old or first line may be said to have been annihilated in the battles which it fought from Brooklyn to Princeton

CHAPTER X.

THE NEW CONSTITUTION AND STATE GOVERNMENT.

In the meanwhile, in compliance with the requisitions of the late convention, elections were held throughout the State on the first day of August, 1776, for delegates to a new convention to adopt a constitution and form of state government. The number of delegates, their qualifications and the qualifications of the voters, the judges of the election and the mode of proceeding were fixed by the resolutions which directed the holding of the elections On the 14th of August this new body assembled and organized by unanimously electing Matthew Tilghman president After having devoted several days to the transaction of general business which had accumulated since the adjournment of the late convention, and having completed their own organization, the convention selected by ballot the president and Messrs Carroll, Paca, Carroll of Carrollton, Plater, Chase and Goldsborough, to prepare and report a declaration of rights and form of government.

While this committee, composed of the ablest and most distinguished patriots of Maryland, were busily laboring at their arduous duty, the convention was directing the whole energies of the State to a vigorous prosecution of the war and at the same time conducting the general legislative and executive branches of the government On the 6th of September they divided Frederick county and erected out of parts of it two new counties, Washington and Montgomery, the latter named in compliment to the great commander-in-chief, and the gallant Irishman who eight months before, under the walls of Quebec, had laid down his life battling for American liberty.

On the 10th the committee reported the bill of rights and constitution, which were laid over, and on the 17th were ordered to be printed and disseminated among the counties for public information and discussion, as well as to enable the delegates to ascertain the sentiments of their constituents upon this all important subject before they proceeded to act upon it, the convention adjourned until the 30th of the month.

When the body reassembled, public business pressed so heavily upon them that the consideration of the constitution and bill of rights was postponed from day to day while matters of more immediate importance were disposed of. The condition of their troops and the lamentable deficiency of arms and ammunition exacted immediate attention. Ample supplies were determined on, and the committee of safety were ordered to import at the risk of the State, four thousand stand of arms, as many good gun locks, fourteen pieces of cannon, twenty tons of powder and forty tons of lead, to be purchased with wheat, tobacco, flour and other Maryland produce to be for that purpose exported by the State.

Congress, moved by the remonstrances of General Washington and satisfied of the inefficiency of hasty drafts of militia in the field, resolved to raise a strong regular army and called on the states to furnish eighty battalions of men. The quota of Maryland was set down at eight battalions numbering four thousand men being one tenth of the whole army. The convention took the matter into consideration and resolved that, although the quota assigned to them, being founded on the joint number of black and white population, was larger in proportion than that levied on the northern states, still, "desirous of exerting the most strenuous efforts to support the liberties and independence of the United States, they would use their utmost endeavors to raise the eight battalions demanded from them." But they refused to vote bounties of land to the recruits, in accordance with the recommendation of congress, lest, not possessing a sufficient quantity of unsettled territory, they should be involved in great difficulty in the fulfilment of such a pledge. They therefore determined to substitute a bounty of ten dollars, payable to each recruit instead of land Four commissioners were immediately despatched to the camp to re-organize the Maryland troops already in service upon the new footing, and to induce as many as possible of the regulars and militia of the flying camp to enlist for the war The independent companies were formed into a second battalion and the two ordered to be increased to the continental standard. The commissioners were furnished with the blank commissions, sent by congress, and required to follow the advice and counsel of the commander in chief in appointing and promoting the officers of the new battalions

Having thus disposed of the necessary military arrangements the convention took up the bill of rights and constitution. They were fully discussed from day to day, revised and amended, and on the 3d of November the bill of rights was adopted On the 8th of the same month the constitution of the State was agreed to, and elections ordered to carry it into effect

While these two instruments were under discussion, Virginia adopted her constitution, and in one of its articles insisted upon certain claims which infringed upon the known rights of Maryland; asserting jurisdiction over the Potomac, the Pocomoke and the Chesapeake and her old claims to the unsettled territory of the west. The convention paused in their discussion to maintain the rights of Maryland, unanimously and in the strongest terms denounced these pretensions, and insisted that "if the dominion of those lands should be established by the blood and treasure of the United States, such lands ought to be considered as a common stock, to be parcelled out, at proper times, into convenient free and independent governments." Again, in November, when addressing congress, they declared that this territory, claimed by the British government, if conquered from them "by the blood and treasure of all, ought in reason, justice and policy, be considered the common stock of all."* Thus, while building up the fabric of their own State government, the sage legislators of

---
* Conventions of Maryland

Maryland marked out for futurity that grand system of expansion of the republic which has since made this union one of the most extensive, flourishing and powerful nations of the earth †

Under the new constitution the government was composed of three distinct branches, the legislative, the executive and the judiciary. The legislative authority was vested in a Senate and House of Delegates whose several powers and privileges were appropriately marked out. The house of delegates was composed of four members from each county and two from each of the cities of Baltimore and Annapolis, chosen immediately by the people, *viva voce,* at elections held by the sheriffs of the counties at their respective court houses The senate consisted of fifteen members, nine from the western and six from the eastern shore, their term of service was extended to five years, and they were chosen by a college of electors composed of two delegates elected *viva voce* by the people of each county, and one from each of the cities of Baltimore and Annapolis

The executive authority of the State was placed in the hands of a governor, elected annually by joint ballot of the two houses of the legislature He was assisted in the execution of his office by a council of five members chosen by the same bodies His authority was simply executive. He possessed no veto upon the legislative proceedings and no means of interfering with that branch of the government By virtue of his office he was commander-in-chief of the military forces of the State, and he was vested with the power of appointing, by and with the advice of the senate, judicial and civil as well as military officers The constitution, besides these and other ordinary powers, conferred upon him authority in matters which now appertain to the federal government

The judicial system of the State was composed of the general court, the court of chancery, and the court of appeals, besides a court of admiralty. The sheriffs of the different counties were elected by the people, and the clerks of the courts

---

† Adams Maryland and the Public Lands

were appointed by the judges The register of wills received his commission from the hands of the governor Two treasurers, one for the eastern and one for the western shore, were selected by the legislature, and a register of the land office of either shore nominated by the governor and approved by the senate.

The elective franchise was limited by a property qualification; for the men of that day, just emerging from monarchical rule, were not prepared for the adoption of manhood suffrage of later times Every voter was required to be above the age of twenty-one years, to possess a freehold of fifty acres of land in the county in which he resided and offered to vote, or property within the State of the value of thirty pounds current money, and to have been a resident of the State for one year prior to the day of election. The qualifications of members of the legislature were still farther restricted. Besides the usual requisites of a voter, the amount of property which the aspirant to the house of delegates must possess to enable him to take his seat, was raised to five hundred pounds instead of fifty Senators were required to be above the age of twenty-five, and to own property of a thousand pounds in value, while it was necessary for the candidate for governor to possess a freehold of lands and tenements of the value of a thousand pounds, to have resided three years in the State prior to his election, and to have reached the age of twenty-five.[*]

In their solemn declaration of rights, the convention of 1776 defined the platform upon which they stood: so fully and so thoroughly in accord with the principles of freedom and justice that the reforms and the progress of subsequent times have been but little more than the evolution of the principles which they then formulated They declared their belief in the popular origin of government, while they insisted upon the submission of the people to the supreme authority constituted by themselves, while they defined those rights of the citizen which no power could absorb. They disestablished the existing State church, and declared that "It is the duty of

---

[*]Original Constitution of Maryland, 1776

every man to worship God in such manner as he thinks most acceptable to Him." If they confined the obligation and the privilege within the limits of Christianity, it was because men could not yet understand a larger liberty.

To introduce the new government the constitution provided that an election should be held on the 25th of November, 1776, for senatorial electors, who were ordered to assemble at Annapolis on the ninth of December, to select nine persons of due qualifications from the western and six from the eastern shore to compose the first senate of Maryland. On the 18th of December an election was to be held in the several counties for members of the house of delegates, and at the same time and place for sheriffs for the respective counties. The 10th day of February was fixed for the beginning of the session of the General Assembly, and the second Monday of November, 1777, and annually thereafter, for the election of governor, by both houses on joint ballot. The legislature, however, was authorized, in the meanwhile, to elect a proper person to act as governor until the regular period appointed by the constitution for his selection should arrive. Having thus provided for the establishment of the new government and appointed delegates to congress, with instructions to maintain unimpaired the independent sovereignty of Maryland while they consented to a confederation with the other states, the convention deposited the supreme power in the hands of the committee of safety, until the new government should rise phœnix-like from the ashes of the old, and adjourned on the eleventh day of November, 1776.

The elections took place at the specified times. And on the fifth of February, five days earlier than the period fixed by the convention, the committee of safety, by virtue of the extraordinary powers vested in them, caused both houses of the legislature to assemble at Annapolis. The nature of their acts explains the pressing necessity which had induced the committee of safety to call them together. During the panic created by the disastrous retreat through the Jerseys, congress, on the 12th of December, had removed from Philadelphia to Baltimore. On the 27th they conferred on General Washington extraordinary powers for the raising of troops and the conduct of the war Great efforts were, in consequence, made to strengthen his army, which was soon further weakened by the battles of Trenton and Princeton The effects of these battles was such, however, as to relieve Philadelphia from immediate fear of the enemy, and in February congress again returned to that city. In each succeeding action the Maryland troops had been further reduced until Smallwood's battalion and the seven independent companies, which had entered the campaign fourteen hundred strong, had been worn down to a mere captain's command In the face of this great loss and the largeness of the drafts made upon Maryland, it required unusual exertions to fill up the quota of eight battalions The legislature, therefore, turned their attention to the recruiting service, which they endeavored to expedite They also made every effort to raise military supplies for the destitute soldiers in camp, and to provide means for transportation of the material of war through the State The provisions of several of these laws very graphically represent the condition of the country at that period, and the slender resources on which the army was compelled to rely. By an act of 1777* the governor was required to appoint in every hundred or district, a blanket collector, whose duty it was to visit every dwelling house and compel the inhabitants to furnish, under oath, a statement of the whole number of blankets which they possessed and of the portion not in actual use. One half of all surplus he was ordered to seize for the use of the army, paying their owners the appraised value in State issues. To favor enlistments in the national or state service every recruit was exempted from arrest for debts under twenty pounds currency, and his property entirely freed from attachment or execution To provide comfortable quarters for the new recruits while preparing for the field, barracks were ordered to be erected at Frederick and the head of the Elk, for the accommodation of two battalions each, and at

---

* Hanson's Laws, ch 3

Annapolis for one. At the same time that they thus provided for defence against the foreign enemies of the State, the legislature wisely turned their eyes upon those equally dangerous domestic foes, who by their restless intriguing and firm adherence to the British crown, weakened and distracted the energies of the patriots. A law was passed to suppress and to punish persons guilty of treason to their country. As at such periods promptness of action is more necessary even than severity, the governor was empowered to commission special courts for the speedy trial of culprits charged with these offences. On the 11th of February the Assembly directed a proclamation to be issued against the disaffected in Worcester county, who, only repressed for a time by the active measures of the committee of safety for the Eastern shore, had again broken out in open insurrection. They offered pardon to all who would submit and disperse within thirty days excepting, however, fourteen of the leaders. As the disturbed condition of the county required active measures, Smallwood and Gist, then in the State superintending the formation of the new line, were ordered to march thither with a Virginia regiment of regulars, the Annapolis independent company, the company of matrosses and Captain Godman's Baltimore artillery. The promptness of these measures secured submission. The disaffected were disarmed, the most influential of them sent in custody to other counties and their estates placed in the hands of commissioners for safe keeping.*

In accordance with the provisions of the constitution, on the 13th of February the two houses proceeded to select a suitable person for governor of the State. Their choice fell upon Thomas Johnson.† On Friday, the 21st of March, 1777, he was publicly proclaimed the first governor of Maryland under a republican form of government. The ceremony of

---

* Journal House Delegates, 1777; Journal of Congress
† The vote for governor was as follows. For Thomas Johnson, Jr, 40, Samuel Chase, 9; Matthew Tilghman, 1, George Plater, 1; William Paca, 1.

inauguration took place at the state house, in the presence of a great concourse of people, the several branches of government, the civic authorities of the city of Annapolis, the military, and many strangers. The announcement was hailed by three volleys from the soldiery drawn up in front of the state house, and a salute of thirteen rounds was fired from the batteries in honor of the new confederacy. A sumptuous entertainment was then partaken, and the festivities of the day were closed with a splendid ball.‡ Thus the new government was fully organized and in active operation; the general and county committees of safety surrendered their powers and the law of the constitution spread its ægis over the State.

The Assembly having fully organized the new seven regiments required from the State and settled the rank of the officers, adjourned on the 20th of April. On the 15th of June, however, they were again assembled for a few days to authorize the governor to detach a portion of the State's artillery companies to Philadelphia to join the continental army, which was then very deficient in that arm. In the following October they took measures to raise an additional quota of two thousand men to serve for three years in the Maryland line, assigning to each county a due proportion to be furnished by it and made further preparations to supply their men in camp with blankets and necessary clothes. With all their exertions, however, the governor and the legislature found it difficult to place their quota upon such a footing as they desired. Besides the regular complement of eight battalions required by congress to complete the army, the State furnished men to many other corps. At the solicitation of General Washington, sixteen additional battalions were raised by congress exclusive of the State lines. Colonel Nathaniel Gist's, and Hazen's regiments —the latter originally intended to be formed of Canadians— and Spencer's, Baylor's, and Lee's corps, were partly raised in Maryland. The legislature always extended to their officers and men in them the same gratuities and the same comforts which they provided for their own line, although those from

‡ Annals of Annapolis

the other states in these corps were too frequently neglected While they were thus busy in raising the material of war at home, their troops, under the new organization, were gallantly doing their duty to their country in the field

CHAPTER XI.

THE CAMPAIGN OF 1777.

After the battle of Trenton and Princeton Washington maintained his position in New Jersey and a constant series of skirmishes was kept up by his reduced army of which scarcely more than a thousand were continentals. So severe had been the preceding campaign that more than two-thirds of the regulars engaged had perished or been rendered unfit for service; and when, by the arrival of the new recruits and quotas from the several states, the army was increased to eight thousand men, at least half of its number were totally ignorant of discipline and had never looked an enemy in the face. Under these conditions Washington feared for the safety of Philadelphia, and with all the militia he could assemble took post at a strong camp near Middlebrook Howe, cautious in all his movements, even to the point of timidity, feared to attack him and resolved to approach Philadelphia by another route After a series of unavailing movements, he embarked his whole force for the Delaware, but changing his design on arriving at the mouth of the bay passed into the Chesapeake on the 21st of August with two or three hundred sail of men of war and transports.[*]

Governor Johnson issued a proclamation calling on the militia of the State to arm He directed that at least two companies out of every battalion should take up their march to the head of the bay "To defend our liberties requires our exertion," declared the appeal, "our wives, our children and

---
[*] Sparks, vol 5, p 46; Annals

our country implore our assistance—motives amply sufficient to arm every one who can be called a man." Although the people everywhere answered the appeal by a resort to arms, influenced by those motives which have always detained the militia in the vicinity of their homes when an invasion threatened them, few could be prevailed on to march to the head of Elk and leave their families unprotected against any sudden inroad of the enemy or his tory adherents. While, therefore, the fleet hovered about the bay the men of the neighboring shores, although armed and ready for defence, refused to be drawn from their homesteads, and the only reliance of the governor for disposable militia was necessarily on the counties of the interior. The hostile fleet, having anchored for a while off the mouth of the Patapsco, proceeded to the head of Elk, where Howe intended to land his army and strike towards Philadelphia

While this invasion threatened the State the Maryland line was engaged in the attack upon Staten Island Upon its increase to seven battalions it had been divided into two brigades the one composed of four battalions was placed under the command of Smallwood who was promoted to the rank of brigadier general, the other, formed of the three remaining battalions and Hazen's regiment, was assigned to General Deborre, a French officer in the service of the confederacy * Colonel Richardson's battalion, in pursuance of an order of Congress, had been marched to Sussex county, Delaware, to overawe the tories of that State and the Eastern Shore. The British force stationed on the island ravaged the main land almost with impunity, and General Sullivan, who commanded the Maryland division then lying at Hanover, conceived the design of attacking and carrying off a part of their force, consisting of a thousand tories stationed on the shore at some distance from the main body. For this purpose he divided his troops into two columns, the first brigade under General Smallwood was to cross at Hasley's Point and attack Colonel Buskirk's regiment, which lay near Decker's Ferry. The sec-

---

* Sparks.

ond, under General Deborre, with a few Jersey militia, under Colonel Frelinghuysen, was again subdivided when it reached the place of embarkation, twenty miles from its encampment. Here the troops found but six boats, three of which were allotted to Colonel Ogden who commanded one detachment of Deborre's column, and Colonels Dungan and Allen, who were stationed about two miles from each other towards Amboy. The remaining boats were assigned to General Deborre, who accompanied by Sullivan was to attack Colonel Barton near the new Blazing Star ferry and then to form a junction with Ogden. All the troops were transported into the island before daybreak.

Misled by his guides, General Smallwood commenced his attack at a different point from that intended and Buskirk's regiment effected its escape. But Ogden and Deborre succeeded in a large measure. Lawrence and Barton were completely surprised and both of them, with several of their officers and men were taken. The alarm being given, it became necessary to draw off the troops as speedily as possible, but from the scarcity of boats, a portion of the rear guard fell into the hands of the British. In killed, wounded and prisoners, the Americans lost 164 officers and men, but carried with them from the island 141 prisoners, of whom eleven were officers. In addition, the enemy suffered severely in killed and wounded in the several actions.[*] On his return from this expedition, General Sullivan received orders to join the commander-in-chief, and the Maryland line once more approached their native State. Finding their homes freed from menace by the enemy the militia of Maryland now began to assemble and march to the head of the bay. General Smallwood was ordered to leave his brigade and lead the men of the Western shore, while Colonel Gist was detached from the line to lead those of the Eastern shore. Until the arrival of these officers, who were marching with the division from New Jersey, the militia were placed under General Cadwallader of Pennsylvania. Colonel Richardson's regiment of continentals was directed to proceed from

---

[*] Marshall, Sparks.

their station on the Eastern shore to the same place of rendezvous Every exertion was made by the State to aid and increase the army of Washington, who was now marching towards the Brandywine, resolved to risk a battle in defence of Philadelphia.

On the 25th of August the British army landed at the head of Elk, and having destroyed the few public stores which had not yet been removed, began their march upon Philadelphia. After several brisk skirmishes the Americans took position behind the Brandywine. There on the 10th of September the British advance found them and attempted to force their position. The main body marched towards Chadd's ferry, where, after a short skirmish, it drove in General Maxwell's brigade which had been thrown across the river to gall their advance parties About eleven o'clock Washington was informed that a strong body of the enemy under Cornwallis having made a detour, was striking for Tremble's and Jeffrey's fords, and formed the bold design of crossing the river and attacking the column in his front But having received conflicting reports from Sullivan he abandoned the attempt About two o'clock it was discovered that the information was authentic, and Sullivan, with the Maryland line and Stirling's and Stephens' division, was ordered to change his position and meet Cornwallis This was effected after a rapid march, but before he could get into formation, his right wing, composed of the Maryland division, was attacked by the enemy Deborre's brigade broke after a slight defence and the centre followed. The right wing attempted to rally but was again thrown into confusion by a brisk charge of the enemy and the whole line gave way Washington with Greene's division hurried to the scene of action only in time to cover the retreat of the army. At the same moment General Knyphausen crossed at Chadd's ford and drove back the forces stationed there to oppose him

The loss of the Americans was 300 killed, 600 wounded and 300 or 400 taken prisoners. That of the enemy was about five hundred killed and wounded. The defeat of Washington's army in this battle has been justly attributed to the confusion created by contradictory intelligence, and the careless manner in which Sullivan brought his men into action. It is certain that the Maryland line, although it behaved gallantly, scarcely sustained its ancient reputation while under him, nor equalled its subsequent glory when led by its own chiefs in the south. Deborre, who commanded one of its brigades was a foreigner, unpopular with his men and entirely without their confidence. His brigade was the first to break, and his behavior was made the subject of inquiry by congress, whereupon he resigned his commission. It must be considered, however, that the division went into action without several of its principal and most popular officers. General Smallwood and Colonel Gist, who possessed the entire confidence of the men, were absent at the head of the militia, leaving their corps without their usual leaders, a material circumstance with inexperienced troops. In addition to this a misunderstanding occurred upon the field between Sullivan and Deborre which necessarily increased the confusion. The night before the battle the men had lain on their arms and slept but little. They were under arms and in line the whole day without food and were hurried into action only half formed after a rapid march and sudden change of position. The expedition of Sullivan against Staten Island had already excited dissatisfaction and an inquiry in his conduct was ordered by congress and he was exonerated.

The American army retired towards Philadelphia and encamped at Germantown for rest; but congress having ordered that another battle should be risked in defence of that city, General Washington recrossed the Schuylkill and advanced along the Lancaster road. General Smallwood, still in the rear of the enemy, was commanded to muster all the forces he could to harass their march, and to cut off their foraging parties. The two armies came in sight of each other at Goshen, and a sharp skirmish immediately ensued, but a violent rain coming up, the ammunition of the Americans, which was badly secured, was rendered unfit for use, and the troops having few bayonets, were compelled to retire. The retreat was continued across the Schuylkill where a new supply of powder could be obtained in time to risk another battle. This movement placed Smallwood's troops in great jeopardy, being left unsupported in the rear of the British army. His force consisted of 1150 militia from the Western shore and 700 from the Eastern shore under Gist, besides Richardson's regiment of the Maryland line. He was ordered to join the army at French creek; but before he could execute the movement, General Wayne was detached to form a junction with him, and thus strengthened he was able to harass the enemy's rear.

On the night of the 20th of September General Wayne bivouacked near Paoli, three miles from the enemy's camp Learning his position from his spies, Howe detached Gen. Grey to surprise him. The picket guards were driven in with the bayonet, but the division again formed and several regiments by sustaining the attack with great firmness, gave time to the remainder to retreat. At the commencement of the action, Smallwood was about a mile distant from Wayne, not yet having joined him His force, principally composed of raw militia, could not be relied on in a night attack; and, upon being assailed by a detachment of the enemy, were routed with the loss of only one man The continentals reformed, but the enemy drew off without renewing the action The American loss was about three hundred men, that of the British only seven.

General Howe now moved to take possession of Philadelphia which he accomplished without opposition Washington, weakened by the absence of Wayne and Smallwood, and not yet joined by the northern regiments, deemed it hazardous to risk another battle in its defence. He however resolved to cut off the supplies of the enemy from their shipping, and to seize the earliest opportunity to strike them in detail. New obstructions therefore were thrown into the Delaware, to prevent the ascent of the fleet, and the garrison of Fort Mifflin was strengthened by a detachment of several hundred continentals under Lieut Col Samuel Smith of the Maryland line.

In the distribution of the enemy's forces a strong body was cantoned at Germantown. Washington considered this post favorable to a successful blow and resolved to take the enemy by surprise The main body of the British was encamped in the fields west of the town and stretching towards the Schuylkill, on the banks of which was stationed a body of Hessians and chasseurs forming their left wing Their right, under Grant, was posted on the east of the town and was flanked by the Queen's rangers. On the night of the 3d of October the American army advanced to the attack. The right wing, under Sullivan, composed of his own division, consisting of the seven Maryland battalions and Hazen's regiment, and Wayne's division, sustained by Stirling's corps, and flanked by Conway's brigade, marched down the Skippack road leading over Chestnut Hill into Germantown, to attack the main body of the enemy. General Armstrong, with a thousand Pennsylvania militia, was thrown along the Schuylkill to assail the Hessians and chasseurs The left wing of the Americans, under Green, composed of his own and Stephens' divisions, marched by the York road to attack Grant's force in front, while General Smallwood and Colonel Gist—who by a singularly perverse policy were still kept from their proper commands in the line—at the head of one thousand Maryland militia, with Forman's Jersey militia, made a large circuit to the left, to strike the rear of his position The whole army commenced its march from the camp at Matuchen hills, at nine in the evening The attack was to commence at all points at break of day.

After maching all night the right wing reached Chestnut Hill at the appointed time, and a regiment from the second Maryland brigade, with one of Conway's, was detached to drive in the pickets at Allen's house. The picket was briskly assailed but was soon reinforced by all the enemy's light infantry The attacking regiments, however, maintained their ground until the whole Maryland division was brought to their assistance. They advanced in gallant style and with such resolution that the light infantry were driven from the field after a close and sharp action of fifteen or twenty minutes, and their encampment fell into the hands of the victorious line, which during these movements had left the road and crossed into the field on the western side of the town The light infantry, however, continued their resistance at every fence, wall and ditch, while the assailing troops were much retarded in their pursuit by the necessity of removing every obstruction as they passed. In the pursuit, a company of the 4th regiment under Captain Daniel Dorsey was thrown across the road and engaged with a body of the enemy, who had sheltered themselves behind the houses. As the Maryland division was pressing on, being already in advance of the rest of the army, Colonel Hall attempted to disengage and bring up Dorsey's company, but was disabled by an accident, and the command of his regiment devolved upon Major John Eager Howard who hurried on his men through the encampment of the light infantry, and captured two six pounders before they reached Chew's house Here they were fired upon by the British, who had thrown themeslves into this strong building, and Colonel Hazen, then in commnad on the left of the Maryland, halted in the rear of that position

In the meanwhile, the remaining regiments of the line, under Sullivan in person, pursuing the flying light infantry. came upon the main body of the enemy drawn up to receive them A severe conflict ensued Sullivan impatient of delay, at once ordered his Marylanders to advance upon them with shouldered arms They obeyed without hesitation and the enemy after a sharp resistance again retired. Wayne had moved along the east of the town and was now ordered to assail the right of the broken troops, which he did with great spirit Maxwell's brigade had been halted at Chew's house and was assailing it gallantly but with great loss Greene's division at length made it appearance on the extreme left, while Stephens' fell in with and joined Wayne's The firing at Chew's house, which had become very heavy, now drew back Wayne's division, and distracted the several corps with the fear that the enemy was in force in that quarter. The morning was dark and hazy and it was impossible to discover the exact position either of the British or of their own columns. The Virginia line, under Stephens, after having fought with great gallantry was thrown into disorder when the enemy were in full retreat, by the approach of a party demanding quarter, and it was found impossible to rally them

The Maryland line, assisted by a regiment of North Carolinians and part of Conway's brigade, by the movement of Wayne were left on their flank, and having continued the pursuit a mile beyond Chew's house and expended all their ammuniton, they found themselves unsupported by any other troops, with the enemy again rallying on the left to oppose them. At this critical moment, with their apprehensions further excited by the heavy firing at Chew's house, a light horseman gave the alarm that the British were in the rear The line perceiving the troops on their right flying from the field, began to retreat in spite of the exertions of their officers. They had already been engaged for three hours in severe fighting, and this, added to the long march of the preceding night, rendered them physically unable to continue the action They, however, brought off all their cannon and their wounded. Their loss was several hundred, principally wounded, Colonel Stone of the 1st and Major Forrest of the 3d regiment, besides many other officers were among the number Smallwood's division of Maryland and Foreman's Jersey militia were unable to form a junction with Greene's division, being detained by a breast work which the enemy had thrown up at Lucan's Mills.

It being impossible to restore order the troops were withdrawn, having sustained a loss of eight hundred killed and wounded and four hundred prisoners. The enemy, according to their own accounts did not lose more than five hundred men. The steady valor of the Maryland troops on this occasion won for them the highest encomiums from their commander, General Sullivan. They were the first in action and were most engaged; and had already routed two bodies of the enemy, and pursued them for several miles from the first point of conflict during the space of an hour and a half, before Greene's division came up, and were still actively engaged when the rest of the army was retiring. To the failure of co-operation, occasioned by the darkness of the morning, and the delay of some of the columns by unforseen circumstances, must be attributed the difficulties of the day, which created a panic and snatched from their hands a victory already won.*

Washington again resumed his position on the Skippack, while the enemy turned their attention to opening their communications with their fleet by the Delaware. For this purpose it was necessary to secure the reduction of Fort Mifflin. In order to compel an evacuation of the work, the enemy erected a battery at the mouth of the Schuylkill. It was immediately silenced by Commodore Hazlewood with his fleet of galleys, in which Lieutenant, afterwards Commodore Barney, of Maryland, served with distinction. On the following night, the enemy crossed to Province island and erected another, which effectually commanded the block-house at Fort Mifflin. The fire of the fleet soon compelled its garrison to strike their flag, but while the boats were conveying the prisoners to the ships, a heavy column of the enemy again took possession of the redoubt in spite of the fire from Fort Mifflin. Colonel Smith now attempted to take it by storm, but was twice repulsed and his numbers reduced to one hundred and fifty effective men by the heavy fire of the redoubt and the severe duty of his post. He was compelled to ask for reinforcements. A Virginia and a Rhode Island regiment were sent to his assistance under the Baron D'Arendt, who was directed to take command of the whole force. Upon being thus superseded, Colonel Smith demanded permission to rejoin his regiment, but being satisfied by the explanation of the commander-in-chief and his just commendations of his gallant conduct, he consented to remain. D'Arendt was soon compelled by ill-health to retire from the island, and he again resumed the command. On the 22d, Count Donop attacked Red Bank with twelve hundred men, but was repulsed with the loss of five

---

* Marshall, Sparks, vol 5, pp 80, 468

hundred killed and wounded At the same time the British fleet and batteries opened upon Fort Mifflin. Their fire was gallantly returned and two of their frigates were destroyed. To reward the brave defence of the Delaware congress voted swords to Colonels Green and Smith and Commodore Hazlewood

But the communication with Philadelphia was too important to the British to be abandoned and General Howe caused floating batteries to be constructed to attack the post from the north, while the fleet and the batteries on the shore kept up a heavy fire on the other sides. On the 10th of November a new and heavy battery was opened from Province Island, and the fleet approached as near as the obstructions in the river would permit The condition of the fort became critical in the extreme. The works were battered to the ground and the men, no longer covered, were killed and wounded in great numbers. Colonel Smith himself was disabled Yet for six days this fort was maintained with the most determined courage. On the night of the 16th, being no longer tenable, it was evacuated Soon after the garrison of Fort Mercer, on the approach of Cornwallis, was withdrawn A part of the flotilla was burned, the remainder escaped above Philadelphia The British obtained complete command of the Delaware

Early in December Howe marched his forces out of the city as if to attack the American army, and a slight skirmish ensued between his advance and the Pennsylvania militia who were soon dispersed. On the seventh he approached near the main army, and Washington, believing a general action at hand, threw Gist, with his Maryland militia and Colonel Morgan's rifles forward to attack their front and flank

The assault was made with great spirit, and, after a severe skirmish the enemy's advance parties driven back, but being strongly reinforced, they in their turn compelled Gist and Morgan to retire. Washington, unwilling to descend from his strong position and fight the battle in the plain below, withheld his reinforcements and prepared for a desperate defence of his camp. On the next day, finding it impossible to take him at disadvantage, the enemy retired to their quarters in the city. Their loss in the action with the Maryland militia and the rifles was upwards of one hundred killed and wounded; that of the militia sixteen or seventeen wounded, and of the rifles, twenty-seven killed and wounded.*

In a few days after the main body of the American army went into winter quarters at Valley Forge. The Maryland line, however, under Smallwood, now reduced to 1400 men, was stationed at Wilmington, to protect the State of Delaware from the incursions of the enemy. While on that service a detachment succeeded in capturing in the Delaware a British brig, laden with stores and provisions, which made their winter quarters comfortable as compared with those of Valley Forge. Among other property thus secured were several valuable medical manuscripts belonging to Dr. Boyes, a British surgeon of the 15th regiment. These papers Washington, with a characteristic nobleness of heart, directed to be returned to Dr. Boyes, saying that he wished to prove to the enemy that Americans did not war against the sciences.†

Howe having resigned, was succeeded by General Clinton, who received orders in the spring to evacuate Philadelphia. France had resolved to aid the struggling Americans against the power of her ancient foe and rival, England. Some of her chivalrous sons, with the great and good Lafayette, were already battling under the folds of the stars and stripes in behalf of liberty; but now the sympathies of the nation were aroused and all France threw herself into the conflict. An alliance offensive and defensive was concluded with the envoys of the United States, and a powerful fleet and army were at once despatched to the American coast. Philadelphia was easily accessible to a French fleet. The British government, therefore, directed its evacuation. This was the first fruit of the new alliance.

---

* Sparks, vol 5, p 182
† Ibid., 196-223

CHAPTER XII.

'78 AND '79

On the 17th of March, 1778, the legislature again assembled at Annapolis. In compliance with the earnest request of the commander-in-chief, Congress had called on the several states for an increase of their forces. The quota demanded from Maryland was two thousand nine hundred and two men. To insure their speedy enlistment, the legislature assigned to each county its due proportion, deducting the two companies of artillery already furnished to the army and the recruits on hand. To render this arrangement effective it was provided that if the counties could not fill their quotas by voluntary enlistments before the 20th of May, the militia should be subdivided into classes, and, if each class did not furnish one man within five days, a draft of one of their own number should be made. The recruits as fast as raised were ordered to be forwarded to the headquarters of the Maryland line, unless otherwise directed by the commander-in-chief.

While this extraordinary draft was thus being filled, Count Pulaski, a gallant Pole, was busily engaged forming his legion, under the authority of congress partly in this State and partly in Delaware. He succeeded in raising a corps which afterwards did good service to the country, and led it on until he perished at its head, victoriously entering a battery which he had stormed at Savannah. It seems surprising at this day how the scanty population of Maryland, distracted as it was by internal dissensions, could have supplied so many demands upon it, and at the same time quelled all domestic resistance. In Somerset county, a great degree of disaffection still continued in spite of the repeated failure of every attempt at insurrection. The legislature now adopted further and more rigorous measures to suppress these outbreaks. The governor was authorized to order out the militia of any county if the occasion required their assistance, to fit out as many of the armed boats or galleys of the State as he should deem necessary to guard the coast, and to raise a permanent independent company of one hundred men to be stationed on the Eastern Shore during the war.* They also conferred upon the executive almost dictatorial authority in case of invasion of the State or of a neighboring State by the enemy; also for raising and arming men and supplying provision, clothes, forage and means of transportation. These extensive powers were placed by the legislature in the hands of Thomas Johnson, who had been re-elected governor in the preceding fall, and whose sterling patriotism and public virtue merited the confidence which was reposed in him.

In addition to these State affairs the governor was fully occupied in endeavoring to supply the exhausted magazines. The northern and southern states had been very slow in sending in their quotas of provisions and it was feared that local supplies for the army at Valley Forge would become entirely exhausted. It therefore required the greatest energy on the part of the executive to strengthen the quartermaster's department. The governor and his council were also occupied in carrying into effect the measures of the legislature to supply the quota of the State to the continental army. The stringency of the act and its speedy enforcement produced beneficial effects. By the middle of June, before the other states had well moved in the matter, except New Jersey, the Maryland line was raised to its full complement.†

New elections having taken place the second General Assembly of Maryland was convened at Annapolis by Governor Johnson on the 19th of October, 1778. The session was important; and was rendered especially interesting by a warm

---
* Hanson's Laws
† Washington's letter, Sparks, vol 5, p 399

controversy between the two houses, excited by an attempt of the house of delegates to increase the pay of its members from twenty-five to forty shillings per day.* The house contended that the insufficiency of the per diem, as it did not cover the actual expense of a member while in Annapolis, would prevent many honorable and efficient men of small means from serving in that body, thus tending to form an aristocracy of wealth in the legislature The senate steadily refused to accede to their proposition, alleging that as the constitution had restricted the right of membership to men of certain property it was clearly intended to place the power of legislation in the hands of persons of independent position, and that in the present burdened condition of the country it was unjust to increase the expenditure of the government. At the same time they offered to provide for the expenses of any indigent members of the lower house by special pay. The house replied with warmth, and the senate, waiving further discussion, the matter remained unadjusted Thus recommenced the struggle between the popular tendencies of the constitution and the old aristocratic ideas—a struggle which has worked out many important changes in that instrument and enlarged the rights and liberties of the people. But while thus sharply contending upon this minor point, both houses united harmoniously in all matters of public importance

Under the constitution the number of judges of the court of appeals was left undetermined and as yet no such tribunal had been erected. As there was a pressing necessity for its establishment, the house proposed to the senate to fix the number of the court at five On the 12th of December, 1778, recommended to the governor and council, Benjamin Ramsey, Benjamin Mackall the 4th, Thomas Jones, Solomon Wright, and James Murray, Esqs, to be appointed judges Both resolu-

---

* 25 shillings = $3 33 1-3; 40 shillings = $5 33 1-3 Seven shillings and six pence, old Maryland currency, were equal to one dollar. The State adhered to this manner of reckoning — by pounds, shillings and pence — until the close of the war of 1812, when the mode of computation by dollars and cents was universally adopted

tions were agreed to by the senate, and carried into effect by the executive By this act was completed the organization of the government under the new constitution.* After providing for the support of officers and soldiers who might be in service and granting a gratuity of one hundred and fifty pounds to the officers of the Maryland line and the artillery, to relieve them from the distresses incident upon the great depreciation of the paper currency, in which they were paid, the legislature took up a question, which had heretofore occupied the attention of the convention.†

Virginia still adhered to her claim to the western lands, and had succeeded in securing, in the articles of confederation, a clause "that no State should be deprived of her territory for the benefit of the United States" Maryland refused to give in her adherence to the articles while that clause existed. The preceding legislature had solemnly protested again this unjust appropriation of the public lands, won by the blood and treasure of all, and directed their delegates in congress to lay their protest before that body and to offer an amendment authorizing congress to fix the western limits of those states claiming to the Mississippi or the South Sea The amendment was rejected, and the protest remained unanswered. The State, however, did not submit A declaration was adopted by the General Assembly setting forth their claims to a portion of the proceeds of these unsettled lands, and urging the other states to open their eyes to their true interests and put at rest at once this vexatious subject. Their delegates were instructed to renew their proposition, to cause the declaration to be printed and forwarded to the different states, as well as laid before the members of congress, and to have it, together with their instructions entered at large upon the minutes of that body.* While thus protesting against any usurpation of their rights they pledged themselves to continue the struggle against the common enemy, and to do all in their power to

---
* Votes and Proceedings.
† Ibid.
* Pitkin, Votes and Proceedings

bring it to a successful termination. In proof of their sincerity they at once took up the consideration of the treaties of alliance, amity and commerce, made between France and the United States, and unanimously approved of them, as equal, honorable and wise, and pledged themselves and the State of Maryland to be bound by these provisions and faithfully to fulfil them as good and true allies.

As the spring advanced, although preparing for a retreat, the British still continued to hold possession of Philadelphia, loath to retire from the capital of the States. The desire was entertained by many that an effort should be made to drive them out of the city. But the weakness of the American army and the backward state of the preparations for the campaign, rendered the attempt impossible, or at least exceedingly hazardous. None of the states except Maryland and New Jersey had yet filled up their quotas for the new battalions, although constantly urged by the commander-in-chief to comply with the requisitions of congress. At length, on the 18th of June, 1778, the British army evacuated Philadelphia and crossed the Delaware. Washington was desirous of striking a blow upon their rear and called a council of war, which, however, opposed his design. Being supported by Lafayette he determined to risk an action, and, having taken up his line of march in pursuit of the enemy, he detached four thousand men under Lafayette in advance, with orders to attack, if a favorable occasion presented itself. Major General Lee, who in council had opposed a battle, being second in command, now claimed the right of leading this body, and was accordingly detached with two divisions to take charge of the whole force. The enemy had encamped at Monmouth Court House in a strong position. Washington determined to attack them the moment they began to retire from their positions and directed Lee to carry this design into execution.*

Sir Henry Clinton, annoyed by the light parties which hovered about his flanks, under Maxwell, and suspecting a design upon his baggage train sent it forward on the morning

---
* Sparks and Marshall.

of the 28th of June towards General Knyphausen, while with a strong body of his best troops, he descended into the plains to attack the advance of Lee's corps. The position of the American force was immediately in front of a morass, passable only at a few points and was scarcely tenable. Retreat in case of defeat would be extremely difficult, while the advance of reinforcements to their assistance would be equally so Lee, however, kept his ground, and the enemy opened a cannonade upon Lieutenant Colonel Samuel Smith's battalion of the Maryland line which formed a part of General Scott's detachment Mistaking the oblique movement of one of the American columns for a retreat and fearful of being left unsupported in this dangerous position, General Scott fell back and began to pass the ravine in his rear. Lee, doubting the propriety of engaging his foe on the ground he occupied, did not correct his error, but ordered the remainder of the troops to retire and regain the heights behind Monmouth Washington, at the first sound of the enemy's artillery, ordered his troops to cast aside their packs and to move on rapidly to the support of the advance After a speedy march of five miles he came upon the front of Lee's detachment in full retreat before the enemy, without having made an effort to maintain their position. Informed that they had fallen back by the orders of their leader, and indignant that he had not been notified of a measure taken in defiance of his orders he rode to the rear and severely reprimanded Lee for his disobedience, The enemy were closely pressing upon the retreating troops, while the advance of the detachment was in danger of throwing the main army in confusion The crisis required promptness of action. Lieutenant Colonel Ramsay's Maryland* battalion

---

* The regiments of the first brigade, which had been without a leader since the resignation of Deborre, seem to have been detailed in the several detachments on this day The divisions engaged were so completely confused and mingled together by the carelessness of the retreat, that it is difficult to trace the several corps. The position given to the third and fourth Maryland regiments, (Lieutenant Colonel Ramsey's and Lieut Col Samuel Smith's) is ventured upon the testimony given in the proceedings of Lee's court-martial —THE AUTHOR.

and Colonel Stewart's regiment were in the rear. Seeing Ramsay, Washington called to him that he "was one of the officers he should rely upon to check the enemy that day," and addressing Stewart in the same manner, he ordered Wayne to form them, and directed Lee to reassemble his detachment and maintain that position against the enemy until he should bring up the main body.

Their artillery now opened upon Ramsay and Stewart who were soon after sharply engaged with the infantry. The action was maintained gallantly, until overpowered by numbers, they were compelled to fall back. Ramsay himself was wounded and taken prisoner But their obstinate defence had given time to the commander-in-chief to draw up the left wing and second line in their rear, on the right of which was stationed Smallwood's second Maryland brigade The right wing of the army under Greene early in the day had been thrown forward by a road to the right of that pursued by the main army and was already in advance of the scene of conflict As soon as he was informed of the retreat of Lee and the present disposition of the forces Greene changed his route, and coming up, took an advantageous position on the right of the main body.

Thus firmly resisted in front the enemy endeavored to turn the left of the Americans But they were met and repulsed by parties of infantry detached to meet them. They then assailed the right but without success; and General Wayne with the regiments he had formed on the centre, was ordered to charge upon them in turn He executed the command in gallant style, and after a sharp action the enemy were driven back

As soon as the scale of victory began to turn, Washington ordered up Patterson's division and Smallwood's brigade* to secure the day The British were driven back to a strong

---

* Captain Jacob of the 6th regiment, and therefore in the 2d brigade, under Smallwood, in his Life of Cresap, speaking of the actions of the Maryland line, says, "We had the pleasure of driving the enemy off the field at Monmouth."—THE AUTHOR

position, on the ground where they had received their first check from Stewart and Ramsay. Determined to follow up his advantage, Washington ordered the artillery to be brought against them and detached several bodies of troops to attack their flanks, but before the arrangements could be completed, night came on The troops slept upon their arms in order to renew the action in the morning; but Sir Henry Clinton, taking advantage of the darkness, drew off his army silently, and made good his retreat, with most of his wounded, to the heights of Middletown. The loss of the British was upwards of three hundred men slain, besides many wounded and a few prisoners; that of the Americans was only sixty-nine killed Fifty-nine British* and several American soldiers perished without a wound, from the extreme heat of the day

Sir Henry Clinton's loss on the field was increased in his march through New Jersey, by upwards of a hundred taken prisoners and more than six hundred deserters After remaining a few days on the heights of Middletown, he continued his retreat towards New York, which he reached on the 5th of July The American army now turned its line of march once more upon the Hudson, where it remained watching the movements of Sir Henry Clinton, until the close of the campaign.

In the meanwhile, Baylor's and Pulaski's corps, which were partly raised in Maryland, were stationed in New Jersey to protect the country from the inroads of the enemy. Both, however, were surprised at different times by parties of the British, and slaughtered with circumstances of excessive cruelty The remnants of Baylor's dragoons were afterwards incorporated in Lieut. Col. William Washington's light horse, which did such good service in the southern campaign. It was now found necessary to post a stronger force in New Jersey for the protection of that state during the winter, and towards the close of November the Maryland line, with several other divisions was marched to Middlebrook, where General Washington himself established his headquarters The route

---

* Holmes' Annals, vol 2, p 284

from the Hudson was rendered difficult and painful by a heavy fall of snow, and the bad roads it occasioned; and the troops suffered severely, whilst preparing the huts in which they were to pass the winter as they had done at Valley Forge. Yet the privations of the army were not equal to those of the preceding season *

In February, 1779, the British landed a body of troops from Staten Island, with the design of taking Elizabethtown. Smallwood, with the Maryland line, and St. Clair, with the Pennsylvania division were immediately ordered to form a junction at Scotch Plains, and reinforce General Maxwell who lay nearest the scene of action. The British, however, failed in their attempt; and, having hurriedly retreated, the troops were recalled The campaign of 1779, opened late and was rather remarkable for a series of manoeuvres than for any brilliant actions with the exception of the storming of Stoney Point by Wayne, in which affair Major John Steward of the Maryland line was honorably distinguished † The moral effect produced by the presence of a powerful French fleet, ready to aid the American army against any point on the seaboard, seemed to paralyze the energy of the British leader, placed between two strong opponents he was compelled to remain inactive and on the defensive The allies then determined to assume the offensive, and the following July the army was concentrated at West Point, the headquarters of the commander in chief, for the purpose of cooperating with the French fleet in any design that might be attempted against the British in New York. The Maryland line formed its right wing It was soon found impracticable to execute any combined movement against the city, and the idea was abandoned ‡

---
* Sparks

† At the head of one hundred volunteers he fought his way into the fort with the bayonet, in front of the left column A gold medal was presented by Congress to General Wayne, and silver medals to Major Steward and Colonel Fleury. The thanks of the Legislature were also voted to Major Steward — Proceedings of Congress and Maryland Legislature —THE AUTHOR

‡ Sparks

CHAPTER XIII.

INTERNAL AFFAIRS

THE withdrawal of the British troops from Philadelphia and the consequent removal of the scene of the campaign to a greater distance from their borders, gave the people of Maryland a breathing time to recover from the constant drain of men, provisions and military supplies, which their vicinity had rendered necessary During the campaign of '77, besides the frequent drafts of militia for the protection of its own coast when the Chesapeake was filled by British cruisers, the State had furnished to the continental service two thousand and thirty regulars and fifteen hundred and thirty-five militia. While the invasion continued most of the people upon the bay shore were under arms and those of the interior in readiness to march to any threatened point. In the ensuing campaign, when the British fleet had withdrawn from the Maryland waters, and their army was still lying at Philadelphia, anxious to place a sufficient force in the hands of Washington, it furnished a body of three thousand three hundred and seven regulars A quota one-third larger than that of any other State, except Delaware, according to the proportions fixed by congress Its quota to the campaign of 1779 was twenty-eight hundred and forty nine continentals Maryland was also looked to for its early wheat which it supplied to the army and which was also largely shipped to the north. To protect this coasting commerce, which was extremely hazardous on account of the supremacy of the British fleet, and to guard the entrance of the bay from the small cruisers of the enemy and the galleys of the lawless tories the State was obliged to keep up a separate marine of some force. It consisted of the ship Defence and several galleys, the Chester, Baltimore, Independence, Conqueror, and a number of others, of different tonnage, besides a sloop of war and four barges. The prize money arising from the captures made by these vessels was placed at the disposal of the governor and council for distribution among the victorious crews—an incentive to exertion, which percepibly increased their usefulness. In July, 1779, Commodore Grason, in the Chester, fell in with a hostile armed ship and schooner, which were endeavoring to make their way into the capes, and after a sharp conflict compelled them to stand out again to sea.

The arrival of the French fleet, however, in considerable strength at a later period rendered it less important to maintain this force, and the immediately pressing condition of the finances of the State caused the legislature in March, 1779, to suspend the fitting out of additional galleys. The Annapolis, which was then getting ready, was laid aside, the State's surplus of powder sold, the ship Defence and the several galleys and boats, with the exception of two of the best galleys and one boat, were disposed of and the money paid into the treasury. At the same time the companies of matrosses, heretofore stationed at Baltimore and Annapolis, were ordered to proceed at once to the headquarters of General Washington, and report as portion of the State's quota for the campaign. But while engaged in carrying out these measures of economy the house of delegates re-opened the controversy of the last session, by a resolution providing for an increase of the pay of the members. They were in their position sustained upon strong grounds. The principal medium of currency had long since become a depreciated paper issued by the State and by congress. The exigencies of the moment could not be met by the proceeds of taxation, and bills of credit were constantly issued with the delusive hope that a favorable turn of affairs would bring about their speedy redemption. As these issues were enlarged their value fell far below that which they bore upon their face and as a matter of course continued to sink lower and lower at each new increase, and this was rendered nominally larger by its depreciation in current value. Every effort was made to support their credit, but in vain. Many of the State made the notes a legal tender in payment of debts. The legislature of Maryland, at the session of 1777 declared that the convention and State issues, as well as continental paper, should be received as legal tenders in payment of debts, at nominal value, but the courts decided that this only applied to the bills issued before the passage of the act. The continental emissions had already increased to the enormous sum of two hundred millions of dollars, and had sunk so low in public confidence that they were rated at forty dollars in paper for one in silver.

The nominal pay, therefore, of a delegate or senator, at twenty-five shillings a day, when reduced to specie value, was utterly insufficient to meet his expenses; and the action of the house bore, on its very face, an argument which seemed irresistible. For a time the senate continued its opposition, but at length yielded, and the amount of the pay was increased to three pounds current money (eight dollars) per day, for the session, and a like sum per day for itinerant charges. Charles Carroll of Carrollton was the only man who persevered in his opposition. He considered the resolve a dangerous precedent for future legislators, for it would take away from men in whom the desire of gain might overcome the dictates of duty and honesty, that dread of the people which alone could prevent them from enriching themselves with the spoils of their constituents. It was, besides, a measure calculated to exempt the lawgivers themselves from those very inconveniences which the people at large were enduring. These were reducing to destitution the gallant soldiers who were shedding their blood in the field, and rendering penniless the brave officers who sustained the honor of the State and defended its liberties, spending in the meanwhile their own fortunes to make up the deficiency of their pay caused by the depreciation.* It was a

---

* Captain Jacob, in Cresap's Life, p. 18, says he was despatched by a party of officers of the Maryland line to Baltimore, to purchase cloth for coats, after great difficulty he bought fifteen yards, for fifteen hundred pounds, which were made into ten regimental coats!—THE AUTHOR

continuance, too, of that "private and selfish spirit which induced the passage of the law making bills of credit legal tender in payment of debts, unnecessary and impolitic at its commencement, injurious and oppressive in its continuance, and alike destructive of public and private faith." This spirited protest produced its effect upon the members of the senate, and when a few days later a second tender law to remedy the decisions of the courts by including in its provisions the issues made subsequent to the passage of the former law, was sent up from the lower house, it was rejected by a vote of five to three

The discussion of these questions led both houses to the consideration of a subject which had already occupied the attention of congress and the nation—the proper recompense and just provision for the officers of the army, who, it was everywhere admitted, were bearing the heaviest burdens of the war, with a pay which scarcely supplied them with the necessaries of life, and were, most of them, now so reduced in estate, as to be frequently dependent upon the gratuity of the State for the clothing they wore. Their condition at the close of the war began already to be looked to. When that happy event should arrive, it would be to them the forerunner of utter destitution. The army would of course be disbanded or much reduced, and these men, broken down by the hard service of the war, wasted in estate and no longer fitted for a business life, would be thrown on the world without support unless provision were made for them by the country in whose cause they had spent their best days. The matter was agitated in congress and several of the States desired that a half pay for life should be granted. But at length the opposing view prevailed, and it was determined to bestow upon them at the close of the war a gratuity equal to seven years full pay. This was afterwards reduced to five years pay. But the legislature of Maryland was actuated by a worthier sentiment Those who had hitherto enjoyed the security won by the sufferings of the army did not permit any feelings of parsimony to interfere with its appropriate reward

The legislature, therefore, upon the determination of the

question in congress immediately resolved that the officers of the Maryland line who should serve to the close of the war should be entitled to half pay during life, commencing after the expiration of the seven years pay voted by congress. They further extended this provision to the widows of such officers as would have been entitled to half pay during their widowhood.

To relieve for the present the wants of the officers and soldiers, the legislature ordered that each commissioned officer should be furnished annually, during the war, with a good uniform and four shirts, besides a daily allowance of a variety of necessaries enumerated in the act, and the privates, rations of rum and tobacco equivalent to twenty pounds per year. In the several reorganizations of the line, disputes had arisen as to precedence. The Assembly now referred the whole matter to Washington, requesting him to settle the rank of all officers in the Maryland line and separate corps, as he should deem most consistent with justice He was also requested to incorporate the Maryland portion of the German battalion and the rifle regiment into one battalion, to appoint proper officers and enroll it in the line of the State For the purpose of hastening the recruiting service, the commander-in-chief was desired to detach suitable officers with active sergeants to enlist men in the State to fill its quota; and the sum of two thousand dollars was immediately appropriated to meet the necessary expense. To each recruit, in addition to the bounty allowed by congress and the State, were presented a hat, shoes, stockings and overall.

The divisions of party already began to make their appearance in the two houses. The legislature, in imposing taxes had directed a treble tax to be levied upon non-jurors, persons who had refused or neglected to take the oath of allegiance to the State The ultra patriots, who were resolved to spare no means to crush the tories and support the army, insisted upon this measure, while the more moderate desired to release the non-jurors from the heavy burdens thus imposed upon them in addition to that of disfranchisement. Some of these non-jurors were clergymen of the church of England, who besides other disabilities, had been prohibited from teaching or preaching the Gospel. Several acts had been introduced for their relief upon taking the oath,* but had always been rejected A resolution for the general relief of non-jurors upon their taking the oaths was now proposed It awakened the most violent opposition, and Samuel Chase, a distinguished member of the house of delegates openly charged that there were tories in the two houses. He was summoned before the senate to make good his assertion, as far as it related to the members of that body He appeared and, having objected to their authority to require his presence, proceeded, at the request of the senate, to make specific charges of disaffection and lukewarmness to the cause of liberty against several members of that body.† As two of the members implicated were absent the affair was referred to the July session of the senate, when, after thorough investigation, the allegations were unanimously declared unfounded But the resolution in favor of non-jurors although it passed the house was rejected by the senate. Subsequently, however, a temporary relief was granted to them.

During the preceding campaign a large number of the German troops in the service of the British had deserted, and some had found their way into Maryland Many foreigners, attracted by service under the American flag, or to partake of the liberty which seeemd to be already established, had arrived in the country, and others were desirous of immigrating if proper inducements were offered them. The legislature, conscious of the great accession of strength such persons would make to the State, passed a naturalization law by which all foreigners, upon taking the oath of allegiance to the State, were admitted to the rights of natural born citizens, save and except the privilege of holding civil office until after a residence of seven years. The governor of the State was directed to cause this act to be printed and circulated in Great Britain and Ireland, and to be translated into German and distributed

---

* Votes and Proceedings, Senate, July, 1779, p 69.
† Votes and Proceedings, March, 1779

throughout the cities and towns of Holland, Germany and Switzerland

Thomas Johnson had now served three years as governor, having been twice re-elected without opposition; the constitutional restriction rendered him no longer eligible. When the time arrived for a new election two candidates were proposed, Colonel Edward Lloyd and Thomas Sim Lee, Esq. On the 8th of November, 1779, the election took place, a majority of votes of both houses being cast in favor of the latter gentleman, he was duly proclaimed governor of the State Desirous of testifying their high estimate of the public conduct and administration of the late governor, the two houses transmitted to him an address, which forms the best eulogy upon his character and services during the critical period at which he presided over the destinies of the new State, and upon his "prudence, assiduity, firmness and integrity," rendering him conspicuous even among the galaxy of distinguished men who then gave luster to Maryland *

The effect of the depreciation of currency, in greatly raising the prices of labor, produce, and all commodities called for some measures of relief, and a joint committee of both houses was appointed to consider the matter. They proposed that a convention of commissioners from the several States should be assembled at Philadelphia in the ensuing January to take measures for limiting prices to a certain standard throughout the country. They also advised that the governor should be empowered to seize provisions, wherever a surplus should be found, and suggested sharp measures against all persons who should buy up grain and produce for the purpose of speculating upon the distresses of the army Three commissioners were accordingly appointed on the part of Maryland, with full powers to agree upon any united action in reference to this important subject, and to report the result of the conference to the next General Assembly, should they deem it proper.

Another question of great importance grew out of the deranged condition of the currency. The weight of the taxes

---
* Votes and Proceedings

already imposed and the overwhelming debt which had been contracted filled the minds of the most ardent patriots with apprehensions Congress at length awoke to the ruinous effect the excessive issues of paper without credit having only a compulsory circulation. They accordingly limited its amount to two hundred millions of dollars, and, determining to cancel as much as possible of this sum, called on the States for their respective shares of one hundred and thirty-five millions, to be paid in nine monthly instalments.* The quota of Maryland amounted to fourteen millions two hundred and twenty thousand dollars, making the monthly instalments, to be paid by the people, reach the sum of one million five hundred thousand dollars The rate of taxation upon the assessment of property to raise this amount, exclusive of the tax of thirty shillings for the State, was twenty-seven pounds on every hundred pounds. But the frightful proportion diminishes when it is remembered that the valuation was made at the old specie or currency rate and the taxes were paid in the depreciated paper, then nearly forty to one

The leaders in the house of delegates, in casting about for some means to meet this heavy draught, resolved, in imitation of the example of other States, to confiscate the property of those who had adhered to the royal cause. It was deemed no justice to seize the estates of such persons, many of whom were wealthy, as the property of either open and notorious traitors, or of British subjects A bill for that purpose was accordingly framed and passed by the house and sent to the senate The November session was now drawing to a close, several of the members were absent, and the senate, considering the question one of too great importance to be hastily disposed of and doubting the justice and expediency of the matter, returned the bill to the house desiring it might lie over to March session of 1780, as they were not prepared to act finally upon it. But the house would admit of no delay, and despatched a delegation of sixteen members to make a strong remonstrance to the senate. They contended that the people were unable to

---
* Pitkin

raise more than nine millions by taxation at the rate of one million per month; and that some extraordinary measure must at once be resorted to. The property of the refugees would sell for at least the balance of five millions this would give time for the taxes to be collected and paid in Unless congress received the expected aid, a further emission would be necessary, and the condition of things rendered still worse. An ably conducted debate followed. The senate rejected the bill for the present, suggesting as a more appropriate source of revenue that congress should make foreign loans and pledge for their payment the western lands which were improperly claimed by certain States. Unable to agree both houses adjourned over to the twenty-eighth of March, 1780.

In the meanwhile the people heartily took up the subject of the confiscation of British property and, when the assembly re-opened its sessions numerous petitions were presented, urging the adoption of the measure. The amount required to be paid had now increased to twenty-three millions, seven hundred thousand dollars, rendering the difficulty of raising it by taxation more evident The States had failed to pay in their proportions and congress, as the house had predicted, was compelled largely to exceed the limit of two hundred millions, which it had assigned for the issue of paper money To meet their quota the people of Maryland would have been obliged to pay a tax of one hundred pounds of paper for every hundred pounds worth of property The house immediately passed another bill for the confiscation of British property, which the senate, after a renewed contest, again rejected

A scheme was then devised for calling in the old issues of continental paper by means of an issue of State paper, at the rate of one dollar of the new for thirty-three and a third of the old, and pledging the faith of the State for its redemption. This measure met with a like fate. After a long session spent in fruitless attempts to effect a compromise, both houses adjourned to the seventh of June having ordered the disputed bills and the messages concerning them to be printed and circulated throughout the State for the information of the people.

HISTORY OF MARYLAND.

The bill for recalling the continental issues was at length agreed to in March and the old were redeemed at the rate of forty to one of the new Few, however, were brought in; and the laws making them currency being repealed, they soon altogether ceased to pass and quietly died in the hands of their holders. In this state of affairs it was impossible to place any value upon currency So that, in fixing the governor's salary, the legislature was compelled to assign it to him in wheat at the rate of forty-five hundred bushels per year.*

The March session passed without an effort to bring up the confiscation bill, and it laid dormant until October, when, after material modification, it was at length agreed to by both houses. That injustice might not be done, an opportunity was allowed the owners to come in and take the oath of allegiance to State, prior to the first of March, 1782. This provision was extended in an especial manner to ex-governor Sharpe, whose deportment as Proprietary governor of Maryland had won him the respect of the people. By another act the quit rents of the Proprietary were forever abolished.†

Early in the revolutionary struggle Benjamin Franklin introduced into congress a plan for the confederation of the colonies which was discussed from time to time until the adoption of the Declaration of Independence. Then a more enlarged scheme of union became necessary, and a committee of one member from each State was appointed to draft articles of confederation The dark and trying struggles which ensued compelled the postponement of the subject to April, 1777. Congress then resolved to devote two days in each week to its examination until a definite conclusion should be reached. On the 15th of November they were finally adopted and printed copies were sent to the legislature of each State for their consideration, accompanied by an address requesting them to authorize their delegates in congress on or before the 10th of March, 1778, to subscribe the articles of confederation. In June, 1778, the delegates were called on for their instruc-

*Votes and Proceedings
† Hanson's Laws

tions upon this subject from their States. New York, New Hampshire, Virginia and North Carolina unconditionally adopted the plan. Amendments were proposed by the others, but all the States except Maryland, Delaware and New Jersey had instructed their delegates to agree even if they should fail to obtain the adoption of their propositions

Maryland was determined not to relinquish its claim to a portion of the public lands and its delegates, in pursuance of their instructions, proposed an amendment, authorizing congress to fix the boundaries of States claiming westward to the Mississippi or the South Sea Upon this question the States were nearly equally divided, Maryland, Delaware, New Jersey, Pennsylvania and Rhode Island were in its favor, Massachusetts, Connecticut, Virginia, South Carolina and Georgia against, and New York undecided. The amendment was therefore rejected In July the articles were formally signed by the delegates of all the States except Maryland, Delaware and New Jersey, who were urged by congress to give their immediate attention to it, as a subject of vital importance New Jersey, in November, directed her representatives to accede to the confederation; and Delaware followed her example in February, 1779 Maryland alone held out; and the legislature resolutely asserted their determination not to accede until their rights in the western lands should be secured As these claims affected Virginia, and their instructions to their delegates particularly pointed to that State, it called forth a strong remonstrance on her part, and the legislature of that commonwealth instructed their delegates in congress, to ratify the union with such other States as would join with them, declaring that it should be binding without the assent of Maryland, allowing the State however a certain time to unite with the confederacy. Connecticut adopted a similar course. But Maryland was no more moved by threats than it had been by remonstrances As many of the States felt a strong interest in the success of its demands they refused to accede to the proposition of Virginia, and the confederacy remained unratified. New York led the way to a settlement of the difficulty and instructed its delegates in February, 1780, to limit the western boundary of the State and cede to congress their claims to lands beyond it, "to enure for the use and benefit of such of the United States as should become members of the Federal alliance of the said States and for no other use or purpose whatever "* This act, the instructions of Maryland and the remonstrance of Virginia were referred to a committee of congress, who reported a resolution calling on the several States to follow the generous example of New York, and thus effectually remove every obstacle in the way of a perfect union, and at the same time time requesting Maryland to accede to the confederacy. In order to give effect to its recommendation, congress afterwards pledged itself that the public lands should be held for the common benefit of the whole, and eventually to be parcelled out into free and independent States In compliance with this request Virginia, on the second of January, 1781, determined by resolution to cede to the United States all her claims to lands northwest of the Ohio.†

While Maryland had thus for two years persevered in holding aloof from the confederation, it had not for one moment relaxed its efforts in the common cause. At the very time when it was thus contesting with Virginia its sons were fighting on the soil of that State for its defence. The Maryland line and the Virginia regiments, side by side, bearing the brunt of the hard fought southern campaigns. But now the State stood triumphant. every difficulty had melted away before its firmness and perseverence On the second of February, 1781,‡ the legislature authorized their delegates in congress to sign the articles in their behalf. This was done on the first day of March, and the union was thereby made complete. Thus was Maryland privileged to point the way to the creation of a great American Commonwealth. "This important event was on the same day publicly announced at Philadelphia, the seat

---

*Pitkin, vol 2, p. 33

† Ibid , p 35, and also Burke, Hist Virginia, vol 4, p 471   The final deed of cession was not made until 1784.

‡ Votes and Proceedings, October session, 1780, p 49

of government, and immediately communicated to the executives of the several States, to the American ministers in Europe, to the minister plenipotentiary of France, and to the commander-in-chief to be announced to the army under his command."*

By the articles of confederation each State preserved its separate and distinct sovereignty while the United States only possessed such authority as was specifically delegated to it No State was to have less than three or more than seven delegates in congress, who were to be chosen annually and were only eligible three years out of six. The votes in congress were to be taken by States; and it required a majority of States to carry a question, unless it related to peace or war, the army, navy, or the coinage of money, when it could only be passed by a vote of nine States. The articles could not be changed, altered or amended, except by the consent of all The States were prohibited from making peace or war, laying imposts, which should interfere with those of the United States, and maintaining an army or navy in peace, without the consent of congress Congress was authorized to make peace or war, raise fleets and armies, coin money, contract loans, and issue bills of credit, and to appoint a committee of one from each State, called a committee of States to sit as an executive committee during its own recess. The great error in the system, as was afterwards abundantly proved, was the want of sufficient federal authority, a defect which was at length remedied by the adoption of the present constitution ten years later

---

* Pitkin, v 2, p. 36

CHAPTER XIV.

THE SOUTHERN CAMPAIGNS

During the year 1779 the southern army had been particularly unfortunate; Georgia and South Carolina were reconquered by the enemy and North Carolina invaded. In this critical state of affairs it was resolved by congress that the Maryland and Delaware lines should be despatched to reinforce that department. In April, 1780, they were accordingly detached under the command of Major General De Kalb, and after marching through New Jersey and Pennsylvania, embarked at the head of Elk river The first brigade passed through the State on the 5th, the second on the 11th of May. They numbered then about two thousand strong. They cheerfully marched on to new fields of glory without pausing to receive the gratulations of friends, or to revisit those homes to which they might never more return The south was calling for their aid, and these veterans of many fights were hastening thither to again cross their bayonets with British steel. To strengthen the southern force as much as possible, the legislature ordered that the three Maryland companies of artillery in the continental service should be formed into four with proper officers, and attached to Colonel Harrison's Virginia regiment. They also passed stringent measures to increase the number of the line by the enlistment or draught of fourteen hundred men, to which a thousand more were added in June. However, the actual number of recruits did not reach the amount called for An additional regiment was raised, and placed under the command of Colonel Alexander L Smith but after it had marched to the south, its officers were recalled and the men drafted into the old regiments The legislature then published an able and stirring address to the people of Maryland, calling on them to come forward at this trying time and reminding them of the outrages perpetrated by the British soldiery on their brethren in New Jersey, recounted the reverses which had befallen the American arms, the reduced condition of their forces in the south, the fall of Charlestown and the conquest of South Carolina, and urged them "to draw new resources and an increase of courage, even from defeats, and manifest to the world that they were then most to be dreaded when most depressed."

The progress of the line was somewhat delayed by the difficulty of obtaining provisions, but the news of their approach preceded them and served at once to raise the spirits of the southern people. At Hillsborough, in North Carolina, they encamped until further preparations were made to facilitate their march to the south, and to give time to the militia of Virginia and North Carolina, under Caswell and Stevens, to join them On resuming their march they were overtaken at Deep river by General Gates, whom congress had desired to be appointed to the southern department. The conqueror of Saratoga was received with the greatest enthusiasm by the army of the south The broken remains of the cavalry which had served through the preceding campaign had withdrawn to North Carolina to recruit, and their officers requested Gates to use his influence to fill their corps; but this he refused to do, thinking Armand's horse, which he had with him, would be sufficient He learned to regret his neglect De Kalb had already selected a route for the army, somewhat circuitous, but through a fertile country, where provisions and supplies could be readily obtained Gates, eager to reach the scene of action, fixed upon a more direct course, through a barren and exhausted district The consequences to the troops were serious in the extreme. The men were compelled to live upon green corn and unripe fruit and suffering and deaths from this cause reduced the effective force. The horses, destitute of forage, were unable to support the forced marches, and the army when it approached the enemy was unfit for immediate service

As Gates advanced towards Camden, Sumpter, Marion, and Pickens, three distinguished southern partizan leaders, rallying their scattered troops, made their appearance in the field. Lord Rawdon, who commanded at Camden, desirous of striking a blow before the Americans should concentrate their forces advanced to a strong post fifteen miles in front of that place, on Lynch's creek But the American general, inclining to the right, and endangering his position, he fell back to Logtown, near Camden. Being desirous of opening his communication with Sumpter, Gates at once advanced to Rugely's Mills, and having learned from that leader that a British convoy of stores and provisions were on their way from Ninety-Six to Camden, immediately detached Lieutenant Colonel Woolford with four hundred men of the Maryland line, and two pieces of light artillery, to form a junction with Sumpter and attack the enemy's train.*

Lord Cornwallis, being informed of the movements of the American General, immediately hastened to Camden and determined to seek battle before his enemy could secure increase of strength. He accordingly marched from that place by night, intending to surprise the Americans. By a singular coincidence Gates had set forward upon a similar design, and the advance parties of the opposing armies met at half past two o'clock in the morning a few miles from Saunder's creek. Armand's cavalry, the van of the American force, was soon driven in by the British guards under Lieutenant Colonel Webster; and the flight of the fugitives threw the leading Maryland regiment into some disorder. But the heavy fire of Porterfield's and Armstrong's infantry upon the flanks gave it time to rally, and the guards were driven back

As if by common consent both armies ceased their fire and drawing back awaited the dawning of day. Immediately the two hostile leaders began to form their lines of battle. The British troops, numbering about two thousand men, were

---
* Lee's Memoirs

posted between two swamps, which protected their flanks and rendered the superior numbers of the Americans of little avail The American left, resting on the morass, was composed entirely of Virginia militia under Stevens whose flight would leave the centre and right wing unprotected, and expose them to be taken in flank and rear. The North Carolina militia, under Caswell, formed the centre, and three regiments of the first Maryland brigade, under General Gist, with the Delaware regiment, formed the right, while the second Maryland brigade, under Smallwood, was stationed as a reserve three hundred yards in the rear of the line. Baron De Kalb commanded on the right and along the line of battle, while Gates retained the general superintendence of the whole to himself, and took post between the main body and the reserve.

As the first streak of day broke in the east the artillery opened fire on both sides and the left under Stevens was ordered to advance. To teach the Virginia militia to stand the fire of the enemy, Colonel Otho H. Williams, of Maryland, with a party of volunteers moved in their front against the British artillery to draw and sustain their fire, and General Stevens, after exhorting his men to use the bayonet freely, led them into action. Cornwallis threw forward his right under Webster with his veteran corps. The Virginia militia, scarcely waiting to deliver one fire broke ranks and throwing away their arms, fled in the utmost disorder. The North Carolina militia followed and Gates. Stevens and Caswell, in vain attempting to rally them were borne from the field by the flying mass of frightened men. One regiment of North Carolinians, under Dixon, an old continental officer, cheered by the firm bearing of the Marylanders, on whom they flanked, alone maintained their ground.

At the same moment that the left wing broke, Cornwallis elated with success, ordered Rawdon to charge upon the right But Gist's brigade stood immovable. For a while the terrific struggle seemed of doubtful issue "Bold was the pressure of the foe," exclaims an eye-witness, "firm as a rock the resistance of Gist. Now the Marylanders were gaining ground"

The gallant Howard, at the head of Williams' regiment, impetuously broke upon the enemy and severing his front, drove the opposing corps before him; and it seemed as if the lost battle was about to be retrieved even whilst the commander-in-chief was flying far from the scene of action. But the eagle-eyed Webster, the best and bravest officer after Cornwallis in the British army, upon the flight of the centre and left brought his veteran guards upon their flank. In a moment they were met by the second Maryland brigade, which Smallwood rapidly brought up to replace the fugitives and the battle was again renewed with undiminished spirit upon the left

Finding his flank once more protected and his Marylanders bearing up with unflinching valor, the brave De Kalb, although outnumbered two to one, resolved to make one great and final effort with the bayonet. The charge was terrific. For a time the two lines seemed mingled with each other, clinging together and slaying with that terrible weapon. But at length the veteran troops of Cornwallis began to retire. At one point they were broken and thrown into disorder and many prisoners were taken. A single corps of cavalry would have retrieved the day, but Gates' folly had rendered victory impossible. The forward movement had again uncovered the left of Smallwood's brigade, and Webster immediately turned the light infantry and the twenty-third regiment upon his open flank Smallwood, however, sustained himself with undiminished vigor; but, borne down at last by superiority of force, was forced to retreat Soon, however, his brigade forced back its assailants and regained the line of battle, again it gave ground and again it rallied. The right under Gist and De Kalb continued to maintain its superiority

Cornwallis, alarmed at the unexpected resistance of the Maryland line, and having before experienced its desperate valor with the bayonet, now concentrated his whole force and brought it upon them The inequality was too great to be resisted The whole British army was poured upon these two devoted brigades, who still maintained their ground, although only numbering eight hundred men,* opposed to more than two thousand British regulars, and surrounded and unsupported, yet still fighting on with unflinching hearts The cavalry were suddenly thrown in upon them, in front and rear, while they were still entangled with the infantry. The moment was critical De Kalb at the head of one regiment attempted to restore the line, but overpowered and falling covered with wounds was made prisoner His life was saved by the generous De Buysson, his heroic aide-de-camp, who threw himself upon his fallen leader and received in his own body the bayonets aimed at his friend Intermingled with the infantry, and trampled under foot and sabred by the dragoons, without space to rally, the ranks of brave troops were broken, and they were driven from the field by successive charges 'To the woods and swamps, after performing their duty valiantly, these gallant soldiers were compelled to fly The pursuit was continued with keenness and none were saved but those who penetrated swamps which had been deemed impassable The road was heaped with the dead and dying Arms, artillery, horses and baggage were strewn in every direction." Brigadier General Gist moved off with a body of one hundred men, still maintaining their ranks unbroken, through the swamp where the cavalry could not pursue them while Colonel Howard effected his escape with a still smaller party.†

The loss was severe. Four hundred North Carolina militia were taken prisoners, and sixty killed and wounded, for a portion of them—the regiment under Dixon—had gallantly continued to maintain its ground on the left of the Maryland line. The Virginia militia, to the regret of all, escaped with only the loss of three men, wounded in the flight, and a few taken prisoners The loss of the Maryland line and Delaware regiment was especially heavy, three or four hundred killed and wounded and one hundred and seventy taken prisoners, most of the latter being of the wounded. The regiment of

---

* It had been reduced by detachments made before the battle —Burke's Hist. of Va, 4th vol, p 400
† Marshall, Lee's Memoirs, Tarleton's Campaigns, etc

Delaware was reduced to less than two companies, and having lost its field officers, Colonel Vaughn and Major Patton, was afterwards formed into one company under Captain Kirkwood.

The brave De Kalb, though treated with every attention, survived but a few days. He spent his last moments in dictating a letter to General Smallwood, who now succeeded him in the command of the Maryland line, "full of sincere and ardent affection for the officers and soldiers of his division, expressing his admiration of their late noble but unsuccessful stand, reciting the eulogies which their bravery had extorted from the enemy, together with the lively delight such testimony of their valor had excited in his own mind. In this endearing adieu, he comprehended Lieut. Col. Vaughn and the Delaware regiment and the artillery belonging to his division, both of which corps had shared in the glory of that disastrous day. Feeling the approach of death he stretched out his quivering hand to his friend De Buysson and breathed his last in benedictions on his faithful brave division."* His death was lamented in Maryland and his memory honored. The legislature, in testimony of their respect and gratitude passed an act granting the rights of citizenship to his descendants, a copy of which they directed the governor to transmit to the Baroness De Kalb, his wife † Congress ordered a monument to him to be erected at Annapolis with an inscription commemorative of his actions and glorious death.

Gates, in the midst of his defeat was cheered by the intelligence that Sumpter and Woolford had succeeded in capturing the convoy of the enemy, but the gratifying news was speedily followed by the announcement that Tarleton had, in turn, surprised and defeated them, killing or taking prisoners the larger portion of the infantry, and dispersing the cavalry. In these two actions the Maryland line suffered greatly in officers, besides its distinguished leader, De Kalb.

Throughout this hard fought but disastrous day, Generals Smallwood and Gist conducted themselves with exemplary

---

* Lee's Memoirs, p 96
† Votes and Proceedings Assembly.

skill and bravery and the thanks of congress were voted to them in a special manner. Lieut. Col Williams, the adjutant general, was everywhere in the heat of action, volunteering to face every danger, although out of the line of his duty, and Lieut. Col. Howard gave proofs of that "solidity of character," * that cool and daring courage which aftererwards distinguished him as one of the first and bravest of Maryland's sons. Gates in vain endeavored to rally the flying militia. Could he have succeeded and brought them back to the aid of the line, the victory would have been retrieved. He halted for a time at Charlotte to gather a portion of the remnants of that gallant army he had so lately led into the south, and then removed to Hillsborough, one hundred and eighty miles from Camden.

Smallwood and Gist remained at Charlotte with about one hundred and fifty officers and men to rally their scattered soldiers. Colonel Williams, with a brigade major, was detached towards the scene of the battle to bring up all the stragglers he could find, and to obtain information of the enemy. Major Anderson, of the 3d Maryland regiment, had succeeded in rallying a portion of his corps not far from the field, and now, learning the point of rendezvous, proceeded to Salisbury by slow marches, to give time to the dispersed soldiers to join their colors. By these cool and skilful measures Smallwood succeeded in ten days in collecting upwards of seven hundred non-commissioned officers and privates besides the larger portion of his commissioned officers, which number was fortunately increased by the recapture of one hundred and fifty continental prisoners taken at Camden, made by the indefatigable Marion, on their way under escort to Charleston.

Cornwallis, crippled by the desperate resistance of the Maryland line, the Delaware regiment and Dixon's North Carolina militia on the 16th of August, was unable to follow up his advantages without further reinforcements. His strength

---

* General Gist was promoted on the 19th of January, 1779, to a brigadiership, and Smallwood, after the death of DeKalb, was made major general on the 15th September, 1780.

was subsequently weakened by the capture of Colonel Ferguson, at King's Mountain, and an advantage which Sumpter obtained over Tarleton. The army, therefore, remained undisturbed at Hillsborough and the commander employed the time in reorganizing the several corps.

In compliance with General Washington's directions, the seven Maryland regiments of the old line were merged into one, to be known as the first Maryland, and Colonel Otho H. Williams given command. The supernumerary officers, under General Gist, for whom there was now no longer any command in the broken conditions of the army, were ordered back to Maryland to take charge of the recruiting stations and to form two new regiments, as rapidly as possible.* The numbers of the new battalions were fixed by the commander-in-chief at five hundred and four men, and the legislature of the State at once set about raising recruits to fill them up.† The militia of the State were again divided into classes, each class being compelled to furnish within five days one soldier, either free or a slave,‡ and thus not a few negroes served throughout the war, not only in the Maryland, but in the lines of other States, with faithfulness and courage.

General Smallwood was retained in the army as second in command; and was detached to the Yadkin to take charge of the militia gathering in that quarter. The Virginia levies soon after joined Gates, increasing his force to about fourteen hundred continentals, which was further strengthened by a corps of volunteer cavalry and two divisions of North Carolina militia. He now moved to Charlotte, and Smallwood was advanced from the Yadkin to the Catawba, while Morgan was thrown forward with a light corps. In the meanwhile congress, dissatisfied with the conduct of Gates, requested General Washington to supercede him, and General Green was at once despatched to the south to take the command. The only re-

---
* Lee's Memoirs.
† Sparks
‡ Hanson's Laws

inforcement which could be spared him from the northern army was Lee's legion composed of three companies of infantry and three of cavalry, numbering about three hundred and fifty men. On his way the new commander passed through Delaware and Maryland, which had been annexed by congress to the southern department, to urge the forwarding of reinforcements In Maryland he was informed that General Gist was indefatigably engaged in raising the new levies, a work which, in spite of every effort on the part of the State, owing to the exhausted condition of the people, proceeded slowly. He held a long conference with the governor and council, and having made his final arrangements hastened to join his army at Charlotte, in North Carolina, where he arrived on the 2d of December. He immediately commenced a series of active and energetic movements Smallwood's detachment was drawn into the main army, while a chosen body of troops was placed under the command of Morgan to operate on the western quarter It consisted of four hundred men of the Maryland line under Lieut Col. Howard, two companies of Virginia militia, mostly discharged continentals, under Captains Triplett and Taite and Lieutenant Colonel Washington's dragoons, one hundred in number. When Morgan reached Broad river he was joined by several parties of militia He took post near the confluence of Broad and Pacolet rivers

Cornwallis had ordered from the north a reinforcement of fifteen hundred men under General Leslie, who was now approaching to unite with him Learning of the movements of the American forces he suspected a design against Ninety-Six, and determined to strike a blow at Morgan, before he could be joined by the hardy mountaineers of the west. Accordingly he detached Lieut Col Tarleton with his legion and other forces, amounting to about one thousand men, to pursue him; whilst he himself put the main body in motion to cut off his retreat if he should escape that active officer. As Tarleton approached Morgan retreated So rapid was the pursuit that the British columns passed through the ground of the American camp only a few hours after it had been abandoned. Leaving his baggage behind him with a guard, Tarleton hurried forward during the night and on the morning of the 17th of January, 1781, came in sight of the Americans encamped at the Cowpens.

Morgan, accustomed to win battles had retreated with reluctance, although a retrograde movement was rendered necessary by the advance of Cornwallis on lines parallel to his route. He had gained sufficient time to risk an action and having been joined on the evening of the 16th by General Pickens with a body of five hundred militia he determined to await the coming of the enemy. The ground was open and favorable to Tarleton, whose cavalry outnumbered that of Morgan three to one, and, fearful lest the American general would again retreat, that energetic officer immediately formed his wearied troops into line and advanced to assail him.

Morgan arranged his men with consummate skill. The Marylanders with Triplett's and Taite's companies of Virginia militia, all old soldiers, composed his main and second line under the command of Colonel Howard, and were posted upon an eminence covered with open wood with Washington's cavalry in their rear as a reserve. The first line consisted entirely of militia, under General Pickens, while a short distance in their front two parties of North Carolina and Georgia militia were stationed as skirmishers. As the enemy began to advance Morgan addressed his soldiers briefly but energetically. He directed the militia to deliver but two or three volleys and then to retire and form behind the main line. The Marylanders he reminded of their past glory and "of the confidence he had always reposed in their skill and courage, and assured them that victory was certain if they acted well their part."[*] Then taking his post he awaited the advance of the enemy.

Tarleton moved rapidly to the assault. The skirmishing parties of militia delivered their fire, and falling back, formed on the flank of Pickens' men. The British pressed on with loud shouts upon the first line, which, however, maintained an undismayed front and poured in a close and destructive fire.

---

[*] Lee's Memoirs, p 131

But the enemy continued to advance with the bayonet and the militia being armed mostly with rifles, retired in haste. A portion with Pickens formed on the right of Howard, while the rest fled to their horses in the rear of the line. Believing victory to be already in their grasp, the enemy in pursuit of the flying militia charged upon the continentals. They were met with unshaken firmness. The conflict became desperate; for a time neither the assailants nor the assailed seemed to give ground. But the unconquerable spirit of the Marylanders at length prevailed and the enemy began to falter. Tarleton ordered up his reserve, and his line, thus reanimated, again advanced, extending its front so as to endanger Howard's right. That officer instantly ordered his flank company to change its front, but mistaking the command, it fell back; upon which the line commenced to retire. Morgan at once directed it to retreat towards the cavalry, and to assume a new position. This manœuvre which was executed with coolness and precision effectually relieved the menaced flank.

The British, mistaking the movement for one of flight, rushed forward with great impetuosity and in disorder to complete their triumph. Perceiving their mistake, Howard, not yet having reached the position marked out by Morgan, suddenly faced about and poured in upon the astonished enemy a close and murderous fire. Their front ranks recoiled under the shock. Seizing the happy moment, Howard, cheering on his men, broke in upon them with the bayonet. The charge was terrible and decisive and the day was won. Dearly was the slaughter of Camden avenged. The whole British infantry was killed or taken. One hundred, including ten officers, were killed upon the field and twenty-three officers and five hundred privates taken in the flight. Almost at the same instant that Howard was winning this brilliant victory over largely superior forces, Colonel Washington was routing the cavalry of Tarleton. This sanguinary corps had pursued the retreating militia to their horses and ruthlessly begun to sabre them when Washington charged upon and drove them before him. With the remains of his cavalry Tarleton fled from the field, closely pursued by Washington, who at one time, in the eagerness of pursuit, advanced more than thirty yards beyond his regiment. Tarleton turned upon him, seconded by two of his officers The officer on the right aimed a blow at Washington which was intercepted by his Orderly Sergeant, Everheart,* who disabled his sword arm. The officer on the left, at the same moment aiming a blow at him, was wounded by a pistol bullet fired by a servant boy. The blow of the third—Tarleton himself—Washington parried with his sword, leaving his mark upon the British leader's hand for life Reining back his horse in rage Tarleton discharged a pistol at him, wounding him in the knee, and continued his flight. His artillery, eight hundred muskets, two standards, thirty-five baggage wagons, and one hundred dragoon horses fell into the hands of the victors, whose loss amounted to about seventy men, only twelve of whom were killed

Never was there a more complete or more glorious victory. The force of Morgan did not much exceed eight hundred men, half of whom only were regulars, and eighty cavalry, while that of Tarleton reached a thousand, including three hundred and fifty cavalry. These were all chosen men, the very sinews of Cornwallis' army. This splendid force was entirely annihilated. Although the militia did good service, "the weight of the battle," says one who served in the campaign with great distinction, "fell upon Howard who sustained himself admirably in those trying circumstances, and seized with decision the critical moment to complete with the bayonet the advantage gained by his fire.' Yet he won the battle without orders, so that after he had swept the field by his glorious

---

* Of Frederick County, Md,— he had served throughout the whole revolutionary war, and was well known in western Maryland long after its close Subsequently visiting Frederick, Colonel Washington sent for Everheart, then residing in Middletown in charge of a congregation, and the two old men met and embraced, with teais in their eyes, recurring to the eventful scenes they had passed through together Everheart died in 1839, aged 74 years, and was buried with every testimony of respect and affection, and with the honors of war.— Sketch of the Life of Everheait, by L. P W B , South. Lit. M — THE AUTHOR

charge Morgan rode up to him and said severely, "You have done well, for you are successful; had you failed I would have shot you." At one moment Howard held in his hands the swords of seven British officers who had surrendered to him. Congress awarded Howard and Washington silver medals, Morgan a gold medal, Pickens and Triplett swords.*

Cornwallis, having been joined by General Leslie and finding himself still superior to Greene, who was unable to profit by Morgan's splendid victory, took the bold resolution of burning his baggage, converting his army into light troops and pursuing the Americans into North Carolina. Morgan hastened to rejoin the main army, and by forced marches crossed the Catawba before his pursuers could reach its banks. The British van appeared in sight just as he had made good his passage, and a heavy rain coming up, the waters suddenly raised so as to become no longer fordable. The freshet continued for two days and gave the Americans time to dispose of their prisoners. call in their detachments and make every preparation for retreat. On the third day the British forced a passage with some loss and pursued the retreating army with great rapidity. As soon as Morgan had crossed the Yadkin its waters also became swollen and impassable from the rains and the British were again delayed. Cornwallis, despairing of striking the light troops before their junction with Greene, determined to cut that general off from the fords on the Dan and force him into action.

The British army numbered twenty-seven hundred men; that of Greene twenty-three hundred, of which five hundred were militia, and two hundred and seventy cavalry including Lee's corps, then in fine condition and mounted on fresh horses purchased in Maryland, and far superior in quality to those of the enemy. Unwilling to risk an action until reinforced from Virginia the American leader determined to retreat towards Guilford Court House, and despatched Colonel Carrington, aided by Captain Smith of the Maryland line, to collect boats for the passage of the Dan, when the army should reach

---

* Lee, p 134, Marshall.

it To harass the march of his enterprising enemy he formed a light corps of his best infantry under Howard, Washington's cavalry, and Lee's legion, with a few militia riflemen, amounting in all to seven hundred men, the command of which he offered to Morgan. But that gallant officer was suffering severely from rheumatism and was about to leave the service The command was then tendered to Colonel Williams. "This accomplished gentleman and experienced soldier accepted it with cheerfulness and yet becoming diffidence,"[*] and fulfilled the duties of his charge with honor and ability.

On the tenth of February Greene began his retreat from Guilford, and Williams, with his corps inclined towards the left, threw himself in front of the advance of Cornwallis Now began a series of masterly manœuvres, of rapid marches, and severe duty Cornwallis, finding a strong corps of horse and foot in his front and uncertain of the object of his enemy, immediately checked the rapidity of his march. Williams selected a route lying between that of Greene, which was on his right or to the east, and Cornwallis on his left or to the west, both armies moving north. The enemy, having condensed his force, renewed the rapidity of his march, and the rear-guard of the light corps under Lee was constantly in sight of the van of the British under O'Hara In the night Williams increased his distance to prevent a surprise. The duty, sufficiently severe during the day, then became painful and trying in the extreme. The necessity of maintaining extensive pickets and numerous patrols, kept half the corps constantly in active service. Each officer and man was allowed by six hours sleep in forty-eight, and sufficient time was afforded them for only one hasty meal a day At three o'clock in the morning they broke up their bivouac and marched rapidly forward to secure time for their hurried repast; and sometimes they were even deprived of this by the sudden appearance of the enemy. At night, when the halting ground was reached, worn down with fatigue, the officers and men cast themselves upon the earth, forgetting hunger in the overpowering weariness which op-

---
[*] Lee's Memoirs

pressed them after forty-eight hours of ceaseless toil and watching *

On the morning of the thirteenth, Cornwallis changed his route towards Dix's ford and fell into the rear of Williams. The pursuit was continued with increased activity as the two armies approached nearer the Dan. Greene was now in the vicinity of that river and Williams suddenly changed his route to the road on his right which had been already traversed by the main army, keeping his corps together ready for a prompt blow against the enemy if any occasion presented itself. The distance between the van and the rear of the two armies began to diminish. More than once were the legion of Lee and the advance of O'Hara within musket shot of each other; and the militia riflemen were with difficulty restrained from picking off the pursuers. Both parties, however, maintained a pacific demeanor and seemed like portions of the same army vieing with each other in rapidity and skilfulness of manœuvre. But that seeming holiday parading was full of interest to the whole south. Had Williams' corps been involved with the advance, the strength of the southern army might have been destroyed, and Greene, shattered and no longer covered by his light troops, would have fallen an easy victory to Cornwallis. The burden, therefore, of the retreat fell upon Williams, and gallantly did he bear it. Never, perhaps, was there made so ably conducted a retreat, considering the difficult nature of the country, conducted with so little loss,—scarcely a single man was killed or captured. This is the more remarkable as the retreat was effected in the face of an active, energetic and superior enemy whose van for days was constantly in sight of the retiring rear.

But its termination was at length approaching. On the fourteenth Williams was informed that Greene had safely crossed the Dan the day before, and, leaving Lee's legion on his former route to amuse the enemy, had struck rapidly towards Boyd's Ferry. His men had been cheered up and inspired by the glad tidings of the safety of that army for which they had endured such unequalled privations and fa-

---

* Lee's Memoirs.

tigues The enemy were still close upon his rear but the light corps crossed without interruption, and were followed by the legion infantry. At nine o'clock the cavalry reached the banks of the river and were safely crossed in the boats which were gathered on the northern shore by the carefulness of Carrington and Smith.

Thus closed this remarkable retreat, unparalleled throughout the war for the consummate skill of the leaders and the patient endurance of the soldiers of both armies From South Carolina to Virginia, through a country thickly settled with hostile tories, in want of provisions and clothing, with only a blanket to every four men, even without shoes, the gallant army of Greene maintained its order in its rapid route, sustaining no loss and experiencing no confusion It reached its destination in safety in spite of every exertion of a superior force under the ablest general the British service could boast From the time of its formation the light corps of Williams never slept under a tent until it crossed the Dan By the light of their watch-fires one-half of these brave fellows, wrapped in their blankets, cast themselves down to their brief repose upon the damp earth while the rest stood guard or were stationed as patrols.

Cornwallis, baffled in his pursuit, rested his army on the banks of the Dan and having selected Hillsborough as his headquarters, returned thither by easy marches. In the meanwhile Greene earnestly set about gathering reinforcements He was soon joined by a brigade of Virginia militia, the second Maryland regiment, just raised, was already on its way to his camp and two new regiments of the Virginia line were preparing to march to his assistance Fearful lest Cornwallis should be enabled to arm the tories of North Carolina he determined to recross the Dan, harass the enemy, and give countenance to the patriots of that State.

On the 18th of February, Lee's legion, reinforced by two veteran companies of the Maryland regiment under Captain Oldham and Pickens' South Carolina militia, crossed the Dan. with orders to gain the front of Cornwallis and repress the loyalists. They fell upon Colonel Pyle with four hundred tories, who were hastening to the British army, and who mistaking Lee for Tarleton, permitted him to draw up his men along their line. Discovering their mistake as he was in the act of passing on to surprise Tarleton they opened their fire upon him The legion and infantry immediately attacked them killing about ninety and wounding and dispersing the survivors. Greene soon after advanced into North Carolina and again detached Williams with a light corps to distract the attention of the enemy By a series of brilliant manœuvres, accompanied with several sharp skirmishes, he completely repressed the rising of the royalists and prevented Cornwallis from filling up his ranks with the disaffected young men of the country In a few days he was joined by the new levies from Virginia under Colonel Green, another brigade of militia from the same State under Lawson, and a body of North Carolina militia The second Maryland regiment soon arrived in camp; his whole force then amounted to forty-five hundred men, of whom about sixteen hundred were continentals. He now determined to risk a battle for the recovery of the south Accordingly, on the 15th of March, 1781, he awaited the approach of his enemy at Guilford Court House.

The American army was drawn out in three lines upon the face of a hill at the foot of which ran a small rivulet On the road within close shot of this stream Captain Singleton was stationed with two six pounders, on his left, across the road, the North Carolina militia under Butler and Eaton were marshalled. The second line, drawn up in a deep wood a short distance in the rear, was composed of the Virginia militia under Stevens and Lawson. The third line consisted of the four regiments of continentals, and was displayed on the right of the road. The Virginia regiments held its right, under General Huger. The first Maryland under Colonel Gunby, and the second under Lieut Col Ford, formed the left, under Colonel Williams. Gunby's was the only veteran regiment; the remaining three were entirely new levies with few exceptions, scarcely broken to camp duties. The officers, however, were able and experienced. The right flank was covered by Washington's cavalry, Kirkwood's Delawares, and Lynch's Virginia militia, the left by Lee's legion and Campbell's Virginia riflemen

As the enemy approached, Singleton's pieces opened upon them, his fire was returned by the royal artillery, and the cannonade continued while Cornwallis arrayed his army for battle. He formed in but one line—the seventy-first and the regiment of Bose on the right, under Leslie, the twenty-third and thirty-third regiments on the left, under Webster, and the light infantry and yagers in the centre The first battalion of guards, under Lieut. Col. Norton, supported the right, and the second battalion and grenadiers under O'Hara, the left The British crossed the rivulet and deployed into line at a quick step, and advanced upon Greene's first position The Americans began to fire at long range, but Leslie pressed on firmly, and at the first discharge the North Carolina militia were seized with a panic and fled in the utmost disorder. Lee and Campbell still continued to maintain their position. The Virginia militia under Stevens stood their ground gallantly. That officer, stung with the recollection of the inglorious flight at Camden, had placed sentinels in their rear with orders to shoot down every man that faltered or turned back They sustained their position with courage and firmness, and it was not until the supporting columns of the enemy had been brought up, that they were driven off the ground at the point of the bayonet.

Webster now approached the third line He was met by Gunby and Howard of the first regiment, and with his usual impetuosity he hurried into close fire, but so firmly was he received by this body of veterans that he was compelled to retire, and wait for the rest of the line The first battalion of guards now made its appearance in front of the second Maryland regiment, and Williams charmed with the gallantry of the first, hastened to cheer up the second by his presence But to his astonishment and dismay the regiment broke and fled in disorder. Gunby, perceiving their discomfiture, immediately turned upon the guards as they were pursuing the fugitives and an animated struggle ensued between them. Webster was at this moment engaged with Hawes' Virginia regiment and Kirkwood's Delawares, and Gunby charged up the hill with the bayonet upon the guards under Stewart. His horse was shot under him, and the command fell upon Colonel Howard, who with his characteristic impetuosity led forward the regiment with such rapidity that Gunby could not again overtake it Washington's cavalry at this critical period fell upon the guards and disordered their ranks while Howard was rushing upon them with the bayonet. Like a torrent the old Maryland regiment broke through their ranks, driving them headlong from the field with terrific slaughter, their leader falling under the sword of Captain Smith The remains of that splendid corps were only saved from utter annihilation by a desperate expedient of Cornwallis Determined to arrest the progress of Washington and Howard he brought up his artillery and opened upon them, although every discharge swept through the flying guards, slaying alike pursuers and pursued. The remedy was effectual, and Howard assumed the position formerly occupied by the second regiment under Ford; but, seeing several columns of the enemy crossing to his rear whilst he was hotly engaged in front, and finding most of the troops withdrawn, he began to retire, carrying off his prisoners with him. Lee's legion and the riflemen had continued to maintain their position with undaunted valor.

Greene, finding the fortune of the day turned against him by the flight of the North Carolina militia and the second Maryland regiment, and Lee's corps severed from the army, conceived it prudent to provide for a retreat. The remaining troops were accordingly recalled. They retired in good order, covered by Green's Virginia continentals who had not been engaged. So costly had been the barren victory of Cornwallis that he found himself upon the field of battle utterly unable to pursue his defeated antagonist. The American loss in continental troops was fourteen officers and three hundred and twelve privates, of whom five officers and fifty-two privates were killed, the remainder being wounded or missing; while of the militia, seventeen officers and seventy-seven privates were killed and wounded. The Maryland brigade lost of this number one major, one subaltern, two sergeants and eleven rank and file killed, five captains, one sergeant and thirty-six rank and file wounded, and three sergeants, six drummers and fifers, and eighty-eight rank and file missing—a total of one hundred and fifty-four officers and men. Among the slain was Major Anderson, a valuable officer of the line. The British general lost nearly one-third of his army: ninety-three were killed, and four hundred and thirty-nine wounded. Such was his crippled condition, that after burying his dead, he left his wounded who were incapable of being moved, about seventy in number, to the humanity of General Greene, and proceeded by easy marches back towards Cross creek. Greene immediately determined to force him to another battle, and detached Lee's corps to harass his retreat, while he himself, after obtaining a supply of ammunition, brought up the main army. But Cornwallis, conscious of his present weakness, was now anxious to avoid an action, and made his escape to Cross river, and thence to Wilmington which was strongly secured. Greene finding himself too weak to attack that place, abandoned the pursuit and dismissing his militia, permitted his army to repose at Ramsey's mill.

The American general determined at length to pass by his antagonist and penetrate to South Carolina where Lord Rawdon was now in command, with the expectation of rallying together the scattered partizan leaders, and redeeming that State from British thraldom. Accordingly, on the 6th of April, 1781, Lee's legion, with Oldham's detachment of veteran Marylanders was ordered in advance to form a junction with Marion, while Sumpter and Pickens were notified by couriers to collect their militia and to join the main body at Camden. On the 7th the army began its march for that post. Cornwallis, thrown into great perplexity by this movement, was undecided whether to follow his antagonist south or by striking into Virginia compel him to retrace his steps for the protection of that State At length he resolved upon the latter course

Greene's army had been reduced by the detachment of Lee's legion from eighteen hundred continentals to fifteen hundred; but confidently expecting to find Sumpter in force to join him, he hastened his march towards Camden, fearful lest Cornwallis might retrace his steps to the south and form a junction with Rawdon. To his surprise, on approaching Camden, he learned that Sumpter had neglected to come in with his men, and disappointed in this expected reinforcement, he was unable to invest that post, although its garrison had been diminished by a detachment of five hundred men under Colonel Watson, thrown out to attack Marion, and now closely watched by that active officer with his partizans and Lee's corps. Greene, therefore, contented himself with sitting down on the north of Camden at Hobkirk's Hill to await his reinforcements. Lord Rawdon, informed of the condition of his army, and aware that every delay would increase its strength and diminish his own, resolved at once to risk a battle On the morning of the 25th of April he marched out from Camden at the head of nine hundred men to seek his enemy

The army of Greene was encamped upon a ridge covered with wood, affording facilities for a surprise to an active officer like Rawdon. When the British van fell upon the American pickets—the first notice of its approach—the troops were engaged in cooking their rations and washing their clothes along the rivulets which traversed the hill side. Captains Benson of Maryland and Morgan of Virginia, who commanded the outposts, offered a gallant resistance, and being supported by Kirkwood's Delawares, made good their position until the army was drawn up The Virginia brigade under General Huger was stationed on the right, the Maryland brigade under Colonel Williams, aided by Gunby, Ford and Howard, held the left The artillery was placed in the centre, and Washington's corps of cavalry and two hundred and fifty North Carolina militia were held in reserve.

As the British appeared in presence of his line, Greene perceived their narrowness of front and ordered his centre regiments to advance with fixed bayonets while Washington's cavalry fell upon their rear. The fire on both sides was hotly kept up, but Rawdon, extending his front, protected his flank, although Washington was furiously assailing his rear. Hawes' Virginia regiment and Gunby's Maryland, still somewhat in disorder from its rapid formation, were now ordered to charge with the bayonet, when the right flank company of Gunby's regiment joined in the fire contrary to orders. It spread along the regiment, a part of which became confused Unfortunately, Gunby ordered its right to fall back and form at the very moment when Captain Armstrong with two sections was charging upon the enemy. The movement was fatal. As the flank company retired, its leader, Captain Beatty, was killed and his men became unable to form; the confusion spread, and the whole regiment began to fall back. Seizing this favorable moment, the British line pressed forward with loud cheers, and the veterans of the first regiment, seized with panic, broke and fled In vain Williams and Gunby attempted to rally them In vain Howard, "who had so often and so gloriously, with this very regiment, borne down all opposition, appealed to their patriotism, the recollection of their past glory, the shame of present disgrace"* Worn by previous sufferings, emaciated from scarcity of food and brought suddenly to a charge when only half formed, these brave men seemed to forget the laurels which they had already won. When at length they rallied it was too late to retrieve the day

The second Maryland regiment had resolutely maintained its ground from the commencement of the action but being left uncovered by the retreat of the first, became somewhat deranged Lieut Col Ford received a mortal wound whilst gallantly endeavoring to re-form them, and they too began to retire. The first Virginia had already fallen back, and Greene, ever cautious to preserve his army, ordered the troops to retreat, covered by the unbroken regiment of Hawes. The loss of both armies was about equal; that of the American was two hundred and sixty-six killed, wounded and miss-

---

* Lee's Memoirs; G W Greene's Life of General Greene, p 247, Johnson's Life of Greene, pp 32. 85

promising officer in the army, was among the slain, and Lieutenant Colonel Ford died shortly after the battle from the effects of his wounds

Greene, mortified at a defeat caused by the defection of a favored and trusted regiment, crossed the waters above Camden and assumed a strong position, so as to cut off Rawdon from his supplies. But the British general having received a reinforcement again advanced to attack the Americans. Greene, however, had assumed another position which was too strong to be assailed. Fearing lest his communications with Charleston should be cut off, the English general prepared to abandon the upper country, and sent orders to Cruger to retire from Ninety-Six to Augusta, and Maxwell to fall back upon Orangeburgh

The American army was now busily occupied in besieging the different strongholds he had left behind him. One by one they fell into its hands, until in the space of a month after Greene's entry into South Carolina the British general, in spite of his victory, held possession only of Charleston and Ninety-Six. This latter post Greene now hastened to invest. It was defended by Lieut Col. Cruger with five hundred men and strongly fortified. After some time spent in making the approaches the garrison was summoned but refused to surrender

At the same time Lee and Pickens invested Colonel Brown at fort Cornwallis near Augusta. On the night of the 28th the enemy made a sally to destroy the American works, and drove the guard before them. But Captain Oldham of the Maryland line coming up with his support, after an obstinate conflict regained the trenches and forced the enemy back to his works Frequent sorties were made, and at length the Americans erected a tower of wood which enabled their riflemen to overlook and command the British works. Oldham's infantry were posted to protect the tower from the attempts of the enemy In the night Colonel Brown made a fierce sortie to destroy it, and fell upon the rear of Picken's militia Olding; that of the enemy, two hundred and fifty-eight Captain Beatty of the Maryland line, than whom there was no more

ham leaving one company to guard the tower, hastened to relieve the militia, whom Brown was forcing from the trenches A severe and bloody conflict ensued, but at length the Marylanders carried the victory at the point of the bayonet. Being now completely cut off, and his defences commanded by the riflemen, Brown surrendered, and Lee hastened to join the besieging army before Ninety-Six.

Learning that Lord Rawdon was rapidly approaching at the head of two thousand men to relieve Ninety-Six, Greene determined to attempt it by assault Lieut Col Campbell, of the Virginia brigade, with the first Maryland, under Captain Benson,[*] and first Virginia regiments, was entrusted with the attack upon the left; Lee's legion and Kirkwood's Delawares, upon the right Lieutenants Duval of Maryland and Seldon of Virginia commanded the forlorn hope of the left. Rudolph, of the legion, on the right. The height of the walls had been increased by bags of sand, and parties were armed with hooks to pull them down, while others carried fascines to fill up the ditches At the signal both divisions rushed to the assault. The storming parties sprang fearlessly into the ditch and assailed the walls which were defended with bayonets and long pikes, while the riflemen kept up a deadly and continuous fire from behind the sand bags. For three-quarters of an hour, in the face of this terrible discharge, the assailants struggled in vain to drag down the sand bags and mount the defences. A heavy cannonade was then opened on their flank, and a sally of the enemy made into the ditch with the bayonet, dispersed the hookmen. Duval and Seldon, after an obstinate resistance, having had nearly all their men killed or wounded, were driven back, and Greene recalled his troops from the assault. On the other side, Rudolph forced his way into the fort and Lee was about to follow when he was withdrawn by his commander. The loss of the American forces during the siege amounted to one hundred and eighty-five killed and wounded, among whom were Captain Armstrong

---

[*] Greene's Memoirs, p 440.

of the first Maryland regiment killed and Captain Benson wounded; that of the enemy was eighty-five.

Greene, anxious to avoid the stronger force of Rawdon, abandoned the siege and retreated towards Charlotte in North Carolina. Rawdon after relieving Ninety-Six, set out in pursuit of the Americans, but finding his efforts to overtake them useless, returned to that post which he determined to abandon. Greene immediately retraced his steps, waiting for a favorable opportunity to strike a blow against his active enemy. Finding the lower country destitute of provisions, his troops being compelled to live upon rice, which was suited to neither the Virginians nor Marylanders, who were often times driven by hunger to resort to the flesh of frogs and even alligators,* he retired again to the healthier regions in the northern part of the State to pass the hot summer months.

On the 21st of August he broke up his encampment and hastened to the south to seek the enemy, now under the command of Lieutenant Colonel Stewart, Lord Rawdon having returned to England. He overtook them at the Eutaw Springs. The American army had been increased by reinforcements to twenty-three hundred men, of whom nearly sixteen hundred were continentals. Stewart's force was about equal to that of Greene. On the morning of the 8th of September, 1781, at four o'clock, the American army was put in motion; its advance soon fell in with a party of foragers, who were entirely cut off. A second detachment met with the same fate, and Stewart was informed by the flying fugitives of the approach of his antagonist. He immediately drew out his army to receive him. Greene advanced in two lines—the militia in front, the continentals in the rear. The North Carolina brigade of continentals was stationed upon the right under General Sumner, the Virginia brigade under Lieut. Col. Campbell, in the centre, and the Maryland brigade under Colonel Williams, seconded by Lieut. Col. Howard on the left.

The militia advanced with spirit and opened a heavy fire upon the enemy, which was soon briskly returned; but they

---
* Greene's Memoirs.

continued to maintain their ground until the British troops pressed close upon them Sumner's North Carolina brigade was immediately ordered up to cover their retreat and check the advance of the enemy. This corps, consisting of newly raised regiments never before in action, pushed forward in good style and the conflict became warmer. Greene now brought up the Maryland and Virginia lines, which advanced with a shout and poured in a destructive fire upon the enemy. Stewart finding the dense line of his antagonist pressing hard upon him called up his reserve. Sumner's North Carolinians, unable to maintain their position, began to fall back, when Greene ordered the Marylanders and Virginians to withhold their fire and charge with the bayonet. At trailed arms, cheering vehemently, these two gallant brigades, led on by Williams, Howard and Campbell, rushed upon the enemy, heedless of the close and terrible fire which was repeatedly poured in upon them as they advanced at a rapid pace The shock was terrible. Howard's regiment was received by the Buffs, an Irish corps which had just joined the army, and here the fiercest struggle ensued Neither would yield, but crossing bayonets, their ranks mingled, the men in opposing files sinking to the earth each pierced with the bayonet of his antagonist Thus they were found, grappled in death and transfixed together upon the field of slain, marking the spot where the Marylanders and Buffs had met in deadly conflict. The officers fought hand to hand. So bloody a strife could not continue long, the rest of the British line had given way, scarcely waiting for the approach of the Americans, and the gallant Buffs unable to maintain the conflict with the veteran Marylanders, broke and fled Delighted with the conduct of this regiment Greene rode up and complimented it and its commander in the midst of the action.

The victors followed up their advantage and pressed the fugitives rapidly before them through their camp, which fell into their hands A party of the enemy under Major Sheridan threw themselves into a large brick house near the scene of action, and maintained a destructive fire upon the pursuers, while Majoribanks seized a strong position on the right, sustained by Coffin. This gave time to Stewart to re-form his line. In the meantime, Howard at the head of Oldham's company continued the pursuit between the house and the head of a ravine, where a portion of the enemy had posted themselves, and recommenced the action, but receiving a severe wound, he was compelled to withdraw from the field. The position which the British now held was almost unassailable, and after a vain effort to batter down the house and to force their lines, Greene determined to recall his men from the action, satisfied that he had won all the honors as well as the benefits of victory.

In the pursuit, three hundred British prisoners were taken, with two pieces of cannon, one of which was captured by Lieutenant Duvall of the Maryland line, a young officer of the highest promise, who was afterwards killed during the action. The battle lasted three hours and was hotly contested; more than one-fifth of the British and one-fourth of the American army were killed or wounded. Greene's loss was stated at one hundred and thirty-seven killed and four hundred and eighteen wounded, of whom sixty fell into the hands of the enemy. Nearly sixty commissioned officers were killed or wounded, seventeen being killed upon the spot and four others dying of their wounds. The British lost about five hundred killed and wounded and as many taken prisoners, making a total of one thousand men.

Greene attributed his glorious success to the free use of the bayonet made by the Maryland and Virginia troops, in their rapid charge in the face of a murderous fire of artillery and musketry.* The thanks of congress were voted to each of the corps engaged, and to General Greene was accorded a gold medal The results of the battle were at once appreciated.

Destroying his stores and more than a thousand stand of arms, and leaving his wounded behind him, Colonel Stewart hastily retreated on the evening of the ninth; and having formed a junction with a corps advancing to reinforce him, took post at Monk's Corner, one day's march from Charleston.

---

* Greene's letter, in Memoirs, Lee's Memoirs; Marshall, etc

Greene endeavored to overtake him before he reached that place, but failing to do so, returned to his camp at the Eutaw Springs

The great number of his wounded, as well as the increased sickness which the hard service of the last few days had produced, determined the American leader to retire to his favorite camp on the high hills of the Santee to recruit his wearied troops. After the fall of Cornwallis he again descended to the lower country, forced General Leslie, who had succeeded to the command of the southern army, to withdraw into Charleston, and blockaded him there; having redeemed North Carolina and nearly the whole of South Carolina from the British sway. The spirit of the enemy was broken, and although many skilful manoeuvres and several partizan contests ensued, British supremacy in the south may be said to have terminated with the battle of Eutaw, overturned in great part by the bayonets of Maryland Governor Rutledge of South Carolina, thinking the time had come for the reestablishment of the state government, convened the Assembly at Jacksonborough. Further reinforcements, composed of the Maryland, Pennsylvania and Virginia troops who had been engaged at the siege of Yorktown, were now received from the northern army, under General St Clair, and General Wayne, who accompanied them, was despatched into Georgia, which he soon freed from the presence of the enemy. General Gist, who had returned to the south, was placed at the head of the light corps, and Greene continued to hem Leslie in Charleston, until that general announced his determination to evacuate it, which he did peacefully, with the consent of his antagonist, on the fourteenth of December, 1781.*

While the Maryland line was thus gloriously occupied in the south, its native State seemed for a time threatened with invasion Arnold, the traitor, had been detached to Virginia at the head of an active body of British troops and had committed great ravages in spite of the militia who assembled to oppose him. Cornwallis, when Greene after the battle of Guil-

---

* Marshall; Lee's Memoirs; Tarleton's Campaigns

ford passed into South Carolina, hastened into Virginia, and forming a junction with the forces there took the whole command upon himself. The Marquis De La Fayette was dispatched by the commander-in-chief to Virginia with a small force to make head against the enemy.

He passed through Maryland on his way and was hospitably received by the merchants of Baltimore Being invited to a ball he was there remarked to be grave and sad On being questioned by the ladies as to the cause of his gloom he replied that he could not enjoy the gaiety of the scene whilst his poor soldiers were without shirts and destitute of the necessaries of a campaign. "We will supply them!" exclaimed these patriotic women. The pleasures of the ball room were exchanged for the needle and on the next day they assembled in great numbers to make up clothing for the soldiers out of materials provided by their fathers and husbands. The distresses of his corps were relieved and blessing the kind hearts and fair hands of the ladies of Baltimore, it hastened to take its share in the severe campaign in Virginia.

The legislature, fearful lest the invasion, open as the bay was, might be extended to the State, caused a select body of twelve thousand militia to be organized, and held out inducements for the formation of a corps of volunteer cavalry in each county. The glory of the southern battles won by their brethren had re-awakened the spirit of the people of Maryland and these measures were effectually and promptly carried out The third regiment of continentals was speedily completed and despatched to the south while the formation of the fourth was accelerated. Provision was made for the defence of the bay and several severe actions took place with the straggling cruisers of the enemy. The fourth regiment under Major Alexander Roxburgh, when raised to its complement of six hundred rank and file, on the 7th of September was ordered to join La Fayette in Virginia.

Washington, having formed the design of destroying Cornwallis, was now anxious to concentrate as strong a force as possible in that quarter, while the French fleet seized the mouth of the bay to cut off the retreat of the enemy. On the eighth, Washington and his suite passed through Baltimore where he was received with demonstrations of the greatest respect An address was presented to him on behalf of the people and the city was illuminated In a few days the commander-in-chief was followed by strong bodies of the northern army, and then commenced those masterly movements which resulted in the surrender of Cornwallis with his whole force of seven thousand men, prisoners of war, at Yorktown, on the 19th of October, 1781, an event which marked the close of the revolution In this hard-contested siege a portion of the Maryland troops was engaged maintaining the honor of the State and the fame of the old Maryland line.

The event was hailed with universal joy. The legislature of Maryland was in session when Washington reached Annapolis on his way to rejoin the northern army To honor his arrival they passed a vote of thanks and appointed a committee to deliver him an address on their behalf A splendid entertainment was provided, and during the two days which he tarried there the venerable city, crowded to overflowing with happy spectators, presented one constant scene of enthusiastic rejoicing. She had the proud honor of first "saluting him as the PATRIOT, the HERO, and the SAVIOUR OF HIS COUNTRY" Maryland had been the first to propose him for the arduous and responsible station which was to result in the freedom and the glory of the new republic, and entitle him to the admiration of posterity. It was meet and just that Maryland should first tender him the gratitude of his country and bestow upon him those titles which were to render his fame universal and never dying. The sons of Maryland had often stood foremost in his lines of battle; they were now the foremost to offer him the proud ovation of a republican triumph.*

---

* Votes and Proceedings

CHAPTER XV

THE CLOSE OF THE REVOLUTION.

THE legislature had made every effort to prepare for the campaign of 1781, and conscious of the impossibility of meeting the necessary expenses by means of the usual paper money, resolved to have recourse to the patriotism of the wealthier citizens. Accordingly it was determined to issue two hundred thousand pounds in bills of credit, for the payment of which double their value of the confiscated lands of the disaffected and British subjects was pledged; and to give additional support to this new issue, an "association and subscription" were offered for the signatures of the patriotic merchants and planters of the State, but the first of which they agreed to receive these notes at their par value, and by the second to take at once, for the purpose of circulation, as much as was set opposite to their names.

The security pledged for the redemption of these bills of credit was ample The amount of the confiscated property was large, and but a small portion had yet been sold by the commissioners appointed for that purpose. In addition to this, the "association and subscription" were extensively circulated. Public meetings were held in the different counties and the pledges were almost universally taken. For a time the scheme was successful, but such was the want of confidence in paper money no matter how issued or in what manner secured, that in three months these bills had depreciated to less than half their nominal value.*

The State, while menaced with invasion by Cornwallis, was also threatened with domestic insurrection, which for a time excited extensive alarm. The fortunate discovery and prompt punishment of the conspirators, however, allayed the excitement and effectually discouraged similar attempts. At the opening of the campaign of 1781 the enemy formed the design of invading the western frontier from Canada. General Johnston with a body of British troops was to strike at Fort Pitt, while Colonel Connolly, already once baffled in his designs in Maryland, was to proceed secretly to the interior, enlist the friends of the crown and assemble a tory force to co-operate with him † It is probable that the preliminary arrangements with the western tories were made through the agency of the British officers of the convention troops, then prisoners at Frederick Large numbers had already been enrolled in that county and in the neighboring states, when the conspiracy was discovered at Frederick. Tradition relates that a disguised British officer was to meet a messenger of the traitors at a designated place, to deliver into his hands papers containing every intimation concerning its progress. The vigilance of the patriots deterred the officer from attending at the appointed place and the papers fell into the hands of an American officer, who by a singular coincidence was at that moment standing where the tory messenger expected to find his correspondent The plot and the names of the leaders were thus at once disclosed. The leaders were arrested and sufficient evidence obtained to insure their conviction On the 25th of July they were brought to trial before a commission presided over by Judge Hanson, found guilty and sentenced to be hanged, drawn and quartered Seven of their number were executed in the courthouse yard of Frederick ‡ They

---

* Hanson's Laws, 1781, ch 23, note
† Marshall
‡ Votes and Proceedings, Senate, November 24th, 1781, manuscript copy of Judge Hanson's sentence

persisted to the last that they were only guilty of doing their duty as lawful subjects of the king of England and that their judges and executioners were more truly deserving of the name of rebels and traitors

After the surrender of Cornwallis at Yorktown, the British government reluctantly abandoned the idea of conquering the United States and only sought to detach them from their alliance with France Accordingly, early in 1782 Sir Guy Carleton was despatched to New York with power to make peace or war "with the revolted colonies" As soon as his arrival had been announced, it was unanimously resolved by the legislature of Maryland that "though peace with Great Britain and all the world was an object truly desirable, war with all its calamities was preferable to national dishonor. That this State could never consent to treat with Great Britain except upon the footing of an equal, and would never enter into any treaty with that power which would sully its own honor or violate its obligations to France, its great and good ally"

At the same time to display still further their affection for the French people, on the announcement to the two houses by the governor of the birth of the Dauphin of France, they resolved that his excellency should be requested to appoint by proclamation a day of celebration of that auspicious event, testifying their wishes that the young prince might prove a blessing to the nation by following the example of his illustrious father, and that he might continue to preserve their affections by perpetuating that happiness which they had experienced from an alliance with a prince and people whose great and good qualities had long since excited their admiration and gratitude *

The bay shores were still infested by armed gallies and barges manned by tories and refugees who plundered the unprotected farmhouses and carried off and sometimes murdered the inhabitants The French fleet, although still lying at Yorktown, could not effectually put a stop to these outrages,

---
* Votes and Proceedings, Senate

for the light draught of their boats enabled the perpetrators to escape where pursuit was impossible. The legislature determined to reestablish its State marine and ordered four barges to be equipped and armed with eight pieces of cannon and manned with two hundred and fifty men, and despatched a member of their body to Virginia to obtain the cooperation of that State in an expedition to clear the bay. The French commander was also solicited to detail an armed brig and sloop to cover the lighter galleys Monsieur Villebrun, then on that station, readily afforded the desired aid The commerce of the bay was soon relieved and the inhabitants protected by these effectual measures.*

Tired of the struggle, England determined to end the contest, which had dwindled down to a little more than the possession of the city of New York and petty marauding expeditions upon the coast A provisional treaty was concluded on the third of February, 1783, though actual hostilities had ceased a considerable time before. No State came out of the contest with a better record than Maryland She had always responded with her quotas to calls for additional troops and she had been equally prompt in her liberal appropriations of money to the common cause. She had furnished all-told twenty-three thousand men, which was one-twelfth of the whole number of men enlisted in the American army, and had spent seven million, six hundred thousand dollars, which was two-thirds of the total value of her real estate. Her loss in population from all causes during the struggle had amounted to sixty-six thousand. In proportion to their number, no body of men suffered severer losses than did the Maryland line, whose achievements have inured to the lasting glory of the State. They were the first to use the bayonet against the experienced regulars of the enemy. This was in their earliest battle and throughout the succeeding engagements they were often called upon to lead the charge with the same weapon. In the battle of Long Island a fragment of a battalion shook

---

* Votes and Proceedings, Senate.
* Gambril

with repeated charges a whole brigade of British regulars. At White Plains they held the advancing columns at bay; at Harlem Heights they drove the enemy from the ground; at Germantown with fixed bayonets they swept through the hostile camp far in advance of the body of the army, at Cowpens and at Eutaw they bore down all opposition with unloaded muskets; at Guilford and at Camden, though they met defeat, they fought with their accustomed courage and won the admiration and elicited the surprise of the enemy. Everywhere they used the bayonet with terrible effect. The two battalions with which they entered into the war became reduced to a single company, again it was swelled to seven regiments, to be again thinned to one Before the campaign had well passed they were once more recruited to four full battalions of more than two thousand men

At least two of their colonels, Williams and Howard, were considered the best officers of their grade in the army, while Gunby, Hall, Smith, Stone, Ramsey and Ford were equal to any in the continental service. Although they were entitled to a major-general and two brigadier generals from their own State, they submitted for a long time to be led by strangers. But upon the death of the brave De Kalb, Smallwood was promoted to the command of his division and Gist, who was followed by Williams, to that of the two brigades Now that the war was over, the remnants of the old line and the new regiments, having already upon the scene of their southern exploits been presented, through General Greene, with the thanks of both houses of the legislature for their gallantry and good conduct, turned their footsteps towards their native state The remnant of the Maryland line, upon arriving in Baltimore July 27, 1783, from Annapolis, to which place they had come a few days before on transports from South Carolina, were received with an enthusiasm which testified to the satisfaction which the people of that town felt in their splendid achievements. The Treaty of Paris, which was signed on September 3, 1783, marked the official close of a strife whose responsibilities Maryland had met with honor. Although depleted in men and resources, she bore with equal credit the obligations which the war entailed.

When about to separate, the officers of the army, anxious to constitute some binding link of brotherhood by which to remember their long service together, determined at the suggestion of General Knox to form a society, to be called in honor of the Roman patriot the "Society of the Cincinnati" After making some preliminary arrangements, on the 13th of May, 1783, at the cantonments on the Hudson a meeting of the general and field officers and of delegates of line officers from each regiment was held and the principles of the association agreed upon. They proposed as their object the preservation of the liberties for which they had fought and bled, the maintenance of the union of the states and the continuance of the friendly relations and good offices which should be cherished between companions in arms and sharers of the long and perilous struggle Their views partook of the highest order of benevolence and prompted them to provide assistance to their needy brethren or to their widows and orphans For this purpose a fund was established, to which each officer upon his admission to the society was required to contribute the amount of one months' pay. Admission to the society was limited to those who had fought in the Revolution and to their descendants, except that civilians might be elected to honorary membership. A branch society was to be formed in each State and the general association composed of five delegates from each of the subordinate societies was to meet at Philadelphia at intervals not exceeding three years General Washington was chosen as first president He immediately wrote to the principal officer in each state advising the formation of a state society *

In compliance with this request, the officers of the Maryland line assembled at Annapolis on the 21st of November, 1783; Gen Otho H Williams was placed in the chair and Lieut. Col. John Eccleston was made secretary. A permanent organization was effected by the election of Major-General

* Sparks, 9-22, Marshall, 5-30

Smallwood as president of the society; Brigadier-General Gist, vice-president; Brigadier-General Williams, secretary, Colonel Ramsay, treasurer and Lieutenant-Colonel Eccleston, assistant treasurer Annapolis was selected as the place of their annual meetings

The society, notwithstanding its patriotic inception and principles, excited the distrust and jealousy of the people, who feared that it might lead to the establishment of an order of nobility. By the advice of Washington, the objectionable features of its constitution, especially that of establishing hereditary right of membership, were altered and the hostility excited against it thereupon subsided.

With the close of the war, a permanent seat for the national government became an interesting object of inquiry. The people of Maryland felt that the central position of their state gave it especial claim upon the honor. The corporation of Annapolis addressed a memorial to the legislature at the April session, 1783, offering their city to the general government The two houses in consequence directed a proposition to be made to Congress, tendering to that body, in case it should remove the seat of government to Annapolis, the use of the statehouse for its sessions They also offered the public square, the governor's house as a residence for the president of the body, thirteen dwelling houses to be erected at the expense of the State for the accommodation of the delegates from the thirteen States of the Union and complete jurisdiction over the people of Annapolis. Congress was affected by several of the reasons set forth in the memorial and resolutions, but, while it determined to fix the seat of government in Maryland, deemed it prudent to select some place other than that already occupied by the state capital However, they accepted for the present the accommodations tendered them by the state and adjourned from Princeton to Annapolis The legislature welcomed them with great cordiality and gave up one of their halls for their use. The Governor, William Paca surrendered the government house to their president The legislature further pledged themselves to take suitable measures for their permanent establishment as soon as the site of the new federal city and its boundaries should be marked out

General Washington had already notified the several states of his intention to resign his commission and retire to private life He now hastened to Annapolis, where he arrived on the 17th of December He was met a few miles from the city by General Gates and Smallwood and the most distinguished citizens of Maryland and was escorted to the apartments prepared for his reception. His arrival was announced by salvos of artillery and he was otherwise greeted with an enthusiasm worthy of the venerable city, the seat of old colonial politeness, learning and splendor The members of Congress tendered him a public dinner and at night the statehouse was brilliantly illuminated A ball was given by the members of the assembly and was attended by the beauty and fashion of the state, as well as the most distinguished men of the Confederacy Addresses were presented to him by the legislature and the city authorities, to which he made dignified and happy response All vied in doing him honor The preliminaries having been arranged, on the 23d of December in the presence of both houses of the state legislature, the Governor and council, many military officers and a throng of spectators, Washington entered the Senate chamber and advanced towards the Speaker's chair In a calm, yet feeling and eloquent manner he addressed the President and members of Congress. When he had concluded, he delivered into the hands of the President the commission under which the liberty and the independence of America had been achieved and commended his companions in arms to the gratitude of his country, and his country to the protection of Almighty God The President, on receiving his commission, testified to him on behalf of Congress and the people of the United States their gratitude for his long, persevering and glorious fidelity to his country and commended him to the blessing of Heaven. Then calmly, as if he had not just resigned the highest place in his country's gift, the great man, now truly greatest in heroism, retired from the hall, to betake himself to the domestic seclusion of Mount Vernon.

The war having closed, the attention of the people and the government was drawn to the condition of the finances. Not only was the treasury of the United States empty and Congress burdened with a debt of $42,000,000 in specie, but the several states were also involved to a large amount. The commissioner of Maryland, Matthew Ridley, had succeeded in 1781 and 1782 in negotiating a loan of three hundred thousand guilders, with the Van Staphorsts, bankers, in Holland. but the legislature, believing the terms to be disadvantageous, in 1783 annulled the contract and directed the agent to repay the money already in his hands The affair was not finally settled for several years The requisitions were collected to a great extent in specific articles which were sold for the benefit of the treasury. Every expedient, however, failed to enable it to meet the demands upon it

In its extremity, Congress called upon the States to agree to the levying of certain duties upon exports to cover the interest of the public debt, estimating the proceeds thereof at $1,000,000, while the balance, $1,500,000 was divided among the several states The proportion of Maryland amounted to $141,517. The legislature immediately passed a law authorizing Congress to levy the required duties and to restore, so far as possible, the credit of the state, ordered the consolidation of all its funds, the collection of the purchase money of the confiscated British estates, the sale of barges and other public property and laid a heavy tax for the ensuing year. Several of the states were not so prompt. New York refused to grant Congress the authority it required, and some states neglected to raise their quota of the annual interest on the public debt. It therefore remained unpaid and Congress was obliged to issue certificates which soon depreciated to one-tenth of their nominal value, as public confidence in the authority and resources of the government began rapidly to decline.

Prior to the war, Maryland had invested the sum of twenty-seven thousand pounds sterling in the stock of the Bank of England. During the Revolution, the legislature had drawn bills of credit upon the trustees for the amounts of the dividend which had been uniformly protested They now appointed an agent, Samuel Chase, to proceed to England to recover the amount of the accumulated dividends and to sell the stock for the purpose of honestly meeting their liabilities as quickly as possible. Difficulties and disputes arose and a considerable period elapsed before success crowned the efforts of the agent The sum of six hundred and fifty thousand dollars being received as the proceeds of the trust estate. Fifty thousand dollars was paid to the late Proprietary, Henry Harford, in commutation of his claims. Harford, together with other loyalists had returned to the State at the close of the war and ex-Governor Eden sought to resume possession of the property which the Lord Proprietary had abandoned at the time of his flight He was restrained in this by legal proceedings instituted by the Governor and council, whereupon Harford appealed to the legislature for a settlement of his claim. His petition was adversely acted upon and the merits of the case were summed up in a Senate message to the House. This document set forth that the Revolution had been occasioned by the unjust acts of the British government of which the memorialist was a subject and to which he had remained attached thereby cutting himself off from any rightful claim for compensation for his losses His claim for quit-rents was disposed of upon the ground that the representatives of the people could not consistently with their duty to their constituents, do or suffer any act which might justify even a remote supposition that the people of Maryland were still tenants of a superior lord. It contended that the former Proprietary had lost his claim to quit-rents upon the Declaration of Independence and that the citizens of Maryland thereafter held their lands upon equal terms with the citizens of other States. This action on the part of the Maryland assembly effectually disposed of the Proprietary's claims. The return of many tories to the State was a matter of grievance to its citizens and a town meeting was held in Baltimore on the 21st of June, 1783, at which resolutions were adopted declaring that it was not right that those who had not borne the burdens of the late strife, but had continued in sympathy with the government now overthrown, should participate in the blessings derived from independence, and the town's representatives were instructed to secure the passage of a law at the next session of the assembly prohibiting the residence in the state as citizens, of all persons who had not allied themselves with the patriotic cause.

The generous attitude of Maryland towards the general government, which was shown by the acts of her assembly, June, 1783, "To invest the United States * * * with the power to levy certain duties on imported foreign goods, wares and merchandise as a fund for the payment of the debt contracted by Congress during the late war" was prompted by a broad appreciation of national needs It was also in harmony with the State's endeavors to reduce to uniformity the conflicting tariffs of the several States, particularly, to come to an agreement with her neighbor, Virginia, in the regulation of commerce. After the Revolution, the Chesapeake became a great highway of trade and it was important that Virginia and Maryland should come to an agreement with regard to their conflicting rights On the 22d of November, 1777, Congress took cognizance of the lack of a uniform price of labor, manufactures and internal and foreign products, and recommended Maryland, Virginia and North Carolina to appoint commissioners to meet at Fredericksburg, Virginia, on the 15th of January, 1778, to confer and to effect an agreement if possible The convention failed to accomplish its object. An effort on the part of Maryland and Virginia the following year to harmonize their differences with regard to the jurisdiction and trade of the Chesapeake was no more successful. It was not until 1784 that the two States agreed upon a compact A bill embodying its provisions passed the Maryland Assembly and was followed a short time after by the adoption by the House of a series of resolutions having for their object the regulation of the currency, as well as the harmonizing of the trade laws of the two states. These resolutions were concurred in by the Senate and sent to the Legislature of Virginia as well as to those of Pennsylvania and Delaware, which, being neighboring states, it was hoped would also be favorably disposed towards a commercial agreement Accompanying the resolutions was a proposition for Virginia to join with Maryland in a petition to Congress for leave to form a compact between the two states for a naval defense on the Chesapeake and the Potomac In these resolutions may be found the inception of the sentiment for a general convention of representatives of all the States To Maryland must be accorded large credit for the influences set at work, which later crystallized in the adoption of the Federal Constitution

The intelligent interest which Maryland displayed in seeking an adjustment of currency and trade relations with proximate States was an index of the general unsettled condition of the country in those respects There was a preponderating sentiment in favor of a new issue of paper money, which should be so hedged about by statutory provisions as to give assurance of its circulation at par This was the great issue of the elections of 1786 Seven of the thirteen states counted a majority of paper men in their Legislatures The consequences were at once apparent No sooner did these men find themselves in power than they hurried through all sorts of bills for the issue of paper In most of the states the opposition sentiment broke down after but a slight struggle, but in a few the strife was bitter and protracted Among these was Maryland. More than a year before, a paper money bill had been passed by the House, but failed of indorsement by the Senate. The rejoicing at the defeat of this measure was more than tinctured with clamor and indignation at the attempt to pass such a bill Nevertheless a petition was sent to the Legislature from Baltimore praying for the emission of paper money This instrument bore the signatures of nine hundred and ten men. Opposed to the paper party was the party of industrial progress. The latter contended that fiat money was but a specious panacea for the ills of the times and that in the building up of manufactures, the encouragement of commerce and the passage of navigation bills was to be found the sources of real economic stability. The strife of words was bitter and the transparent arguments for "easy money" awakened as fanatical a spirit among those who were influenced by them as later characterized the "greenback era." The Maryland Gazette was the organ of the opposition and in its columns appeared expositions of the fallacy of the paper money position which aided in holding in check the tide of sentiment that set in that direction. In the midst of the discussion came the expiration of the term of the Senate. The campaign centered about the currency and both parties carried on an extensive pamphleteering canvass for votes for their respective candidates. When the heat of the battle was over and the ballots counted, it was found that the House of Delegates was made up almost entirely of paper men and that the hard money men were in the majority in the upper house, although many of the old advocates of specie had lost their seats. The situation of course created a deadlock. Credit-bills passed by the House of Delegates were thrown out by the Senate and in the fall election of 1787 the currency was again the paramount issue.

Notwithstanding the burdens which rested upon the people by reason of the large war expenditures and the derangement of foreign and domestic trade, rendered heavier by a clause in the peace treaty pledging to British subjects the payment of debts due them, Maryland soon showed signs of an industrial revival. The most significant indication of a reawakened spirit of progress was a project to construct a canal from the Pennsylvania line along the Susquehanna to tide water. A company for this purpose was duly incorporated under the name of The Proprietors of the Susquehanna Canal.* The rich lands of the West and its mild climate had already attracted the attention of the settler and crowds of hardy emigrants flocked thither to make the wilderness bloom with civilization. It became a matter of serious importance to open a convenient route for travel and transportation between the Atlantic and the growing frontier settlements. The position of the Potomac

---

* Hanson's Laws; Votes and Proceedings

on the map pointed it out as one of the most eligible means of effecting this desirable object. The idea was favored by the greatest men of the day. One of its most ardent friends and supporters was Washington. To carry it into effect Virginia and Maryland appointed conferees who assembled at Annapolis on the 22d of December 1784, to devise some form of united action General Washington and General Gates appeared in behalf of Virginia , Thomas Stone, Samuel Hughes, Charles Carroll of Carrollton, John Cadwallader, Samuel Chase, John De Butts, George Digges, Philip Key, Gustavus Scott and Joseph Dashiell on the part of Maryland The result of this meeting was the formation of the Potomac Company. It was incorporated by Virginia and confirmed by Maryland, its actual organization being effected at Alexandria, Virginia, on the 17th of May, 1785 George Washington was chosen its president.

The principal work undertaken by the Company was to make navigable the Potomac as far as Cumberland. From that point on to Ohio, transportation was to be facilitated by a wide road Thus it was proposed to connect the rapidly filling west and the seaboard and to promote economic interest as well as amity between the two sections. To put the new company on a secure basis, it was proposed that Maryland and Virginia should each subscribe fifty shares of stock and direct a survey of the route to be made at their joint expense.* With the adoption of these proposals, it was felt that the project was encouragingly financed. Washington had such profound interest in the projected canal that he assisted in person to survey the river.† It was then supposed that the Potomac could be rendered navigable by locks and dams and short canals, and the works for this purpose were very soon undertaken But experience proved the fallacy of the idea. The death of Washington had its influence in dampening the ardor of his associates and soon after it became evident that the company

---
* Votes and Proceedings, Legislature, 1784, p 24
† Tradition.

could not meet the requirements of its charter with respect to the time when the river was to be opened for navigation. The Legislatures of the two States were indulgent and the time limit was repeatedly extended. So things went until 1819. After an existence of thirty-five years and the expenditure of seven hundred thousand dollars, including stock, debts and tolls, with the payment of but one dividend of thirty thousand dollars in 1811, the Potomac Company applied to the Board of Public Works of Virginia for relief.*

Canal construction was not the only aspect of the transportation and highways problems which engaged the interest of Maryland. Prior to the second war with England, communication between Baltimore and Washington was regarded as fairly satisfactorily established by a light coach and three horses, making the journey in a day and a half. The mail wagon, which was regarded as a marvel of celerity, left Pennsylvania Avenue, Washington, at five o'clock in the morning and arrived at the Baltimore post-office at eleven at night. The delay in land traveling was due to the wretched condition of the roads, ruts were deep and there was little or no attempt at grading. It was no uncommon thing for travelers to have to alight and assist the driver to extricate the vehicle from the mud. From the village of Rising Sun to Philadelphia the road was execrable, part of it being nothing more than a quagmire of black mud. Along the York Road teamsters customarily unhitched their horses to aid one another in pulling their vehicles through the mire. A solution of the bad roads problem was frequently sought by turning teams out of the road entirely and traversing the fields until past the bad stretches. The people of Maryland were not oblivious to the need of better highways and with the growth of sentiment gradually took hold of the situation.

Improved methods of locomotion did not attract considerable attention in the United States until after the first decade of the nineteenth century but to Maryland belongs the credit

---

* Ward, "Chesapeake and Ohio Canal," J. H. U Studies, 17th Series, pp. 13-17

of producing the inventor of the first steamboat. This was James Rumsey, a native of Cecil County, who in 1784 secured from the Maryland Legislature the passage of an Act granting him "an exclusive privilege and benefit of making and selling new invented boats on a model by him invented."* Washington, who saw a trial of the boat, in which it successfully moved against the current of the Potomac, gave to Rumsey a certificate of its efficiency. At this time the boat appears to have been propelled by paddles and setting-poles, the motion being communicated by hand; but, during the following winter, the inventor directed his efforts to the utilization of steam and built a boat on the Potomac in the vicinity of Shepherdstown, which in December, 1785, he brought down the Shenandoah to Harper's Ferry There, upon the 14th of March, 1786, was made a trial of the first steamboat. One of the pleasant incidents of the year which witnessed the organization of the Potomac Company and the initiation of Rumsey's endeavors for improved water navigation was the visit to Annapolis of the Marquis de Lafayette † He accompanied Washington thither and the inhabitants of the capital vied with each other in doing them honor. Addresses were presented to the Marquis by the Governor and council and by both Houses of the Legislature. To testify further their gratitude for his generous devotion to the cause of American liberty, they passed an Act to naturalize him and his heirs male, forever; thus bestowing upon them those rights of citizens of Maryland, which he had so nobly aided in defending. They also ordered the Governor to procure a full length portrait of General Washington, painted by Charles Wilson Peale, a native of Annapolis, in pursuance of a resolution passed in 1781, to be placed in the hall of the House of Delegates.

Connected as the colony had been with England, several of its religious denominations were subject to spiritual superiors in that country. The Catholics of the State were under the jurisdiction of a vicar, appointed by the Catholic bishop of

---

* Scharf " History of Maryland," vol. 2, p 526
† Annals of Annapolis, p 215

London, and the Episcopalians were subject to the Anglican bishop of the same city; while the Methodists looked to Mr Wesley of England for ministerial appointments.* It now became desirable to establish separate ecclesiastical organizations, and the Catholic clergy assembled at White March on the 27th of June, 1783, to draw up a system for their government After several meetings these articles were completed, and the Rev. John Carroll, at their request, received from Rome the necessary powers of spiritual superior A few years afterwards he was appointed a bishop, was consecrated in England, whither he went for the purpose and returned to his see of Baltimore in 1790, the first bishop of the United States. In 1810 his see, having been divided into several bishoprics, he was elevated to the rank and dignity of archbishop.

The Episcopal church had suffered much during the Revolution from the impossibility of obtaining ordination for its clergymen. It was a common want throughout the country, and the Rev Samuel Seabury, of Connecticut, was dispatched to England in 1784 to obtain consecration as a bishop of the Episcopal church. Many obstacles were thrown in his path, but he returned the ensuing year Several others in due time were consecrated and in 1789 the Book of Common Prayer, as now used, was ratified and adopted by a convention of that church. The application of the Methodists to Mr. Wesley resulted in the appointment of Dr. Thomas Coke as superintendent.

While these steps were in progress for the furtherance of the organization of the religious bodies, the cause of learning and science was not neglected A college had been established at Chestertown, on the Eastern Shore—named in honor of the Father of his Country, Washington College. An additional college in connection with it and under the patronage of Rev Drs Carroll, Smith and Allison was opened at Annapolis under the title of St John's College; and the two were erected into the University of Maryland.

---

* Annals of Baltimore

The land office was again opened and the bounty promised the soldiers of the line laid off for them. The officers were not neglected. The depreciation of their pay was made good to them and those who had served in the independent corps were placed upon the same footing with regard to half pay and pensions as the officers of the line. Upon their commander a higher reward was bestowed. After the expiration of the term for which William Paca was eligible, in 1785, Major-General Smallwood was elected governor; and continued in the office during three consecutive years. He was succeeded by Col. John Eager Howard, whose terms extended into 1791 —ample proofs of the affectionate regard of the people and Legislature for the gallant men who had won so much glory for Maryland.

A canal project, which proved more successful than that undertaken by the Potomac Company, called the Chesapeake and Delaware Canal because it was to furnish communication between those two waters, was conceived of at a very early date. In 1679-80 Dankers and Sluyter, two commissioners sent out to Maryland by a peculiar religious denomination of New Netherlands called the Labadists, entered in a journal which they kept of their travels an observation upon Maryland traffic and the desirability of a water way between the Delaware River and the Chesapeake Bay. After commenting in particular upon the geography of the region, they say. "What is now done by land in carts might then be done by water for a distance of more than six hundred miles."* They realized, however, the magnitude of the undertaking and spoke of the digging of the canal as a matter to be considered by the highest authorities in control of the region. Little attention was paid to the canal project until nearly a hundred years later, when various routes were surveyed. In 1806 Mr. Benjamin H. Latrobe, who made the survey of the route finally determined upon, mentioned that thirty-two surveys had previously been

---

* Memoirs of Long Island Historical Society, vol 1, p 209. James, the Labadist Colony in Maryland, J. H. U Studies in His and Pol Science, 17th Series, p 32.

made and this number was subsequently added to by fifteen more. On the 7th of December, 1799, the Legislature of Maryland passed an Act of incorporation of the Chesapeake and Delaware Canal Company, authorizing the cutting of a canal between the Chesapeake Bay and Delaware River. The company was empowered to receive subscriptions to the amount of half a million dollars in shares of two hundred dollars each. The coöperation of Delaware and Pennsylvania was first to be secured before the company could begin work

It was not until May, 1803, that the organization of the company was completed by the securing of a sufficient number of shareholders The stockholders then met at Wilmington and elected William Tilghman, of Pennsylvania, President, and associated with him as directors a number of prominent gentlemen, among whom were Messrs. Chew, Gale and Adlum of Maryland Benjamin H. Latrobe and Cornelius Howard, brother of Gen John Eager Howard, were among the engineers and surveyors selected to carry out the undertaking The Elk River route was chosen. Work was commenced upon the canal on the 2d of May, 1804, and it was completed on the 4th of July, 1829, when water was admitted into the whole line

CHAPTER XVI.

MARYLAND A FEDERAL STATE

WE have seen that the Confederation in its need had appealed to the States to come to its aid by imposing a tariff upon imports and that Maryland had generously responded to the call, although the majority of the States had not been so forward to accord the degree of recognition of the general government which the adoption of its fiscal recommendation would have implied. The efforts of Maryland to harmonize its trade and currency differences with Virginia, resulting in a compact which was referred to Delaware and Pennsylvania for their concurrence, was well received by those States, which immediately appointed commissioners in accordance with the sixth and seventh resolutions of the Maryland-Virginia compact.

Virginia, however, when it came to consider the appointment of commissioners to meet those of the other interested States, broadened the plan to include a general conference by commissioners from all the States of the Union to take into consideration the trade of the United States and to consider how far a common commercial agreement would be conducive to the harmony and interest of the states. It was proposed that the commissioners should meet at Annapolis the following September. The Maryland Senate, however, refused to concur in the Virginia proposition upon the grounds that the congressional fiscal proposition of 1783 ought to receive the indorsement of the states as a relief measure and that the proposed convention was an acknowledgement to the world of the weakness of the American Confederation, and further that it was needful only to confer upon Congress the power to formulate a uniform system of trade regulation. But Maryland was ready to go into the convention provided that it was not confined to fiscal measures but should have purview of the whole plan of union for the correction of its defects.

The convention for which Maryland declined to appoint representatives met in Annapolis on the 11th of September, 1786, and continued in session three days. Five states were represented, New York, New Jersey, Delaware, Pennsylvania and Virginia. In consequence of the limited number of states represented, the convention contented itself with a statement of the defectiveness of the federal government and an exhortation to all the states to take action in the appointment of commissioners to meet in Philadelphia on the 2d day of the following May to devise provisions for the needs of the Union Congress approved the recommendation of the convention, as did all the states excepting Rhode Island On the 23d of April, 1787. the Legislature of Maryland selected five delegates to represent the state in the convention about to assemble with power to revise the articles of confederation. They were Robert Hanson Harrison, Charles Carroll of Carrollton, Thomas Stone, James McHenry and Thomas Sim Lee. Several of these gentlemen having declined, others were elected in their stead and on the 26th of May, when the act of appointment finally passed, the delegation was composed of James McHenry, Daniel of St. Thomas Jenifer, Daniel Carroll, John Francis Mercer and Luther Martin.*

On the 14th of May the convention assembled at Philadelphia and organized by electing Washington president of the body. The delegates, generally, admitted the pressing necessity of change. But, while one party was inclined to strengthen the State authority at the expense of the general government, dreading too great a centralization and a gradual destruction of freedom and State independence, the other, principally those who had served during the war, hoped to derive from an efficient national government that unity which would insure pros-

---
* Votes and Proceedings

perity and that stability which would demand respect from abroad and secure at home the blessings of peace, order and good government Various plans were proposed This was natural, as some had entered into the convention with monarchical sentiments and others were advocates of a partition of the confederacy. The northern states in particular, were greatly agitated over their incubus of debt for which they had sought to provide by renewed issues of paper money instead of by imposing taxes as had been done by Maryland Even in Maryland the people were much disturbed over the recent proposition which had found favor with the House of Delegates for the issuing of bills of credit by the State to the amount of three hundred and fifty thousand pounds, and which had precipitated a violent controversy leading to the dissolution of the House of Delegates in resentment at the failure of the Senate to concur in its measure. The proceedings of the Philadelphia convention need not concern us further than to record the prominent participation in its debates by Luther Martin of Maryland, who was a leader of the opposition to the conferment of greater powers upon the federal government *

On the 7th of September, 1787, the convention concluded its labors and agreed upon the present constitution and form of government of the United States, which was laid before Congress That body immediately directed that copies of the constitution should be transmitted to the several legislatures to be submitted to a convention of delegates, chosen in each State by the people in conformity with the resolves of the convention.

The Legislature of Maryland, in compliance with this resolve, on the 1st of December in the same year, by resolution recommended the people of the State "to submit the proceedings of the federal convention to a convention of the people for their full and free investigation and decision." For this purpose they further recommended "that such of the inhabitants as were entitled to vote for delegates in the Assembly should choose four persons for each county and two for the

---

* "Luther Martin, the Federal Bull Dog," Md Hist. Soc Publications

cities of Baltimore and Annapolis in the mode prescribed for holding other elections, to serve in the said convention." The qualifications of delegates were that they should be citizens of the State, twenty-one years of age, having resided therein at least three years and in the county twelve months before the election. The convention was directed to assemble at Annapolis on the 21st of April, 1788,—if they approve the constitution, "to ratify it finally in behalf of the State and report their action to Congress."

On Monday, the 21st of April, the convention organized by the election of Hon George Plater, president. The few anti-Federalists present could not do anything positively to prevent the convention from taking favorable action so that they sought by a policy of obstruction to wear out the patience of the members and then to bring in a motion to adjourn. With a show of commendable caution they urged that Maryland should defer action until Virginia or New York or some other state more directly concerned in the proposed change should have taken action. The Federalists, however, were on the alert and estimated the attitude of their opponents at its real worth. They were determined to sit out all parliamentary obstructions and, although their patience was sorely taxed by the protracted harangues of their associates, they resolved that the convention should not dissolve without giving its ratification to the new constitution. After sitting for a week, the convention ratified the constitution by a vote of sixty-three to eleven. On motion of Mr. Paca, a committee of thirteen, was appointed to draft amendments, a series of which, thirteen in number, were agreed to in committee, while fifteen others were rejected by the majority. Mr. Paca read to the convention the amendments agreed upon. A vote of thanks was tendered to the President and the convention then adjourned.[*]
By its action, Maryland expressed its confidence in the general government and its willingness to accord to it those powers, the lack of which had shorn it of strength and had deprived it of respectable status among the governments of the world.

---

[*] Elliot's Debates on the Federal Constitution, vol 2, p. 547

The acceptance of the larger measure of authority evinced the wisdom of those who shaped the decision, but by many of these the new plan of government was looked upon askance. It was natural that those who had broken from the tyrannical government of England should fear lest they were forging chains for their own serfdom as a state, when they ratified a document which gave undoubted sovereignty to a general body which they had created and been accustomed to look upon simply as the servant of the State.

By the 2d of July, 1788, the constitution had been ratified by nine states and was laid before Congress, which immediately took steps for carrying it into effect The States were directed to appoint their electors on the first Wednesday of January, 1789, who were to assemble at New York on the first Wednesday of February to cast their votes for the President and Vice-President of the United States, and the month of March was fixed as the time, and New York the place for inaugurating the government under the new constitution On the 22d of December the General Assembly of Maryland passed an act providing an elective system. By this law the State was divided into six electoral districts. The first election was to be held on the first Wednesday in January, but thereafter on the first Monday of October every second year. The electors were to consist of eight persons, five to be residents of the Western Shore and three of the Eastern Shore. There were to be six representatives, to be selected from their own districts, but each voter should have the right of voting for the six persons. The elections were to be free and made *viva voce* After considerable discussion concerning the election of senators, it was agreed that the two men for this office should be elected by a joint ballot of both houses. Upon the day appointed for the election, December 9, thirteen members of the Senate and seventy of the House of Delegates came together and it was resolved that "one senator should be a resident of the Western and the other of the Eastern Shore." After three ballots, John Henry and Charles Carroll of Carrollton, of the Eastern and Western Shores respectively, were elected the first senators from Maryland under the new federal constitution.

The elections of 1788 over, the people of the United States looked to Washington as the one man fitted to first grace the office of chief magistrate of the perfected Union It was feared, however, that he would be unwilling to leave the pleasures of his retirement again to enter the arena of arduous effort in behalf of his country. Before the assembling of Congress, he received many letters urgently pressing upon him the nation's hope that he might consent to become their civil, as he had gloriously been their military chieftain. Thomas Johnson wrote: "We cannot do without you, and I and thousands more can explain to any one but yourself why we cannot do without you." Such was the feeling throughout the country, so that the action of the electors was a foregone conclusion Assembled at New York on the 6th of April, 1789, where, since the 4th of March it had been awaiting a quorum, Congress gave official pronouncement of the decision of the electors When the votes were counted in the Senate, it was found that Washington was the unanimous choice, while John Adams received the majority vote for the second place. Maryland cast her six electoral votes for Washington for president and Robert Hanson Harrison for vice-president. Messengers were despatched to inform Washington and Adams of their election Charles Thompson, the Secretary of the Continental Congress, bore the letter of notification from John Langdon, temporary president of the Senate. He arrived at Mount Vernon on the 14th of April, and upon the 16th Washington set out for New York, feeling, as he confessed, the weight of responsibility which developed upon him and for which he apprehended he would not be equal. His journey was marked by a continuous ovation. At Baltimore he was greeted by the ringing of bells and volleys of artillery; a numerous cavalcade of citizens forming an escort to his carriage. A committee of prominent men presented him with an address of congratulation, to which he made feeling and dignified response, breathing the spirit of devotion to the cause of his country which had endeared him to his countrymen On the 30th of April, 1789, he was inducted into the duties of his high office, upon taking the solemn oath prescribed by the constitution With rare discretion, he associated with him in the executive offices of government men of the highest competency Robert Hanson Harrison, who during the War of Independence had been one of his trusted secretaries, was appointed to the Supreme Bench pres ded over by the distinguished jurist, John Jay. Other Maryland appointments were William Paca, judge of the United States District Court, Richard Potts, United States district attorney; Col N Ramsey, marshal; Capt. Joshua Barney, clerk, Gen. Otho Holland Williams, collector of the port of Baltimore; Robert Purviance, naval officer; and Col. Robert Ballard, surveyor *

The national government had not yet adopted a permanent residence Several States had made tender of locations, Maryland, as we have seen, being one of them That State now made another proposition to the new Congress and directed its representatives to cede to the United States a district of ten miles square in any portion of its territory which Congress might select After a good deal of hesitation and of conflict of the rival claims of the Delaware and the Potomac, the latter was chosen. The arguments in its favor, as advanced by Washington, Madison, Lee, Carroll and other advocates, were that the seat of government ought to be removed from the neighborhood of populous cities, and yet be as centrally located as possible. The selection of the site also had reference to the project of a canal from the tidewater on the Atlantic to the great west. When this enterprise should be carried out, it was urged that Washington would then be advantageously located for communication with the western frontier

Messrs. Johnson, Stewart and Carroll in 1790 were appointed commissioners, and, under their direction the district was laid out on both sides of the Potomac, its territory being equally divided between Virginia and Maryland and including in its area the towns of Alexandria and Georgetown The new

---

* Annals of Baltimore

city whose site was selected for the national Capitol was named in honor of the Father of his Country, the city of Washington On the 18th of September, 1793, the cornerstone of the north wing of the Capitol was laid by President Washington with Masonic ceremonies, he being prominent in the councils of that order Congress met there for the first time in November, 1800, but before that date Washington had ended his labors and passed to rest, leaving a memory revered and a name that should be the heritage of the centuries

Finding that the duties on imports were insufficient to supply the needs of the Treasury, Congress determined to levy an internal excise Whiskey, as one of the most common and deleterious articles of consumption, was selected as the principal subject. The tax met with great opposition, especially in western Pennsylvania. One of the objections to the law in that section was that an accused person suffered the hardship of traveling several hundred miles to Philadelphia to stand trial On June 5, 1794, Congress passed an act for the relief of this grievance, providing that offenders against the internal revenue law might be tried in the state courts. But before this law could be made practically effective, the United States marshal had received a large number of writs to serve on persons in the western part of the State, summoning them to Philadelphia. When he attempted to execute the services, the people of the county raised the cry "the federal sheriff is taking away people to Philadelphia." The popular resentment rose to a high pitch, the marshal was captured by a mob and compelled under threat of death to promise to serve no more such writs west of the Alleghanies. He made his escape and by a circuitous route arrived in Philadelphia with the intelligence of the grave nature of the uprising. Word was received by Washington that on August 1 a mass meeting attended by seven thousand persons had been held to protest against the enforcement of the excise law. The issue was clearly presented: was the constitution of the federal Union to be regarded in the same way as the flimsy affair which had furnished the basis of the old confederacy, or was it to be respected as the authoritative expression of a government that stood firm for its enforcement There could be but one answer to the challenge, on the part of Washington. There were those in the government, however, who seriously questioned the advisability of using the radical means which the President advocated and employed. The argument was advanced that Virginia was also infected with resentment at the law and that the disaffected classes generally would rally about those who gave them an issue with the government If the State militia were to be employed for the suppression of the uprising, these persons doubted that the citizen soldiery from the other states would serve It was even argued that the disaffectants might turn to the British for succor and so plunge the country again into international strife. Edmund Randolph was the leading exponent of these views. Although Hamilton had greater confidence in the loyalty of the people to the general government, he yet entertained fears as to the response of the States to the call upon them to take up arms against the citizens of one of their number. Writing in 1799, he says: "In the expedition against the western insurgents, I trembled every moment lest a greater part of the militia should take it into their heads to return home rather than to go forward" However, when the requisitions were made on the Governors of Pennsylvania, New Jersey, Maryland and Virginia for quotas of fifteen thousand men, they responded. An attempt at conference failed, and, it being reported that the insurgents were gathering in force at Cumberland, Maryland, for the purpose of marching on the arsenal at Frederick, whither the arms of the State had been removed at the close of the Revolution, an immediate call for the troops of Maryland was made by the Governor and was promptly answered. Five hundred men marched from Baltimore alone and the remainder of the requisition was filled up by the militia of the counties. The point of rendezvous was Cumberland. There the Maryland soldiers, joined by those of the other States, were placed under the command of Governor Lee, of Virginia. Their appearance crushed the insurrection without the necessity of a battle, only two men were killed and they in personal conflict with the soldiers, for which the latter were punished. It is to the discredit of the men of that day, however, that upon their arrival at Philadelphia, the leaders of the insurrection who were taken prisoners were paraded through the streets with the word "Insurgent" on their hats and during the night were treated with the greatest cruelty by the soldiers on guard. The whiskey insurrection derives its importance not from its magnitude, which was too insignificant for it to deserve the name, but from the fact that it represented a great issue, the importance of which was little understood by those concerned in it.

In the meanwhile Maryland was advancing in commercial and industrial importance, and the trade of the State was becoming concentrated at Baltimore, which was the geographical center of the United States. As early as 1784, an attempt had been made to invest the community with municipal dignity, but the endeavor was thwarted by the rivalry of the people of Fell's Point.* But in 1796 the General Assembly granted Baltimore Town the incorporation it sought and which proved the basis of a stimulated prosperity and rapidly increasing population. The English merchants, after the treaty of peace had lifted the restraints upon commerce with America, eagerly sought to regain that lucrative trade. In consequence of their efforts and those of a number of Holland merchants, who had established branch houses in Baltimore, with offices in the principal towns of the State, trade in tobacco, corn, wheat and flour, which were the staple products of Maryland, revived and surpassed anything in the previous trade history of the State.† Baltimore, as the principal shipping port, was thus brought into great commercial prominence. With the growth of trade, shipbuilding advanced, and the "Baltimore Clippers" became famous, and carried the name of the city to the principal ports of the world. They frequently showed a speed that is now surpassed only by swift ocean steamers. No other single fact contributed so much to the rise of Baltimore as did the fame

---
* Scharf II, p 603
† "Picture of Baltimore."

and service of the ships built upon the model which was distinctive to the shipbuilders of the Chesapeake region.

The difficulties which had arisen in Europe out of the French Revolution were reflected in the contemporary feeling and sentiments of the people of the United States Genet, the minister of the French Directory, relying upon the pro-French sentiment in the country for support, was guilty of contemptuous indifference and insolence towards the President, which resulted in his recall. A large portion of the nation, actuated by feelings of gratitude for the past assistance of France, were disposed to overlook the outrages of that people against American commerce, while similar acts upon the part of England engendered feelings of deep hostility. In national politics, the Democrats sided with France. while the Federalists were desirous of punishing her infringements of the nation's rights. The latter being more powerful, active measures against the Directory were resolved upon Congress ordered an increase of the army, the command of which President Adams bestowed upon Washington, who once more left his retirement at Mount Vernon to draw his sword in his country's cause Col John Eager Howard was selected by him as one of his brigadier generals Two or three French ships were captured and the French Directory at length consented to receive an American minister This and other subjects of dispute being satisfactorily arranged, the war cloud passed over.

In the meanwhile a contest had arisen in Maryland for the enlargement of the right of suffrage. The restriction of a property qualification was justly obnoxious to a large class of the population The question went back to the close of the Revolution, although even prior to that in contests between the House and the Senate the former body frequently displayed the popular tendency towards a more liberal construction of the rights of franchise; while the latter body, from its composition and mode of selection, was strongly conservative. Before the year 1800 it had become the leading topic in state politics and in that year the popular party succeeded in having passed through the House of Delegates a bill to extend the right of suffrage to every free white male citizen, twenty-one years of age, who had resided twelve months in the state and six in the county prior to the election. The Senate voted to amend the measure by requiring that the voter should also have been assessed and paid a tax twelve months before the election and that he should have had two years' residence in the state. These amendments, the House contended, would make the bill an empty gift. For it would not only retain but enlarge the property qualification, and would deprive of the right of suffrage many who already possessed it—those whose property was greater in value, but was still under the limit of that upon which taxation was imposed. The two bodies being unable to harmonize their differences, the bill failed.

The controversy, however, only became the more bitter and at the ensuing session of the Assembly, in 1801, practically the same bill was re-introduced into the House, where it was passed by a vote of forty-eight to fourteen. At the same time, the committee, who reported the bill, intimated that the part of the constitution referring to the Legislature might profitably be altered, so that the Senate should be made more responsible to the people. That body was elected for a period of five years with the power of filling its own vacancies. Other modifications were suggested. As the manner prescribed by the constitution for its alteration would make it a constitution only to be found in acts of assembly, they advised that a bill recommending a convention to assemble in 1803 should be passed, to take effect if confirmed by the succeeding Legislature. Stimulated by the threat of the House, the Senate concurred in a suffrage bill which was passed on the 28th of December. The act of confirmation introduced early in the session of 1802 was passed by a large majority of the House and unanimously by the Senate. Maryland thus became invested with a suffrage law equalled in liberality by that of only one other state, Vermont. At the same time that the unrighteous restriction was removed from the suffrage, the *viva voce* method of voting gave place to the system of secret ballot. Property qualification was still thrown around the state offices, but in 1809 all clauses of the constitution containing such restrictions were repealed by an act which was confirmed at the fall session of the Assembly of the same year.

With the evolution of the franchise went along the development of the judiciary. The state was divided into six judicial districts, presided over by a chief, with two associate justices, for the county courts throughout the districts. The court of appeals was constituted of the chief justices of the six judicial districts. To secure impartiality in its decisions, it provided that the judge who had given an opinion in the lower court should withdraw from the bench at its trial in the court of appeals. Its sessions were to be held both on the Eastern and Western shores.

The international relations of the United States began every day to grow more gloomy. The aggressions of the Bashaw of Tripoli had been promptly resented. The more trying oppressions of England were borne in the hope that remonstrance would obviate more active measures. The triumph of Napoleon over all the nations of Europe except England had made that country arrogant in her use of the great fleet which served to preserve her independence of the autocrat of Europe. The United States resented her seizing of property and the impressment of citizens as violations of the rights of neutrals. The relation of neutrality, however, gave the United States such important trade advantages and added so much to the wealth of the country that many persons, who upon general grounds of patriotism resented the insults of Great Britain, were willing to swallow their wrath and to raise their voices in deprecation of proposals to call Great Britain to account.

Jealous of the growing naval power of the United States, England at length determined that American vessels bearing French products were lawful prize and laid most of the ports of France under embargo. France retaliated by the famous

Berlin Decree of November, 1806, declaring the British Islands in a state of blockade and all neutral vessels trading there liable to capture.* The claim of the British Government to the right of impressment resulted in the United States ship of war Chesapeake being fired upon because of the refusal of her commander to submit to a search. Popular indignation ran high and public meetings to protest against the indignity done the national honor were held throughout the country. President Jefferson was importuned to resent the insult by a declaration of war On the 2d of July the United States manifested its displeasure by declaring an embargo against British vessels, thus closing to that nation the ports of the United States The English government disavowed the outrage, but the embargo continued. The Maryland House of Delegates in 1808 joined other of the maritime states in instructing its representatives in Congress to vote for a suspension of the embargo, but the Senate stood resolute for the necessity of the measure, a position that both houses of the legislature agreed to at the next session. Foreseeing that war was inevitable, the Assembly sought to foster home industries in order to render the state independent of those things which it had customarily imported from Europe They further directed their representatives in Congress to support the administration of the new President, Madison, in every retaliatory measure The people earnestly, indorsed the action of the legislators Associations were everywhere formed for the encouragement of domestic manufactures and in Baltimore a company was incorporated under the name of the "Athenian Society" with a considerable capital to establish a warehouse for the reception and sale of such articles. To aid in the advancement of this design, it further offered annual premiums for the best domestic productions, and members of the legislature as well as the people at large made it a matter of pride to appear clothed in the fabrics of the State†

---

* McMaster, pp 249, 270, 292
† Annals of Baltimore, Votes and Proceedings

CHAPTER XVII.

THE WAR OF 1812

On the 18th of June the American Congress formally declared war against Great Britain, assigning as the causes of its action the right of search of American ships claimed by the British, the impressment of American seamen, the lengths to which the system of paper blockade was carried and the gross injustices perpetrated against neutral commerce under the sanction of the British Orders in Council The last of these grievances was removed a few days after the President's proclamation of the action of Congress. But that body was not mollified and alleged that the action of the British was not inspired by consideration for the American attitude towards the obnoxious British policy, but by regard for the needs of their own population The other grievances remained unredressed and furnished ample justification for hostilities. But this sentiment was not universally entertained in the United States, at Boston the declaration of war was made the occasion for general mourning. Throughout New England the people met to express their displeasure and to demand the restoration of peace Flags on the shipping in the harbors were displayed at halfmast A peace party was organized and adopted every method to discourage the advocates of the war and to cripple its progress. The pulpit as well as the press was arrayed against it and there were some who went to the length of advocating that the Northern States might profitably sever a tie of union which had long since been virtually dissolved.

The session of the twelfth Congress was largely taken up with war measures. For several years the military establishment of the country had been upon the basis of three thousand men, and the navy, whose achievements were so largely to determine the conflict in America's favor, numbered but ten frigates and ten sloops of war, with about one hundred and fifty gunboats suited for harbor defense. At this session of Congress the several states and territories were laid under requisition to furnish their quotas of one hundred thousand militia. In compliance with this action, Gov. Robert Bowie convened the General Assembly of Maryland on the 15th of June to provide for the raising of Maryland's contingent of six thousand men The Legislature took this action and also passed an appropriation bill of twenty thousand dollars. The defense of Baltimore was pushed, the guns at Fort McHenry were mounted and extraordinary measures taken for the security of the emporium of the State. The war enthusiasm was so strong that the recruiting officers were compelled to suspend enlistments by companies and to give preference to old military organizations

When the war fever was at white heat, its opponents in Baltimore occasioned through their injudiciousness an act of violence that remains one of the most regrettable occurrences in the city's history. The publishers of a journal called the Federal Republican had irritated public feeling by their attacks upon government measures and, the day after the proclamation of war appeared, one of the owners of the paper, Alexander Contee Hanson, in a censorious article bitterly inveighed against the measure and impugned the motives of its advocates. The time of the appearance of this article was Saturday, June 27. The other papers upon the following Monday replied to the Federal Republican's attack and the excitement, which had partially subsided, was again aroused. Having intimation of a proposed attack upon their office, Jacob Wagner, the associate of Hanson, removed the books of the firm from the building. About nine o'clock in the evening the gathering of a crowd of men and boys with noisy demonstrations was followed by a desultory attack upon the structure, which, however, soon became a determined purpose to destroy both the plant and the building, which was located on the corner of Gay and Second streets. The house, which was of frame, was razed to the ground, the presses were destroyed and the type thrown into the street. The rioting thus begun expressed itself in deeds of destruction of everything that the mob regarded as connected with British sentiment Several vessels lying in the docks, bound for Spain and Portugal, were dismantled, the mob having the impression that they were to set sail under British licenses. After the destruction of its Baltimore office, the Federal Republican was issued at Georgetown, but Mr. Hanson was not content to allow his principles to be repressed by the action of a mob. He unfortunately returned to Baltimore and upon the 27th of July renewed the issue of his paper in that city, although it continued to be printed in Georgetown.* The editor commented upon the conduct of the authorities and the people of Baltimore in the same violent strain that had before awakened popular feeling He made no secret of his determination to preserve such freedom of speech even to the point of actual hostilities. It was a matter of public knowledge that he had introduced into the house in which his office was located a company of friends and a number of stands of arms In the excited state of the popular mind, this action was construed as a direct challenge, and, as night approached, a large crowd gathered about the house and began to make assaults upon it. After having several times warned them to desist, the besieged persons fired upon the crowd, wounding several of them and killing one. Some of the men in the street then brought a field-piece to bear upon the office, but were dissuaded from firing by persons of prominence and by the assurance that their enemies were ready to surrender While being conducted to the jail, the prisoners were subjected to great indignities and that night the prison was broken into by the excited mob, who vented their spleen upon them by acts of the greatest cruelty. One of the unfortunates, General Lingan, who had served his state and country with credit in the Revolutionary War, was killed Others escaped actual death by feigning it The passion of the mob by this time was raised to such a pitch that

---

* Baine's "History of the Late War"

they even threatened the postoffice because several of the obnoxious papers were said to have been deposited there. The people of Baltimore had already obtained unsavory notoriety for outbreaks of popular feeling; they had burned Aaron Burr in effigy upon the discovery of his supposed treason and this new act of violence gained for their city the unenviable title of "Mob Town." The Baltimore disorders led to a great change in the political sentiment of the State, so that a number of counties which had been Democratic elected Federal delegates to the next legislature.

In the prosecution of the war, the government planned to garrison and defend the seacoast towns largely by state militia, while the regular forces, aided by such militia as were not needed for coast defense, were employed upon the northern frontier. In these operations in the North, Maryland had no particular part, although her sons were in the regular forces and aided in achieving such victories as were won by the American army. In the meanwhile the State was actively pushing defense measures. The general government was relieved of the necessity of detailing any of the regular troops for this purpose by the generous and patriotic action of the Maryland government in assigning to its own militia the work and providing for their pay from the funds of the State. In this way the forts of Annapolis and Baltimore were garrisoned. But Maryland did not confine her activities to self defense. Within six weeks after the declaration of war a company of Baltimore city and county artillery, under the command of Capt. Nathan Towson, was marching to the front. After General Hull's ignominious surrender of the fort at Detroit, Maryland, feeling keenly the sting of shame which this defeat brought upon the states, hastened to join in wiping out the disgrace by tendering to the President a number of companies, which, however, could not be accepted because of the low state of the national treasury until the state itself should provide for their comfort. Baltimore met this requirement by promptly raising fifteen thousand dollars, with which she equipped for service nearly a regiment of men and sent them to the front under Col. William Winder. Shortly after, these were joined by another company of volunteers. Not only did these men from Maryland go out provided with everything needful for their comfort, but they carried with them as well a flag made by the ladies of Baltimore as an inspiration to them to fight bravely for the honor of their State. It is invidious to make comparisons to the discredit of a sister state, but this action of Maryland deserves the foil which is supplied by the attitude of Massachusetts. Concurrently with Maryland's prompt response to the nation's needs, the latter state was engaged in seeking to evade all responsibility for the general welfare upon the ground that their militia was not subject to the behest of the President and could not lawfully be compelled to serve outside of the state

Recovering from the shock of Hull's defeat, the American army prepared for another expedition into Canada While arrangements for this undertaking were in progress, two Marylanders became the heroes of an exploit which compensated in part for the army's loss of prestige. Lieut. Jesse Duncan Elliott on the 7th of September was sent to join Gen. Van Rensselaer on Lake Erie to aid him with advice as to the construction of ships for the command of the Lake. The young officer was at this time but twenty-seven years of age, and felt profoundly the honor conferred upon him by so important an assignment While he was engaged at Black Rock, the place selected for the building of the ships, the Caledonia and the Detroit, two British armed brigs anchored under the guns of Fort Erie Elliott immediately conceived a plan for their capture and submitted it to the commanding officer, General Smythe, who proceeded to put it into effect For this purpose, he detailed Capt. Nathan Towson with fifty Maryland volunteers The expedition was fitted out in two boats; one under the command of Lieutenant Elliott, with whom were associated Lieutenant Roach of the engineers and Lieutenant Presstman, of Baltimore, in command of the infantry The other boat was commanded by Sailing-Master Watts with twenty sailors and twenty-eight artillerists commanded by Captain Towson. Silently ascending the Lake with muffled oars, they planned to make a simultaneous attack upon the two brigs and carry them by boarding The project was successfully consummated The enemy was taken completely by surprise and in ten minutes time, as Elliott wrote, the prisoners were "all seized, the topsails sheeted home and the vessels under weigh" The expedition, however, had drawn the fire of the enemy upon the Caledonia Sailing-Master Watts supposed that his pilot had not kept close enough to the shore to make a successful attack upon the Caledonia and ordered him to pass on. But Towson intervened and peremptorily ordered the pilot to lie alongside of the vessel. The attempt to grapple with the Caledonia was not fully successful and the boat was exposed to a raking fire from the brig But, nevertheless, the boarding party were soon upon the decks and received the surrender of their foe. The adventure had a sequel in the grounding of the brigs in the Niagara River close to the Canadian shore, where they were exposed to a severe fire from field pieces mounted ashore. Captain Towson lightened his vessel, whose cargo consisted principally of furs, and succeeded in getting it afloat and under sail; only to ground it a second time, but eventually he was able to get beyond the enemy's reach and presented the Caledonia not only as a prize of American valor, but as an addition to that fleet with which Perry was to win his signal victories Lieutenant Elliott had not been so successful with the Detroit and, after burning that brig, had sent word to Captain Towson to take a similar course with regard to the Caledonia This order the resolute commander disregarded The total loss of the Americans in the expedition was two killed and five wounded. This brilliant exploit reflected great credit upon the enterprise and valor of the Americans and served to expiate to a degree the discredit of their late reverses

This invasion of Canada, however, was not successful and General Smythe again prepared to undertake it, but once more met with failure. Colonel Winder's regiment had been detailed to cross the river five miles above Fort Erie, capture the guard, kill or take the artillery horses and to return to the American shore, while a second division under the command of Captain King was sent up the river to storm the British batteries King's division was discovered before it reached the shore and met with signal defeat. The rapidity of the current and the floating ice effectually frustrated Colonel Winder in his attempt to cross the river, and had he succeeded in doing so, he would have found it impossible to put into effect his plan, owing to the alertness of the enemy along the whole shore, who were aroused by the fire upon King. Filled with chagrin and disappointment at the repeated reverses which he met in his campaign against Canada, General Smythe ordered the volunteers to go home and the regular troops into winter quarters.

The land reverses were atoned for by the achievements of the navy and of that irregular branch of the naval service of the times, the privateers. The latter harassed and annoyed their adversaries in every quarter of the globe, crippling the British fleets and preying upon commerce. Their depredations of this sort, as well as their destruction of millions of dollars' worth of property, were potent in bringing about a permanent peace.* Among those who achieved contemporary fame, but whose exploits, being outside of the arena of regular service, have not gained for them permanent recollection in the memorials of the nation, were Boyle, Stafford, Murphy, Wilson, Wiscott, Pratt, Southcomb, Veasy, Levely, Grant, Dawson, Moore, Richardson and many other sons of Maryland, while in the regular service Decatur and Barney gained imperishable glory.

The first notice which America received that England had taken cognizance of her declaration of war by the adoption of offensive measures, was the passage of an order in council on the 26th of December, 1812, declaring the ports and harbors of the Chesapeake to be in a state of blockade. It was not until the 4th of the following February, however, that any considerable force of the enemy appeared in American waters. It was then that Admiral Cockburn, entering the Virginia Capes, took possession of Hampton Roads. By the end of the following month, his fleet was sufficiently augmented for him to declare a state of blockade against the whole coast of the

---

*Coggeshell's History American Privateering; Scharf, vol 3, p. 32

United States, with the exception of Rhode Island, Massachusetts and New Hampshire

In the meanwhile the blockading squadron at the mouth of the Chesapeake sent marauding expeditions up the bay, plundering and burning farm houses and carrying terror to the hearts of the people. Frenchtown, Havre de Grace and Fredericktown and Georgetown (on the Eastern Shore) were plundered and burned. Upon the arrival of the enemy in the Chesapeake, the Governor of Maryland had manifested the deepest concern for the defense of the State. Baltimore was practically at the mercy of the foe. In a letter to the Secretary of War on the 5th of March, 1813, the Governor said that the forts were poorly garrisoned and asked for an assignment of troops. Receiving no reply, on the 20th of the same month he again broached the matter to the Secretary of War, calling attention to the defenseless condition of the state and his anxiety to be informed as to what aid might be expected from the general government in the emergency of an attack upon any of the principal towns.[*] To this inquiry he received the reply that a battalion of militia had been ordered for the particular defense of the city of Annapolis and that a strong body of militia had been organized for the protection of Baltimore. These generalities were followed by other evidences of a lack of concern for the critical position in which Maryland was placed and deep indignation was engendered among the people, which found expression in angry articles in the press. Much anxiety was felt at Annapolis, when upon the 1st of April, 1813, the fleet of the enemy moved up the bay. The Governor called out the militia and again made earnest representations to the Federal authorities of the need of adequate protection. On the 16th of April the fleet threatened the city of Baltimore and so far from evoking sympathy, its plight elicited from some quarters expressions of satisfaction, whose animus was the rapidly developing commercial importance of the Maryland metropolis. The annihilation of trade, necessitating the cessation of many forms of industry had thrown out of employ-

---
[*] Ingraham's Capture of Washington, pp 1-20.

ment large numbers of mechanics and caused even the necessaries of life to rise to prohibitive figures. Many citizens preferred to emigrate with their families rather than to face the situation of want and terror. When the Federal government persistently refused to aid the State, Maryland asked reimbursement for the funds expended in the common defense, but this request, too, was denied. Yet when the government applied for a loan of sixteen millions of dollars, the patriotic merchants of Baltimore subscribed three millions.

Wherever the plundering expeditions of the British appeared, they were met with valor, although the few militia and raw troops hurriedly gotten together could not successfully combat the superior and trained force of the enemy. On the 29th of April thirteen British barges manned by four hundred men made an attack upon Frenchtown, opposite Elkton in Cecil county. Putting to flight the small force of defenders, the British marauders plundered and burned and then passed on to White Hall and from there to the battery erected at Elk Landing, where, after an exchange of shots, they retired and reimbarked. They next appeared at Havre de Grace on the west side of the Susquehanna near the head of the bay. It was then a thriving town of about fifty houses, protected by an insignificant battery of one nine and two six pounders. A small battery was placed at Concord Point and also at Point Comfort. On the 3rd of May, early in the morning, nineteen barges of the enemy's squadron suddenly appeared and opened fire upon the slumbering town. The air was lurid with the glare of shells and rockets. The same scenes of pillage and barbarity were repeated that had discredited the British in all such expeditions. Many acts of personal valor on the part of the defenders of the little town showed the determined spirit of the American fighter. A gallant defense was made by an Irishman named O'Neale, who manned one of the batteries himself and kept up a hot fire upon the barges until he was disabled by a wound in the leg received from the recoil of the cannon which he was firing. He then continued the fight with two muskets, which he loaded and fired until he was captured by the enemy. They threatened to hang him as a

British subject found in arms, but the determination of the Americans to execute two British soldiers in retaliation induced them to spare his life, and the "true and brave adopted citizen" was received as a prisoner of war. Passing up the Sassafras, Cockburn and his troops attacked the villages of Fredericktown and Georgetown At the former place he made an offer to Colonel Veasy that if the shore battery did not fire upon the boats, he would content himself with burning the vessels and the storehouses To this proposition Colonel Veasy made a contemptuous rejoinder; whereupon Cockburn soon put to flight the militia with a severe fire from his guns.

On the 1st of June, Cockburn's fleet was reinforced by a considerable contingent under Admiral Warren, whose ships bore a large force of troops and marines under the command of Sir Sidney Beckwith Thus the State was kept in a condition of serious alarm It became apparent that Baltimore could not hope long to escape attack, and companies of militia were mustered for its defense In the latter part of May Governor Winder convened the Legislature in extra session and laid before them the correspondence which had passed between him and the United States authorities. In his message to that body, he pointed out the recreancy of the general government in not providing for Maryland the protection from the invasion of a foreign foe which the federal compact guaranteed. This portion of the Governor's message was referred to a special committee which a few days later reported, confirming the Governor's complaint and charging the general government with a spirit of partiality in its disbursements to the states for defensive provisions The report of the committee was adopted, and the sum of one hundred thousand dollars was appropriated, or such part thereof necessary to meet the expenses of the state militia already in service

The British contented themselves with depredations along the coast until the reinforcements to the fleet and the addition of large bodies of troops gave them courage to enlarge the scope of the campaign In the meanwhile the American Commodore Barney had been assigned to the defense of the Chesapeake.* This was in the summer of 1813. His flotilla of gunboats was fitted out in Baltimore He soon found himself in command of twenty-six such vessels and barges and a force of nine hundred men, officered by shipmasters and mates of the port of Baltimore In May he proceeded down the Chesapeake with the intention of attacking the enemy at Tangier Island Sailing out of the mouth of the Patuxent River, he fell in with several vessels of the enemy and was compelled to retreat, being pursued by the foe Barney retired to St Leonard's Creek, where on the 10th of June he accepted the challenge of the enemy to an engagement and gallantly bore a tremendous fire, yet without sustaining much injury. The flotilla, however, had done creditable execution upon the enemy, one large schooner being put out of service The experiences of Admiral Cockburn in the waters of the Chesapeake and its tributaries encouraged him to believe that the expedition might be widened to include not only the destruction of Barney's fleet, but also the capture of Washington The British admiral ordered the troops to be in readiness to land and to be provisioned for three days and supplied with fresh ammunition as well as arms and accoutrements Everything being in readiness, on the 19th of August the British troops five thousand strong under General Ross made landing at Benedict on the Patuxent.† In this act they met with no opposition, as there were no American troops within miles of the place General Ross commenced his march towards Washington Immediately the militia of the State and the District of Columbia assembled to the number of about three thousand men under General Winder to oppose their progress But this small and undisciplined force was compelled to retire until they reached the village of Bladensburg on the 24th of August. In the meanwhile the advance of the British had brought destruction to the little fleet of Commodore Barney. General Ross had shown a strong reluctance to concur in Admiral

---
* Scharf, vol 3, p 61
† Ingraham, 14, Gleig's Narrative, p 95.

Cockburn's suggestion of an attack on Washington, but his objections were overcome The destruction of Barney's flotilla was not effected by the British, but was heralded to them by dull, distant explosions The brave commander, rather than permit his ships to fall into the hands of the enemy, to be turned against the Americans, had abandoned and destroyed them

When the British arrived at Bladensburg, they found the Americans assembled in force. General Winder had been reinforced by a body of twenty-one hundred men under General Stansbury, including the gallant Fifth Regiment of Baltimore under Col Sterret, several rifle companies commanded by Major Pinckney, two companies of artillery under Myers and Magruder and by the sailors and marines under Commodore Barney. General Stansbury was stationed on the left of the road leading to Washington with his artillery in a breastwork near the bridge over the Western Branch, with the Baltimore volunteers in advance Colonel Beall, with eight hundred militia was placed on the right of the road, while Winder in person commanded the main body a short distance in the rear The heavy artillery, under Commodore Barney, was posted on an eminence commanding the road President Madison reviewed the army, but, upon the approach of the enemy, withdrew to the city, where he prepared an elaborate collation for the American generals when they should return to the city elated with victory

As soon as the enemy appeared in sight they formed and moved towards the bridge, but were received with a destructive fire from the batteries and the Baltimore rifles The road battery did tremendous execution. When it opened fire upon the British swarming over the bridge, almost an entire company went down under the first fire, but the accuracy of its aim was not sustained and the British troops forced their way across the bridge and, having overpowered the rifles and the Fifth after a brave resistance, they drove back General Stansbury's force, capturing one of the pieces of artillery. Thus the advance or light brigade became established on the opposite side of the river. Flushed with victory, they lightened themselves by casting aside their knapsacks and haversacks and, extending their ranks to show an equal front to that of the enemy, they rushed on to attack the second line of defense, but the Americans, standing firm, received them with a heavy artillery fire followed by musketry, and at the same time advanced to recover the ground which they had lost In this way the precipitate retreat of Colonel Beall's militia and a detachment from Annapolis was prevented from carrying confusion to the main body of the army. The heavy fire poured into the flank of the foe from the battery and the muskets was delivered by Barney and by his marines under Colonel Millar In seeking to avoid the cannon, the British grenadiers fell under the fire of the marines The volleys were too galling to be endured and the confident enemy was driven back upon the main body in disorder. The moment was critical, but, for the want of a sustaining force, the Americans were unable to follow up their advantage, and Ross, having rallied his men and called into action the second brigade, debouched upon the left flank of the Americans and succeeded in turning it By a concerted assault upon the front and the right flank, at the same time the left weakened, the marines were forced to give way; Colonel Millar being wounded, Captain Sevier ordered them to retire. Barney, no longer sustained by a column of infantry, was unable to maintain his position, although his gallant marines continued to work their guns as coolly as upon shipboard, until they were surrounded and some of their number bayoneted at their posts. Then only they retired, leaving their gallant commodore, covered with honorable wounds, a prisoner in the hands of the enemy

Thus far, at least, defeat had not brought disgrace Even while Barney and Millar seemed to be on the point of driving back the foe, the main body of the militia and a body of regular cavalry and infantry never brought into action had been ordered to fall back. The men who had chafed at the folly of their leaders in withdrawing them almost in the moment of victory, now that their backs were turned upon the foe, were seized with panic, broke ranks and dispersed, many of them returning to their homes.* So complete was the rout that the "Bladensburg races" became a favorite theme for the satirists of the day. The American force numbered seven thousand, the British forty-five hundred, although the latter were seasoned troops This battle, which decided the fate of the American capital, began about one o'clock in the afternoon and lasted until four The British accorded the highest praise to the marines under Commodore Barney Their quick and precise serving of the guns, their resolute stand and cool nerve saved the Bladensburg engagement from being a wholly ignominious defeat The loss to the Americans was thirty killed, fifty wounded and one hundred and twenty taken prisoners, although the British estimates placed the numbers much higher.

While the main body of the enemy was thus employed, one detachment plundered Alexandria Another, under Sir Peter Parker, made an inroad upon the Eastern Shore, but with a very different result. Two hundred militia had been collected under Colonel Reed, an officer of the Revolution, and Sir Peter determined to surprise them The British advance, however, found them fully on their guard They were received with heavy fire Pressing towards the right, they attempted to gain the flank of the militia, but were again repulsed Having exhausted the ammunition, Colonel Reed fell back to obtain a fresh supply The enemy, crippled by their severe reception and the loss of their leader, Sir Peter Parker, who was mortally wounded and died early in the action, abandoned their expedition and retreated to the boats, leaving fourteen killed and twenty-seven wounded The Americans suffered a loss of but three men wounded.

With the victory of Bladensburg, every obstacle in the way of the British was removed and their approach to Washington was a triumphal progress. Arriving at the outskirts of the city, General Ross sent in a flag of truce with terms

---
* Ingraham, 23-25; Gleig, 116-123

for capitulation. Claiming that the Americans had fired upon the flag of truce and that his own horse had been shot from under him, General Ross laid aside all thoughts of accommodation and hurried his troops into the town, where, having first put to the sword all persons found in the house from which it was alleged that the shots were fired, they proceeded to burn and destroy everything that in the remotest degree was connected with the government.* At the advance of the British, President Madison and his cabinet had made their escape from the city across the Anacostia bridge, which they caused to be destroyed so that it might not be used by the enemy in pursuit. The people of Washington thus had their exit cut off in either direction and were thrown upon the clemency of their foes. Aside from the alarm of their situation, however, there was no suffering inflicted upon the citizens The destruction of the public records and the library of Congress and public buildings was an act of vandalism of which the British themselves were ashamed and for which the firing upon the flag of truce did not furnish justification, even if that claim was not an afterthought to mollify the feeling engendered against the victors † The capture of Washington was more spectacular than serviceable, as it was impossible for the enemy to hold it Its chief value was the deep impression which it made not only in England and America, but also in France and other parts of Europe. It was hoped by the British that the spirit of their foes would be crushed by the loss of their capital and that they would sue for peace Had the British, instead of proceeding to Washington, pursued the Americans after the defeat at Bladensburg, it is probable that the little army would have met with such chastisement as would have more than compensated in practical results for the temporary abandoning of the Washington expedition

Having triumphantly despoiled the capital of the Union, General Ross turned his eyes towards the flourishing and

---

* Ingersoll, Hist War of 1812, vol. 2, p 167
† Ingersoll, 35-37; Gleig, 124

wealthy city of Baltimore Anticipating his design, the governor had ordered the militia of the State to hold themselves in readiness and large bodies were marched to the city for its defense.* About seven hundred regulars, and several volunteer and militia companies from Pennsylvania and Virginia increased their strength to about fifteen thousand men They were commanded by Gen. Samuel Smith, who had distinguished himself in the Revolution by his gallant defense of Fort Mifflin. One division of the army was confided to General Winder, the other to General Stricker As soon as it was announced that the British were approaching the city, the militia, irritated by the disaster at Bladensburg and the sacking of Washington, flocked in from all quarters in such numbers that neither arms, ammunition nor provisions could be supplied them, and the services of many were of necessity declined As it was expected that the enemy would land and attack the town from the east, heavy batteries were erected on the high ground in that direction and an intrenchment thrown up, in which the main body of the militia was posted. On the water side the city was defended by Fort McHenry, garrisoned by a thousand men under Major Armistead Two small batteries were erected on the south side, while the channel was obstructed by a number of sunken vessels It was September 11, 1814, when intelligence of the arrival of the enemy's fleet was announced to the people by the fire of three cannon, which rudely disturbed the Sabbath stillness. Congregations were dismissed, drums beaten, men on horseback galloped to and fro, rousing the people and every man was mustered to his place. A reconnoitering party was sent out to "feel the enemy" The young men to whose valor this trust was committed unfortunately fell into the hands of the British general The troops, full of enthusiasm, marched out of Baltimore as though upon dress-parade. At seven o'clock on Monday morning, the 12th, General Stricker, the commanding officer of the division, received word that the enemy, under cover of their guns, were debarking at North Point at the mouth of the Patapsco, four-

---

* Scharf, vol 3, pp. 102-7, Dr. Emmon's "Defense of Baltimore."

teen miles from Baltimore. He immediately sent back his baggage under a strong guard and prepared to give the British a warm reception. His force was composed of the fifth regiment under Colonel Sterrett, the sixth, under Colonel McDonald, the twenty-seventh, under Lieutenant-Colonel Long; the thirty-ninth, under Colonel Fowler; the fifty-first, under Colonel Amey, also, one hundred and fifty riflemen, under Colonel Dyer, one hundred and forty cavalry, under Lieutenant-Colonel Biays, and the Union Artillery with six field pieces. In the regiments of the brigade were incorporated Spangler's York, Metzgar's Hanover, Dixon's Marietta and Quantril's Hagerstown Uniformed Volunteers. General Stricker took a position about eight miles from the city, his right resting on Bear Creek and his left covered by a marsh. The fifth and twenty-seventh regiments formed the first line, the fifty-first was posted three hundred yards in the rear of the fifth; and the thirty-ninth in the rear of the twenty-seventh. The sixth was held in reserve. The artillery, comprising six four-pounders, was planted on the main road, and a corps of riflemen pushed in advance as skirmishers. The rifles soon fell in with the van of the enemy, and a sharp skirmish ensued, during which General Ross was killed. The death of the British general filled his army with horror and dismay. The command now devolved upon Colonel Brook. Under him the British continued their advance and at half past three the action commenced with the main body by a heavy cannonade. General Stricker ordered his artillery to cease firing until the enemy should get within close cannister range and brought up the thirty-ninth on the left of the twenty-seventh, while the fifty-first was ordered to form at right angles with the line, resting its right near the left of the thirty-ninth. The fifty-first, in attempting to execute this order, fell into confusion, which, however, was soon remedied. Colonel Brook, perceiving his advantage and hoping to produce a general rout, charged with vigor, the Americans reserving fire until the foe was near enough for their artillery to belch forth its death-dealing "grape and cannister, shot, old locks, pieces of broken muskets, and everything which they could cram into their guns "*

Weakened by the desertion of the fifty-first and two companies of the thirty-ninth, the defenders numbered hardly more than fourteen hundred men. The whole line, undismayed, maintained its ground with the greatest firmness pouring in a destructive fire upon the advancing columns of the enemy. The artillery reopened with terrible effect upon their left, which was opposed to the fifth, while that gallant regiment proudly sustained the laurels which it had won at Bladensburg. This close and hot fire was kept up without intermission for nearly an hour, in the face of a foe more than treble their numbers in action. Their volleys were deadly, for they fired not only by order, but each man at his mark and the front ranks of the enemy were frequently observed throwing themselves upon the ground to avoid the unerring bullets.

Finding that his foe, uncovered on the left flank, was no longer able to make head against the superior strength of the enemy, and having accomplished the main object of his detachment by the severe check which he had given them, General Stricker ordered his line to retire to the position of the sixth, his reserve regiment. This was accomplished in good order, but the fatigued condition of the troops who had been in action, and the exposed position which he occupied, determined the general to fall back still nearer the city The enemy, crippled by the severe contest, did not attempt pursuit, and the brigade, feeling that it had gathered the benefits of a victory, assumed its position near the lines.

The American loss was heavy Adjutant James Lowry Donaldson, a member of the legislature, fell in the hottest of the conflict Lieutenant Andre was killed, Captain Quantril of Hagerstown, Captain Stewart, Major Moore, Lieutenant Reese, Joseph R. Brookes and Ensign Kirby were wounded. The American loss was twenty-four killed, one hundred and thirty-nine wounded and fifty prisoners, a total of two hundred and thirteen The loss of the enemy was nearly twice as great.

---

* Gleig, 175-178

On the morning of the 13th of September, the British made their appearance within two miles of the entrenchments on the Philadelphia road, as if endeavoring to gain the flank of the American position, but, baffled by the skilful manoeuvres of General Smith, after throwing forward a reconnoisance and threatening the lines in front, they retired towards their former position, deterred from the attempt by the strength of the works.

Having thus failed to take the city by land, the enemy hoped that an attack by water would be more successful and on the evening of the 13th the fleet began to bombard the fort, its main defense. The garrison was composed of three companies of United States artillery and three volunteer city companies, under Captain Berry, Lieutenant Pennington, and Captain Nicholson, besides six hundred infantry; in all about one thousand men under Colonel Armistead. For a time the garrison were compelled to receive the fire of the fleet in silence, anchored, as it was, two miles from the fort and beyond the reach of its guns. At length, however, some confusion being created in the southwest bastion by the bursting of a bomb, several vessels were brought within range to follow up the supposed advantage; but the batteries immediately opened upon them with such effect that they were driven back to their former position. At this safe distance they poured a continuous storm of shells upon the gallant defenders of the fort, who held their posts in stern silence, ready to repulse any nearer approach. During the night, several rocket vessels and barges, with fourteen hundred men, supplied with scaling ladders, passed silently by the fort and entered the harbor. Little dreaming of the resistance of the six and ten gun batteries, as they drew opposite to them, the foe, by order of their commander, Lieutenant Webster, opened upon the batteries with a terrific fire. This the fort and the ten gun battery returned with spirit, and for two hours a furious cannonade was kept up, while the heavens were lighted with the fiery courses of the bombs from the fleet and the barges. The havoc was dreadful. One of the barges was sunk and the cries of the wounded and drowning could be plainly heard upon the shore. The rest, in the utmost confusion, retreated precipitately to the fleet.

It was under these circumstances that Francis Scott Key wrote "The Star Spangled Banner." He had gone on board a vessel of the British fleet under the protection of a flag of truce to effect the release of some captive friends and was himself detained. His immortal poem is descriptive of the scenes of that dreadful night and vividly portrays the mingled emotions which thronged his own breast. As the struggle ceased, upon the coming of morn, uncertain of its result, his eye sought for the flag of his country, as he asked in doubt:

> "Oh! say can you see by the dawn's early light,
> What so proudly we hailed at the twilight's last gleaming?
> Whose broad stripes and bright stars through the perilous fight
> O'er the rampart we watched, were so gallantly streaming?
> The rocket's red glare, the bombs bursting in air,
> Gave proof through the night that our flag was still there.
> Oh, say does that star spangled banner still wave
> O'er the land of the free and the home of the brave?"

And then, as through "the mists of the deep," dimly loomed that gorgeous banner fluttering in the first rays of the morning sun, he triumphantly exclaimed:

> "'Tis the Star Spangled Banner! oh long may it wave
> O'er the land of the free, and the home of the brave."

Baffled by land and water, Admiral Cockburn and Colonel Brook determined to abandon the expedition. On the 15th and 16th, the troops were embarked and the hostile fleet dropped down the Chesapeake, leaving the liberated city filled with joy at her triumphant preservation. After burning and destroying the property of the defenseless citizens for some time longer, and threatening the towns on the coast, Cockburn at length withdrew. The gallant defense of Baltimore saved the other Atlantic cities from attack and renewed general confidence in America's defenders when led by brave and skilful officers.

CHAPTER XVIII.

INDUSTRIAL AND GOVERNMENTAL DEVELOPMENT.

EARLY in the ensuing year the war closed by an honorable peace, signed at Ghent on the 24th of December, 1814, and ratified by the United States on the 17th of February, 1815 Maryland once more turned her energies to the great work of fostering her own growth and increasing her strength and resources It was a veritable golden age in the history of the State and Baltimore particularly went forward by leaps and bounds in commercial importance This is not surprising when the situation of Baltimore, her commercial advantages and the enterprise of her citizens are considered The most rapid and considerable increase in the population and wealth of the State took place in that city and in no other period did she stride forward so rapidly as during that of the great European wars, when commerce was thrown principally into the hands of the Americans In 1790 her population had numbered but thirteen thousand. Yet, in ten years it had doubled and in ten years more had almost quadrupled Such rapid growth for so long a period was unprecedented A spirit of activity and progress pervaded every class of society and touched and invigorated all industry During the war the vessels belonging to the port had become scattered in various parts of the United States. Prevented by the blockade from entering the port of Baltimore, the fleet clippers carried the trade of other ports and thus continued to make money for their Maryland owners These were now called home and the trade with China, Batavia, Bengal and other parts of Asia was resumed and greatly extended, as was commercial intercourse with the various countries of Europe The products of a large section of the country were brought to Baltimore for foreign disbursement European imports were greatly augmented and Great Britain particularly sent to Baltimore her diversified manufactures. The same impetus which characterized the trade of Baltimore during the years following the war gave to real estate a higher appreciation in value than it had ever before possessed To accommodate the increasing population, many dwelling houses were erected and their rents for that time were exorbitant

Baltimore, however, was but participating in a wave of prosperity that swept over the whole country and, if her gains were considerable, they were due to her fortunate situation It was impossible that such sudden prosperity should not possess fictitious elements; in fact there was considerable inflation in it. The conditions upon which it was based were not in a real sense normal, and, when the inevitable reaction set in, Baltimore suffered severely Business was curtailed, property depreciated in value, and, when in 1818 the panic set in which brought ruin to many persons and caused the stock of the Bank of the United States to drop one-third in value in the space of a few weeks, many Baltimore business men were among the principal sufferers. Those who were not ruined by the collapse had their spirit of enterprise so shocked that they became as hesitating and timid in making business ventures as they had before been confident and aggressive The setback which the commerce of the city had experienced was but temporary and, if Baltimore's after progress was less buoyant, it was more stable

The part which Baltimore played in the War of 1812 was in the highest degree honorable Her ready financial response to the needs of the nation evoked from President Madison the encomium "The claims of Maryland for her expenditure during the war stand upon higher ground than those of any state in the Union" The burden of the war, however, had laid upon the State a necessity which it had not before experienced.

namely, that of imposing taxation upon its citizens The fund of $1,500,000 to her credit in the Bank of England at the close of the Revolutionary War had furnished sufficient revenue to meet the needs of government; while Baltimore City found the licenses upon retail trade and similar sources of revenue sufficient for her municipal needs. After the war, however, the State's obligations were too large to be met without recourse to the method in use in all of the other states. In 1816 her citizens were required to pay a rate of twelve and a half cents on the hundred dollars.

The rapid growth of Baltimore and the increasing strength and population of the western counties, whose inhabitants had frequently declared their opposition to certain features of the constitution, at length brought the question of its reform into greater prominence and made it the engrossing topic of discussion and the great object of political movement By the system of that day, the senate, the governor and council and the majority of the legislature itself could be elected by a minority of the people As the legislature was composed of four members from each county and two from the cities of Baltimore and Annapolis, the smaller and less populous counties had as much influence in that body as the larger. Six members of the eighty, which at that time composed the house of delegates, were elected from Baltimore city and county; while these paid about one-third of all the funds of the State, excepting such as were derived from sources other than taxation Ten counties, with perhaps little over one-third of the population of the state, could cast a majority of votes. The same held good in regard to the senate, which was chosen by a body of electors of two from each county, and, as the governor and council were selected by the two houses on joint ballot, the influence of the ten smaller counties, if brought to bear, could outweigh that of the larger. The Assembly was thus a confederation of counties with equal voice without regard to population or wealth This disparity had existed from the adoption of the constitution, but, with the rapid growth of Baltimore and the western counties and the diminution of the smaller, it became more glaring. The mode of electing the senate was particularly objectionable As early as 1807 a strong effort had been made to effect an alteration in the system It was corrected so that one member from each county was elected by the people and in the bill for that purpose which passed the house an attempt was made to incorporate a provision regulating the number of delegates for each county in proportion to population. This measure, however, was opposed by the senate and the house ordered the rejected bill to be published in the votes and proceedings for the information of the people * A similar bill met with a like fate in the ensuing year and the struggle seems to have been absorbed by the more exciting questions which occupied the public mind prior to the breaking out of hostilities

No sooner was peace declared, however, than the old disputes were revived Complaints arose from all quarters about the inequality of the system under which the State was governed The dissatisfaction extended to other features besides the organization of the house and senate The mode of electing the governor, the tenure of many offices, particularly those of the county clerks and registers of wills—profitable offices held during good behavior, in effect for life—became the subject of violent opposition For years, however, efforts to effect a change were frustrated. Both of the political parties in the counties which advocated the reform united to secure their object, but in vain The discordant elements of such ill-assorted alliances militated against cohesive effect Finally, however, united effort brought about practical results through the instrumentality of a convention of reformers, of which we shall speak particularly later. This was the reform convention of the 6th of June, 1836

The growth of Baltimore in population, drawn from many sources, naturally resulted in the introduction of many features of social life and organization, to which these persons had previously been accustomed. The most notable result of an effort to establish former affinities was the organization in Baltimore,

---

* Votes and Proceedings.

in April, 1819, of the first lodge of Odd Fellows in the United States The honor of its institution is due to Thomas Wildey, a London mechanic, who came to America in 1817 In order to secure a sufficient number of persons for the organization of a lodge, an advertisement was inserted in the papers, and this resulted in an organization's being effected at "The Seven Stars" tavern, a building which remained standing, an object of veneration to the order until finally destroyed in the great Baltimore fire of Feb 7, 1904. In February, 1821, the Grand Lodge of Maryland and of the United States was organized in Baltimore, but later divided itself into two bodies

The year which witnessed the introduction of Odd Fellowship into Baltimore is notable also for a visitation of quite another character. A malignant epidemic of yellow fever prevailed in most of the large cities of the country, which were put under severe quarantine Baltimore suffered peculiarly in that it was early visited with the plague and the terror of the infection led the authorities of neighboring cities to refuse shelter to refugees The fever, however, was confined to the less healthful portions of the city, and finally came under control. While it lasted, however, business was brought to a standstill and the hills in the northeastern suburbs of the city were dotted with tents for the reception and isolation of the plague-stricken persons *

The interest in internal improvement in Maryland continued to center in canal projects † The immense mineral resources of western Maryland, the rich mines of iron ore and the inexhaustible supply of coal which its mountains contained made it a matter of peculiar importance to Maryland that the designs of the Potomac Company should be carried out, aside from the growing trade with the West But, as we have seen, the Potomac Company had not been successful nor were its plans feasible It was therefore proposed that the Potomac Company should surrender its privileges to a new corporation, to be formed for the purpose of making a canal along the river

---
* Scharf, vol 3, pp 146-7
†Adams, Maryland's Influence in Forming Commonwealth, pp. 109-112

to its head and thence to the waters of the Ohio This was an undertaking of vast magnitude The advocates of the project felt their way along and made the necessary preliminary surveys. In 1821 the states of Virginia and Maryland appointed a joint commission to examine into the affairs of the Potomac Company, and, upon its report of that Company's insolvency and its failure to comply with the conditions of its charter, the Potomac Company on the 3rd of February, 1823, adopted a resolution expressing their willingness to surrender their charter. At the same time a bill was introduced into the Maryland Legislature for the incorporation of a new association to be called the Potomac Canal Company The bill met with active opposition from Baltimore; not because its citizens were not favorable to a canal, but because it called for the appropriation of large funds or credit of the State, one-third of which they would be compelled to pay without receiving commensurate advantages, many even being apprehensive of actual loss through the diversion of the city's trade to Georgetown This apprehension arose from the fact that the canal was to terminate at Georgetown and the company was to have ceded to it the right to the waters of the Potomac River, which would prevent the city of Baltimore from making connection with the canal at any future time Baltimore insisted that, according to the original intention, the canal ought to terminate there instead of at the tidewater of the Potomac Nevertheless the Maryland Legislature approved the design and a convention was called at the city of Washington of delegates chosen by the people of the different counties of Virginia, Maryland and Pennsylvania to consider the best means of effecting the object Fourteen delegates were present, eight of whom were from Maryland, besides representation from the District cities. This was upon the 6th of November, 1823. As a result of their deliberations, it was resolved that a company should be formed to construct a navigable canal by way of Cumberland to the coal banks on the eastern side of the Alleghanies and thence, as soon as practicable, to the highest point of navigation on the Ohio or the Monongahela. It was proposed to have the project put into effect by inducing the federal government to cooperate with the three states for the completion of the canal Subscriptions from private stockholders were also to be received The "Chesapeake and Ohio Canal" was the name finally adopted During the sessions of the convention a communication was presented from two delegates from Ohio proposing a further extension of the work by a canal from the Ohio through that state to the Great Lakes of the north This portion of the design was finally accomplished by that state unaided.

In conformity with the recommendations of this body, an act was passed by Virginia on the 27th of January, 1824, to incorporate the Chesapeake and Ohio Canal * Maryland, Pennsylvania and the federal government confirmed Virginia s action The agitation of Baltimore for consideration of its interests was fruitful in having embodied in the provisions for the canal the reservation of a right for Maryland at any time to construct a lateral section through the District of Columbia and terminating at Baltimore Maryland also had strenuously insisted upon the expediency of the general government's fostering and aiding the completion of the canal as a great national work. It authorized the state treasurer to subscribe in its behalf five thousand shares of stock at one hundred dollars per share on certain conditions It was proposed to construct the canal from Georgetown to the coal banks without delay. The estimated cost of this undertaking was two million, seven hundred and fifty thousand dollars

Books were opened by commissioners appointed for the purpose at a second convention of delegates from the interested states and the District, and the requisite amount of stock was subscribed by June, 1828, at which time the stockholders formally organized and accepted the charter The United States subscribed for ten thousand shares of stock and Congress authorized the District cities to become stockholders They accordingly took an aggregate of fifteen thousand shares The amount of the subscription of Virginia was only seven hun-

---

* Canal records and proceedings, acts, etc

dred and seventy-seven shares These subscriptions, together with the stock taken by individuals, brought the sum total to thirty-six thousand and eighty-nine shares, representing a capital of three million, six hundred and eight thousand, nine hundred dollars It had been estimated that the whole work could be completed to Cumberland on the scale at first contemplated namely, to afford the canal a width of forty feet at the top, twenty-eight at the bottom and a uniform depth of four feet, at a cost of four million, four hundred thousand dollars. The dimensions, however, were afterwards increased, at the suggestion of the general government, to six feet in depth and the width to range from sixty to fifty feet The route was selected and work commenced.

While these measures were in progress, the people of Baltimore because of their fears that the work would interfere with their prosperity and build up the District cities at their expense and their doubts as to the feasibility of constructing the lateral canal turned their attention to the construction of a steam railroad to the waters of the Ohio River In February, 1827, a public meeting was called in the city and a memorial presented to the Legislature It was asserted that the route of the railroad was the only practicable one and that it was shorter by one hundred and forty miles than that adopted for the canal. It was argued that the railroad project could be put into effect at an expense of seven million dollars less than would be needed to complete the canal. A charter was granted by the Legislature for the construction of the road ten days after application had been made

It was soon found that the best route was by the banks of the Potomac. This, however, had already been surveyed for the canal and presented hardly sufficient way for the construction of both works, where the mountains and the river upon the Maryland side came close together The railroad company procured the condemnation of the lands in that section in advance by means designated in their charter. The surveys and other proceedings were taken with such rapidity

---

* Mayer's History of B & O R. R, pp 10, 30, 52 (note)

that they were completed before the Canal Company could procure and serve a writ of injunction. A legal contest ensued, which resulted in the success of the Canal Company, but a compromise was effected by which the Railroad Company was allowed to lay its tracks parallel with the canal to Harper's Ferry, at which point it crossed the river to the Virginian (now West Virginian) shore Several years elapsed before the settlement of this vexatious dispute, which considerably retarded the progress of both works. In order to bestow an equal encouragement upon the railroad, the State subscribed for five thousand shares of its stock, and authorized the city of Baltimore to subscribe for thirty thousand.

The spirit of improvement had now taken hold of the Maryland people and projects of various sorts were advanced. A railroad was projected from Baltimore to York and a company incorporated for its construction under the name of the "Baltimore and Susquehanna Railroad." A branch of the Baltimore and Ohio was laid to Washington. With it was connected a lateral road to Annapolis. Large schemes for draining, improving and canaling on the Eastern Shore were entertained, and on the Western, the rendering of the Monocacy navigable A lateral canal to Baltimore and another to Annapolis were dreamed of as accomplishments for the near future. The schemes which were actually undertaken were liberally subscribed to by the State, which thereby incurred a heavy public debt

In the meanwhile the progress of governmental reform showed as great activity as industrial development. We have seen that on the 6th of June, 1836, the dissatisfaction of Baltimore city and some of the counties with the ratio of representation in its relation to taxation had culminated in a convention where concerted action was resolved upon. Delegates from Cecil, Harford, Baltimore, Frederick, Montgomery and Washington counties and Baltimore city assembled at Baltimore and adopted resolutions advising the people to elect delegates at the ensuing election pledged to introduce into the Legislature a bill to take the sense of the people upon the amendment of the constitution, and providing for the calling of a convention for that purpose in case a majority of the popular vote demanded it. They further proposed that the time for electing the delegates to the convention should be fixed as the first Monday in June, 1837, and that they should assemble on the 4th of July and prepare a constitution to be submitted to the people for their approbation at the October election following They empowered their president to re-assemble the body if the Legislature failed to act upon the matter within forty days "to take such ulterior measures as might be then deemed expedient, just, proper and best calculated without the aid of the legislature to ensure the accomplishment of the desired results."* The preceding Assembly had passed laws which tended to enlarge the representation of the more populous districts, and which only needed the confirmation of the succeeding Legislature, to become effectual. Two additional delegates were by these measures given to Baltimore City, and the new county of Carroll was erected out of portions of Frederick and Baltimore, thus securing four more representatives to the people formerly embraced in those two counties. But this item of incidental reform, only made the reformers more urgent in their demands, and the people seemed disposed to sustain fully the recommendations of the convention.

But these movements suddenly took a most unexpected turn The presidential election was approaching; the spirit of party was at its height, and it was scarcely possible that united action in favor of reform could long be looked for The term of the old senate of Maryland was about to expire and the time had arrived for the election of a college of senatorial electors to choose a new one Party spirit dominated the contest, and upon its close it was ascertained that, although the senate counted a majority of reformers, twenty-one Whig and nineteen Van Buren electors had been chosen † On the third Monday of September, as provided by the State constitution, the

---

* "Brief Outline, etc, of The Nineteen Van Buren Electors"

electors gathered at Annapolis Only twenty-one, however, qualified by taking the official oath As the constitution required the presence of at least twenty-four members to complete the organization of the college, nothing could be done.

The nineteen Van Buren electors having met together in caucus determined, in accordance with instruction from several primary meetings to secure a majority of the senate "of a similar complexion with the people electing them and entertaining the same opinions and sentiments." That, as they represented counties which contained a large majority of the voters, it was right that they, although in minority in the electoral college, should have the nomination of eight members, this being a majority of the senate. Accordingly, they addressed a note to Mr Heard of St Marys, one of the twenty-one electors then sitting in the senate awaiting their presence to proceed with the business of the session In their communication they exacted a pledge from the majority that they would select eight gentlemen, whom they should name. They declared that otherwise they would refuse to qualify, with the result that a senate could not be chosen They affirmed that the immediate consequence of such action on their part would be a disorganization of the government, so that it would became necessary to call a convention for the remodeling of the constitution Mr. Heard promptly declined to receive the letter or to present it to his associates. The latter also refused to hold communication with the nineteen, until they should have qualified according to the requirements of the constitution; whereupon those gentlemen took the further revolutionary step of promulgating an address to the public, announcing their determination not to take part in the election of a senate They set forth the reasons for their course and called upon the people of Maryland at once to elect six delegates, from each city and county, to meet at Annapolis, in convention, and form a new constitution. A counter address was immediately issued by the twenty-one In taking such a radical stand the Van Buren electors rightly interpreted the people's desires, but they were wholly wrong in their confidence that the revolutionary proceedings they proposed would meet with sanction. The people of the State were not disposed to tamely submit to the inverting of the order or relationship between themselves and their legislative representatives The electors were ' mere agents of the people of Maryland selected for a specific purpose, the performance of a single and well-defined duty " They were besides "under the most sacred and solemn obligation to execute a trust faithfully and conscientiously Therefore the people of the State were indignant at being approached "with a proposition of bargain touching the performance of their duty and made reply, 'we never for a moment entertained the idea of trafficking upon such a subject'."* Indeed the sudden and violent movement thrilled the State with excitement and alarm. It was pronounced by men of both parties as a commencement of a revolution, bloodless as yet, but which, if persisted in, must eventually lead to civil commotion and anarchy It was everywhere felt that a crisis was at hand. State credit and public business were disastrously affected, the minds of many were filled with forebodings, while those of firmer moods, on either side of the exciting question braced themselves for the struggle.

Public meetings were convened in many places, and in Baltimore, the center of reform sentiment, a mammoth meeting was held at Monument Square, at which Hon John V. L McMahon spoke in behalf of a series of stirring resolutions endorsing the action of the Whig electors, "in a strain of unsurpassed eloquence and force." The strongest disapprobation of the course of the nineteen recusant electors was expressed and sentiments of strong attachment to peaceful and constitutional reform avowed by all of the speakers. Having nominated candidates for the house of delegates, they called on all good and true citizens to come forward at the ensuing election and by their votes prove their love of law and order Similar proceedings were taken in Frederick, Wash-

---

* Bernard C Steiner, "The Electoral College for the Senate of Maryland, and the Nineteen Van Buren Electors," House Documents, U S Cong, vol 62, p 145

ington and Alleghany counties; and men of both parties pledged themselves to sustain the supremacy of the law.

In the meanwhile, the supporters of the obstructing electors took measures to carry out the schemes proposed for assembling a convention. Meetings were called in several places to nominate candidates and a circular addressed to the people of the counties urging the execution of the project was sent out by a central committee from Baltimore. In fact, many delegates were elected by votes printed on blue tickets, cast at separate polls, opened for the purpose on the day of the November election; a proceeding in which the opponents of the movement took no part.

The twenty-one electors continued at Annapolis, adjourning from day to day, patiently awaiting until a sufficient number should qualify to enable them to proceed to business. They were at length joined by one of the nineteen, who qualified and took his seat. On the 7th of November, the presidential election took place; on the 8th, Governor Veazy issued his proclamation denouncing the proceedings of the remaining eighteen and their supporters, calling upon the people and the militia to hold themselves in readiness to support the law, and convened the old senate and house of delegates to meet on the 21st of November, and solemnly proclaimed "that the constitution of the State must be preserved and the government maintained, as they then were, until altered, changed or abolished in the manner constitutionally provided for." This proclamation was cordially responded to in every part of the State. The people of Prince George's organized and equipped a company of dragoons, under Major John Contee, and offered their services to the Governor to sustain the power of the law; but their aid was never required. On the 12th of the month another of the nineteen entered the college, and was followed in a few days by five others which permitted the election of the senate, and so the storm passed over.

The senate which was elected stood for reform. The lower house had advocated such action for several years and now no further obstructions were thrown in the way of the desired amendments As the new senate had been chosen the old one called to convene at Annapolis did not meet. The deputies to the reform convention, however, still asserted the power to remodel the constitution in the way they had proposed. They met at Baltimore on the 16th of November and passed a set of resolutions declaring that the meeting of the General Assembly would render it inexpedient for them to take further action until it was ascertained what course would be pursued by that body. After expressing their belief that at no distant day a fuller convention than their own but with similar organization would be necessary, they stated the reforms which they desired and adjourned to meet at Annapolis on the 1st Monday of January, 1837, unless otherwise notified by their president. Their adjournment was the act of their expiration. They never again met. It is of interest to notice the nature of the proposals they advanced. These were "the election of the governor by the people, and the abolition of the council; the election of one senator from each county and the City of Baltimore directly by the people; the re-apportionment of the house of delegates so as to do justice to the populous districts, and at the same time to give to the small counties and the City of Annapolis ample power to protect their interest, the abolition of all offices for life, the appointment of judges for a limited time by the joint action of the governor and senate, the election of the clerks and registers by the people, limitation and restraint on the power of the legislature, in the grant of further charters, and the whole constitution to be so arranged and digested as to be free from uncertainty and obscurity "*

When the Legislature assembled it immediately entered upon the work of reform; the result of its deliberations was the adoption of most of the amendments contemplated by the reform movement The governor was made electable by the people, his term of office was fixed at three years, and the State was divided into three gubernatorial districts, from each of which in turn he was required to be taken The Eastern

---

*" Brief Outline of the Nineteen Van Buren Electors."

Shore counties composed the first district; Frederick, Carroll, Harford, Baltimore, Washington, and Alleghany counties the second, and the remaining counties with the City of Baltimore the third. The council was abolished and a Secretary of State provided to supply the place of the clerk of the council. The senate was entirely reorganized on the plan proposed in 1807; one member being assigned to each county and to the City of Baltimore, to be elected immediately by the people. The first election was to be held at the October elections of 1838, and in order that there might be a periodical change in that body, the senators first elected were to be divided into classes, by lot, who were to serve two, four or six years. Upon the expiration of the terms of the different classes their places were to be filled through new elections held in their respective counties, and the term of office of their successors was fixed at six years. So that, always thereafter, at each period of two years, one-third of the whole body would be elected by the people. Thus permanency in policy would be secured as well as frequent accountability of representatives to their constituents. The qualification of a senator was the same as that of a delegate, except that he should have arrived at the age of twenty-five years and have been a resident of the county or city from which he was elected for three years.

The constitution of the house of delegates was materially altered. Five members were assigned to Baltimore City, and the same number to Frederick and Baltimore counties. Four each were given to Anne Arundel, Dorchester, Somerset, Worcester, Prince George, Harford, Montgomery, Carroll, and Washington, and three to each of the remaining counties. Annapolis was assigned one. This arrangement was only intended to last until after the official promulgation of the census of 1840, when, and also at every second census thereafter, the number of delegates was to be apportioned upon a specified basis. This was that every county with a population of less than fifteen thousand according to the federal returns, should elect three delegates; every county with a population of fifteen thousand, and less than twenty-five thousand, should elect four delegates, while every county with a population of twenty-five thousand and less than thirty-five thousand should be entitled to five delegates. Those counties having a population above thirty-five thousand should be entitled to six delegates and Baltimore City as many as the most populous county. After the year 1840 the City of Annapolis was to lose its separate representation and to be considered a part of Anne Arundel county.

The term of service of county clerks and registers of wills was reduced to seven years and their appointment conferred upon the governor who was to act by and with the advice and consent of the senate These alterations were all confirmed at the ensuing session of the Legislature, and became portions of the constitution. The movement of the nineteen recusant electors although repugnant to the constitution had brought to settlement questions which had long divided the sentiments of the people, but more positively of their representatives in the State Legislature. The disputes of more than half a century had now become composed. The unparalleled boldness of these nineteen radicals had shaken the very foundations of the government and of itself had shown the need to some precautionary change in the constitution in order that at no future day a body of men by their independent action should be able again to arrest the machinery of government. The danger of vesting too great powers in the hands of a few had become apparent. Although the motives of the projectors of the revolutionary movement were assailed by opponents as corrupt and their measures as designed to secure the ascendency of their party in the state, there is no reason to believe that they are not to be credited with a measure of the lofty purpose for the regeneration of the constitution which was attributed to them by their friends and supporters.

Having considered the rapid movement of constitutional progress we can turn our attention to industrial matters. The canal was already completed some distance beyond Harper's Ferry when its resources failed The national government determined to withdraw its assistance and Virginia also declined to give it further aid. Maryland was placed in the position of being responsible for the continuance of the work if the project was not to be abandoned before the mineral resources of the western part of the state could be tapped. Another canal convention was called to meet at Baltimore in December, 1834. It was attended by many delegates from the several interested states. They directed estimates to be made of the amounts necessary to complete the canal and the York Railroad and a memorial to be presented to the ensuing legislature asking assistance.* The estimates were two millions of dollars for the canal and one million for the railroad. The legislature granted their prayer and directed the state treasurer to issue the necessary amount of bonds bearing an interest of six per cent., which should not be sold at less than fifteen per cent above par. This premium was to be invested in good stocks to form a sinking fund for the payment of the bonds when due. The tolls of the works were pledged for the payment of the interest on the loan.

It soon became apparent that the two million dollars estimated as necessary to complete the canal to Cumberland was entirely inadequate, and "aid was given by Maryland in the famous eight million dollar bill passed June 4, 1838. In accordance with the provisions of this act the canal company received three million dollars."* The bill provided for a subscription of three millions to the Chesapeake and Ohio Canal, three millions to the Baltimore and Ohio Railroad, half a million to the Maryland Cross-cut Canal, half a million to the Annapolis and Potomac Canal and one million to the Eastern Shore Railroad. The Chesapeake and Ohio's share of the eight million loan, proving unsalable in England, had to be converted by a subsequent legislature into five per cent. bonds. The difficulties of the company were added to by the panic of 1837, during which specie payment was suspended. Like an improvident child, the canal company was again found humbly

---
*History of Public Debt of Maryland, pp. 7-10
*Ward, Chesapeake and Ohio Canal, J H U Studies, Seventeenth Series, p 109

petitioning aid from the Legislature at the session of 1838. With remarkable confidence in the power of the supplicant ultimately to perform its promises, the Legislature granted a subscription to the amount of one million, three hundred and seventy-five thousand dollars. Even in those days of magnificent schemes and extravagant loans, the large and repeated issues of state bonds startled the Legislature, particularly was this the case with regard to the eight million dollar bill It was only after an adjournment of the Legislature in order that the delegates might feel the sentiment of their constituents, that the bill was passed at all The amount of the State's interest in the canal in 1839 amounted to the enormous sum of seven million, one hundred and ninety-seven thousand dollars

In this liberal distribution of favors other companies were not forgotten One million of dollars in state bonds were loaned to the Tide Water Canal Company, for the interest of which its tolls were pledged, and seven hundred and fifty thousand dollars to the Baltimore and Susquehanna Railroad to enable that company to assist in the completion of the York and Wrightsville Road By this time the successive issues of state bonds had reached the appalling sum of sixteen million and fifty thousand dollars Three million, two hundred thousand dollars of this remained in the possession of the Baltimore and Ohio Railroad undisposed of. As long as the companies to whom these loans have been made were able, either from the profits of their works or the proceeds of the bonds which they sold from time to time, to pay the interest falling due upon those already issued, the people were not alarmed at the frightful load of debt But at length the Chesapeake and Ohio Canal Company, having exhausted its resources and become involved in almost irretrievable ruin through issuing over half a million dollars in worthless scrip, was no longer able to meet the calls for interest Other companies were in a similar condition. The prodigality of the State's expenditures for public works received a check of a nature which aroused the people to a consciousness of the bad character of the investments which they had been making, when it was announced that by the 1st of December, 1840, there would be a deficit in the State treasury of five hundred and fifty-six thousand three hundred and eighty-seven dollars and thirty-eight cents *

How was this deficit, almost double the annual revenue of the State, to be made good? Politicians shrunk from the idea of direct taxation as a solution. To postpone the issue for a while, it was proposed to apply to the payment of the interest that portion of the surplus revenue distributed by the United States, which had been received and set apart by Maryland for the school fund, and its bank stock, representing the remainder of the proceeds of the Bank of England stock reinvested in the State. This temporary expedient could at best have met only two years' interest The design was abandoned and it was resolved to have recourse to direct taxation. At the session of 1841 the Legislature, after seeking to minify the State's financial distress, was forced to recognize the gravity of the situation and to have recourse to the only expedient available. On March 23, 1841, an act was passed, supplemented in the following December, levying for the first year a tax of twenty cents on the hundred dollars of assessed value of real and personal property and for the three following years, twenty-five cents. It was expected thus to derive a revenue of four hundred and fifty-six thousand dollars per annum. Certain other laws productive of revenue were expected to realize two hundred thousand dollars more When it is borne in mind that before the passage of the act of March, 1841, the citizens of Maryland had not in any previous year been called upon to pay more than sixty thousand, eight hundred and eighteen dollars in direct taxation, the effect of that levy can be well understood It was contested upon all hands and the State found itself opposed and its efforts frustrated in every direction To make provision for the payment of the interest accruing before any receipts could be expected from the new tax levy, the State treasurer was directed to borrow, upon an issue of bonds of the State, five hundred thousand dollars.

---

* Governor's Messages, 1840-1844

The prostration of the canal company and the frequent failures to complete the work after repeated assistance by the State had thoroughly discredited the enterprise in the mind of the public. Propositions were made to dispose of the State's interest in this and other public improvements to the highest bidders, payment to be made in State bonds at their par value, although at the time they had depreciated fifty per cent. Another scheme which found favor in many quarters was the compulsory transfer of the canal to the holders of the bonds in liquidation of the debt Some few persons openly and avowedly promulgated the doctrine of the unqualified repudiation of the whole debt The consequences of the State's bankruptcy were soon perceived in a pronounced corruption of public feeling. Several counties flatly refused to pay their taxes, collectors failed to act; and, in some places, the people even banded themselves together to resist the execution of the law * The unsoundness of public opinion had, as we have observed, made ineffective the revenue measures, and the machinery for their execution was rendered inactive. All the while the arrears of interest rapidly accumulated

Such a condition could not long continue and it is creditable to the sounder judgment and truer morals of the more serious element of the people that the process of virtual repudiation was checked and public opinion educated to more healthy views The repudiators became an ineffective minority The legislature elected in the fall of 1844, assembled at Annapolis the following December imbued with the determination to restore the credit of the State and to pass such laws as might be necessary for that purpose. They were supported and encouraged in their patriotic resolve by the newly elected governor, Thomas G Pratt, who in his inaugural address recommended the passage of new revenue measures with stringent provisions for their enforcement. A certain degree of confidence was restored. Three years of taxation, discussion, opposition and gradual submission to its necessity during the administration of Governor Pratt's predecessor, Gov-

---
* Short History of Maryland Public Debt (1845)

ernor Thomas, had prepared the people for the policy of the new executive and, finding himself sustained by the trend of public opinion, he was enabled to point the way from the path of repudiation to the honorable restoration of faith in the State's fidelity

Public attention was once more directed towards the Chesapeake and Ohio Canal Company, which showed renewed energy. The canal had been completed from Georgetown to Dam No. 6, fifty miles from Cumberland, and nearly all the remaining space had been partially excavated. It required about a million and a half dollars to insure its completion. By this time the railroad had been constructed as far as Cumberland, but its available resources, like those of the canal, were exhausted. The president of the company made every effort to sustain the work. As it had reached Cumberland and been brought into connection with the western trade and travel, it yielded sufficient returns to keep it from becoming so much involved as the canal company. Both companies renewed their efforts to reach the termini of their routes,—the railroad to the Ohio, the canal to Cumberland.

In 1843 James M Coale, who had been elected president of the Canal Company, by his well considered and active measures, gave a new impulse to the work. He effected an arrangement with the railroad company, by which he secured for the time the transportation of the coal trade from Cumberland to Dam No 6. In consequence of the measures adopted, a marked increase of tolls resulted and the economical administration of the affairs of the company enabled it for the first time to meet its annual expenses from its revenues and, to some extent, to pay off the accumulations of preceding years. The completion of the canal and the restoration of the public credit were intimately related matters, the success of the one depending upon that of the other. Therefore while the Legislature, in compliance with the recommendations of Governor Pratt, had adopted prompt and efficient measures to meet the annual interest of the State without recourse to a direct tax, it was compliant to the earnest representations of Mr Coale in behalf of the canal and, upon the 10th of March, 1844, passed an act waiving the state liens in favor of seventeen hundred thousand dollars worth of bonds, which were to be issued by the company at par in the event that a guarantee should be given to the company that for a period of five years after the completion of the canal, not less than one hundred and ninety-five thousand tons should be transported annually upon it. The energy of the company was directed to securing the guarantee and, aided by the exertions of the western counties and of the District cities, it succeeded Having received the approbation of the state's agents and the governor, a contract was made for the completion of the canal to Cumberland After considerable difficulty, the funds were raised and in November, 1847, work was resumed. At about the same time the railroad company commenced its surveys to the Ohio

In the meanwhile the condition of the finances had rapidly improved. The measures adopted by the Legislature, although objected to for a time, overcame opposition through the ample success which attended them Accumulated arrears of taxes were paid Every county in the State hastened to redeem its credit and the effects of the new spirit were evident in the increased value of Maryland bonds at home and abroad Yet the interest of the debt was still discharged in certificates or coupons, which were received in payment of taxes; but because of their depreciation, the creditor of the State did not receive his full due The condition of the treasury had now become firm and prosperous. Every year a greater sum was received than was needed to pay the current interest, and the surplus was devoted to reducing the arrears of former years. The governor, confident of the ability of the State to meet all of its liabilities, recommended the Legislature to fund the arrears, to repeal the coupon law and to resume cash payment of the interest upon the debt *

'In the spring of 1847 this desirable measure was adopted The arrears of interest during three years had been reduced from one million, four hundred and fifty thousand dollars to

---

* Scharf, vol 3 p. 214

less than nine hundred thousand, and this sum was funded. The accruing interest for the three years was paid and the sinking fund largely added to with the prospect of the liquidation of the whole debt of the State in less than thirty years, this too without the aid of the annual surplus which might be in the treasury. To Governor Pratt, whose wise recommendations to the legislature had much to do with the adoption of the financial measures which rehabilitated the State's credit, was due the fact that on the 1st of January, 1848, the State was able to resume the regular payment of its interest at home and abroad. The incoming governor, Philip Francis Thomas, in his inaugural address felicitated the State upon its financial reorganization.

While the people of the State were occupied with the struggles for the reform of the constitution and constructive works, they were not unmindful of the interests of education. It had been the early pride of Maryland that its metropolis, the ancient city of Annapolis, in colonial days had won the title of the "Athens of America," and the people had long turned their attention to the fostering of education. But the provisions made in those times became entirely inadequate and schools and colleges were erected and sustained by public and private munificence. In 1812 the State Legislature made the first serious effort to provide a fund for the encouragement of primary schools. At that time the charters of the banks were extended to 1835 and they were required to make annual payment of twenty thousand dollars, which was "pledged as a fund for the purpose of supporting county schools."* This sum was apportioned among the banks according to their capital, and was equally divided among the several counties of the state. In 1813 a change was made in the law, so that each bank was required to pay twenty cents upon every hundred dollars of capital stock which it actually paid in. In 1816 nine "commissioners of the school fund" were appointed for each

---
*Bernard C. Steiner, "History of Education in Maryland." U. S. Bureau of Education, Circular of Information, No. 2, 1894. Acts of Assembly, 1812, 1816, 1825.

county to superintend the application of the money, and "a moderate tax on the wealthy for the education of the poorer classes of society" was imposed and constitutes the first resort to direct taxation for the maintenance of schools

The system adopted at that early date was subsequently much altered by local legislation and was finally superseded by the formation of the primary school organization in 1825 This was much more comprehensive. It provided for the appointment by the governor and council of a state superintendent, an office which has recently been revived Nine commissioners of primary schools were established in each county, who were appointed by the justices of the levy courts. A number of "discreet persons," not to exceed eighteen, were constituted inspectors of primary schools The commissioners were empowered to lay off, alter or regulate the school districts, to receive the money apportioned to the county and divide it among the districts, to hold property as a corporate body for the use of the primary schools, and, with the inspectors, to examine and qualify all applicants for the position of teacher. The taxable inhabitants were directed to assemble in their respective districts upon notification by the commissioners and to choose a district clerk, a district collector and three trustees The district meeting also designated the site for the schoolhouse, voted a tax upon the resident inhabitants for its purchase and the erection of a schoolhouse, which the trustees were to keep in repair and for which they were to employ qualified teachers and pay their salaries out of the money placed in their hands by the commissioners. They were required to report semi-annually to the commissioners, who in turn reported annually to the county clerk the condition of the schools. It was made the duty of the inspectors to visit the several schools quarterly at least and to examine into the proficiency of the pupils and the good order and regularity of the sessions. The powers exercised by the levy courts in the counties were vested in the mayor and city council of Baltimore for the regulation of the primary schools of that city. Finally the law erecting this extensive system was required to be submitted to the people and was to be in force only in those counties where a majority of votes were cast in its favor at the ensuing election. The revenues assigned for the purpose were to be divided among the counties and the city of Baltimore in proportion to their white population

This general school system was soon adopted in several counties, but the differing needs of localities effected a modification of its for better general adaptation. When the public debt of the United States had finally been paid off, Congress determined to distribute the surplus revenue among the states. Maryland invested more than six hundred thousand dollars of the amount which she received for the benefit of the schools. The interest of this money, with the former funds and new contributions from the banks, raised the amount annually distributed from the State treasury for public education to sixty-five thousand, six hundred dollars This system gradually went into general operation and in its essential features is still maintained

During the period which this chapter covers a number of events occurred which demand passing mention, either for their wide significance or for their immediate impression. Of such was the laying of the corner-stone of Washington Monument in Baltimore on the 4th of July, 1815, and that of the Battle Monument and the monument to Major Armistead. The first of these was erected after a plan by Robert Mills, and the money for its building was raised through a lottery, permission for the holding of which was obtained by several citizens from the State Legislature The Battle Monument, erected to the memory of the slain in the battle of North Point, is the more closely associated with that notable battle by the date of the laying of its corner-stone, which was the 12th of September, 1815. The Armistead Monument was erected in a Gothic niche in the building at the rear of the old City Spring on Calvert Street, in Baltimore, now the site of the City Hospital. The laying of the corner-stones of these various monuments was attended by impressive ceremonies in each instance.

As early as 1820 the use of oil for lighting began to be superseded by the newly discovered illuminating gas. A company for the manufacture of the new illuminant was formed in Baltimore, and Peale's Museum, on Holliday Street, which building afterwards raised to the dignity of the City Hall, was the first structure in Baltimore so lighted. Many persons paid an admission fee for the privilege of viewing the new light.

In 1825 Maryland had the honor of again and finally receiving General Lafayette as its guest. The man to whose devotion the country was so largely indebted for the independence which it had secured was shown every honor which an appreciative people could bestow. On the 17th of December he came to Annapolis and was conducted to the statehouse by an imposing guard of honor, where addresses of welcome were tendered him in behalf of the corporate authorities, the members of the legislature and the people in general.

Although Maryland was the original home of religious liberty in America, yet until the year 1826 no Jew was allowed to hold any office either civil or military under the state government. The history of the agitation for the enfranchisement of the Jews is an interesting record of a struggle for a right which to-day is so manifest that it is difficult to appreciate the grounds for its denial at any time. In fact the basis of such denial was the force of prejudice. In 1818 a resolution was introduced into the legislature by Mr. Thomas Kennedy, of Washington county, providing for the appointment of a committee to examine into the justice and expediency of conferring upon persons professing the Jewish religion the same privileges that were enjoyed by Christians. A bill embodying the committee's favorable report suffered defeat. However, the issue was a live one and came up at each succeeding session of the legislature until, in 1822, it triumphed. According to the constitution of the State, it was necessary that it should be confirmed by the legislature of 1823 before it could become a law. As the measure was extremely unpopular, many of those who had voted favorably for it failed of re-election.

Finally, at the end of the session of 1824, a bill to alter the constitution so as to afford relief to persons from political disqualification on account of their religious opinions again passed the Assembly This bill was ratified by the Assembly of 1825, and by it the Jews attained the status of freemen in Maryland. From that time on Jewish names in the city council of Baltimore, the State Legislature and in connection with the various public offices became a familiar fact

In 1844 telegraphic communication was inaugurated by the construction of a telegraph line between Baltimore and Washington. Samuel Finley Breese Morse had exhibited a working model of telegraphy in 1835 and received a patent for the same in 1837, followed by an appropriation by Congress of fifty thousand dollars for the construction of an experimental line One of the first messages sent over the newly installed line contained the announcement of the nomination of James K. Polk for President of the United States by the Democratic National Convention then in session in Baltimore

From colonial days much attention had been given in Maryland to the cultivation of the soil. The State's natural wealth in this respect had induced an evil system of husbandry which was productive of the worst results. The author of a "Relation of Maryland," published shortly after the settlement of the colony, said that "the soil was generally rich, and in many places two feet of black rich mould with scarcely a stone, under which there was a loam, whilst there was much ground fit for meadows and plenty of marl both blue and white' Tobacco and corn formed the staple agricultural produce, and these two crops were raised alternately without due regard to the preservation of the soil by a judicious system of cultivation. The consequence was that the richest lands in time became impoverished and those of less strength, entirely unproductive Wide tracts of "old fields" were thrown out into common, as their enclosures fell into decay. leaving a melancholy line of sickly verdure to mark where the slovenly "worm-fence" had stood and rotted. The neglected homestead dropped into ruins slowly and steadily, and at length its owner, deserting his native state and all of its associations, migrated to the new lands of Ohio, Kentucky, or western New York. These desolate wastes met the eye in almost every portion of Maryland and excited the forebodings of men to whom the prosperity of their native state was dear.

It was necessary that an effort should be made to arouse public attention to the agricultural evil and to awaken the husbandmen from their apathy. Agricultural societies were formed throughout the counties, a state association was organized and an excellent journal was established to advocate the cause of improved agriculture. Men of enterprise turned their attention to the restoration of the barren wastes and as a result of their wise efforts and direction the "old fields" were renovated The judicious use of lime, guano and composts soon restored them to almost their original fertility. Many of the streams of Maryland were brought into requisition for the running of mill wheels and to furnish power for the propelling of other machinery, so that manufacturing plants became greatly increased throughout the state, and Maryland's commercial and agricultural importance rapidly advanced

CHAPTER XIX.

ERA OF POLITICAL ACTIVITY.

Upon the fourth of July, 1845, the Republic of Texas was admitted to statehood, adding her "lone star" to the flag of the Union, an act, which, in view of the fact that Mexico had never relinquished her claim to the territory, was tantamount to a declaration of war. Neither country shrank from the encounter General Taylor assumed a position opposite Matamoras. Hostilities were precipitated between the two armies by the murder of Col. Trueman Cross, of Maryland, quartermaster general in the army, who, while riding out for exercise, was attacked by a company of banditi. On the eleventh of May, President Polk sent a special message to Congress, setting forth "that American blood had been shed upon American soil, and that by the acts of her generals, Mexico had proclaimed that hostilities had commenced," and two days later Congress declared war. President Polk issued a call for volunteers and this action was followed in Maryland by the issuance by Governor Thomas G Pratt, of a proclamation summoning the citizens of the State between the ages of eighteen and forty-five to enroll themselves. John R Kenly, a Baltimore lawyer, opened a recruiting station in Baltimore, and the attractions of a campaign in the southwest in behalf of the issue which centered about the erstwhile little republic, whose name had become illustrious through the fame of the deeds of Houston and that band of hardy pioneers to whose Americanism the acquisition of Texas is to be credited, proved to be so strong that volunteers in large numbers enrolled themselves for the patriotic cause.* The two

---
* Kenly's Memoirs of a Volunteer, p 22.

regiments called for from Maryland were not used, but the few men who were received into active service were organized into a body called the Battalion of Baltimore and Washington Volunteers This was composed of six companies, four of which were recruited in Baltimore and two in Washington. Embarking on June 13th from Washington for Brazos Santiago, they proceeded from thence to Matamoras, and took up the line of march a hundred and thirty miles across the country to Camargo, where they joined the army under General Taylor They arrived at that place after eight days of indescribable horror, due to the extreme heat, the burning sand, the lack of water and the mismanagement of the quartermaster and commissary departments

On the first day of September, 1846, General Taylor was prepared to march with an army which both in numbers and in spirit proved sufficient for the achievement of victories which added glory to the American arms and thrilled the United States with enthusiasm Arriving before Monterey on the 19th, he and his staff mapped out the plan of campaign Approaching the city by a devious road through the mountains the Americans found themselves frowned upon by a gloomy citadel The position of the enemy was an extremely strong one. The road along which the Americans advanced brought them in such relation to the citadel and Fort Taneria as to lay them open to a scathing enfilating fire. Nevertheless, the Americans proceeded undaunted and, although many of their number fell under repeated and deadly volleys and their line formation was necessarily broken by reason of the obstructions to their advance, they made their way into the city, where they sought refuge from a fire unremitting and unerring. At the end of the first day's battle, the brigade of General Garland, of which the Maryland battalion formed a part, found it necessary to retire before the storm of missiles Kenly, with his lieutenants, Schaeffer and Aisquith, made their way with the main body of the battalion out of the town under fire of the citadel which opened its guns upon them with redoubled fury. Colonel Watson and Lieutenant Oden

Bowie, however, with a few of the men, becoming separated, sought another exit They met Mitchell's First Ohio Volunteers marching to the support of Garland and joining them, returned to the assault Colonel Watson fell a few moments later, struck in the neck by a bullet and instantly killed.

The city held out four days, although the second day's engagement went far towards determining the victory of the Americans.* On the 25th of September a tribute was paid to the valor of the Baltimore contingent of the troops when the flag which had been presented to the battalion by the patriotic women of Baltimore was unfurled in place of the Mexican colors which had flaunted defiance from the tower of the Bishop's Palace It was not an empty honor which was accorded to the men of Maryland for not only had their valor been illustrious but their losses had been severe. Maryland had now dedicated itself to the patriotic cause by the deaths of Ringgold, Watson and Ridgeley The first had fallen in the battle of Palo Alto, and the last, who had won the admiration of the army by his courage and the reckless exposure of his person to the fire of the enemy, met his death a few days after the fall of Monterey, by being thrown from his horse †

Upon the death of Colonel Watson, Major Buchannan of the Fourth U S Infantry was assigned by General Twigg to the command of the Baltimore battalion. In assuming command he declared that "A native of Baltimore and a citizen of Washington, his only desire was to make the battalion worthy of the cities which sent it forth" Major Buchannan was a man fitted by temperament for military direction and by education as well, being a graduate of West Point and having made a splendid record in the war of 1812 at the battle of North Point. On the 10th of December the first division was reorganized for a march to Victoria, 200 miles to the southwest, and the Baltimore battalion was incorporated with it By the 29th their destination had been reached and the

---

*Kenly, pp 95-100, 105-113, 121-132.
†Kenly, p 160

town taken Baltimore's colors were again given the place of honor, waving proudly from the statehouse. On January the 11th General Scott succeeded General Taylor in command of the American forces in Mexico, the latter returning to Monterey to direct the operations of the army of occupation Pressing on to Tampico and finding that place already in the possession of the Americans, it having been captured by Commodore Connor of the Navy, General Scott marched his forces upon Vera Cruz, which fell on the 29th of March. The Baltimore battalion did not take part in this engagement, having been left behind as part of the garrison at Tampico, an assignment of duty regarded by the men as a high honor The campaign on the Rio Grande had been ended on February 25th by the victory of Buena Vista, which not only added imperishable laurels to the renown of General Taylor but left General Scott free to operate from a new base After performing garrison duty until the 30th of May, the Baltimore battalion was mustered out of service and returned home with a record of achievement which won for them the gratitude of the people of their native state. On the 10th of July, under fitting circumstances the flag which had floated from Monterey was presented to the city of Baltimore and accepted in behalf of its citizens by Mayor Davies *

By arrangement between the war department and the governor of Maryland, a new battalion was raised to take the place of the troops mustered out of the service, and upon his arrival in Baltimore Captain Kenly was commissioned major of the battalion, of which Brevet-Major George W. Hughes, of the U. S. Army, was appointed by the President lieutenant-colonel On the 24th of July the battalion sailed from Baltimore under command of Major Kenly. Arriving at Vergara August 26th, Major Kenly was assigned to the command of the forces at that point. On the 1st of September Colonel Hughes arrived, and upon the 6th the line of march was taken up to join Scott before the City of Mexico, On the 9th Colonel Hughes surprised the enemy at National

---
* Kenly, pp 272-5

Bridge, one of the strongest natural passes in Mexico, and the rendezvous of numerous guerilla bands. This effectually disposed of a system of irregular warfare which was a principal reliance of the enemy.

On the 10th of August General Scott moved to the assault of the City of Mexico with ten thousand men It was a daring undertaking, because of the natural strength of the city, its splendid fortifications and its garrison of select troops, under General Santa Anna; a force which numbered 35,000 men. After a hot engagement lasting from the 12th to the 14th and marked by many instances of courage upon both sides, the city surrendered.

On November 5th the Baltimore battalion left National Bridge to join Scott at the City of Mexico, but on November the 22nd they were ordered to Jalapa as a portion of the garrison of that place. Upon his surrender, Santa Anna came into the American lines and the Baltimore battalion was assigned to escort him to the coast.* On the 2nd of February, 1848, the treaty of Guadalupe Hidalgo was signed. With the end of the war the active labors of the Baltimore battalion were brought to a close, but it could not at once be relieved of garrison duty, and not until June 16th did it leave for home, being mustered out of service at Pittsburg on July 12th. The men were received with honors in Baltimore, and the State felt that although its numerical representation in the war had been small, its achievements were vastly out of proportion to its numbers On the 29th of January, 1850, the General Assembly passed a vote of thanks to its valiant troops The territory which was gained by the United States through the war with Mexico was a gain in geographical area but it afforded new opportunities for friction when the great issue of slavery extension sundered the counsels of a great and free people. Maryland's part in the acquirement of that territory was indeed another contribution of the state towards that problem, but also towards the crowning glory of ultimate American union and progress

---

* Kenly, p 391

As a result of the War with Mexico, General Taylor became the logical candidate for the presidency. Although it was conceded that his qualities were not those of the statesman but of the soldier, it was felt that he was worthy of the highest distinction that the nation could bestow and that the affairs of state might with safety be intrusted to him. The fact that he was a "no-party" man did not detract from his availability, but rather was a further reason for his general popularity. Maryland shared in the prevailing sentiment. Upon the 26th of April, 1843, a "Taylor State Convention," which was composed of prominent and influential gentlemen irrespective of party affiliations, met and put in nomination General Taylor for the presidency of the United States. Although the general was induced to say that he was a Whig, the party managers derived little advantage from the declaration, for he insisted that "he would not be the president of a party but the president of the whole people."* When the new president made selection of the members of his cabinet, Reverdy Johnson of Maryland was tendered and accepted the portfolio of attorney-general.

The great overshadowing question in Maryland, as well as throughout the country generally, was that which resulted in the break up of the old political parties and the recasting of affiliations—the question of slavery. The admission of Missouri into the family of states had brought the issue sharply into the national arena, and the sectional nature of the question of whether the applicant should be admitted with or without a slavery stipulation ranged the states of the North and those of the South into antagonistic camps. New England spoke in no uncertain tones for a prohibitory provision. On the other hand, Virginia and Kentucky as earnestly declared for the recognition of slavery. Maryland's sympathies went with Virginia. Nevertheless, the position which that state was to occupy upon the gravest subject in the country's entire history was forecast by division of sentiment which was significantly

---

* Rhodes Hist of U S, from the Compromise of 1850, vol 1, p 99

shown by an assemblage of citizens in Baltimore presided over by the mayor, which petitioned Congress against the further extension of slavery The geographical situation of Maryland indicated for the State a neutral position upon the matters at issue Her division of sympathies was consequently intensely acute These facts make an recital of the place of the State in the mighty movements of the time more difficult than that of any other State in the Union.

Until the issue of slavery took the form of a sectional question, Maryland's relation to the institution was not different from that of the other states which by reason of the nature of their industries became large employers of slave labor. Negro slaves had been brought into Virginia in the infancy of that colony and from there introduced into Maryland. The first slaves imported into Maryland were brought from Bermuda in 1634.* The first mention of slaves by the Maryland General Assembly was in 1663, at which time the planters were profiting greatly by slave labor. So much so in fact, that eight years later an act was passed to encourage their importation The great influx of negro slaves, however, necessitated the passage of restraining legislation, so that in 1695 the Assembly imposed a per capita tax of ten shillings upon all slaves brought into the State, the proceeds to be devoted to the building of a statehouse. A circumstance which greatly influenced the slave traffic in its relation to American development, and so influenced politically and economically the State of Maryland, was the treaty of Utrecht, by which Spain guaranteed to England the monopoly of supplying negro slaves for the Spanish-American provinces. The importations of large numbers of slaves into those dependences made them bases of supply for the North American colonies The negro population of Maryland continued to grow and various disability acts were passed to arrest miscegenation and other evils.† In 1760 an act of the Legislature declared it impossible for a negro to secure his freedom by becoming bap-

---
* Rhodes, vol 1, p 3
† Rhodes, vol 1, p. 11.

ized Heretofore this had been popularly but erroneously supposed to afford an easy and rapid method of emergence from servile condition

Just prior to the breaking out of the American Revolution in 1775, the negro population of Maryland was 20 per cent. that of the white, and this was about the same proportion that obtained in other of the British colonies [*] By a British order in council, passed in 1770, the colonial governors had been instructed to assent to no law whose object was the restriction of the importation of slaves, but in 1783 we find Maryland, keenly sensitive to the evils of a large servile population, putting upon its statute books an absolute prohibition of further importation of slaves.

With the end of the Revolutionary War and the ratification of peace with Great Britain the American Congress found itself called upon to legislate for a vast territorial area which was ceded to the federal government by the several states which claimed it under their colonial charters. The cession of the Northwest Territory to the general government stands as a monument to Maryland's high conception of the Federal Compact. As it was largely responsible for federal territorial sovereignty, Maryland was thus indirectly responsible for the creation of the great issue which in its finality threatened to sunder the Union. For it was in the territory thus ceded that the question of slavery became critical Whether or not the ægis of the constitution should cover the institution of slavery in territory specifically national was the question that precipitated the great historical debates in the national forum and gave occasion for those decisions of the Supreme Court which to no small degree helped to precipitate the Civil War In 1784 Thomas Jefferson introduced an ordinance providing for the prohibition of slavery into the ceded territory after the year 1800. This proposed interdiction covered the territory from which was subsequently carved the States of Alabama, Mississippi, Tennessee, Kentucky, as well as the Northwestern territory The anti-slavery clause was lost by

---

[*] Bancroft, Hist U S, vol 2, pp. 270, 290

one vote, which circumstance drew from Jefferson an expression which told how ardently devoted he was to the restriction of slavery. In a letter written two years later he said: "The voice of a single individual would have prevented this abominable crime Heaven will not always be silent, the friends of the rights of human nature will in the end prevail" In 1787 a substitute for Jefferson's act of 1784 was passed restricting the anti-slavery prohibition to the Northwest territory. It provided also for the yielding up of fugitive slaves. This ordinance partook of the nature of a compromise and received the support of the representatives of four of the Southern States It was in no way regarded as an anti-slavery triumph. At this time slavery was regarded as a decadent institution. It had been abolished in seven of the states and the man would not have been regarded as fatuous who should express a conviction that in his lifetime he would see Maryland, Virginia and Delaware free states Although the evolution of sentiment seemed to mark the end of slavery by a gradual process there was an industrial circumstance which fastened the institution upon the Southern States with a tenacity it had never before possessed. This was the introduction of Eli Whitney's cotton gin.† Its contribution to the manufacture of cotton fabrics made the cotton crop throughout the Southern States the great source of wealth of that section. Immediately there was created a great demand for cheap field labor which could not be met under the existing social economy except by the extensive employment of slaves. The talk of gradual self-purgement by the Southern States of the institution of slavery ceased. Maryland, bound by hooks of steel to her Southern sisters came under the influence of the revulsion of feeling and whatever prospect there had been that Maryland by voluntary action would become a free state passed away. Nevertheless there was not wanting a party within the state to strenuously fight for the emancipation of the slaves of Maryland. In 1789 anti-slavery sentiment crystallized in

---

† Rhodes, vol. 1, pp 25-27, Webster's Works, vol 5, p. 338

the organization of an abolition society * This society rapidly increased in membership and in 1797 numbered two hundred and thirty-one persons including many of the best people of the State It was then the third largest organization in the country. However meritorious was the purpose of the abolitionists of Maryland, the effecting of an organization with a strong arraignment of slavery and a declaration of a purpose to bring about its overthrow, served to correspondingly strengthen the position of those who did not share such sentiments

Charles Carroll of Carrollton was one of those who bitterly lamented the existence of slavery and although he himself was a large slaveholder, he would have been glad to have had some satisfactory plan adopted to relieve the country from the evil He was especially concerned for the abolition of slavery in Maryland. In 1797 he introduced into the Senate of Maryland a bill to that end It provided for a purchase by the State of all the female children of slaves who were to be educated to the point of appreciation of freedom and usefulness and to be bound out until twenty-eight years of age, at which time they were to be given full liberty. At a given date all persons in servile condition under forty-five years of age were to be free. The bill however failed to pass. Washington was another of the illustrious men of his day who hoped to see Maryland rid of slavery and believed that it would come to pass.† But as we have already said, all such optimistic hopes were frustrated by the invention of the cotton gin. The session of Congress of 1820 marked the beginning of a brilliant series of political orations unsurpassed in the history of public debate. To Maryland belongs the honor of having had one of her sons deliver a speech which although it was never printed, has come down to us in contemporary opinion

---

* Maryland Journal, Dec 15, 1789
† Letter of Washington, expressing his belief that Maryland and Virginia would soon gradually abolish slavery. Spark's "Washington,' vol 12, p 326

as one of the most thrilling ever delivered in the halls of Congress † Senator Pinckney, to whom this reference applies, spoke against the imposition of the restriction of slavery on Missouri as a condition of its admission to statehood Although Pinckney always made careful preparation, he sought to have his rhetorical periods have the air of spontaneous eloquence A student of great application, he had the curious craving to be regarded as an elegant man of leisure, to whose natural genius alone was to be attributed his splendid forensic ability

An organization which sought to relieve the country of the incubus of slavery in a progressive and peaceable way had been organized in Washington in 1816. This was the American Colonization Society. The purpose of the benevolent gentlemen comprising it was the colonizing of the free people of color of the United States in Africa It was proposed that as masters manumitted their slaves this society should secure their transportation to the free state they sought to organize in the dark continent

In 1831 the Orion was fitted out by the State Colonization Society in Baltimore and sailed for Monrovia. It carried thirty-one emigrants. The scheme had taken hold upon the interest of the well disposed people of the State, and the Legislature made the annual appropriation of ten thousand dollars for twenty-six years for the transportation of emigrants and their care after their arrival. Thus Maryland gave an exhibition of practical effort for the welfare of the colored race and assessing itself above a quarter of a million of dollars in its behalf. Even at the time of its financial embarrassment when the interest upon the public debt could not be met, this annual appropriation was sustained. And at the expiration of the term for which the appropriation was made, the act was successively renewed for periods of six, four, and six years. At the expiration of the last extension the breaking out of the war gave another aspect to the problem In respect to her interest in and expenditure for the colonial experiment and her laws permitting the manumission of slaves, in addition

---

† Benton's "Thirty Years' View," vol 6, p 20

to various statutes for the amelioration of their condition, Maryland, for a state whose affiliation and environment were Southern, must be credited with having taken high ground in her attitude toward the subject race.

It would be difficult to exaggerate the effect upon public opinion in Maryland of the servile insurrection which was attempted in Virginia in 1831 by Nat Turner, a fanatical slave of exceptional capacity, who, construing an eclipse of the sun into an omen, preached from it a crusade among his fellow slaves, exhorting them to rise and slay their enemies, who he declared had deprived them of their freedom. Maryland deeply sympathized with her sister state in the scenes of murder and distress which were thereby wrought. It was not strange that these social disorders were attributed to the preaching of abolition and it is highly creditable to the states concerned that although feeling ran high against those to whose influence the negro unrest was attributed, they read in such disorders the portent of calamity and sought to rid themselves of the coils of slavery.

The practice of kidnapping of slaves prevailed in the border states and led to interstate controversies, the merits of which came before the Supreme Court of the United States for decision through the case of Edward Sprigg, which was appealed from the Pennsylvania courts to that august body. In 1839 Sprigg had carried out of the State of Pennsylvania a colored woman named Margaret Morgan and her three children, who had fled from servitude in Maryland six years before. He delivered them to the claimant. For this Sprigg was brought to trial and convicted of the breach of a Pennsylvania statute. Justice Story delivered the opinion of the bench that the Pennsylvania act was unconstituional and void for the reason that the constitution in the clause providing that fugitives from labor should be delivered up, thereby created a new right over which Congress had sole jurisdiction Inasmuch as the clause was not in the state constitution and did not make demand upon the state authorities, the national government was bound to its execution, and the rights of the owner not being affected by state boundaries, he might seize and recapture his slave wherever he might be, provided that in so doing he did not make breach of the peace or commit an act of illegal violence. To this decision Chief Justice Taney dissented upon the ground that it invalidated the act of Congress of 1793, which provided for the recovery of fugitive slaves through the agency of the proper judicial officers of the state in which they were apprehended or those of the United States *

The organization of the American Anti-Slavery Society in 1833 in Philadelphia represented an attempt to give greater force to the advanced position of such abolitionists as Garrison and his associates In the Declaration of Sentiments they drew up, the doctrine of abolition was fortified with argument and brought by analogy into relation to the declaration of independence. Yet even that organization did not contemplate national interference with slavery in the states. This meeting was looked upon by the people of the South and even by many of those in the North much as to-day an assemblage of anarchists would be regarded.

During all this period of agitation and partly because of it there had been a gradual revolution of Southern sentiment. The apologetic tone towards slavery had changed to one of confident assertion that its perpetuation was bound up with the interests of that section. This new attitude was strongly reflected by the Southern representatives in the national council In 1840, William Cost Johnson, of Maryland, introduced the so-called "gag rule" in Congress, which effectually put an end to the reception of anti-slavery petitions † A further significant sign of the massing of pro-slavery sentiment was given by a convention of the slaveholders of the State, held at Annapolis, in 1842. Feeling that their rights had been subjected to such serious attack as to demand from them some united action, they not only endorsed the institution of slavery but recommended to the Legislature more stringent laws in regard

---

* Scharf, vol 3, pp. 326-7, Smith, Political History of Slavery, vol 1, pp. 66-69
† Rhodes, vol. 1, pp 69-70   Morse's Life of John Quincy Adams, p 251

both to slaves and free negroes. By 1844 the pro-slavery sentiment in Maryland found concrete expression in the passage by the State Legislature of a series of resolutions in endorsement of slavery.*

The question of slavery had come up in connection with the reform of the constitution in 1836. It was feared by many that the convention might touch the relation of master and slave and those vitally interested in the question took care to have an additional guard thrown around their rights. To this end a provision was engrafted upon the constitution "That the relation of master and slave in this state shall not be abolished unless a bill for that purpose shall be passed by a unanimous vote of both branches of the general assembly, be published three months before a new election, and be unanimously confirmed by the succeeding legislature." Even then it was required that full compensation should be made to the master for the property of which he would thereby be deprived. The insertion of this provision was due to the feeling of resentment engendered against the abolitionists because of their aggressive propoganda. Such was the constitutional position of Maryland upon the subject of slavery at the time the "Wilmot Proviso" sounded the call of the sections to their hostile camps. As the whole subsequent history of slavery and the strife of the Civil War are related to that epoch-making provision, we may leave for awhile its consideration and take up a topic which while only indirectly connected with the subject of slavery nevertheless forms an integral part of the political history of the period.

The slavery agitation had been productive of a theory of nationality such as had not before been entertained by the people. The sturdy assertion of the doctrine of States' Rights was the answer of the Southern section of the country to the dogma of national supremacy. It is a curious circumstance, however, that coordinantly with the sentiment for State sovereignty there was awakened in some of the South-

---
* Scharf, vol 3 p 328
† Von Holst, "Constitutional History of the United States," vol 3, pp. 285-8.

ern States—together with the Northern—a feeling of conservative nationalism which found expression in the odd political movement popularly known as Knownothingism. It is also a singular circumstance that many of the leaders of this movement in Maryland, which was one of its strongholds, thereby became broadened out of their States' Rights attitude, and, when the great conflict was precipitated, abandoned their former position and fought for the preservation of the Union For a number of years opposition to the vast increase of foreign population due to immigration had been slowly taking form. In 1844 Baltimore contained about fifty thousand persons of foreign birth, one-fourth of its total population The magnificent opportunities offered by the United States had turned thither a tide of immigration which, at first welcome, had subsequently become a source of irritation to many who saw in it a menace to the privileges of themselves and the safety of their posterity. It was seriously believed by a great many that it was a part of the policy of the European governments to send over to this country the undesirable elements of their population so as to weaken the national character as well as the national tie and thereby sow disorders in the country. After the revolutionary outbreaks in Europe in 1848 great numbers of Germans came to America to await the passing over of the storm and then to return to their own country, they did not seek naturalization and some of them even vaunted that they would establish German states in the west and defy the government of the United States. These sentiments took on an alarming character in the popular imagination and opposition to them found expression in the halls of Congress, where many earnest anti-foreign speeches were delivered Various German organizations were formed in Baltimore and other cities and schedules of "reforms" were promulgated, embodying the various demands of the foreign born elements of the population. These in the main reflected the socialistic opinions current in Germany and France.

As early as 1844 the Baltimore Clipper had announced its advocacy of an American Republican Party in opposition to immigration.* This party was organized and in 1846 polled three thousand, three hundred and forty votes for a state ticket, and though it proved short-lived, the anti-foreign sentiment remained Distrust of the large foreign element in the State was greatly intensified by the introduction in the Legislature in 1852, of a measure known as the Kerney School Bill, for the division of the school funds between the public and parochial schools †

The rise of the Knownothing or American party is involved in obscurity by reason of the fact that for a long time members of its secret lodges would not admit its existence and when interrogated with regard to it would invariably reply "I don't know." This gave name to the movement. The first lodge in Baltimore is supposed to have been organized in 1852. This secret party had for its tenets opposition to the progress of the Roman Catholic Church and the advocacy of a longer term of residence for foreigners, before extending to them the privilege of naturalization Its watchword was a saying attributed to Washington, "Put none but Americans on guard to-night" The Knownothings had vigorously opposed the Kerney School Bill and under the title "The United Sons of America," had addressed a circular to the candidates for election to the legislature. asking them if they favored the passage of that bill. The Democrats would not commit themselves but the temperance candidates announced their opposition Accordingly, a combination was effected resulting in the election of the entire city legislative ticket. The following year the Knownothings carried the election in Hagerstown and also put in nomination Samuel Hicks for Mayor of Baltimore, electing him by a majority of two thousand "Unannounced to the public, unknown to the press, with no published account of its proceedings, no one possessing any information concerning it, except the delegates, this new party * * * met in a secret convention and put forth

---
* Baltimore Clipper, Nov 5, 1844
† H D Journal, 1852, pp 607, 768, 1853, pp 330, 577

its candidates."* The election was characterized by great disorders in some of the wards; the Democrats attempted to carry their ticket by the same discreditable measures which were employed by their opponents. The streets were paraded by the two parties who met at Fayette and Exeter Streets in a battle in which pistols, clubs and stones were freely used.

It became impossible longer to disguise the existence of the party or to preserve secret its tenets or its personnel. In 1855 the Knownothings came out as a distinct party, held a convention in Philadelphia and promulgated a platform.† Almost every state in the Union was represented. All secret machinery was abolished and the party went before the country with a set of principles which centered in a demand for "more stringent naturalization laws" and resistance to the "aggressive policy and the corrupting tendencies of the Roman Catholic Church" The reading of the Bible in the public schools was upheld and a declaration was made in favor of the existing slavery laws and denying the right of Congress to legislate upon the slavery question

In the elections of that year Henry Winter Davis, the Knownothing candidate for Congress from the fourth Maryland district, was elected. The party carried thirteen counties and the city of Baltimore The clause of the Knownothing platform which gave most serious offence in Baltimore was that which declared opposition to the Roman Catholic Church, many persons in the state who were pronounced Protestants did not favor an indictment against a faith which had given to Maryland the majority of its founders and had produced such peerless characters as Charles Carroll of Carrollton and Roger Brooke Taney. The Knownothing party denied the charge of intolerance, and asserted in its defense, that the Roman Catholic Church had identified its interests with one of the leading parties, and that in various parts of the country its representatives had been guilty of indiscretions which menaced the public school system, and which had not been repudiated by

---

* Schmeckenbier, History of Knownothingism in Maryland, p 18, Balto Sun of Sept. 27 and Oct. 12, 1854
† Schmeck, pp 21-22.

the authorities of the church. On the other hand, a declaration was elicited from the Archbishop and Bishops of the Province of Baltimore in which the strongest assertion of allegiance to the civil authority was made and the charge emphatically denied that the head of the church at Rome was regarded in any other than a spiritual capacity. The political atmosphere, however, was not cleared by these respective declarations. The Legislature in 1856 showed an overwhelming Knownothing majority in the house although that party was barely strong enough to effect an organization in the senate. Hardly had the Legislature convened when Governor Ligon, who was a Democrat, sent a message to the body in which after reviewing the affairs of the State he added that he would be recreant to his duty if he did not call attention to "the formation and encouragement of secret political societies."[*] He pointed out that some of the most cherished principles of the government were thus endangered and added "If on one hand we permit brute force to control the ballot-box and violence to deter the quiet and peaceably-disposed citizens from the exercise of their right of suffrage, or on the other hand allow a citizen to be proscribed on account of his religious faith we poison the very fountain of public security, our Constitution becomes a solemn mockery and the Republic a cheat and a delusion whose very essence is despotism." This part of the Governor's message raised an issue between him and the majority of the legislature and resulted in the appointment of a committee to summon witnesses and receive evidence in regard to the Governor's charges, from which nothing, however, of material value resulted.

The following year witnessed exciting scenes in Baltimore. There were riots at Lexington Market and the Washington Monument. Four persons were killed in the melée. That year Thomas Swann, the Knownothing candidate, was elected mayor by a majority of seven thousand. Political clubs were numerous and on both sides were chiefly noteworthy for the number of reckless and desperate characters included

---
[*] Scharf, vol 3, pp 246-9, Schmeck, p 50, Gov Message, 1855

in their membership The following extract from the diary of Dr. L H Steiner, under date of October 8th, will suffice to give a picture of a situation which unfortunately was true not of a single day but in its essential features of that whole unfortunate period: "This has been one of the most disgraceful days for Baltimore. From early in the morning until very late at night, both parties have been drawn in deadly array against each other, and Plug Uglies and Rip Raps and Eighth Ward Blackguards have endeavored to see which could be vilest and most inhumane The so-called American party seems to have the most villainous material in its composition, while the other side has never been deficient in that article A number of men have been killed to-day and over fifty wounded, more or less dangerously At some of the polls, only such as were of the party predominating at the polls were allowed to vote. Affairs going on in this way and the elective franchise will become a humbug "* In view of the approaching state elections, Governor Ligon in 1857 addressed a letter to Mayor Swann, calling his attention to the disorders attending the municipal and presidential elections of the preceding year and asking him in view of the apparent inadequacy of the police department what further measures he would take to prevent a repetition of such scenes. Receiving a rebuff from the mayor, the governor issued a proclamation addressed to the citizens of Baltimore in which he reviewed the disgraceful occurrences of the year before and stated that in discharge of his duty to insure to the voter the rights guaranteed him by the constitution, he had directed the proper military authorities to enroll and hold in readiness their several corps The city was thrown into a high state of excitement by the Governor's proclamation and the mayor hastened to obtain legal opinions as to the validity of his action, as did Governor Ligon himself.†

In compliance with the urgent appeal of a committee of citizens, the mayor issued a proclamation in which he set forth

---
* B C Steiner, "Citizenship and Suffrage in Maryland," p. 39
† Scharf, vol 3, pp 252-262, Schmeck, pp 74-87

just what extraordinary provisions he contemplated for the preservation of order and honesty of elections; which, being satisfactory to the governor, led to a further proclamation from him disavowing a purpose to place the elections under military control. The threat, however, had had a salutary effect and the elections were remarkably peaceful The usual election devices, however, were resorted to and corruption was rampant Hicks, the Knownothing candidate, received seventeen thousand, eight hundred and fifty votes as against eight thousand, two hundred and eleven cast for his opponent, Groome. The state vote went for the latter so that Hicks owed his election to his vast city majority. Mayor Swann was, at the same time, re-elected. The Knownothing party had reached the height of its power and the Reform movement which took aggressive shape in 1859 marked its downfall, George William Brown, the Reform candidate, being elected mayor the following year, by a decisive majority.* Meanwhile, the Knownothing movement was paralleled by the slavery issue by which it was finally overshadowed. In spite of its incongruities, it had aided in cultivating a larger national consciousness and at its dissolution the majority of its members passed into the new Republican party. In this way Knownothingism contributed to swell the numbers and to increase the forcefulness of that element of the State that stood for the strengthening of the national tie. At the same time the gross disorders which brought disrepute upon Baltimore during the period of party animosity pointed the way to the appreciation of a purer electorate †

When William Pinckney delivered his famous speech in the Congress of 1820, he brought to a sharp issue the question of whether Congress had the right to refuse admission of a State and whether if admitted, it had authority to impose upon it discriminating conditions. He declared that to impose on Missouri slavery prohibition, would be to shackle it with a condition of statehood, foreign to the letter and spirit of the Constitution The argument so cogently put, was answered

---

* Schmeck, p. 113. Balto Sun and American, Oct 20, 1860
† Schmeck, p. 115

by the adoption of the famous Missouri Compromise, by which that state was admitted without anti-slavery restriction, but with the declaration that slavery should forever be prohibited in that part of the Louisiana Purchase which lay north of the latitude 36° 30', excepting the portion included within the bounds of the proposed state This Compromise was regarded as a Southern concession and indeed the right of Congress to fix the status of newly created states was unanimously agreed to by the brilliant men who composed the President's cabinet Among these was William Wirt of Maryland.

The close of the war with Mexico again raised to prime importance the question of the status of acquired territory with regard to the subject of slavery. Mr. Brinkerhoff, of Ohio, drew up a proviso, extending to any territory which might be acquired by the United States through its war with Mexico, the prohibition of slavery, which was based upon the Ordinance of 1787 As this proviso was offered by Mr Wilmot of Pennsylvania, it received his name.[†] This proposal led to the famous Compromise of 1850, which was offered by Henry Clay, who, now an old man, had once more returned to the senate His passage to Washington was in the nature of a continuous ovation. At Baltimore he made an address of some length in which he gave expression to views afterwards embodied in his Compromise He expressed the opinion that under no circumstances was slavery likely to be introduced into California or New Mexico. In the senate this opinion took the form of one of a set of resolutions, which among other things declared "that as slavery does not exist by law, and is not likely to be introduced into any of the territory acquired by the United States from the Republic of Mexico, it is inexpedient for Congress to provide by law, either for its introduction into, or exclusion from any part of the said territory " The bill embodying the Clay resolutions provided for the admission of California with a free state constitution, the establishment of territorial government for New Mexico and Utah, without the Wilmot Proviso, the settlement of the boundaries

---

[†] Smith, vol 1, p 83

of Texas, as well as for an efficient fugitive slave law and the prohibition of the slave trade in the District of Columbia Although this omnibus bill, as it was called, failed of passage, its provisions were enacted in separate measures *

The country did not have to wait long for illustration of the working of the fugitive slave law Edward Gorsuch, a resident of Baltimore county, accompanied by friends, his son and a United States officer, all heavily armed and bearing the warrant of a commissioner at Philadelphia, went to Christiana, Pennsylvania, to effect the arrest of two negroes who had fled from servitude three years previous. When they attempted to apprehend the men they were opposed by a party of free negroes, who fired upon the posse, killing Mr Gorsuch and seriously wounding his son † From fifty to one hundred negroes joined in the defence of the fugitives, so that the affair assumed the dimensions of a small-sized riot The men whom the posse sought to arrest made good their escape. Immediately, under orders from the President, the United States marshal, district attorney and commissioner from Philadelphia, with forty-five marines from the navyyard hastened to the scene of disorder. This force was augmented by a large body of special constables and the country was scoured, with the result that twenty-four arrests were made of persons supposed to have been implicated, two of them white and the rest colored. The white men were brought to trial for treason and acquitted The other prisoners were never tried The effect of this decision upon Maryland was to excite the minds of the people and to call forth an inflammatory appeal from the Governor to the Legislature ‡

The famous Dred Scott decision is too familiar to need recital other than a sketch of its salient features. Its importance lies in the fact that it was made an abstract political question and evoked from a son of Maryland, Roger B. Taney,

---

* Rh, vol 1, pp 1, 122-129, 147.
† Scharf vol. 3, p. 333 Rh, vol 1 pp 223-4, Smith, vol 1, p 147 N Y. Tribune, Sept 15, 1851
‡ Scharf, vol. 3, 334

one of the few great historic decisions of the Supreme Court of the United States Dred Scott had been taken by his master, an army surgeon in Missouri, to Rock Island, at that time in the portion of the territory of Wisconsin which had formerly been a part of the Louisiana Purchase, where with the consent of his master he had married On returning to Missouri several years later, Scott brought suit in the local court of St. Louis to recover the freedom of himself and his family The decision was in his favor Whereupon his master appealed to the State Supreme Court, which reversed the decision of the lower court Scott was later sold to a citizen of New York, and sued for his freedom in the United States Circuit Court. The case was decided against him and he took an appeal to the Supreme Court. The decision of this body was that Scott being of African descent, was not a citizen of Missouri in a constitutional sense and therefore the case was not within the purview of the United States Circuit Court. In a learned opinion Chief Justice Taney reviewed the constitutional aspects of the case in their political relations and declared that, as slaves had been recognized by the Constitution as property, Congress was bound to protect their possession rather than prohibit their presence in the territories. This opinion, which declared invalid the Missouri Compromise, carried the point of the Southern contention to its maximum value and evoked from the North a storm of violent protest.* It is but fair to the memory of the eminent jurist to repudiate the perversions of his meaning in his famous expression that the African race in the United States possessed "no rights which the white man was bound to respect." Chief Justice Taney was a man of high character and humane sentiments and was far from sharing the too-prevalent opinion of the day that the negro was below the human plane, or that he was not to receive the considerate treatment to which his humanity entitled him and for which his unfortunate status made eloquent appeal. The real mean-

---

* Rh, vol. 1, pp 250-270, Smith, vol. 1, pp 245-9

ing of the words ought not to have been missed by any fair-minded person. They simply set forth the incontrovertible fact that, as related to the rights guaranteed by the constitution, the negro was an extraneous person.

In the high state of public excitement over the slavery issue, it was impossible for general feeling not to be influenced and swayed by appeals directed solely to the passions. Many books, pamphlets and addresses were published by intemperate persons in the North which grossly libeled the people of the South and evoked in response violent declarations which were undisguisedly seditious. A publication of this kind which achieved the distinction of violent antipathy from the South and which in a sense became a political issue in Maryland, was Helper's "Impending Crisis." It was an economic argument against slavery from the point of view of the non-slaveholding white. It undertook to give a description of the Southern slaveholders, their social and private lives and to point the way, by its black portrayal of the Southern situation and feeling, to the liberation of slaves regardless of any consideration other than the accomplishment of that fact. The book was an economic arraignment of slavery, and contended for its abolition not from humane motives, but from a desire to lift from the white labor of the South the crushing incubus of slave-labor competition. The state of feeling in Maryland with regard to Helper's book was reflected the year after its appearance in the Police Reorganization Bill for Baltimore City, which passed the legislature and contained a provision that "no Black Republican or indorser of Helper's book shall be appointed to any position by said board."* 1859, the year in which Helper's publication appeared, witnessed the attempt of John Brown to incite a servile insurrection in Virginia and Maryland. This futile effort to spread revolt among the slaves of the vicinity of Harper's Ferry, the scenes of violence which resulted, the movement of troops, and the execution of Brown and some of his misguided followers, thrilled the country and

---

* Act 1860, ch 7, sec 6

more than any other single circumstance led the nation to realize the dark and forbidding chasm which lay before it*

In the excited state of public feeling the Democratic National Convention convened at Charleston, South Carolina, June 23, 1860. It represented a house divided against itself Democratic councils were made discordant by the issue which recognized as sacred no association or tie which could not stand its test It was impossible for the committee on resolutions to effect an agreement and therefore a majority and a minority report were presented The former declared that it was the duty of the federal government to protect when necessary slavery in the territories. The slogan of the Southern Democracy in the convention was "slavery is right and it ought to be extended." On the 9th of May a party of mediation styling themselves the Constitutional Union party and embracing the remnant of old-line Whigs and Americans, met in convention at Baltimore It was a gathering notable for its high respectability, as well as ability. It was noticeable for the all-but-total absence in it of young men. It was inspired by a patriotic spirit, and, alarmed at the growth of sectional feeling, its appeal was to those matters in common between all lovers of their country, it went before the people upon the simple platform "the Constitution of the country, the union of the States and the enforcement of the laws." It put in nomination Bell, of Tennessee, for President and Everett, of Massachusetts, for Vice-President.† In the meanwhile the strife of the Charleston Convention echoed throughout the country and was heard in the United States Senate, where the principles of both Douglas and Davis sections of the Democratic party were urged with great eloquence and vehemence.

The Democrats, after the disagreement at Charleston, had adjourned to meet in the Front Street Theater, Baltimore, where it was found impossible to harmonize the factions and the minority withdrew to the Maryland Institute and there

---

* Scharf, vol 3, pp 341-4; Rh, vol 2, pp 161, 165, 236, 354, 394, 404
† Scharf, vol 3, p 355, Smith, vol 1, p 293.

nominated Breckenridge as their candidate.* The regulars, left free to carry out their program, affirmed their platform and named Stephen A. Douglass as their standard bearer.

The Republican National Convention was held at Chicago, and Abraham Lincoln was tendered and accepted the nomination for the Presidency.†

---

*Scharf, vol 3, p 354, Rh, vol 2, p 473
†Rh vol. 2, pp. 456-472, Smith, vol 1, pp 284-292; Blaine's "'Twenty Years in Congress," vol 1, p 164

CHAPTER XX.

A BORDER STATE IN THE CIVIL STRIFE

THE growth of secession sentiment in the cotton states was strengthened by the nomination of Abraham Lincoln upon an anti-slavery-extension platform which involved the practical repudiation of the Supreme Court decisions. Particularly in South Carolina, where chronic disaffection had for a long time existed, the course of events and the tide of feeling had become ominous. It there found culmination in the unfurling of the "palmetto" banner upon the 26th of November, 1860. On the 20th of December, the South Carolina Convention passed the Ordinance of Secession, and, in commenting upon this action, the Charleston Mercury, voicing the sentiment of the people of the state, observed, "The tea has been thrown overboard—the revolution of 1860 has been initiated."* Thus was that state by its deliberate action constituted the leader of the secession movement and the irresponsible unfurling of the "palmetto" flag by some hot-headed individuals a month before given the seal of official action. To an invitation extended by some South Carolina volunteers to the people of Maryland to enroll themselves under the new flag, the Baltimore Exchange, the leading Southern journal of the city had made response, "Most of all do we protest against any enrollment of any portion of our people, no matter how insignificant, under the 'palmetto' banner. The good old blood of Maryland is a wine that needs no such bush. If ever—which God forbid —a time should come when our people would be unwilling to let the flag of the Union float over them, Maryland has a ban-

---
* Rh., vol 3, pp 114-7, Crawford, "History of Fort Sumter," pp 45-50

ner of her own, red with the glories of the Revolution, and well known to South Carolina, which she can unfurl and be proud of its memories, though she sorrow over the need of its return."

Maryland's position as a border state had made it a principal ground of sectional strife. A slave-holding state, with strong devotion to the Union, and confident that in the constitution wisely interpreted was to be found a sufficient solution of difficulties which had grown to appalling proportions through intemperate leadership and virulent utterances within and without the national legislature, she was in no mood to look upon the destruction of the Union as a panacea for the national disorders. Her contributions to that Union had been too great and too significant for her to belie her history by repudiating the Federal Compact. There were not wanting many serious-minded men in her councils who looked back to the formative period of the national commonwealth and saw in Maryland's sturdy advocacy of the cession to the national government of the vast western territory a sacred obligation thereby imposed upon her to maintain the coherence of the Union whose life was now threatened by issues which had largely arisen in that very territory which indicated the highwater mark of Maryland's national appreciation. Strong as were Maryland's southern sympathies, four-fifths of the people of the State regarded the attitude of the cotton states as radical and ill-advised. It was deemed important, however, that as the other border states had declared their convictions, Maryland likewise, should leave no room for doubt as to her position upon the great issue. In the face of the petition of a large number of the citizens of the State, Governor Hicks, steadfastly declined to convene the Legislature, upon the ground that it would not faithfully reflect the sentiments of the majority of the people. He feared that to make the Republican program an occasion for the calling of an extra session of the Legislature would be to invite the adoption of some revolutionary measure adverse to the conservative and safe position which Maryland had heretofore maintained. Personally, Governor Hicks, by all the earlier associations and traditions of his life was a States' Rights man Nevertheless, his prominent identification with the Knownothing movement had led him to commit himself to the idea of conservative nationalism to a degree that raised his appreciation of his duty to the country at large above all other considerations. Swayed by the conflicting emotions of duty to his country and devotion to his section, he, of necessity, made himself subject to misunderstandings and attacks. But when the issue of the times ranged the men of Maryland upon one or the other side, Governor Hicks' position was no longer ambiguous. He cast his fortunes with those of the Union.*

The Hon S Teackle Wallis was one of the foremost opponents of Governor Hicks in his refusal to convene the Legislature. Mr. Wallis was a constitutional unionist, nevertheless, he was a thorough believer in the right of peaceable secession and when the war left him no alternative action, he allied himself with the cause of the Confederacy, throwing the onus of his action upon the Federal Government, whose denial of the right of peaceable withdrawal from the Union on the part of the dissatisfied states led him and many thousands of Marylanders to oppose the government which they would otherwise have been glad to have upheld

In the excited condition of the public mind, rumors of all sorts of dire plots took hold of the popular imagination and became greatly exaggerated even in cases where they had some actual basis of fact It was asserted that a plot was afoot to prevent the inauguration of Lincoln Another story passed from mouth to mouth that the capital was in danger of seizure and it was seriously believed by Governor Hicks and many others that a well-devised plot for the assassination of President Lincoln on his passage through Baltimore had been formulated. These rumors took hold upon the minds of all those who were ready to give credence to whatever tallied with their own belief as to the motives and methods of their adversaries. Seward is found writing in a

---
* Rh, vol 3, p 301

confidential letter, "Treason is all around and amongst us and plots [exist] to seize the capital and usurp the government." "One friend came in this morning to tell me," he wrote, later, "that there are two thousand armed conspirators in the city, and the mayor is secretly with them"* Such apprehensions were not unnatural in the light of views like those to which the Richmond Enquirer gave expression: "Can there not be found men brave enough in Maryland to unite with Virginians in seizing the Capitol at Washington?"†

Upon the convening of Congress on the 3rd of December, 1860, President Buchanan transmitted to that body a message in which he called attention to the perilous condition of the country, whereupon one of the Virginia representatives moved the reference of that part of the document to a special committee comprised of one representative from each of the states Hon Henry Winter Davis, of Maryland, was the representative of that State The senate also deemed that portion of the President's message worthy of special consideration and referred it to a select committee of thirteen, the membership of which represented all the political elements of that body. This attempt to reach some positive conclusions was unfruitful, and no better results were derived from a Peace Convention which was called by the governors of fourteen states and which was in session from the 4th to the 27th of the following February ‡ This convention was remarkable for the number of able and representative men which it included. Among those from Maryland were Reverdy Johnson, Augustus W. Bradford, William T. Goldsborough, John W Crisfield and J Dixon Roman. All these attempts to stem the tide failed because the time for compromise had passed. The feeling on the respective sides of the great issue had gone too far towards crystallization for the effective working of those affinitives which at one time might have served to hold the sections together

---

*Rh, vol 3, p. 300
†Richmond Enquirer, Dec, 25, 1860
‡Cambridge Modern History, vol 7, p 448

The issue had passed from the compromise to the apologetic stage The respective factions now sought to vindicate their positions Their appeal was no longer for Union as between themselves, but for the collection of all persons and concentration of all forces representing their particular views On the 10th of January, 1861, two meetings were held in Baltimore which were significant of the divided sentiment and position which Maryland was to hold in the coming civil strife. The one was a convention of Union sympathizers, which endorsed the position of Governor Hicks in declining to call a special session of the Legislature, and affirmed its devotion to peace. The other was a smaller assemblage which met at the invitation of several prominent gentlemen of Baltimore. It was a body of Southern sympathizers and its principal object was to impress Governor Hicks with the strength of the demand in the State for the convening of the Legislature to authoritatively define Maryland's position Sentiments of devotion to the Union were freely expressed and the meeting put itself so on record *

Popular feeling in Maryland was in a high state of tension over the prospect of the passage of Abraham Lincoln through Baltimore, and this was largely due to the fact that the many rumors to the effect that the President-elect's course would be arrested by assassins had, seemingly, taken more definite form. Intelligence was conveyed to Mr. Lincoln from two different sources that his public passage through that city would be fraught with imminent peril. Yielding to the counsel of his advisers he consented to an alteration of his program and passed secretly through the city. This he was able to do without breach of etiquette as he had received no official invitation from either City or State It is needless to remark that Mr. Lincoln's action was not dictated by a feeling of personal concern but "by a sense of the highest prudential duty to the people and the government over whose destiny he had been called to preside "† However, this was a tactical mistake on

---
* Scharf, vol 3, pp. 383-4
† C M H, vol 7, p 449, Rh, vol 3, p. 304; Scharf, vol 3, pp 384-397

the part of a President-elect, for had he carried out his original program and paused long enough in the city "to express the kind feelings which were in his heart with the simple eloquence of which he was so great a master he could not have failed to make a very different impression from that which was produced not only by want of confidence and respect manifested towards the city of Baltimore by the plan pursued but still more by the manner in which it was carried out "*

On February 18th Congress, by a two-thirds vote, recommended as a thirteenth amendment to the Constitution that "No amendment shall be made to the Constitution which will authorize or give to Congress the power to abolish or interfere within any state with the domestic institutions thereof, including that of persons held to labor or service by the laws of said state." This amendment, which Lincoln in his inaugural address approved, was promptly agreed to by the legislatures of Maryland and Ohio, but had no effect on the course of the South, though it would have permanently protected the institution of slavery in the states in which it then existed.† On the same date as the proposal of this amendment, a convention of the seven seceding states, assembled at Montgomery, Alabama was listening to the inaugural address of President Jefferson Davis, who had two weeks previous been chosen chief magistrate of the new Confederacy. He declared that "it was wanton aggression" that justified the course of the Southern people, a statement which the speaker amplified by the declaration that "we have vainly endeavored to secure tranquillity and obtain respect for the rights to which we were entitled As a necessity, not a choice, we have resorted to the remedy of separation "‡

The inauguration of Lincoln was carried out under circumstances whose dramatic effect was increased by the feelings of the assemblage gathered to do him honor, which were too tense for expression in the exuberent ways which commonly

---

* Brown, "Baltimore and the Nineteenth of April"
† Rhodes, vol 3, p 313.
‡ Rhodes, vol 3, p 293; Schouler, vol 5, p 490

characterized such gatherings. The presence of the decrepit Chief Justice Taney, the careworn Buchanan, and the two defeated candidates, Breckenridge and Douglas, had a solemnizing effect upon the assemblage. Representatives of an old order, their appearance on this occasion served to deepen the popular consciousness of the untried eventualities of the future When President Lincoln gathered about him his executive associates, Montgomery Blair of Maryland was given the seat of postmaster-general at the cabinet table. All phases of current political faith were there represented, but Blair was the most aggressive of them all in his advocacy of immediate and thorough-going measures for the preservation of the Union A true disciple of Andrew Jackson, he was so radical as to give offense to Seward, who at first refused the commission tendered him rather than have the Marylander as an associate, and was only pursuaded to reconsider his action, by the assurance from Lincoln that Blair should be held in check.*

When on the 12th of April, 1861, at 4 A. M Brigadier-General Beauregard, who was in command of the Confederate forces at Charleston, S C., ordered Fort Sumter to be fired upon, the first overt act of hostilities was committed and the long impending conflict between the states precipitated. Three days later, on Sunday, April 14th, "with colors floating and drums beating, and saluting the flag of the Union with fifty guns," Major Anderson evacuated Sumter. His forces were transferred to the Steamer Baltic which immediately sailed for New York. The news of this overt act was the signal for energetic action on the part of President Lincoln His call for troops and the news from Sumter appeared simultaneously in the newspapers of the 15th The breaking out of hostilities found the Confederacy better prepared for immediate action than the Federal government For some time before the attack upon Fort Sumter, recruiting stations had been opened in the border states and Southern cities for the enlistment of men for the Southern cause. A number of Marylanders recruited at a station in Baltimore had participated in the opera-

* Schouler, vol 6, p 8, Rh, vol. 3, pp 319-20

tions which brought about the reduction of Fort Sumter.*

With the call of the government for troops appeared the announcement in the Northern press that Maryland was to be compelled to adhere to the Union   The State was in a condition of intense excitement, and the bitterness of the partizan feeling threatened to produce scenes of riotous disorder in Baltimore, so that on April 17th Mayor Brown issued a proclamation in which he exhorted all good citizens to refrain from any act which could offer excuse for violence, to refrain from intemperate speech and to sustain the public authorities   It was inevitable, however, that scenes of disorder should be consequent upon the state of public feeling and for a number of days the city was often in the hands of contending factions. The whole country was interested in Maryland, whose strategic position commanded all the routes to the national capital, and if these should not be kept open Washington must certainly be captured by the forces of the Confederacy   At the beginning of the war this was the great stake for which both sides played.

On the 17th of April Virginia seceded from the Union. On the 18th five hundred unarmed Pennsylvania militia passed through Baltimore without attracting attention. On the 19th occurred an event which was second only to the fall of Sumter in deepening the feeling and solidifying the determination of either side to vindicate the supremacy of the cause which it held dear. On that day the Sixth Massachusetts Regiment, while being transferred from one station to another, was assaulted on the streets of Baltimore by a mob which wounded twenty-five of the soldiers, some fatally. That the attack was not more serious in its consequences was largely due to the efficiency of the police under the command of Marshal Kane   Colonel Jones, the commander of the Massachusetts troops, had instructed his men that they would probably be molested in their passage through Baltimore but they were to refrain from retaliation, unless actually fired upon, in which event they were not to fire promiscuously into the crowd, but to

---

* Crawford, "History of Fort Sumter," pp 309, 310

drop any man whom they saw aiming at them Had the Massachusetts troops like the Pennsylvania regiments marched through the city in a body the probability of molestation would have been reduced and protection could better have been afforded them But, according to the custom of the day, the cars were detached from the engine and each one was hauled through the streets by horses for the distance of a mile between the two stations; this laid the soldiers open to attack in detail. At first obstructions were put upon the track which effectually prevented the passage of the troops and compelled their return to President Street Station By that time a dense and angry crowd had collected so that when the soldiers advanced afoot along President street they were subjected to a shower of missiles, pistol shots were fired into the ranks and one soldier fell dead. The order "Fire!" sent a volley into the crowd The Mayor of Baltimore put himself at the head of the troops in order to afford them the protection of his person, but it was impossible to restrain the wrath of men who had passed beyond all bounds of caution and who were uninfluenced by fear. The fire on both sides was scattering and a number of innocent bystanders were among those injured When the troops had gotten to the vicinity of Light Street, Marshal Kane appeared at the head of fifty policemen and forming a rear guard to the troops succeeded in awing the crowd sufficiently to enable the regiment to reach the station * Well did Baltimore show its regret for this attack upon the citizen soldiery of another state who offered no provocation, when the same gallant regiment again passed through Baltimore in behest of the call of President McKinley for troops to effect the redemption of Cuba from the tyranny of Spain No soldiers could have received a more splendid ovation than was tendered the Sixth Massachusetts Regiment at that time. An earlier evidence of the same spirit was the reception accorded the regiment when visiting Baltimore April 19, 1880

Following the attack upon the Massachusetts troops, Governor Hicks and Mayor Brown sent a joint telegram to the

---

* Brown's "Baltimore and the Nineteenth of April"

President praying him not to send any more troops through the city and giving assurance of their ability to maintain order. A mass meeting was held in Monument Square at which the prevailing sentiment was opposition to any attempt at coercion of the Confederate States. The War Department strongly resented the attack upon the troops advancing to the defense of Washington and had issued an order for more troops to be forwarded to that point prepared to fight their way through if necessary. Fearful of the consequences if the troops were not stopped, Mayor Brown and Marshal Kane came to a decision that it would be wise to burn some of the bridges of the Philadelphia, Wilmington and Baltimore and the Northern Central Railroads. To this proposition Governor Hicks, whose ambiguous attitude had not yet been changed into one of open espousal of the Union, gave reluctant assent. This resolution was carried out at midnight on the 19th.* A committee had been sent to the President and General Scott to impress upon them the desirability of not aggravating further the people of Baltimore by bringing troops to that city. They returned to report "We have a letter from the former [the President] to the mayor and governor, declaring that no troops shall be brought through Baltimore, if in a military point of view, and without interruptions from opposition, they can be marched around Baltimore." This response was deemed unsatisfactory and another committee was sent to Washington. In the meantime the city was put in a state of defense and Mayor Brown requested from the citizens contributions for that purpose. There was a strong feeling that the dispatch of Northern troops across the soil of the state would constitute a grievous offense to the Southern feeling of its inhabitants.

The opposition to efforts of the government to mass troops at Washington dwindled with the subsidence of the first feeling which had engendered it. The Seventh New York was hurried to the capital and other troops soon followed, so that Washington assumed the aspect of an armed camp.

---

* Rhodes, vol. 3, pp 363-7, Schf, vol. 3, p 411, Brown's "Baltimore and the Nineteenth of April"

HISTORY OF MARYLAND.

In the meanwhile the pressure upon Governor Hicks to convene the Legislature had become too strong to be denied, and that body was convened in special session at Frederick on April the 26th, the reason assigned for the temporary change of the capital being the presence of Federal troops in Annapolis. The pro-Union bias of Hicks was shown in his selection of a town in which such sentiments predominated rather than the more natural place, Baltimore. In his message to the Legislature, the governor expressed his strong conviction that the correct attitude of Maryland was one of neutrality, and this was the policy which was adopted by that body. At its adjournment Maryland remained officially attached to the Federal government. It had placed itself on record as affirming that it had no constitutional power to pass an ordinance of secession.

May the 13th found General Butler in Baltimore with a large portion of his command and in possession of Federal Hill, his occupancy of which was not disputed. In so doing Butler had acted on his own responsibility and called out a severe censure from General Scott, who rebuked him for an enterprise fraught with such great hazard.[*] This characteristic action on the part of Butler did not seriously discredit him with his superiors and received the plaudits of the North. The activity of the Union forces in Maryland was responded to by Confederate movements. Captain Bradley T. Johnson of Frederick organized a Confederate company, May 8th, which was mustered into service on the 22nd of the same month. They were without arms or supplies of any sort, but the wife of Captain Johnson, a native of North Carolina, undertook and succeeded in accomplishing a mission to the governor of that state by which these needs were met. The organization of the Frederick company was followed by other Maryland enlistments for the Confederate army.

The suspension of the writ of habeas corpus, within limits, came to be recognized as a military necessity, and by proclamation the writ was formally suspended throughout the United States in certain cases. Chief Justice Taney denied the

---
[*] Butler's Autobiography

right of the President to suspend the writ and filed an opinion to that effect in a case which came before the Supreme Bench. It was a Maryland case and wide indignation was excited in the State. The feeling was deepened by the subsequent arrest of Hon Ross Winans and other prominent citizens The State Legislature on the 22nd of June passed a series of resolutions remonstrating against the assertion and exercise of military jurisdiction within the limits of Maryland on the part of the United States government. The proximity of Maryland to the seat of Federal authority gave to this action of its legislators almost heroic quality. The protest of committees of remonstrance appointed to wait upon the President were ineffective, being regarded simply as the obstructionist efforts of recalcitrants. The position of the President upon the subject is well illustrated by the case of Vallindingham, a Democratic member of Congress from Ohio, whose opposition to a general conscription law passed by Congress March 3rd, 1863, led to a charge of contumacy being preferred against him and his incarceration in a military prison An application for a writ of habeas corpus was denied by the judge of the United States Circuit Court upon the ground that if the President, under whose military authority the arrest had been made, had transcended that authority, redress could properly be had only by a process of impeachment of the President The prisoner's sentence was modified to expulsion beyond the Federal military lines The answer of the President to a committee of New York Democrats, who joined a very general expostulation at the President's proceeding, was succinct, "Must I shoot a simple-minded soldier-boy who deserts, while I must not touch a hair of a wily agitator who induced him to desert?"*

On June 10th General Banks assumed command of Baltimore, being placed in charge of the Department of Annapolis. Alleging that there were within his military jurisdiction unlawful combinations of men for resistance to the United States authority, General Banks undertook to ferret out and to suppress them On the 27th of June, Colonel Kane, the marshal

---
* The Cambridge Modern History, vol 7, pp 573-575.

of the police, was placed under arrest and the police board was superseded by the appointment of Colonel Kenly as provost marshal. On July 1st the deposed police commissioners were also placed under arrest. No specific charges were preferred against the men who were thus subjected to the hardship of military arrest A resolution introduced into the House of Representatives requesting the President to communicate to the body "the reasons and evidence" for the arrest of the commissioners and their detention at Fort McHenry, only elicited the response that it was "incompatible with the public interest" to do so Mayor Brown was the only member of the board of police commissioners who had not been deprived of liberty and he expressed to General Banks his willingness to undertake the management of the police department, but his offer was declined and throughout the war the police department of Baltimore City was administered by the Federal government.*

On July 16th, pursuant to the plan of campaign decided upon and which was expressed in the popular cry, "On to Richmond," the Federal army moved towards the Confederate capital Their march, however, was not to be a holiday affair. Arriving at Bull's Run July 21st, General McDowell, the Federal commander, found that Beauregard and Johnston had effected a junction which he had been above all things anxious to prevent. The battle of Bull Run was fought on Sunday, July 21st, and the tide was turned in favor of the Confederate army by the timely arrival of Elzey's brigade, which included the First Maryland regiment.[b] General Sherman declared the battle of Bull Run to have been one of the best planned of the war and one in which both armies were fairly defeated. Nevertheless the North was greatly chagrined and the South correspondingly exultant

Fearing that the fall meeting of the Maryland Legislature would show a preponderance of secession sentiment, the Sec-

---
* Scharf, vol 3, 435-437
* Schf, vol 3, p 448, Rh, vol. 3, pp 349-354, C M H, vol 7, pp 464-6.

retary of War adopted a course for which there was no justification and sought to coerce a free state in the exercise of its sovereign capacity to elect such representatives as it saw fit and who should maintain their right of adopting such measures as in their judgment might appear to be wise He ordered the arrest of all or such part of the members of the Legislature as well as other citizens of the State as the military authorities might deem necessary to prevent the Legislature from passing an act of secession. The border states were the pawn in the game of strategy being played by Lincoln and Davis and this high-handed measure was but one of the unwarranted moves which there was no higher power to call.†

The course of the war was taking a wider reach Gen. George B McClellan had been assigned to the Army of the Potomac, and the lines of war were settling hard and fast upon the sections. McClellan, inordinately inflated with self-conceit, did not have his complacence diminished by an engagement at Ball's Bluff on the Potomac above Washington, in which through mismanagement the Union forces met defeat. The casualties were not considerable, but, nevertheless, they included some of the finest and most promising young men of the army, the loss of whom spread a feeling of discouragement throughout the North No Maryland troops were engaged in this battle, but on the 22nd the First Maryland regiment, under the command of Colonel Kenly, which had been sent to the succor of Brig.-Gen. C P Stone at Edward's Ferry, who had been sent over the Potomac to act in conjunction with Colonel Baker's command, performed heroic work throughout the night in reconducting across the river the brigade which was in imminent peril of being cut off and destroyed Colonel Kenly, in his report, paid a warm tribute to the work and worth of the Maryland men After the performance of this service, Colonel Kenly with the rest of General Banks' division was ordered into winter quarters near Frederick, but later was given the active assignment of garrisoning the military posts near Hancock and Williamsport. Confederate batteries had

---

† Scharf, vol 3, p 441

been erected on the Potomac at Quantico Creek and other points, and effectually blockaded the river. Their presence was a source of annoyance to General Hooker's corps on the other side of the river and it was proposed to capture them; but a reconnaisance showed this to be impracticable.

The control of the Potomac river by the Confederates threw a vast amount of freight, which otherwise would have had water carriage, upon the Washington branch of the Baltimore and Ohio Railroad, a larger freight business being done upon this road during the war than upon any other in the United States. At times it amounted to a daily average of over four hundred cars. To further meet the demand for better transportation between Baltimore and Washington, wagon trains of nearly one hundred wagons were established So far as approach from the sea was concerned the national capital was in a state of siege

A naval descent upon the coast of South Carolina and Georgia to be cooperated with by a land force under Gen W T. Sherman was planned and the fleet with its transports left Hampton Roads on the 27th of October for its execution. Especial interest in this movement was aroused in Maryland from the fact that the land forces to the number of fifteen thousand were collected at Annapolis A movement, however, in which Maryland was more directly concerned, was the occupation of Accomac and Northampton counties on the eastern shore of Virginia. General Dix, under whom this was accomplished, was prompted to the movement by the fact that the Federal authority had been set at naught by Confederate sympathizers

The election of November 6th, 1861, for state officers, could have had but one result under existing conditions. The "Union" ticket, headed by Augustus W Bradford was elected Under the military rules which were issued for the detection and apprehension of persons attempting to vote who were known to have given active aid to the Confederate cause, the vote polled was small and the majority for the "Union" ticket large Many persons had their right of ballot challenged and were placed under arrest. It was clear to all that the policy pursued by the administration toward Maryland was to be adhered to and the state prevented from having an opportunity to throw in its fortunes with the Confederacy if it so listed. In his inaugural address delivered January 8th, 1862, Governor Bradford denounced in strong terms the spirit and acts of secession. Early in March the Legislature adopted a series of resolutions in endorsement of the Federal policy for the preservation of the Union and committing Maryland to the loyal support and furtherance thereof Nevertheless, that body was far from being under the influence of abolition sentiment and while it pronounced against secession, it again at the same time in an appeal to the Northern States, issued upon Washington's birthday, urged that the agitation in Congress for the devisement of schemes for the abolishment of slavery in the rebellious states should be frowned upon. At that time the anti-slavery advocates were active in seeking to secure the passage of an abolition bill for the District of Columbia Nevertheless a bill to that effect, reported to the Senate February 13th, passed both houses, and was signed by the President on the 16th of April On the 5th of March Maryland sought to redeem itself from the opprobrium it had come under by its treatment of the Sixth Massachusetts regiment. At that time the Legislature passed a bill introduced by Hon. J V L Findlay appropriating seven thousand dollars for the relief of the families of the soldiers who were killed *

At the beginning of 1862 General Dix was still in command of Baltimore and Hooker was in Charles county to the south of Washington General McClellan was stationed southwest of that city, while Generals Keys and Casey occupied the capital and its environments General Stone was at Poolsville and General Banks at Darnstown, while detachments of the Federal troops were on the Potomac in the vicinity of Williamsport General Kelly had his headquarters at Cumberland. When General Lander, arriving at Cumberland for the relief of General Kelly, took charge of the forces there

---

* Scharf, pp 466-7, Schouler, vol 6, p. 43, note

stationed he found the Confederate general, Stonewall Jackson, encamped on the opposite side of the Potomac, having driven out a body of Federal troops which he found at Bath, Virginia   The Federal administration had determined upon a vigorous prosecution of the war, having become convinced that half-way measures could not restore the Union. At the same time it had become thoroughly demonstrated that the North was a unit in support of the position of the Federal authorities   This had not been the case at the first and there had not been wanting Northern men of prominence and organs of influence to openly declare that the Southern States were not transcending their rights under the Constitution in seceding. Some expressions had gone even further than this and threats had been made that the movement of troops upon the seceding states would be a signal for a reactionary movement in the North and that if the principle of secession was made the issue of the conflict it would have to be determined in other quarters as well as those where the immediate provocation to depart from the Union was found   The cry had now gone up that loyalty to the Union could not contemplate secession even as an abstract right   Feeling assured of the solid sentiment of the country above Mason and Dixon's line the administration was prepared to prosecute the struggle whether it was done under or outside of the Constitution   It was a condition where the preservation of the Union was not simply the paramount but the only issue   Should war measures demand the ignoring of that instrument the fact itself would be ample justification for the proceeding. Maryland's attitude at the special session of the Legislature in declaring that it had no constitutional warrant for seceding from the Union was an evidence of a much more tender regard for that basic fact of the American Commonwealth than was evinced by those who entered upon the suppression of the rebellious states   New views of the constitution were fast taking form in the North. It was coming to be felt that although the Constitution was a written document, "the letter killeth but the spirit giveth life," and the conception of the Constitution as a flexible instrument which was then formed not only prepared the way for Lincoln's emancipation proclamation but was the first sprouting of the old stock into a vigorous growth—the beginning of the era of liberal interpretation of the national document

The political situation had its effect upon the commerce of all of the coast cities but this was especially true of Baltimore. The Union troops had not been able to prevent the Confederates from obstructing the immense traffic of the Baltimore and Ohio Railroad and the embargo placed upon commerce by the military authorities of the city had a repressing effect upon the shipments of the port The financial institutions of Baltimore became conservative to a degree and their unwillingness to afford the usual accommodations to merchants obstructed the channels of trade Maryland's commercial relations with the South and the complications in that quarter added to the express intention of the Confederate Congress to sequestrate all money and debts due to Eastern merchants furnished considerable justification for the attitude taken by the Baltimore banks It is true that in its course towards the Eastern centers, discrimination had been made by the Confederate Congress in the case of the city which had so strongly reflected Southern sentiment but it could not be hoped that Baltimore would continue to receive the immunity which had been accorded it, even by the Southern privateers. On the other hand the government had become sufficiently satisfied with the loyalty of the State as evinced by its Legislature to put into circulation a great deal of money in Maryland A number of vessels were fitted out and expeditions sent from Baltimore and Annapolis for operations in the South and large purchases of stores made in Baltimore

The early months of 1862 were occupied by both parties in playing for position On March 8. 1862, occurred the naval engagement between the Merrimac and the Monitor, destined to revolutionize naval warfare and which in a day rendered obsolete all the warships in the world. When the Norfolk Navy Yard was destroyed the steam frigate Merrimac, one of the finest warships in the United States navy, had been scuttled and sunk. Later she had been raised by the Confederates, cut down to the hull, covered by a slanting roof of railroad iron, extending two feet below the water, and armed with ten heavy guns. Under the command of Captain Buchanan, a Marylander, she steamed into the mouth of the James on the morning of Saturday, March 8, 1862, and when darkness settled over Hampton Roads it found the Union cause wellnigh hopeless The Cumberland had been sunk "with the Stars and Stripes floating victorious in death," the Congress had been burned, the Minnesota and St Lawrence were aground, and the ironclad Merrimac was the undisputed mistress of the sea. But a little before midnight the cry sprang from man to man, "The Monitor has come" This was the little vessel designed by Captain Ericsson, and which the Confederate contemptuously called "a cheese box on a raft," a comparison not inapt, for her hull extended but a few inches above the water line and was surmounted by a revolving turret containing two heavy guns. Early Sunday morning the Merrimac advanced to complete her work of destruction, but a solid shot weighing 160 pounds was the little Monitor's challenge to a duel, which after four hours of incessant firing left the Merrimac a crippled giant.

The principal operations of the land forces in Maryland during the spring of 1862 was the passage of the Potomac by Kenly's First Maryland in connection with General Banks' campaign around Harper's Ferry and the battle of Front Royal, in which Johnson's First Maryland Confederate regiment defeated and captured Kenly's First Maryland Federal regiment. This was the first engagement of the war in which Marylanders measured arms. Its issue created intense excitement throughout the state and was signalized by a number of disgraceful encounters in Baltimore which certainly did not diminish the ill-repute of that city as a place of boisterous outbreaks. Baltimore was not the only place in Maryland where turbulence prevailed and highhanded and disgraceful acts were perpetrated Judge Richard Bennett Carmichael, judge of the circuit comprising the counties of Kent, Queen Annes and Talbot, had had the courage to instruct the grand jury to present parties who had been guilty of making arrests without show of authority within the borders of his circuit the previous fall during the elections. Major-General Dix ordered James L. McPhail, provost-marshal of Baltimore, to proceed to Easton and arrest Judge Carmichael. This order was executed with great brutality by McPhail and his force of one hundred and twenty-five men. The judge was imprisoned in various military forts until December 4th, when he was unconditionally released without either having had charges preferred against him or having been brought to trial.

During July were fought the battles of Beaver Creek, Mechanicsville, Gaines Mills, Malvern Hill, and Harrisons Landing. The battle of South Mountain followed on August 9th and on August 25th was fought the battle of Manassas or second Bull Run. In this engagement the Maryland batteries of Dement, Brown and Brockenbrough performed good service and aided materially in adding the laurels of Manassas to the list of Confederate victories. September opened with Lee's invasion of Maryland, which occurred upon the fifth of the month. He entered Frederick City upon the 6th. Everywhere the Confederates were greeted with enthusiasm, the strains of "Maryland, My Maryland," "Dixie," and "The Bonnie Blue Flag" thrilled the repressed spirits of Confederate sympathizers until their ardor vented itself in the jubilation of men who saw in anticipation, the victory of the cause dearest to their hearts. Frederick was garrisoned by one company under Captain Faithful, who retired at the approach of the Confederates, leaving behind him a conflagration in which was consumed everything that could be of value to the enemy which the Federal troops were unable to remove. The Confederates established martial law. Orders were given to rigidly respect private possessions and Colonel Bradley T. Johnson, a native of the place, was appointed provost-marshal. Lee issued an address to the people of Maryland, setting forth his reason for the invasion of the State and alleging the desecration by the Federal government of the dearest rights of the people, and calling upon them to freely decide their own destiny without constraint In a spirit of true nobility, he closed with the words, "This army will respect your choice whatever it may be, and while the Southern people will rejoice to welcome you to your natural position among them, they will only welcome you when you come of your own free will."* Had the call of Lee been issued from a section of the State where Federal opinion was less prevalent than in Western Maryland, responses to it might have been more satisfying. In Baltimore thousands hastened to enroll themselves under the banner of the chivalric leader of the Confederate forces, but the military domination established by the Federal administration had brought the citizens of that city and other secessionist sections of the State under such close surveillence that it was difficult to effect a concerted movement in response to Lee's invitation. Nor did the appearance presented by the Confederate troops inspire faith in the ultimate success of their cause Ragged and barefooted, many of them leaving in blood-tracks along the turnpike the signs of their weary march, they were little calculated to inspire with the spirit of martial ardor the Maryland sympathizers with whom the habit of caution had become a custom of life

The presence of Lee in the State and his appeal evoked from Governor Bradford a proclamation reciting the fact of the presence of the Confederate forces and calling upon the citizens to enroll themselves in a military organization for the defense of Baltimore. The action of the governor was given effect by Mayor Chapman and a number of prominent citizens, a great many persons volunteered for service and the defences of the city were rapidly put in a state of efficiency. In the event of the Confederates gaining control of the city preparations were completed for its reduction to ashes. The appearance of Lee in Maryland had almost as great an effect upon the neighboring state of Pennsylvania, which was thrown in a state of anxiety at the prospect of the Confederates cross-

---
* Scharf, vol 3, p. 498.

ing the line and securing lodgment in a state unequivocably Northern. It was indeed believed that the Confederate army purposed marching on Harrisburg and thence to Philadelphia. Lee, however, had hoped that upon his entrance into Maryland the Federal troops would evacuate Harper's Ferry and thus open to him a route to Washington, as they did not do so, he felt it incumbent upon him to dislodge them by force. The immediate purpose of Lee's coming into Maryland, which was to cause a rising among the Maryland secessionists, had failed and there was no longer reason for his presence in the State. The impossibility of capturing Washington was apparent, the question that presented itself to him in his situation was in what direction could he move his troops to the best advantage. McClellan aided him to an answer. Lincoln had committed to that general the opposition to Lee's advance. Lee's audacity kept everyone guessing as to his plans and it was only a peculiar piece of good luck which enabled McClellan to obtain a copy of Lee's general order of September 9th by which he obtained full information of the latter's movements and intentions. From this source he found that Lee had divided his force, sending one section of his army to effect the capture of Harper's Ferry and to open up the route to Richmond, while the other remained in Maryland.

With good roads and good weather and the spur of a telegram from the President not to allow the enemy to elude him, and with the knowledge that Lee's weakened vanguard was within twenty miles of him, McClellan nevertheless dissipated two days in indecision, so that when he met the enemy at Antietam it was not to engage a divided foe but to face the guns of Lee's reunited forces full of the spirit of their agile and resourceful general. Even then McClellan entered the engagement with but a third of his forces, the remainder of his army being brought into action piecemeal. The battle was hotly contested and the slaughter was terrific. At the close of the day honors were about equal, although the proportionate loss of the Confederates was greatest. It was McClellan's opportunity but he failed to avail of it. A hasty retreat on the part of Lee was impossible because of the Potomac in his rear. But upon the 19th when McClellan renewed the attack, he found the enemy had eluded him by crossing into Virginia, and the complacent general, with a show of great satisfaction, reported that he had driven the enemy beyond the Potomac and saved Pennsylvania. In the battle of Antietam quite a number of Maryland commands had been engaged on either side. The Third Maryland Federal regiment, which occupied the right of the line, was subjected to a galling fire and came out of the engagement with but two hundred effective men. The Fifth regiment under Major Blumenburg fought gallantly and also suffered heavy losses, while the Seventh regiment under Lieutenant-Colonel Duryea also distinguished itself for its valor and suffered severely. Large gaps had been made in its numbers by other engagements, notably at Newbern, N. C., and after the battle of Antietam it was reduced to two hundred and fifty officers and men. The Purnell Maryland Legion was complimented by the general of the brigade of which it formed a part for conspicuous gallantry, while the First Maryland Federal artillery also achieved distinction in this memorable battle.

In the Confederate army the Maryland troops were no less signalized for their bravery and performances. The state was well represented by the First Maryland artillery, the Chesapeake artillery, the Baltimore Light artillery, and several cavalry and independent companies.

The victory of Antietam furnished Lincoln the opportunity to issue his famous proclamation of emancipation, which had been drafted some time before and which he had laid aside until an important success should give its issuance greater effect. The Confederate army had been driven out of Maryland and now he proposed to dedicate the soil of that State as well as all other slavery territory over which the authority of the government extended and so far as might be that of the states in rebellion, to the doctrine of freedom as enunciated in the Declaration of Independence rather than as expressed in the Constitution. The proclamation was issued September 22nd, to go into effect January 1st, 1863

The South was keenly sensitive to this action of the President and resented bitterly his arraying their former slaves against them Lincoln had been urged to the action he took by the press of the North. In a characteristic reply to a letter of Mr Greeley's, urging a policy of emancipation and declaring that to seek to put down the rebellion without touching slavery would be "preposterous and futile," he had said, "If I could save the Union without freeing any slaves, I would do it, if I could do it by freeing all the slaves, I would do it, and if I could save it by freeing some and leaving others alone, I would do it" In a response to a body of Chicago clergymen who visited him on the 13th of September, he pinned his future course of action to the turn of events in Maryland and declared that he would construe the expulsion of Lee's army from that state as an evidence of God's will that he should proclaim freedom for the slaves Thus Maryland became once more a pivotal factor in the fixing of the national policy upon the greatest question in the nation's history *

After McClellan, with an army of seventy thousand, had allowed Lee, with little more than half that number, to rob him of the advantages of victory, Lincoln personally visited the army to ascertain why such an immense force could not find more serviceable occupation than the policing of Maryland. The inert McClellan, however, in spite of the urgency of his superiors, continued idly complaining, while the bold Confederate cavalry leader Stuart crossed the Potomac, rode entirely around the army and recrossed the river at a lower point. He captured a large number of horses and other stores and took with him a number of prominent citizens and officials to hold as hostages for the Southern citizens whom the Federal authorities had taken from their homes and incarcerated in Northern prisons. On the 26th of November an order from the Secretary of War secured the release of all Maryland

---

* Schouler pp 225-5, 277-9; Smith, vol 2, pp 94-5, C M H, vol 7, pp 591-5

state prisoners The prominent Baltimoreans who had so long suffered the hardships of imprisonment were received in Baltimore with a greeting cordial and sincere. To prevent future abuses of power, General Wood, now in command of Baltimore, issued a special order declaring that thereafter no persons should be arrested within the limits of his department except by his personal order and in such cases the charges against the accused would have to be sworn to before a justice of the peace

Burnside, who succeeded McClellan in command of the army of the Potomac, in turn gave place to General Hooker, on January 26th, 1863 The early months of this year were largely taken up on the part of both armies with preparations for the summer campaign. Lee, however, had managed to secure a strategical victory at Chancellorsville. The Federal army retreated northward bearing with it its commander, who had been seriously wounded in the engagement The victorious Confederate general thereupon undertook a fresh invasion of Maryland His ultimate purpose was to afford relief to the Shenandoah Valley and to transfer the scene of hostilities to the north of the Potomac If he could succeed in doing this the Union troops about Vicksburg would be drawn off and that otherwise doomed city be saved Besides these objects Lee hints at other ends in the words, "It was hoped that other valuable results might be attained by military success"[*] Just what ambitions are hidden in these ambiguous words may never be known, but certainly hope welled strong in the breast of the Confederate commander that Maryland, the child of Southern love, would be aroused by the clarion call of Confederate conquest upon her soil This constant hope of the Confederacy had an influence upon the course of the war which can never properly be estimated. Though possessed of little profit, the speculation is full of interest as to what changes in the campaigns of the Civil War would have been made and with what effect upon the final result if from the start the Confederate government and its military leaders had realized

---

[*] Schouler, p 351,

the futility of seeking to range Maryland upon the side of secession. "The movement into Maryland was of course a more direct threat upon Washington. Besides, at that period there was still a prevalent belief among Southern leaders that Southern sentiment was strong in Maryland, and that an important victory within her borders might change the Confederate camps into recruiting stations and add materially to the strength of Lee's army. But the Confederate graves which were dug in Maryland's soil vastly outnumbered the Confederate soldiers recruited from her citizens."[†]

After crossing the Potomac near Harper's Ferry, Lee and his army proceeded toward Hagerstown where they made a short rest and then crossed the Pennsylvania line and encamped near Chambersburg. He threatened Harrisburg, occupied York and Carlisle and seized large quantities of grain and cattle, tendering payment in Confederate notes. In the meanwhile Hooker had kept informed as to his adversary's movements. The Union army had been reinforced through the call of the President for one hundred thousand militia to be recruited from Maryland, Ohio and West Virginia. Hooker's cavalry leader, Pleasanton, harassed the Confederate flanks and won the battle of Brandy Station. He then concentrated his forces at Frederick, Maryland. In the meanwhile discord in the councils of the high military authorities led Hooker to tender his resignation upon the same day, June 27th, that witnessed Lee's passage into Pennsylvania. His successor, Major-General Meade, spread out his several corps along the roads pointing towards Gettysburg and, pressing on, headed directly towards the Confederate columns of Hill and Longstreet. Each army was to a great extent ignorant of the location and movement of the other. On July 1st Meade occupied Gettysburg.

The feeling in Maryland with regard to the Confederate army and its prospects had greatly changed from what it had been at the time of Lee's earlier advent into the State with his bedraggled troopers bearing laurels too few to be prophetic

---

[†]Gordon, "Reminiscences of the Civil War," p. 138.

of an ultimate crown of victory. Although the possibility of awakening a general response in the State to the open invitation of the Confederate leader to unite with him for the redemption of Maryland from Federal control was forever passed, nevertheless the gallant Lee created great enthusiasm, and his Southern sympathizers boldly predicted the capture of Baltimore The Maryland authorities hastened to put the city in a state of strong defense. The anxiety created by the general uncertainty of the situation was fatal to all business and resulted in a practical suspension of the commerce of the city Governor Bradford on June 17th issued a call for volunteers and received in response the enlistment of six thousand citizens as "Loyal Leaguers." Several thousand negroes were set to work to dig entrenchments on the outskirts of the city Forts McHenry, Federal Hill, and Marshall were strongly reinforced, troops for this purpose being sent to Baltimore from New York and other Northern points Nor were the fears of Baltimore without strong foundation. The Confederates approached close enough to the city for its residents to imagine at least that they caught the smell of gunpowder. Col Harry Gilmour, who had attacked a few squads of United States cavalry at Westminster, utterly routed them, chasing the fugitives as far as Pikesville, but eight miles north of Baltimore

During the first three days of July was fought the battle of Gettysburg. Upon the issue of that tremendous conflict Lee staked and lost Its result had great moral influence upon Baltimore The incubus of dread was lifted and while the authorities and Federal adherents rejoiced at the passing over of the most ominous war cloud which had as yet darkened the sky, the Confederate sympathizers, glad as well that Baltimore should have escaped the horrors of battle, were greatly depressed over a defeat that seemed portentious of the final outcome of the strife betwen the states. Until four o'clock of the afternoon of the first day the tide of battle seemed to favor General Heth, the Confederate commander; his opponent Reynolds had been killed and General Doubleday was in temporary command until the arrival of General Howard with reinforcements. At four o'clock Hancock also arrived and was followed by Slocum, who assumed general command. All that night the Union columns concentrated in that vast natural theater where the struggle resolutely begun was to assume Titanic proportions. Meade himself arrived shortly after midnight. Lee appeared upon the scene in time to witness from Seminary Hill the new position occuped by the foe who had been made to retreat in the earlier part of the engagement of that day. He sent word to General Ewell to attack Seminary Hill if he thought it practicable. Throughout the morning the contending forces maneuvered for position, but four o'clock in the afternoon Hood's division swept up the slopes of Little Round Top to attack the Federal extreme left under General Sickles. At nightfall the Federal army held a seemingly impregnable position from Little Round Top to Cemetery Hill. In their respective councils the leaders of the opposing armies decided to maintain their positions and await the break of dawn. In the meanwhile Lee had received the reinforcement of the fresh troops of Pickett. The issue of the second day had brought the Confederate army a sufficient measure of success to commit it to a continuance of the battle with some apparent hope of victory.

The third day opened with Meade's dislodging Johnson's troops from Culp's Hill, which they had captured, and from the Baltimore pike. This seriously disorganized Lee's plans. The Confederate commander determined to bring into action his massed infantry under the protection of a tremendous artillery fire. At mid-day the lull which had followed Meade's coup was broken by the concentrated roar of one hundred and thirty Confederate guns in the greatest cannonade ever heard upon any battlefield. It was responded to by about half the number in the Federal lines. In the meanwhile the gallant Pickett had massed his seventeen thousand men in wedge-shape formation, and after the artillery duel had ended, hurled them at the heights of Cemetery Ridge. From both directions the Union artillery enfilated the advancing column. But undeterred by the hail of iron, it swept on, passed the stone fence which furnished cover to its foe, and forced the gunners from their guns It was a magnificent specimen of heroism, but the "high-water mark" of Pickett's charge was not only the turning tide of the battle but marked as well the decline of the cause for which that magnificent exhibition of American valor was given It was impossible for Pickett to carry his tremendous rush-line further into the enemy's ranks. He gave the order to retreat The next day found Lee rapidly heading for the Potomac to seek the security of the Virginia shore The invasion of the North was at an end * Among the Maryland commands which took part in the battle of Gettysburg were the Second Maryland Confederate infantry, the Chesapeake Maryland artillery, the First Maryland artillery and Colonel Maulsby's Potomac Home Guards

The terrible results of the battle made demand upon the sympathies of the people of Maryland and they handsomely responded Wounded soldiers, Union and Confederate, were brought into Baltimore in large numbers. A committee was appointed to solicit and forward relief supplies The city council appropriated six thousand dollars which went to swell the sums contributed by citizens of Baltimore to a total of fifty thousand dollars in cash, besides many serviceable articles. A large number of surgeons hastened from Baltimore to the battlefield and the Sanitary and Christian Commission which, under the direction of Mr Goldsborough S. Griffith, did much for the alleviation of the distress of sufferers from the war, also went to the same place with quantities of medicinal stores, clothing and delicacies. The Adams Express Company likewise established through its local superintendent an efficient hospital corps, while the charitable impulses of various religious organizations made quick response to the distressing need

Anti-slavery sentiment in Maryland had been rapidly on the increase and on May 28th, 1862, a Union convention was held in Baltimore which recommended the adoption of a new State constitution to embrace an emancipation provision. Upon

---
* Schouler, vol 6, pp 359-369

April 20th, 1863, at a Union mass meeting held in Baltimore, a resolution was adopted that "slavery should cease to be recognized by the law of Maryland." Upon September 28th another Union mass meeting was held in the same city at which a demand was made for the immediate emancipation of slaves. In the midst of the civil strife, an election was held in Maryland, resulting in the success of the Unconditional Union party. The principal feature of this election was the controversy as to the limits of the military authority which arose between Governor Bradford and Major-General Schenck An order was issued by the latter to the provost-marshals to summarily arrest any persons whom they found approaching the polls of whose loyalty they were not assured. Governor Bradford resented this interference with the functions of the judges of election as well as the virtual placing of the liberty of citizens in the hands of the provost-marshals whose judgment alone was sufficient to cause an arrest. Lincoln was appealed to and modified the order of the military commander, without, however, materially affecting the points of grievance The curious spectacle was represented of the President expressing unlimited confidence in the loyalty of Maryland, the military commander vieing with the governor in asserting his conviction that the issue of the elections was not a matter admitting of doubt, and yet the polls being under the close espionage of the military authorities

At an early period in the session of the Maryland Legislature of 1863 a bill was introduced calling a State convention with a view to the abolition of slavery On the 28th of January it passed both houses The bill provided for the submission of the question of the calling of such a convention to the voters at a special election to be held the first Wednesday in the following April This election was held and the convention proposition received the endorsement of a large majority of the voters. On the 27th of April the constitutional convention convened at Annapolis, State Comptroller Henry H Goldsborough presiding The most important changes in the constitution as adopted were the express acknowledgment of paramount allegiance to the United States, the abolition of slavery and the emancipation of slaves, the imposition of a test oath upon voters and officeholders, the increase in the number of the judges of the Court of Appeals from four to five, the establishment of thirteen instead of eight judicial districts, the institution of county courts and the increase of Baltimore's representation in the legislature from one to three senators and from twelve to eighteen delegates Pursuant to the method prescribed by the new constitution for its ratification, an election was held on October 12th, 1864, and a majority of votes were cast for it. However, the result was contested upon the ground of the alleged illegality of the soldier vote, the elimination of which would have resulted in the rejection of the constitution A writ of mandamus was asked for but was rejected and Governor Bradford issued a proclamation setting forth the adoption of the constitution. It went into effect November 1st, 1864

The summer of 1864 witnessed the third invasion of Maryland. General Early with twelve thousand troops left Staunton, Va in order to draw off the troops about Petersburg by a feint of marching against Washington. Gen. Bradley T. Johnson, in command of Early's advance, crossed the Potomac at Sharpsburg, July 5th The following day General McCausland occupied Hagerstown and made demand upon the citizens for twenty thousand dollars as well as the surrender of all government effects under threats that he would burn the city His demand was complied with The country surrounding Sharpsburg was scoured and everything in the nature of serviceable supplies appropriated At Middletown Johnson encountered a Federal force which fell back on Frederick. Johnson accordingly attacked that city on July 7th and Colonel Clendening evacuated the place a few days later, carrying with him all his stores. On the 9th the Confederates took possession and exacted of the residents a levy of two hundred thousand dollars. On that same date the Union army under Gen. Lew Wallace met defeat at the hands of the Confederates at Monocacy. Baltimore was again thrown into a paroxysm of fright. Consternation reigned supreme. Governor Bradford issued a hurried call for volunteers. General Johnson destroyed the railroads and bridges throughout Baltimore county and advanced towards the city as far as Charles Street avenue, within five miles of the corporate limits. Here he afforded himself the satisfaction of burning Governor Bradford's house, justifying his act upon the precedent set by the Union army.

Early's sally against Washington was brought to an end by the warning given him by Johnson of the arrival at Baltimore of the Sixth and Nineteenth army corps. Sending part of his command on a raid into Pennsylvania he retreated into Virginia. The Confederate force which Early had left behind carried out its instructions and also made an attempt upon Cumberland, Md., where it was repulsed by General Kelly.

The incidents of the final campaign of principal note in relation to Maryland was the gallant part taken by the Maryland brigade of Warren's corps in General Grant's final operations about Richmond and the heroic efforts of the Maryland Confederate troops to cut their way through the victorious Union lines. The struggle was now over, Richmond was evacuated, and on April 9th, 1865, Lee surrendered his army at Appomatox.

The National Republican Convention had met at Baltimore on Tuesday, June 7th, 1864, and renominated Abraham Lincoln, who was elected. Upon the 14th of the following April President Lincoln was assassinated by John Wilkes Booth, an actor, in Ford's Opera House, Washington, D. C., and in accordance with the provision of the Constitution, Vice-President Johnson succeeded to the office of the martyred President.

The principal results which were derived from the Civil War were the emancipation of the slaves, the establishment of the doctrine of an indissoluble Union, which involved the overthrow of the idea of state sovereignty, and the recognition in a general way of the supremacy of the national government in the arena of national issues. Maryland had been preserved to the Union and although subjected to the uncertain fortunes and divided sentiments of a border state had nevertheless maintained a position of credit It had contributed materially to both the Federal and Confederate sides of the issue and its sons had found themselves compelled to cross swords on more than one bloody field. Maryland had never been a large slaveholding state, and, had not the issue of slavery assumed a sectional aspect she would not have felt called upon to give her sympathies to the maintenance of the institution of slavery Her Southern proclivities caused her to sympathize deeply with her Southern sisters while her prominent part in the formation of the American commonwealth and the adoption of the Federal Constitution prevented her from ever endorsing the doctrine of secession

CHAPTER XXI.

AFTER THE CIVIL WAR.

During the dark days of reconstruction in the South, Maryland was compelled to bear many of the afflictions of her recreant sisters. The distress incident to military control of the state during the continuance of the war have been sufficiently dwelt upon. Now to the efforts of the Federal government to insure the civil control of Maryland to its adherents was added a measure whose searching discrimination as to the past conduct and even the opinions of the voting population made it a matter of hazard for anyone to attempt to cast a ballot who had not by some actual contribution to the Union cause placed his "loyalty" beyond impeachment. This word had been for so long the test-word in the state that it had assumed something of the character of a fetich. Those who could pronounce their shibboleths in an approved manner, albeit many did so with hypocrisy in their hearts, were *ipse facto* regarded as devoted sons of the Union. One of the most unfortunate features of Maryland's forced position in the civil strife was the equivocation which it bred. When the display of Confederate colors in the ribbon of a nurse girl's hair was a sufficient cause for her arrest and that of her tender charge and when the failure to display a bit of Union colors was a sufficient cause for the arrest of entire households it was impossible that many men with strong Southern sympathies the expression of which would not only have been futile but fatal, should not have learned too well the art of taking their harps from the willows and playing the Lord's songs in a foreign land.

The act to which reference is here made was directed to the scrutiny of the registry lists It propounded to applicants for registration twenty-five questions which probed into both conduct and conscience A single false statement or one which could be so construed rendered the person making it liable to confinement in the penitentiary for not less than one nor more than eight years and rendered him forever disqualified from voting or holding office To these penalties was added the suggestion to possible derelicts of the moral opprobrium they would be brought under and the future punishment they would be subjected to for false swearing. It is not surprising that the value of the franchise which during the war presented too many perils for it to be generally courted, should now have been reduced in popular appreciation to a point considerably lower than ever before Out of forty thousand persons qualified to vote in Baltimore only ten thousand had the hardihood to present themselves for the prescribed examination. An election held under such conditions was but a perfunctory performance At a mass meeting held in Howard County under the leadership of Montgomery Blair, the registration act was severely denounced. A test case was brought before the Court of Appeals and passed upon adversely On January 10th, 1866, Governor Swann convened the legislature in special session, but recommended to it that no radical modifications should be made

The people now sought mitigation of their grievances in recourse to a State Convention, which was held on the 24th of January and was presided over by Hon Montgomery Blair, and included representative citizens from every portion of the state The Baltimore Sun referred to the gathering as one of the most representative in intelligence and influence which had ever convened in Baltimore The general sentiment of the convention was that efforts should be directed towards the securing of peace and harmony and that measures such as the registration act which were designed to perpetuate the issues of civil strife in the state ought to be repudiated. Thus was begun a popular movement for the restoration to confidence of a large proportion of the citizens of the State who accepted the arbitrament of war and who, in a spirit of devotion to Maryland, desired only to have an opportunity of exercising the common right of franchise. The cry of the convention was let by-gones be by-gones and permit the citizens of Maryland to get together in the common work of assimilating the elements of the state and bringing about a return of that homogenity which had been destroyed by fratricidal strife* The convention appealed without avail both to the general government and to the Legislature. Nevertheless, a practical modification was brought about through a more liberal interpretation of the law and a consequent milder application of it. At the October election, however, the actual votes cast for mayor were only seven thousand, nine hundred and ninety-three. The judges of election, acting upon the advice of the attorney-general of the state, debarred from voting the registered voters of 1866, upon the ground that that registration had not been complete. A meeting of citizens was held on the 16th of October and a committee was appointed to investigate the official conduct of the police commissioners and their appointees, who were charged with having committed grave misdemeanors in connection with the recent election. A memorial accompanied with numerous affidavits was presented to Governor Swann, who took official cognizance of the cases of the commissioners. The latter declined to appear upon the 22nd, the day set by the governor for trial, they denying his jurisdiction. Upon the 1st of November the governor summarily removed them in the exercise of the power with which he conceived himself to be clothed, and appointed a new board. The city was in a fever of excitement, and the discredited commissioners, adhering to their position, mustered in a force of thirty-five hundred special policemen and placed under arrest the members of the new board as well as the sheriff. Fearing that the controversy which had stirred the feelings of the citizens of Baltimore to their depths might result in an "insurrection,"

---

* Reports of Convention in Baltimore Sun and American, Jany. 24, *supra*, 1866.

President Johnson, through the war department, called the attention of General Grant to the situation in Baltimore and that official, after directing General Canby to proceed to the city in the interest of order, arrested the progress of certain troops passing through Baltimore enroute from New York, and also held an infantry regiment at Washington in readiness for immediate service. On the 5th, General Grant appeared upon the scene in person. The seriousness of the situation as it appeared to him is denoted by the telegram which immediately upon his arrival in Baltimore, he sent to Secretary Stanton: "This morning collision seemed almost inevitable." On the same day that Grant sent this telegram the warden of the jail declined to honor a writ of *habeas corpus* which the court had issued in behalf of the imprisoned officials. In so doing he was acting in concert with the displaced board whose purpose was to remain in charge of the police machinery of the city until after the approaching election. This election was held on November 6th, and in spite of the fact that the ballot box was "hedged round by restriction and kept in custody of those who, by the judgment of the law, had forfeited all right to its guardianship," resulted in the election of the conservative candidate for State Comptroller, Col. William J. Leonard, by a majority of one thousand and twenty. In view of the incitement to disorder which the circumstances of the election furnished, the success of the conservative ticket was aptly referred by the Baltimore Sun as a "triumph of popular forbearance." Two days after the election the warden of the jail brought the imprisoned police commissioners into court and upon the 13th of the month Judge Bartol delivered an opinion granting release to the prisoners, who thereupon entered into the unobstructed exercise of their functions.

Maryland was not distracted by her political difficulties to the extent of neglecting her duty of love. The ravages made by the Civil War throughout the South had laid that once fertile and prosperous section under tribute to the locust and the cankerworm. Maryland's ever generous response to need prompted her to liberal contributions for the relief of destitute persons in the states laid waste. It is to the credit of the Northern States generally that they, too, sent large relief funds into the stricken sections, which proved to be veritable peace offerings and went far towards effecting a conciliation of feeling on the part of the people of the South towards their northern brethren. In April, 1866, a Southern Relief Fair was held in Baltimore at the Maryland Institute, at which about one hundred and sixty-five thousand dollars was realized. The following January the State Legislature appropriated one hundred thousand dollars for the same purpose. In addition to these, large contributions were sent through private channels. The commiseration felt by Maryland for the South was prompted by a generous feeling towards the section with which it had so much in common, to which it had made contributions of men and money, and for which it had suffered during the dark days of the war.

The suffrage agitation which had been going on in the State bore fruitage in a bill which passed the Legislature on the 24th of January, 1867, the object of which was "to restore to full citizenship and the right to vote and to hold office, all persons who may be deprived thereof by the provisions contained in the fourth section of the first article of the constitution of the state." The only test remaining for the exercise of the right of suffrage was simply an oath to support the Constitution and laws of the United States. A bill for the holding of a new election in Baltimore City was also passed but was reconsidered before it received the governor's signature.

The popular demand for a new constitution resulted in the calling of an election to decide that question. This was held April 13th, 1867, a majority of votes being cast in favor of the proposition. The convention was held May 8th of the same year, in the hall of the House of Delegates in the statehouse. Judge Richard Carmichael, of Queen Annes County, presided over the body. The convention remained in session until August 17th, at which time it had agreed upon and had drafted a new constitution for the state. On September 18th it was submitted to the people for ratification and received a majority vote of twenty-four thousand, one hundred and sixteen On October 5th it went into effect. Among the more important changes provided for in the new constitution were those relating to the electorate and judiciary. In conformity with the fifteenth amendment of the national constitution, the total population of the State was made the basis of the representation in the Legislature, instead of, as formerly the white population. The number of judicial circuits was increased from eight to thirteen, with three judges instead of one in each circuit. The circuit judges were to be elected by the people of the several circuits instead of upon a general state ticket These judges were also to constitute a Court of Appeals. The five judges of Baltimore City, now eight, were associated in a Supreme Bench of Baltimore City, with certain appellate jurisdiction. The first election held under the new constitution was the municipal election in Baltimore at which R T. Banks was elected mayor. This was on October 23rd The 5th of the following month Col. Oden Bowie was elected governor of the State by a majority of forty-one thousand in a total vote of eighty-five thousand At the same time two-thirds of his associates upon the Democratic-Conservative ticket were elected to the legislature. The triumph of the section of the Union party which continued much of the traditions of the antebellum democracy must be attributed to the votes of those Democrats with Union sympathies whose support had been lost to their party during the Civil War.

Although the elections of 1866 had as their issue the freedom of the ballot box and by their result established the popular vindication of the right of men to vote whom it was customary for their opponents to refer to as "rebels and rebel sympathizers," nevertheless, the struggle for the resumption of political rights by the lately disfranchised element of the electorate had yet to be continued in the face not only of strong adverse sentiment but of actual measures proposed in Congress for Federal governmental control over Maryland Defeated in the state elections, the radical party with ex-Governor Francis Thomas as their leader, carried the contest into

Congress where they hoped to receive active support by reason of the strong Republican preponderance in that body. Charges were presented against Governor Swann of the employment of revolutionary tactics subversive of the true intent of the registration law and of the interest of the "loyal" element of the state and their principles in general. A circumstance of the factional strife in Maryland was a proposal which was made in the House of Representatives to remove the Naval Academy from Annapolis. Although ex-Governor Thomas was swayed by intense Union sentiment in his contest for the supremacy of the radical party in Maryland, he nevertheless, in connection with General Phelps, made an earnest fight against the sinister plan to deprive Maryland of the Naval Academy as a punitive measure. General Phelps in an earnest speech vindicated Maryland's right to be regarded as a loyal state and eloquently recited her contributions to the Union cause, "Fifty thousand men in the Union armies. $30,000,000 thrown into the breach, with eighty-seven thousand of her slaves as a voluntary sacrifice to the Union at the time it was imperilled," said he, "is the answer to the libel." He concluded with a peroration whose satire was most cogent in disclosing the disingenuousness of the advocates of the measure than argument: "If the results of elections from time to time are to have this effect upon works requiring stability for their success, upon great public institutions demanding permanence for their utility, then you must put the Military Academy at West Point, the Naval Academy, the United States Mint, and every other public institution, upon wheels, and move them from state to state, whenever the result of an election may be objectionable to the dominant majority in Congress." This was not the last time that the permanency of the Naval Academy at Annapolis was threatened by those who envied Maryland the distinction. Nevertheless it still remains and the immense sums since spent in the improvement of the Academy places beyond future question its continuance upon the banks of the Severn.

Although the efforts of the advocates of reconstruction for Maryland failed of effect because of the definite refusal of Congress to regard that state as a subject for the application of the stringent measures which were applied to those states lately in rebellion, Congress had the benefit of a campaign of enlightenment upon the situation and sentiment in the state which while it could hardly have been edifying, was not without value in fixing clearly the attitude of the administration towards the state. It was again the eloquence of General Phelps which made clear the injustice of the attack upon Maryland As in the case of the Naval Academy, so in the matter of the electorate, General Phelps made clear the injustice of the action which Congress was urged to take and reaffirmed his declaration of the essential loyalty of the State

The Committee on Judiciary to which all the testimony relating to the Maryland question had been referred never returned a report, so that the December session of Congress of 1867 saw the end of the attempt to further the demands of the minority element of the State whose motives, however, sincere, were based upon an exaggeration of the situation even from their own point of view, and, certainly, were rested upon a wholly mistaken apprehension of the needs of Maryland

With its political status definitely assured, the State experienced a period of quiet and constitutional legislation In 1868 the Congressional elections were fixed as at present on the first Tuesday after the first Monday in November It was enacted at that time that it should be the duty of policemen in Baltimore City to report to the police board the name and residence of every male person known by them to have died within the bounds of their districts during the year in order that these lists might be furnished to the registers This was the beginning of the system of police census Many minor changes were made by the Legislature during these and subsequent years in an attempt to eliminate the objectionable features of the elective machinery and to remedy the abuses to which it had been subjected

An element of interest in the Legislature of 1868 was the selection by the new body of a United States senator to succeed the Hon. Reverdy Johnson, whose term of office was to expire upon the 4th of March, 1869. Hon. William T. Hamilton received the necessary vote and was duly declared elected. In the meanwhile, however, the distinguished abilities of Reverdy Johnson led the President to tender him the appointment of Minister to England. The seat in the Senate which was thus made vacant was filled by the appointment by Governor Swann of William Pinckney Whyte, of Baltimore, for the unexpired term.

A circumstance of the year 1868 which made a deep impress upon the minds of the citizens of Baltimore and serves to mark an epoch in its social experience was a disastrous flood which visited the city, carrying terror to the minds of all and resulting in loss of life as well as the destruction of much property. Jones Falls has always played an important part in the history of Baltimore, but it has frequently been a source of danger to the city. Coming from the hilly country towards the northwest, it winds its course through the very heart of the city. When swollen by freshets it frequently has overflowed and inundated the low-lying sections of the city. On the 24th of July, as the result of a downpour of rain throughout the day, the Falls rose with great rapidity, overflowed into the contiguous streets, inundated dwellings, and became a raging torrent, carrying before it every form of movable property. The destruction of property was estimated at $3,000,000 and the distress was so deep and widespread that the Maryland Legislature and the Baltimore City Council adopted relief measures, large contributions being also made by generous citizens. Another event of quite a different nature and which furnished a beginning of a practical political problem for the State was the casting of the first ballot by colored men at any election in Maryland. This was at the local election held at Towson, Baltimore county, April 4th, 1870, for the selection of five town commissioners. Although it was the first occasion of the exercise by colored men of the right of franchise given them under the new constitution, it was not the first instance of the colored population exercising the right of ballot within the territorial limits of the state of Maryland. Prior to 1666 a few colored men had voted as citizens of the colony. Maryland in bestowing the ballot upon the freedman was but reviving the liberal attitude she had held towards the colored race more than two hundred years before. The colored voters were not slow to avail themselves of their newly acquired right for at the fall elections of 1870 thirty-six thousand negroes voted

On July 9, 1872, the National Democratic Convention was held in Baltimore, at which Horace Greeley was put in nomination for the Presidency. The contest between Greeley and Grant, the Republican nominee, was hotly fought and had about it elements of peculiar bitterness In Maryland the voting sentiment was evenly divided so that although Greeley secured the State's electoral votes he did so by the narrow margin of nine hundred and twenty-seven. The year following has passed into the economic history of the country as one of disaster by reason of the panic which bore down upon the tide of misfortune many financial institutions of New York, Baltimore and other cities and which gave to September 19th of that year the name "Black Friday."

In 1874 the Board of Police Commissioners underwent a fresh modification The law remained substantially as it was in 1867 at which time the board, as we have seen, consisted of three persons elected by the legislature for four years. It was now changed to provide for six commissioners, one member retiring biennially The State had not yet forgotten the disorders incident to the Knownothing rule in Baltimore, at which time the administration of its police was taken out of the hands of the city. In spite of continuous protest on the part of Baltimore against what it regards as a usurpation by the State of an important feature of its local rule, the city is still denied the right to have control of its own police department

The attitude of Maryland in the memorable Hayes-Tilden contest was reflected in a resolution introduced into the House of Delegates by Montgomery Blair, instructing the Attorney-General of the State to take appropriate action looking to the bringing to the attention of the Supreme Court of the United States, the facts with regard to the late Presidential election in Maryland and to pray the court to declare the returns of the Electoral Commission with regard to the states of Louisiana and Florida fraudulent and void and to decide the contest in favor of Tilden and Hendricks. Pursuant of this resolution, Mr. Kimmel of Maryland introduced a bill in the House of Representatives providing a form of action by which the title to the office of President and Vice-President might be tried before the Supreme Court in the name of any of the states of the Union. This attempt of Maryland to make the office of President a proper subject for litigation failed to receive the sanction of Congress.

In 1877 occurred the great strike of the employees of the Baltimore and Ohio Railroad, this action on their part being the result of a 10 per cent. reduction in their pay. For a decade industries and general business throughout the country had suffered depression, largely the effect of a reaction from the fictitious prosperity incident to the close of the Civil War. The situation bore heaviest upon the working classes. Large numbers were thrown out of work and in almost all lines of employment there were reductions made in wages. The railroads of the country, suffering from the reduction of transportation, sought relief by effecting economies in administration. The Baltimore and Ohio Railroad, instead of resorting to the practice followed by some of the other systems of reducing the force of its employees, sought to retain their men in their employ and made the cut in their wages in order to do so. The men were not satisfied to take this view of the company's action and quit work on July 16. Two days later the governor of West Virginia appealed to President Hayes for troops with which to suppress the riots at points upon the railroad line in that State. At the same time President Garrett made a similar appeal upon the part of the railroad, and the national executive deemed the situation serious enough to respond. He issued a proclamation calling upon the rioters to desist from their unlawful proceedings. This action being without effect, on July 20th eight companies of United States troops were sent to Martinsburg, West Virginia. In the meanwhile Governor Carroll of Maryland had called out the Fifth Maryland regiment This crack militia command was despatched to Cumberland, where it acquitted itself with credit. The governor also issued a proclamation to the rioters within the borders of the state to refrain from further acts of violence. This unfortunate strike was characterized by many scenes of disorder and violence in Baltimore Sections of the city were placed under virtual military rule. The clashing of the rioters and militia resulted in a number of distressing casualties By July 28th the strike had spent its force in Baltimore and an attempt was made to run cars in the State The better spirit of the men had by this time reasserted itself and they offered no serious opposition. The election for governor and other state offices in November, 1879, resulted in a sweeping Democratic victory. The issues were fairly and dispassionately presented Hon William T. Hamilton, the candidate of the Democratic party received a majority vote of 22,208 over his Republican opponent, Hon James A. Gary.

From the 12th to the 19th of January, 1880, festivity reigned supreme in Baltimore. The city spent its energies in a round of pleasureable and spectacular events, in celebration of its one hundred and fiftieth anniversary. The sesquicentennial was the greatest celebration ever held in the city The weather conditions were perfect and multitudes of visitors, not only from the State itself, but from the South generally entered with the keenest enjoyment into the spirit of the occasion. The civil, military and trades processions and the water pageantry was upon a scale of elaborateness and extensiveness that proved a vertible revelation to Southern merchants of the resources of the metropolis and did much to strengthen the commercial ties between Baltimore and the South

One of the features of the celebration was a parade of ten thousand school boys This was significant of the place which public education had come to hold in the economy of the city and state. The development of the school system has been noticed in part. An adequate treatment of the history of education in Maryland and the steps by which there came to be grouped in the State, and particularly in Baltimore City, a large number of general and technical schools of high grade is not possible in the brief limits assigned to a particular topic in a state history. No one single thing, however, has so contributed to the high regard in which Baltimore is held and the estimation abroad of its spirit of progress as its educational institutions. No city in the country has so large a proportion of student population or a greater diversity of educational opportunities. With Maryland's appreciation of the institutions for the higher and special branches of learning has gone han-in-hand a generous and wise provision for primary and secondary instruction.

The Act of 1825 to provide for public instruction of the youth in public schools throughout the state soon gave proof of its inefficiency. The governor in his message in 1828 called the attention of the Legislature to the fact that the law was believed to be so defective that there had not been more than a partial attempt to carry out its provisions and that without revision and material amendment it would prove useless. It was not adapted to the habits of the people of Maryland and it was based upon an artificial system. The matter of principal interest in the act was its acceptance of the principles of modern public education and although the State's entrance upon large schemes of internal improvement led to such financial embarrassment that appropriations for schools were not at all times adequate, nevertheless, the way was prepared for the adoption of a state system of education. The various enactments passed between the year 1825 and the breaking out of the Civil War show that public education in Maryland was in a tentative and formative state. It was moreover lacking in uniformity, both as to consistency in the various counties and the grades of schools to which state aid was rendered. In 1856 Governor Ligon in a message to the legislature declared that the system of public instruction in the

state was in a condition of utter and hopeless prostration *
He recommended the reconstruction of the system upon a plan
of uniformity and supported by state and county resources and
under a central controlling and supervisory power.

It was not until 1865 however that the state secured a
comprehensive school system The system then adopted was
strongly centralized. Instead of the school funds being divided
among the several counties and administered according to
different systems there was created a state Board of Education.
This was to consist of the governor, lieutenant-governor,
speaker of the House of Delegates, and a state superintendent,
an appointee of the governor This formidable assemblage
of dignitaries was given supervision of all colleges and schools
receiving state donations They had the selection of the school
equipment, prepared a code of regulations for the government
of the county school boards, appointed such school commissioners for each county as the state superintendent might direct
and had the power of removal of any commissioners found
guilty of failing to act in harmony with the superintendent
"All property, estate, and effects, all money, all funds, all
claims, all state donations, now vested by law in any county
or school district, any board of school commissioners, any
board of inspectors of primary schools, any trustee or trustees
of primary schools, or any other body of persons whatsoever,
for the use and benefit of public, primary, free, or high
schools in the county," was transferred to the board of school
commissioners of the county The counties were divided into
school districts with one commissioner in control of each,
who had the appropriate duties of such an office, the appointing
of teachers from persons having proper certificates, the supervision of certificates and the hearing of charges affecting the
morals or competency of teachers. The law provided for the
establishment of a high school in each county and St John's
College, Washington College, the Agricultural College, the
Faculty of Arts and Sciences, and the Law School were brought
together to constitute the University of Maryland It was

---

* Steiner's "History of Education in Maryland."

designed that the courses of instruction in the county high schools should prepare students for matriculation in some one of the schools comprising that University. The school law of 1865 further provided that the state appropriations to the counties for the maintenance of the academies and schools should constitute "together with such other donations as from time to time may be made and annually appropriated by the county board, a high school fund." In its operation it was soon found that the Act of 1865 had carried centralization too far and a new school law was passed in 1868 which restored the right of local self government in school matters and left the endowed schools as they had been before 1865. The provision for the county high schools remained and gradually a number of the academies became incorporated with the public schools. The institutions furnishing higher education which date back in their history to the formative period of Maryland's educational system had experienced the vicissitudes consequent upon the changes in the state's attitude towards public education.

Washington College, Chestertown, received its charter in 1772 and at its foundation absorbed the Kent County School. Two years later the western shore emulous of educational opportunities equal to those of the other side of the bay secured through its representatives in the Legislature in 1784 the charter of St. John's College. Public appropriations were made for these institutions. The ambition to have within its borders a university such as were to be found in several of her sister states was shown in the act creating St. John's College by a provision by which it was associated with Washington College to constitute the University of Maryland. The institution which was to continue the name of University of Maryland developed from a medical faculty. As early as 1789 there was organized the Medical Society of Baltimore. In 1812 a College of Medicine of Maryland was duly constituted by an act of legislature, which also provided for a faculty of divinity, a faculty of law and a faculty of the arts and sciences which thus united should constitute a University by the name and under the title of the University of Maryland. The organization of the new University was, however, too loose to be effective, and the only faculties which became established on a permanent footing were those which continue to-day, the schools of medicine and law, to which was later added a school of dentistry.

The Peabody Institute, whose aims are broadly educational and which has had a wide influence, not only upon the intellectual life of Baltimore, but of Maryland and the South, was the gift, in 1857, of Mr George Peabody, a native of Massachusetts, but an adopted son of Maryland, who, recognizing his indebtedness to the city of Baltimore as the place in which he had laid the foundation of his great fortune, sought to repay his obligation in part by the establishment of an institution which should provide means of higher culture for the youth of the State. He appointed trustees for the proposed institution and placed in their hands the sum of $300,000 towards the erection of a building and the providing of necessary appliances. Upon the 16th of April, 1869, the corner stone of the Peabody Institute was laid and on October 25, 1866, the building was dedicated in the presence of a vast assemblage, including 18,000 pupils of the public schools By various donations Mr Peabody increased the endowment of the Institute to $1,400,000 This magnificent foundation sustains a free public library, courses of lectures, a school of music, and a gallery of art. The library was formally opened to the public in 1866 and the building was finally completed in 1869 The library is entirely used for reference and is one of the finest of its kind in the country.

The Johns Hopkins University was one of the latest educational foundations of Maryland. It owes its existence to a Baltimore merchant, Johns Hopkins, who acquired a large fortune by industry and sagacity At the request of Mr. Hopkins an incorporation was formed on August 24, 1867, under a general statute "for the promotion of education in the state of Maryland " This liberal authorization permitted the projected institution to assume as wide a range as its incorporators might care for it to take Upon the death of Mr.

Hopkins it was found that he had bequeathed $3,500,000 for each of two institutions which were to bear his name—the Johns Hopkins University and the Johns Hopkins Hospital. The gift to the University included Mr. Hopkins estate, "Clifton," which was eventually sold to the city for a public park. The trustees of the new University were fortunate in securing as its first president Daniel C. Gilman, who was called from the presidency of the University of California to practically create the University whose existence at that time was simply on paper. President Gilman brought with him to Baltimore not only wide and diversified scholarship, enthusiasm and ideals, but a conception of an American University such as had never yet been developed. With the full concurrence of the trustees, Dr. Gilman made the matter of the housing of the new university a secondary consideration and devoted himself to gathering about him a faculty composed of men bred in the methods of the German universities and a corps of graduate students the high competency of which was assured by the method of selection; a number of fellowships being offered with competitive requirements. As Dr. Gilman had selected his teaching associates with rare discrimination, so with splendid tactfulness he organized them into a unit of action, yet without limiting in any degree the full expression of their varied genius, industry and enthusiasm. The wisdom of the new experiment of a university organized upon the graduate idea has been justified by the results achieved. For it did not require any considerable length of time for the worth of the Johns Hopkins University to challenge the respect of older foundations throughout the country and to be accorded preeminence among American educational institutions by universities abroad. The Johns Hopkins Hospital also started with distinctive ideals and its achievement of high renown has fully justified the exceptional standards for hospital service which it established. At the time of its foundation it surpassed in buildings and equipment all other institutions of its kind in this country. The original purpose of establishing a medical school which should be in connection with the university and offer its students all of the opportunities of hospital training could not be carried out, for want of an adequate endowment, until 1890, when, through the beneficence of Miss Mary E Garrett and other women, a fund of $119,000 was tendered the trustees for that purpose. The gift carried with it a stipulation that "women should be admitted upon the same terms as may be prescribed for men " The trustees accepted the gift with its condition, but the sum proving inadequate for the purpose toward which it was to be directed, Miss Garrett increased the amount to $500,000. The Johns Hopkins Medical School was then organized as a department of the University.

In 1866 the State Normal School for the training and equipment of teachers for the public schools was organized in conformity with an act passed by the legislature the year before. This school has since then done a wide work in fitting young men and young women for teaching positions Its graduates are allowed to teach in any of the counties of the state without having to take an examination for a county certificate

Western Maryland College, located at Westminster, Md, was developed from a private academy, which, after having come under the direction of Rev J T. Ward, D D., received the sympathy and practical aid of the Maryland Conference of the Methodist Protestant Church, with which Dr. Ward was connected. Under its new control and with the name Western Maryland College the former academy entered upon an era of prosperous development The succession of Rev T H Lewis, D D, to its presidency was followed by a still greater development, until in 1903 the college had a plant and equipment worth above $200,000 A unique feature of this college is its successful attempt to train the two sexes in separate departments, thereby gaining the principle benefits of co-education without experiencing its objectionable features Western Maryland College has never received an endowment and its high place among institutions of learning in the state is due altogether to economy in administration Like some of its sister colleges, however, it receives state aid in the form of scholarships, the recipients of which engage to teach in the state after graduation The college sustains close relations with the Johns Hopkins University, its graduates being received for graduate work in that institution upon the basis of their diplomas

The Woman's College of Baltimore has given to the city the creditable distinction of being a leading center of female education. Although in close affiliation with the Methodist Episcopal Church it is undenominational in its teaching corps and in its appeal. Its inception was a memorial foundation growing out of the first centenary of American Methodism, but it is indebted to the inspiration of Rev Dr John F. Goucher, its president, for its rapid rise to a leading place among similar institutions. The first building was opened in 1888 The college comprises a group of granite buildings centered about a massive church structure, forming a collection which for architectual effectiveness is unsurpassed by anything else in the city, with the exception of the Johns Hopkins Hospital In addition to these institutions the State is fortunate in having within it a number of sectarian institutions, which, while emphasizing their particular religious affiliations, are yet splendid factors in doing the general work of education of the youth

Resuming again the general subject of Maryland events the political action of Baltimore in relation to the judiciary in 1882 is to be noticed. It had long been felt that a non-partisan judiciary was an imperative need Under the prevailing system the administration of justice had frequently been open to just criticism Baltimore with its strenuous and often turbulent political activity was especially in need of non-partisan judicial administration This feeling found concrete expression in the call of a town meeting, which was held October 18, 1882, at which, after thoroughly canvassing the subject a non-partisan "New Judge" ticket was nominated and at the ensuing election the entire ticket received the endorsement of the voters by a majority of about eleven thousand

On January 21, 1886, the hall of the House of Delegates

in the old statehouse at Annapolis was the center of interest to the people of the State. The occasion was the election of Hon. Henry Lloyd as governor of the state to fill the unexpired term of Governor McLane, who had resigned to accept the post of Minister to France, and the re-election of United States Senator Arthur Pue Gorman, who had been first elected to the Senate in 1881. Political feeling in the State was at a high tension and the re-election of Mr. Gorman was regarded as a personal triumph. Referring to the event the Baltimore Sun declared editorially that "In view of the bitter personal opposition to Mr. Gorman which developed itself in the recent city and State campaigns, the unanimity with which he had been chosen * * * is a compliment of which he has every reason to be proud."* The political contest of the following year resulted in another Democratic victory and that party seemed to be intrenched in an impregnable position in the State. The strength of Democratic control was not entirely due to the bitterness engendered by the Civil War, although the "wavers of the bloody shirt" made noisy demonstrations at every election, but was rather to be attributed to the fear of "negro domination." Not that the colored population in the state was so formidable in numbers, but the genius of the Republican party gave strength to the apprehension that its elevation to power would be followed by negro appointments to public office. When the ballots were counted it was found that Elihu E. Jackson, of Wicomico County, had carried the state by a majority of eight thousand.

The rapid growth of Baltimore City after the war had resulted in the creation of a more or less thickly populated "belt." This suburban population almost encircled the city and extended for varying distances into the limits of Baltimore County. Following the tendency towards corporate expansion prevalent in municipalities throughout the country, Baltimore, through its representatives in the legislature, clamored to have submitted to this contiguous population the question of annexation to the city. The Legislature granted such authori-

---
* Balto Sun, January 20, 1886

zation on February 21, 1888, and upon May 15th of the same year the residents of the "belt" with the exception of the Canton district on the southeast water front, voted favorably upon the question. The actual annexation took effect June 1, 1888. Thereby the population of Baltimore was increased by thirty-five thousand nine hundred and eighty. One of the conditions of the annexation was that the "belt" property should continue to be assessed at the prevailing county rate of sixty cents on the hundred dollars until after the expiration of thirteen years when the city rate was to apply, with certain exceptions in favor of unimproved lands. The question of the constitutionality of the "belt" annexation was raised and was passed upon by the Court of Appeals on November 3, 1888, and was affirmed, six of the judges concurring. The main points of the decision were that the Legislature had power to extend the limits of the city at the expense of the county, and second that it could prescribe a different rate of taxation in the annexed territory from that existing in the city proper. The principle of equality of taxation was declared to be fully gratified by establishing a uniform rate within the limits of each individual taxing district. During the same year the laws of the State were codified by Hon. John Prestiss Poe, one of the foremost jurists of the state, acting under authorization of the Legislature. The simplification and codification of the statutes was not only a clear gain for jurisprudence but it was one of the indications of the larger consciousness which had been awakened in Maryland since the Civil War.*

In 1889, the Chesapeake and Ohio Canal again became a disturbing factor in the economy of the State. It had been greatly damaged by the spring freshets of that year, and the agitation of the question of its future culminated on February 5, 1890, in Governor Jackson's message to the legislature, recommending the acceptance of a bid for the canal made by the Cumberland and Washington Railroad Company, who desired to obtain a perpetual lease of the property for railroad purposes. This action, however, threatened the

---

*Hollander, "History of State Taxation in Maryland."

State, which was the chief bondholder, with tedious and expensive litigation, as it involved the rights of the "bondholders of 1844." These took the matter into court and secured decisions both in Maryland and the District of Columbia authorizing the "bondholders of 1844" to restore the canal to a serviceable condition upon their having given bond in penalty of $600,000 that the canal should again be opened for traffic by May 1, 1891.

The agitation in favor of ballot reform which had been growing in force for a number of years found effective expression in the passage by the legislature at its session of 1890 of a modified Australian ballot law. The salient features of the new law were the erection of polling booths, with desks and curtains, in which the voter might prepare his ballot so as to insure the principle of compulsory secrecy. The printing by the State of "blanket ballots" containing in parallel columns the names of the nominees of the several political parties, with a small square at the right of each name in which the voter might place a cross mark, thus indicating the persons for whom his vote was to be counted. A square at the right of the party names and emblems enabled him to mark his ballot for the whole ticket if he so desired. The act was made to apply only to Baltimore City, and Allegany, Anne Arundel, Calvert, Cecil, Charles, Howard, Frederick, Prince Georges, Queen Annes, Somerset and St. Marys Counties.

This law was amended by the Legislature on April 2, 1896, making its administration bipartisan and throwing greater safeguards about the secrecy of the ballot. To this end, glass ballot boxes and the use of white paper for ballots, containing coupons with the signature of the election judge, etc., were prescribed. In the case of sworn illiterates assistance was to be rendered by two clerks, one from each party. In counting the ballots, the intention of the voter, when such could be arrived at by the election officials, was to govern their action. The legislature also provided for annual registrations in Baltimore City and registration at eight year intervals in the counties.

On May 14, 1891, a reception was tendered Senator Gorman by the people at the Fifth Regiment Armory in Baltimore, in recognition of his services in accomplishing the defeat of the Federal election bill, popularly known as the "force" bill The occasion of this bill was the complaints of the Republicans of the South that a system of intimidation existed which proved an effectual deterrent to negroes attempting to vote. The proposed legislation would have placed the elections in those states under the control of armed Federal deputies.

The state election of 1891 resulted in democratic success and the induction of Hon Frank Brown into the gubernatorial office. He received a majority of twenty-five thousand and thirty-one. In that year amendments to the constitution were adopted, the principle one of which invested the governor with power to veto particular items of an appropriation bill. The year 1892 was marked by destructive fires in several towns of the state On July 6th Pocomoke City, in Wicomico County, was visited with a conflagration in which $125,000 worth of property was destroyed This town was particularly unfortunate, as in 1888 it had suffered by fire a loss of a half million dollars The Pocomoke City fire was followed by one which brought upon Cambridge, Dorchester County, a loss of $65,000. This fire occurred on the 30th of July and was succeeded by a similar calamity at Delmar, a little town in Wicomico County, lying partly in Maryland and partly in Delaware. Almost the entire place was destroyed and a loss of $100,000 was entailed

The financial depression which prevailed throughout the United States during the first part of the last decade of the nineteenth century was keenly felt in Maryland Yet the financial institutions of the State maintained a strength and stability due to conservative management which evoked the praise of the moneyed centers of the country She safely weathered the storm and came out with her financial character and credit unimpaired The financial depression was reflected in industrial lethargy, and thousands of men, willing to work, were unable to find employment. Various panaceas, political and economic, were proposed for the betterment of the country's distressing conditions The most grotesque of these was

"Coxey's Army of the Commonwealth" which traversed the state in its approach to Washington, where its leader purposed to petition Congress to enact certain remedial legislation The industrial army gained no recruits in Maryland, and after the dispersion of the little band of three hundred and thirty-six men that finally reached Washington on May 31st, the ragged remnant encamped at Hyattsville Md , until as an act of mercy they were arrested and sent to the house of correction

In the spring of 1894 the industries of Western Maryland became involved in the strike of the soft coal miners which extended throughout the country. Upon June 5th Governor Frank Brown, responding to an appeal addressed to him by the sheriff of Alleghany County, called out the Fourth and Fifth Regiments and sent them to quell the disorder and to preserve the peace in that region The brigade under the command of General Stewart Brown proceeded to Frostburg, Maryland, where it remained for two weeks, at the expiration of which time it was relieved by the First Regiment under the command of Col L Allison Wilmer The prompt action of the governor without doubt tended to preserve the region from scenes of riot in which large losses of property and perhaps of life might have occurred

One of the principal causes of the financial depression and industrial unrest throughout the country was the business uncertainty consequent upon the long struggle in Congress over the passage of the Wilson Tariff Bill of 1894 That measure involved such considerable modifications of the tariff laws of the country as to amount to a virtual reversal of its economic policy. It passed the House of Representatives and was considered by the Senate which returned the bill with six hundred and thirty-four amendments Some of these were so radical that the bill was virtually emasculated, but the House was compelled to acquiesce in the action of the Senate and the bill was passed on the 13th of August. President Cleveland refused to give his endorsement to the measure in its amended form and allowed it to become a law without his signature A prominent historian and publicist alluding to the Wilson

Bill, says: "It was not the general increase of rate effected in the Senate that held the attention of the country, so much as the very noticeable activity of a group of senators in the interest of the sugar manufacturers and dealers. These headstrong, stubborn rejectors of political obligations wrecked the Democratic program and utterly discredited their party.* This citation accurately reflects a very wide contemporary opinion as to the true inwardness of the measure as amended.

During the thirty years which had elapsed since the close of the Civil War, the Democratic party had been in possession of the government of Maryland. The Republicans had met with repeated defeats. But with the lessening importance of the issues which grew out of the Civil War, new questions arose which compelled a realignment of men and parties. The commercial and financial depression to which reference has been made bore fruit in the old cry which had frequently been heard in the political history of the country—"more money and greater flexibility in its issue and circulation." The "free silver" movement of 1896 was its concrete expression. The Democratic and Populist conventions united in nominating Hon. William Jennings Bryan, of Nebraska, on a platform which pledged the Democratic party and its ally to "the free and unlimited coinage of silver, at a ratio of sixteen to one." The Republican national convention took an equally positive position in favor of "sound money" currency based upon the single or gold standard, and put in nomination as its candidate Hon. William McKinley, of Ohio, whose name had been associated with an important revenue measure. The "sound money" wing of the Democratic party went before the country on a separate ticket with Senator Palmer, of Illinois, as its candidate. The third ticket, however, was not largely voted, that section of the Democratic party which could not follow the silver champion preferring to give its support to the Republican candidate. Rarely in the history of the nation has the presidential contest so stirred the feelings of the people; the result was the complete triumph of the "sound money" cause and the

---
*Woodrow Wilson, "History of the American People," vol. 5, pp. 228-9.

election of Hon. William McKinley to the presidency of the United States Maryland now swung from her former allegience and cast a Republican majority of twenty-one thousand Hon Lloyd Lowndes, the Republican candidate for governor of the state, was also elected, together with a majority of the legislature Maryland could no longer be counted with the Solid South, but had entered the column of "doubtful states" Indeed a new era of political history had been entered upon and the state learned to cherish the greater prerogatives which the people might exercise by maintaining an independent vote, unorganized and for that reason less calculable and controlable

In 1897 an active propaganda in favor of the grant by the Legislature of a new charter for the city of Baltimore was carried to successful issue. It was felt that the city government was archaic, cumbersome and inadequate The needs of the city could no longer be satisfied with the form of city control of the past, which, while it did not give rise to serious scandals of administration, was nevertheless too loose for the honest and faithful conduct of the municipal departments. Accordingly the legislature appointed a charter commission and authorized it to draw a new instrument of government for Baltimore City The personnel of the commission was of high order. It embraced men of breadth of spirit and varied experience. In due process the charter commission made its report which was accepted and the new government for Baltimore went into effect. Its salient features were provision for the election of a mayor to hold office for four years with a large measure of personal responsibility for the proper conduct of the several departments of the government; a city council of two branches with ordinance-making powers which, however, were limited by reserving certain of its powers for the Boards of Estimates and Public Improvements The charter provides for departments of finance, law, public safety, public improvement, parks and squares, education, charities and correction, and taxes and assessments. To the Board of Estimates was given the preparation of the annual estimates of the expense of conducting the municipal government. It was constituted a board of reference for the city council in the consideration of application for franchises. All ordinances relating to new improvements whose cost would be above $2,000 had also to be approved by this board. The Board of Estimates was to embrace the mayor, city solicitor, comptroller, president of the second branch of the city council, and the president of the Board of Public Improvement. Other boards specified were the Board of Public Safety, to be composed of the president of the fire commissioners, the commissioner of health, the inspector of buildings, the commissioner of street cleaning and the president of the board of police commissioners; the Board of Public Improvement to consist of the city engineer, the president of the water board, the president of the harbor board and the inspector of buildings; the Board of Park Commissioners; the Board of School Commissioners, and that of Charities and Correction. There were also constituted a Board of Review and Assessment, to be composed of the president of the appeal tax court, the president of the commissioners for opening streets and the mayor. It was given simply advisory powers. Other city officers named were the city librarian, superintendent of lamps and lighting, surveyor and constables, superintendent of public buildings and the art commission.

In 1898, the call to war once more thrilled Maryland with patriotic responsiveness. Cuba, the last remnant of the magnificent empire, which Columbus, Pizarro and Cortez had given to the crown of Spain, appealed in her extremity to the United States for relief from the crushing tyranny against which she had long struggled. The appeal was not in vain, but the action of this country was stimulated by the mysterious destruction of the United States battleship Maine in Havana harbor, February 15, 1898. This act was popularly attributed to the Spanish, either with or without official cognizance. On the 21st of the following April Congress declared war with Spain and President McKinley issued a call for volunteers. Two days later Governor Lowndes called the Maryland troops to their colors and on the 25th they encamped at Pimlico. On May 13th the state naval militia, numbering two officers and two hundred and thirty men, were mustered into service and embarked on the cruiser Dixie at Norfolk, Va. On the 19th of May the Fifth Maryland regiment, now officially enrolled in the service of the nation, left Pimlico for the concentration camp which the War Department had established at Chickamauga, Tennessee. The rapid movement of events and the monotony of victory gave but a small part of the United States Army mobilized at Chickamauga and at Tampa, Florida, the opportunity to see active service. The Maryland regiments were not included in the favored minority. Nevertheless, Maryland's proud record of achievement upon the seas in the battles of the nation was gloriously sustained by the performances of a son of Western Maryland, Admiral Winfield Scott Schley, who won a great naval victory off Santiago, July 3d, 1898 sharing with the conqueror of Manila the brightest laurels of the Spanish-American war. On August 12th the peace protocol was signed at Washington. The treaty of Paris between Spain and the United States was ratified by the Senate on April 11th, 1899, less than a year from the time of the declaration of war. One of the gratifying features of this war was the bringing together upon the battle ground in a common cause of the men who had worn the Grey and those who had worn the Blue.

On November 2, 1899, the verdict of the people which placed the Republican party in power in the state was reversed by the election of Hon. John Walter Smith as governor. The United States census of 1900 having disclosed evidence of fraud in the enumerations made in some of the southern counties with apparent ulterior political intent, the governor called a special session of the legislature to take action in the matter. This was an extraordinary recourse which had been resorted only once before in the history of the State. This body assembled at Annapolis and authorized the taking of a state census, and before adjourning proceeded to formulate and adopt new election laws which added more stringent conditions to the exercise of the electoral franchise. In this legislation the main features of the Act of 1896 were retained, but party emblems were removed from the ballots, the names of candidates grouped together in alphabetical order and a separate cross mark was required to be placed within the square next to the name of each candidate for whom the vote was cast. In a test case, the Court of Appeals decided that these marks must be of a uniform character, be entirely within the square, and that there must not be any extraneous marks or blemishes of any nature. The effect of this decision was to deprive the "intention of the voter" of any weight in determining the validity of his ballot. No help was permitted to be given illiterates, and even those physically incapacitated were required to orally name the candidates for whom they desired the clerks to mark their ballots. The party responsible for the framing of the new election law disowned any intention of making the conditions as rigid as they came to be under the court's interpretation. These extreme features were mainly intended for the disfranchisement of the illiterate negro vote, but they worked general hardship. In the next state election, November 5, 1903, an appalling number of ballots were thrown out by the judges and the work of counting the vote was so considerable that it was the morning of the third day after the election before the result was definitely known. In some precincts of Baltimore City the count required nearly forty hours. In this campaign both parties pledged themselves to the reform of the ballot law, while the Democrats based their appeal to the electorate principally upon the cry "Maryland is a white man's state." The contest resulted in the election of Hon. Edwin Warfield, the Democratic candidate for governor; a large majority of the legislature chosen being of the same political faith. The 13th of January witnessed the inauguration of the new governor.

INDEX.

Alexander, Robert, delegate to Congress, 159

Allegheny County, erected, 91.

Allen, John, captain of rangers for protection of frontier, 71.

Altham, Father John, accompanies colonists, 15.

Andros, Sir Edmond, assumes government, 79

Annapolis, becomes seat of government, 78; made a city in 1708, 79, council of Colonial Governors meets at, 104; Washington received at, 251, offered to general government for capitol, 258. Washington resigns his commission at, 259; attempt to remove Naval Academy from, 398

Annapolis & Potomac Canal, 321

Anne Arundel County, founded in 1650, 66

Antietam, Battle of, 381.

Ark & Dove, set sail from Cowes, November 22d, 1633, 16.

Armistead Monument, 329.

Armstrong, Captain, killed, 246

Army of the Revolution, reorganization of Maryland Troops, 178-179; Maryland Troops in Congressional Army, 185; composition of Maryland Line, 188.

Assembly called by Governor in 1635, 30, summoned by Governor in 1638, 31, vetoes laws of Lord Baltimore, 32; new assembly called in 1639, 41; constitution of, 42, convened by Puritans at Patuxent 1657, 62

Association of Freemen of Maryland, 151

Associators, organization known as, 132.

Australian ballot, 413.

Avalon, province of, granted George Calvert, 13.

Ballard, Robt, surveyor, 277

Baltimore, addition to in 1732, 88, town laid out 1729, 88; Congress removes to, 182;

Baltimore clippers, 280; defense of 1812, 300; growth of, 307; yellow fever epidemic, 309, convention of Unionists meets at, 363, Republican convention 1864 meets at, 390, sesqui-centennial, 403, annexation act, 1888, 411, flood of 1868, 400; National Democratic Convention, 1872, 401; new charter, 417.
Baltimore, Lord. See Calvert and Proprietary
Baltimore County, founded in 1659, 66.
Baltimore & Ohio Railroad, 312, 321.
Baltimore & Susquehanna Railroad, 313, 322.
Banks, Gen, assumes command of Baltimore, 370.
Barney, Commodore, taken prisoner, 297.
Barney, Capt. Joshua, 277.
Battle Monument, 329.
Beatty, Capt., slain, 244.
Beauregard, General, 365.
Benedict, British troops land at, 295.
Bennett, Richard, head of Puritan colony in Anne Arundel, 53, receives commission to reduce Virginia and Barbadoes, 54, declared governor of Virginia, 55
Benson, Captain, 245.
Bill of Rights. adopted Nov. 3d, 1776, 179.
Black Friday, 401.
Blackstones Island, colonists land on, 19.
Bladen. Thomas, governor 1742, 90
Blair, Montgomery, postmaster-general, 365; 393, 401
Boundaries of Maryland, 94
Boundary disputes. 95-100.
Bowie, Lieut Oden, 335
Braddock, Gen., meets Colonial Governors, 105; killed, 107.
Bradford, Augustus W., 362, governor, 373
Brent, Giles, appointed lieutenant-general. 44.
Brent, Mistress Margaret, administratrix of Gov. Leonard Calvert, 49.
Brooke, Richard, brings colony to Charles, 54; commander Charles Co., 54.
Brooke, Robert, president of council and acting governor, 55
Brown, Frank. elected governor, 414
Brown, Geo. Wm., 352.
Brown, Gen. Stewart, 415
Bryan, W. J., 416.
Buchanan, Capt., commands the Merrimac, 377.
Bull Run, battle of, 371.
Butler, Gen, stationed at Federal Hill, 369.

INDEX.   423

Cabot, Sebastian, starts on voyage of discovery, May, 1498, 6; probably visited Worcester County, 7; touches American Continent, 7, discovers Newfoundland and Island of St. John, 7.

Cabot, John, license issued to, Feb 3d, 1498, to seize English ships, 6.

Calvert, Benedict Leonard, nominal governor, 1684, 74; becomes Lord Proprietary, Feb 20th, 1714, 84; dies April 16th, 1715, 84.

Calvert, Benedict Leonard, governor 1727, 90.

Calvert, Cecil, infant son of Charles Calvert, nominal governor, 73.

Calvert, Cecilius, receives charter, 14; rejects laws submitted by assembly and prepares others, 31, grants people right to originate laws, 41; re-establishes proprietary government, 57; government restored to, after Puritan rebellion, 63, dies Nov. 30th, 1675, 72.

Calvert, Charles, becomes governor in 1662, 66; becomes Lord Proprietary, Nov. 30th, 1675, 72; returns to England in 1676, 73, returns to Maryland in 1680, 73, appoints council of 9 deputies, 74; returns to England in 1684, 74, dies 20th Feb, 1714, 83.

Calvert, Charles, April 16th, 1715, becomes Lord Proprietary, 84; governors under, 90; dies in 1751, 90

Calvert, Charles, governor in 1727, 90.

Calvert, Frederick, becomes Proprietary in 1751, 101, dies in 1771, 144

Calvert, Sir George, interested in London Company, 12; early life of, 12-13, royal commissioner of Virginia Company, 13; sails to Newfoundland, 13, sails to Virginia, 13, explores Chesapeake, 13; prepared charter of Maryland, 14

Calvert, Leonard, appointed governor, 15; authorized to approve laws, 41; returns to England, 44, returns to Maryland, 45, compelled to flee to Virginia, 46, retakes St Marys, 47; dies in St. Marys, 48

Calvert, Philip, appointed secretary of province, 61; appointed governor, 64, superseded by Charles Calvert, 1662, 66, commissioner to settle boundary dispute, 95.

Calvert County, founded in 1654, 66

Cambridge, great fire, 414
Camden, Lord, resolution of House of Delegates commending, 133.
Campbell, Captain, raises company for Canadian expedition, 90.
Canada, expedition against, 90.
Carmichael, Judge Richard, 396.
Carmichael, Judge Richard Bennett, 377.
Capitol, corner-stone laid Sept 18th, 1793, 278.
Caroline County, erected, 91.
Carroll, Charles, commissioner to purchase Indian lands 87; Baltimore on lands of, 88; commissioner to Albany convention, 102.
Carroll of Carrollton, Charles, 139, member of correspondence committee, 148; opposes increase in pay of delegates, 210; 272; first U S. senator, 275; opposition to slavery, 342.
Carroll, Charles, barrister, member of correspondence committee, 148.
Carroll, Daniel, 272
Carroll, Rev John, first Catholic bishop, 268
Carroll County, erected, 91.
Cecil County, erected, 91.
Charles County, founded in 1658, 66

Charter of Maryland, prepared by George Calvert, 14; issued to Cecilius Calvert, 14; provisions of, 14, bill in Parliament for reduction of, 81.
Chase, Samuel, delegate to Congress, 142; member correspondence committee, 148; delegate to Congress, 159
Chesapeake and Delaware Canal, 269.
Chesapeake and Ohio Canal, 311, 321, 412.
Chesapeake Bay, discovered in 1585 by Governor Lane of Virginia, 7, explored by Captain John Smith, 9, explored by John Pory, 11; George Calvert explores, 13, blockaded by British, 1812, 291.
Cincinnati, Society of, 257; Maryland officers, 257.
Civil War, Massachusetts regiment mobbed, 366; Capt. Johnson organizes Confederate company, 369, Battle of Bull Run, 371, Battle of Front Royal, 377, Lee invades Maryland, 379; Battle of Antietam, 381, Battle of Gettysburg, 385.
Claiborne, William, first rebellion, 27-30 sent to England for trial, 29; attainted, 33; presents petition to

King, 34, takes possession of Kent, 45; obtains possession of province, 46; receives commission to reduce Virginia and Barbadoes, 54; declared secretary of Virginia, 55; Kent and Palmer's Islands, delivered to, 55; with Richard Bennett takes possession of Province, 57.

Clergy, tax for support of, 92.

Coale, Jas. M., president C. & O Canal, 325

Coke, Dr. Thomas, superintendent of Methodist Church, 268

Colonists, names of first, 42.

Committee of Correspondence, 151.

Committee of Safety, 151; given supreme power, 182; surrenders its powers, 185.

Confederation, articles of signed, 217-19.

Confiscation of British property, 215-16

Congress, colonial representatives to, 126; proceedings approved, 128, meets in New York, 128, delegates to, 148

Conolly, John, appointed Lieutenant-Colonel by General Gage, 154.

Constitution, new constitution and State government, chapter X; constitutional convention, 160, committee to report on form of government, 177, agreed to by convention, election ordered, Nov 3d, 1776, 179; judicial system, 180; government and elections under, 180-181, constitution ratified, 274, amendments of 1840, 320 constitution of 1867, 396

Convention, assumes government, 147.

Coode, John, attempt to excite rebellion, 74; heads Protestant revolution, 75.

Copley, Sir Lionel, appointed governor, 76, succeeded in 1691 by Nicholson, 79.

Cornwallis, Captain, commands vessels of Calvert against attack of Claiborne, 29, appointed to command expedition against Indians, 45.

Court, established in Kent, 31, established in St. Marys, 1639, 41.

Cowpens, battle of, 231.

Coxey's Army, 415

Cresap, Michael, 152.

Cresap, Col Thomas, Indian fighter, 112.

Cresap, Jr, Joseph, 152

Crisfield, John W., 362.

Croft, Captain, raises company for Canadian expedition, 190.

Cromwell, Oliver, Baltimore and Puritans appeal to, 60.
Cross, Col. Trueman, 333.
Cuban War, 418.

Dagworthy, Colonel, commands Fort Frederick, 111.
Dagworthy, Capt., asserts right to command at Cumberland, 109.
Darrell, Thomas, 42
Davis, Henry Winter, elected to Congress, 349.
Davis, Richard, 152
Declaration of Independence, 159.
De Kalb, death, 227; monument to, 227.
Democratic National Convention, 1860. 357
Democratic Convention 1872 at Baltimore, 401.
Deputies of Charles Calvert, appointment, 74; dissatisfaction with, 75.
District of Columbia, laid out 1790, 277.
Dorchester County, erected, 91.
Dorsey, Col Edward, 80.
Dred Scott decision, 354.
Dulany, Daniel, opposes taxation of colony, 127
Dulany, Patrick, lays out town of Frederick, 88.
Dunmore, Gov., schemes of against patriots, 153-4, raises companies to support royal cause, 154, arrested, 154.
Dutch of New York, drive out settlers beyond Schuylkill, 41.
Duties, port, 66.
Duvall, Lieut, killed, 248

Eastern Shore R. R, 321.
Eden, Robert, Gov, 144; commanded to leave the colony, 157
Elkridge Landing, 88.
Electoral College for the Senate of Md. and the Van Buren electors, 314-319.
Elliott, Lieut. Jesse Duncan, 289.
Eltonhead, William, sent by Lord Baltimore with instructions to Gov Stone, 57; heads party sent to recover records, 58; shot by Puritans, 60.
Elzey, John, commissioner to make settlements on Eastern Shore, 94
Emancipation Proclamation, 381.
Episcopal Church, first bishop in America, 268.
Evelin, Capt George, appointed commander of Kent, 31
Everheart, Sergeant, 233.

Fairfax, Nicholas, 42.
Fell, Edward, addition to Baltimore on lands of, 88.

INDEX.

Fendall, Josias, heads party sent to recover records, 58; appointed governor July 10th, 1656, 60; arrested by Puritans, 61; schemes to deprive proprietary of powers, 64, attempt to incite rebellion, 74.
Findlay, J. V. L., 374.
First settlement of Maryland, 16.
Fitzhugh, Colonel, commands forces against French, 103
Fleet, Capt. Henry, accompanies Gov. Calvert as interpreter, 21.
Ford, Lieut Col, 238; mortally wounded, 243
Ford, 256.
Fort McHenry, 286.
Fort Mifflin, attack upon, 196.
Fort Sumpter, fired upon, 365.
Fort Washington, defense of, 171.
Fox, George, preaches in Maryland, 70-71
Frederick, laid out 1745, 88.
Frederick county, erected, 91.
Frederick county, erected, 91
Fredericktown, burned by British, 292.
French and Indian War, chapter VI, appropriation for, 103; battle at Monongohela, 106; forty thousands pounds appropriated by Maryland, 110; settlements in Western Maryland abandoned, 112; English defeated at Fort Duquesne, 118
Frenchtown, burned by British, 299
Front Royal, battle of, 377
Fuller, Captain, commander expedition, 56; placed at head of Province by commissioners, 57.

Garrett, Mrs. Mary E., gift to J. H U., 409
Gary, Jas. A., 403.
Gas Company, formed, 330
Genet, minister of French Directory, 281.
Georgetown, laid out in 1751, 89
Georgetown (on Eastern shore) burned by British, 292
Gerard, Richard, 42
Germantown, attack upon, 193-196
Gettysburg, battle of, 385.
Genalles, John, commands party sent to watch insurgents, 45
Gilman, Dan C, Pres J. H. U, 408.
Gilmour, Col Harry, 385.
Gist. Genl. 249, 256.
Goldsborough, Robert, delegate to Congress, 142.
Goldsborough, Wm S., 362.

INDEX

Gorman, Arthur Pue, re-elected to U. S Senate, 411.
Goucher, Rev. John F., pres Woman's College, 410.
Government under first Constitution, 180
Grants of lots in City of St. Marys and tracts in interior, terms of, 30.
Greeley. Horace, presidential nominee, 401.
Green, Henry, 42.
Green, Jonas, printer to the Province; issues Maryland Gazette, 88.
Greene, Thomas, appointed governor of Maryland, 48; proclaims pardon for all rebels but Ingle, 49, issues proclamation directing seizure of corn, 49
Griffith, Goldsborough S., 387
Gunby, Col., 238; 256.

Habeas Corpus, writ of suspended by Lincoln, 370.
Hall, John, member correspondence committee, 148
Hall, 256.
Hamilton, Wm. T., 400, elected governor, 403
Hancock, Fort Frederick erected at, 111.
Hanson, Alex Contee, 286
Harford County, erected, 91.
Harford Henry, province devised to, 144.
Harrison, Robt. Hanson, 276; 272; justice Supreme Court, 277.
Hart, John, governor 1715, 90
Harvey, governor, visits St. Marys, 27
Hatton, Thomas, secretary of Province, slain in battle with Puritans March 25th, 1655, 59.
Havre de Grace, burned by British, 292
Hawley, Jerome, 42
Heamans, Capt., commander of the "Golden Lyon," 58
Henry, John, U S senator, 275
Heron Islands, colonists land on, 19.
Hicks, Gov, sides with Union, 361.
Hill, Captain, appointed Governor by council, retires to Virginia, 47
Hill, Capt. John, 42.
Hood, Zachariah, compelled to resign as stamp distributor, 125
Hopkins, Commodore, commands first Continental fleet, 157
Howard, Col, 240
Howard, General, 233, 256
Howard, John Eager, 281.
Husbands, Edward, charged with attempt to poison gov-

ernor and assembly, 73.

Indented apprentices, 69
Indians of St Marys, account of, 23.
Indians, missionaries to, 35; Tayac baptised, 37; Nanticokes, 38; Indian tribes in Maryland, 38, expedition against in 1639, 39, uprising of Nanticokes, 55, treaty with Susquehannahs, 55; Senecas invade Maryland, 71, required to pay tribute to Proprietary, 86, laws for protection of, 86, purchase of lands from Six Nations, 87, co-operate with Maryland troops, 115.
Industries, act to encourage, 92, pig-iron, 123.
Ingle, Capt. Richard, stirs up insurrection, 45, captured, 45, 49.
Insurrection against whiskey tax, 280

Jackson, Elihu E., elected governor, 411.
Jamestown, founded May 13th, 1607, 8.
Jenifer, Daniel, of St Thomas, 272.
Jews, religion of not tolerated, 146, enfranchised, 330.
Johnson, Capt Bradley T., 369, 378; 390.
Johnson, Reverdy attorney-general, 338, 362, minister to England, 400.
Johnson, Thomas, 135, elected governor, 184; 276, address of legislature in honor of, 214.
Johnson, William Cost, 345.
Johnson, Jr., Thomas, member correspondence committee, 148, delegate to Congress, 159
Jones, Thomas, judge Court of Appeals, 201.
Johns Hopkins University, 407
Jones Falls, 400.
Jordan, Captain, raises company for Canadian expedition, 90.
Joseph, William, president of council of deputies, 74.
Judicial System, under constitution 1776, 180
Judiciary, Court of Appeals organized, 201

Kane, Col., arrested, 371
Kane, Marshal, 367.
Kenly, Col, 372; appointed provost marshal, 371; 334; 336.
Key, Francis Scott, composes Star Spangled Banner, 304
Key, John Ross, 152
Kent County, founded in 1650 66
Kent Island, court established

in, 31, Capt Evelin appointed commander of, 31; Calvert makes expedition against, 31.

King, Dr. Robert, commissioner to purchase Indian lands, 87

King Williams School, established 1696, 80.

Knownothingism, 347.

La Fayette, entertained at Baltimore, 250; visits Annapolis, 267; naturalized, 267; visits Maryland in 1825, 330

Latrobe, Benj H, surveys canal route, 269.

Laws, important acts passed in 1639, 41; summary of laws passed in 1663-4, 67; revised and ascertained, 72; codified, 412.

Laws of England, declared to be in force in Province, 67.

Lee, Robt E., invades Maryland, 379

Lee, Thomas Sim, elected governor 1779, 214.

Leonard, Col. Wm. J, 395.

Lewger, 37; 46.

Lewis, Rev. T H, pres. Western Md. College, 409.

Lexington, battle of, 149.

Lincoln, Abraham, emancipation proclamation, 381.

Lloyd, Col Edward, candidate for governor, 214.

Lloyd, Henry, elected governor, 411.

London Company, founded in 1606, 8; fleet of, sets sail from Blackwell, Dec 19th, 1606, 8; letters patent issued to April 10th, 1606, 8; fleet of, driven into Chesapeake, 8; 2d charter issued May 23d, 1609, 11; 3d charter issued March 12th, 1610, 11, writ of quo warranto issued against in November, 1623, 11.

Long Island, battle of, Maryland troops in, 162-166.

Lowndes, Lloyd, elected governor, 417.

McClellan, Gen Geo. B., 372

McHenry, James, 272.

Mackall, Benjamin, judge Court of Appeals, 201.

McKeasy, Alexander, 112.

McSherry, Rev. Wm., 24

Maryland, first settlement of, 16.

Maryland Cross-cut Canal, 321.

Maryland line, Col. Otho H. Williams, given command, 229, battle at Eutaw Springs, 247, 251; part taken in Revolution, 255.

Marine, State marine re-established, 255

Martin, Luther, 272; 273.

INDEX.

Mattapany, missionary station established at, 34; 35; expedition against Nanticokes, ordered to rendezvous at, 56; deputies besieged at, 75
Medcalf, John, 42.
Medical Society of Baltimore, 406
Mercer, John Francis, 272.
Merrimac and Monitor, engagement between, 377.
Methodist Church, superintendent appointed in America, 268.
Mexican War, Col. Freeman Cross murdered, 333; City of Mexico, assaulted, 337.
Mint established, 65
Missouri Compromise, 353
Money, paper money issued, 93, tobacco, legal tender, 93, paper money issued by convention, 151, Continental issues redeemed, 217; bills of credit issued, 252, paper currency, issue of 1786, 263-4.
Monmouth, battle of, 203, 206.
Monongahela, battle at, 106.
Montgomery County, erected, 91, 177
Murdock, William, representative to Colonial Congress, 126.
Murray, James, judge Court of Appeals, 201.

Naturalization, laws passed in 1666, 70; 213.
Naval Academy, attempt to remove, 398.
Naval affairs, Colonial, engagement between vessels of Baltimore and Claiborne, 29, 58; expedition against Spanish dominions, 89; Revolution, first continental fleet, 156-7; Chesapeake fleet, 1777-9, 208; War of 1812, capture of Caledonia and Detroit, 289; Chesapeake Bay blockaded, 291, British fleet in Chesapeake, 293; Commodore Barney destroys his fleet, 296. Civil War; Merrimac and Monitor, 376
Newfoundland, George Calvert sails for, 13.
New-Judge movement, 410
Newport, Capt. Christopher, commander of fleet of London Company, 8
Newspaper, Maryland Gazette issued 1745, 88
Nicholson, Francis. governor in 1691, 79.
Nicholson, commands the Defense, 156, given command of the Virginia, 157.
North Point, battle of, 300.
Notely, Thomas, appointed deputy governor, 73

Odd Fellows, organized in

Baltimore 1819, 309.
Ogle, Samuel, governor in 1727, 90.
Ohio Company, grant to, 101.
Oldham, Capt., 244.

Paca, William, 135; delegate to Congress, 142, member correspondence committee, 148, delegate to Congress, 159, judge U S. District Court, 277.
Peabody, George, 407.
Peabody Institute, 407.
Peggy Stewart, burning of, 142
Pheypo, Mark, commands party sent to watch insurgents, 45.
Piscataways, territory of, 35.
Pitt, William, resolution of House of Delegates commending, 133.
Piater, Geo., president Constitutional Convention 274.
Plymouth Company, founded in 1606, 8, letters patent issued to May 10th, 1606, 8
Pocomoke City, great fire, 414
Poe, John P., 412.
Population of Province, 66, in 1671, 82; in 1748 and 1756, 91, in 1761, 123
Pory, John, explores Chesapeake, 11
Port Tobacco, 37.

Post, public, established 1695, 80.
Potomac Company, 265; surrenders its charter, 311.
Potomac River, explored by Capt. John Smith, 10.
Potts, Richard, U S. district attorney, 277.
Preston, Richard, 58
Price, Thomas, 152.
Prince George's County erected, 91.
Princeton, taken by Americans, 175.
Printing Press, established 1726, 88
Proprietary, veto power, 33; attempt to deprive of rights, 77. opposition to duties levied by, 85; quit rents of abolished, 217; $50,000 paid in commutation of claims, 261
Protestant Revolution, chapter II; chapter IV
Providence, Puritans settle at, 53, expedition, sent by Gov. Stone against, 58; becomes seat of government, 78; name changed to Annapolis, 78.
Public School System, 404.
Pulaski, Count, forms his legion, 199
Puritans, settle in Anne Arundel, 53; send representatives to St. Marys, 54, Gov. Stone sends expedition

INDEX. 433

against Providence, 58; convene Assembly at Patuxent 1657, 62; ascendency of ended 1658, 63.
Purviance, Robt., 277.

Queen Anne's County, erected, 91

Ramsey, 256
Ramsey, Col N, 277
Rawlings, Col. Moses, 152.
Redemptioners, 69
Religion, toleration guaranteed by oath of office, 50, act of Assembly to protect freedom of worship, 50-53; Catholics disfranchised by Puritan government, 57; intolerance of Puritans, 57; Episcopal Church denounced by Puritan Assembly, 57; pledge of Lord Baltimore not to repeal law in favor of toleration, 62; religious toleration extended to "Friends," 70, first attempt to establish Episcopal Church, 73. Episcopal Church established May 10th, 1692, 76; persecution of Catholics, 77; toleration not extended to Jews, 146; state church disestablished by convention 1776, 181; ecclesiastical organizations in America, 268
Restoration of the Province, chapter V

Revell, Randall, commissioner to make settlements on Eastern Shore, 94.
Revolution, depredations on Bay counties, 153, regular force formed by Maryland, 151; powder mills erected, implements of war manufactured, 153, merchant vessels armed, 155; the Defense recaptures prizes, 155; Defense captures the Otter, 155; batteries erected near Baltimore and Annapolis, 155, instructions given delegates, 159; Maryland raises more troops, 160; Maryland troops at Long Island, 162-166; covers Washington's retreat, 167; Battle of White Plains, 169; Trenton and Princeton taken, 173-175; insurrection in Worcester County, 184; attack upon Fort Mifflin, 196; attack upon Germantown, 193-196, Maryland line stationed at Wilmington, while main body of troops at Valley Forge, 198, Battle of Mommouth, 206; Maryland's part in, 255; campaign of 1777, chapter XI, Southern campaigns, chapter XIV.
Revolution, Protestant, chapter II

Ringgold, Thomas, representative to Colonial Congress, 126
Roman, J. Dixon, 362
Rumsey, Benjamin, judge of Court of Appeals, 201.
Rumsey, James, invents first steamboat, 267

St Clements, colonists land on, 19.
St Marys City, colonists settle at, March 27th, 1634, 21; grant of lots in, 30; seat of government removed from, 78, possession obtained by Baltimore. 61.
St Mary's County, founded in 1634, 66.
St Mattapany See Mattapany
St Gregory, Potomac given name of, 19.
St Johns College, 406
Saire, William, 42
Scarborough, Edmond, commissioner to make settlements on Eastern Shore, 194.
Schley, Winfield Scott, 419.
Schools and colleges—King Williams School, established 1696, 80.
School System, adopted, 329.
Secession, Northern views on right of, 375.
Senators, election of, 275; one to be from each shore, 275.
Sharpe, Gov, commands forces against French, 103.
Slavery, laws relating to passed 1663-4, 67-68; introduction of, 68; in Maryland, 339, ordinance introduced by Thomas Jefferson, 340; Abolition Society, 342; Colonization Society, 343; insurrection of Nat Turner, 344, Wilmot proviso, 354; Helper's Inpending Crisis, 356, Maryland Constitution of '64 abolishes, 389, slaves serve in Revolutionary army, 229
Slye, Robert, associate in Fendall's rebellion, 64
Smallwood, William, 135, given command of battalion, 151, wounded 169, succeeds to command of Maryland line, 227, 229; 256, elected governor, 269
Smith, Capt John, explores Chesapeake. 9, explores Potomac, 10
Smith, Capt. 240
Smith, 256
Smith, Gen Samuel, 300
Smith, John Walter, elected governor, 419
Somerset County, erected, 91.
Spain, expedition against Spanish dominions, 89.
Stamp Act, 124, Assembly

protests against, 125; stamp distributor compelled to resign, 125, declared unconstitutional, 132; 133.
Star Spangled Banner, 304
Statehouse, provision for erection, 43; destroyed by fire, 80, house of Col. Ed. Dorsey used, 80.
State Sovereignty, convention instructs delegates to maintain, 182
Steamboats, invented by Rumsey, 267
Stevenson, Col., 152.
Stewart, Maj. John, receives medal for gallant conduct at Stoney Point, 207.
Strike on B. & O. R. R, 1877, 402.
Strike of 1894, 415.
Stone, Thomas, delegate to Congress, 159; 272
Stone, 256.
Stone, William, appointed governor, 50, commission seized and removed from office, 55; reinstated in office, 55, sends party to recover records, 58; wounded in battle with Puritans, March 25th, 1655, 59.
Suffrage, right of extended, 282
Susquehanna Canal, 264.
Susquehannahs, treaty with, 55.
Swann, Thomas, elected governor, 350.

Talbot County, founded in 1660-61, 66.
Taney, Roger B., Dred Scott decision, 354; denies right of president to suspend writ of habeas corpus, 370.
Tasker, Benjamin, commissioner to Albany Convention, 102.
Taxation, Province exempt from taxation by Crown, 14, Lord Baltimore granted duty on tobacco, 73, opposition to duties levied by Proprietary, 85, tax on bachelors, 111; contest between Assembly and Proprietary as to right to impose, 122; Stamp Act imposed, 124; Congress levies tax on whiskey, 278; whiskey insurrection, 280.
Tax on tea, levied by Parliament, 134; resolutions of Maryland Assembly, 135; agreement of people for non-importation, 136, "The Good Intent" compelled to return, 136; the "Maryland Jane" returned to London, 142, the "Peggy Stewart" burned, 142
Tayac, chief of Piscataways, converted to Christianity, 35.
Taylor, General, elected presi-

dent, 338.
Telegraph, constructed from Baltimore to Washington, 331.
Tide Water Canal Co., 322.
Tilghman, Edward, representative to Colonial Congress, 126
Tilghman, Matthew, 135, delegate to Congress, 142; on correspondence committee, 148, delegate to Congress, 159, president of constitutional convention 1776, 177.
Tithes, collection of opposed, 137
Tobacco, inspection house for, 89 legal tender, 94.
Tories, taxation of, 212; property confiscated, 215-16, insurrection of, 253
Towson, Capt. Nathan, 288, 289
Trade, with foreign governments prohibited, 56.
Treaty, with "Six Nations," 87.
Trenton, taken by Americans, 173-4
Trueman, Major, commands expedition against Seneccas, 72, impeached for putting Indian chiefs to death, 72

Union of colonies, plan for disapproved, 102.

University of Maryland, 405; 406
Upper Marlborough, records removed to, 155

Verazzini, Giovanni, first to cross mouth of the Chesapeake, 7.
Virginia Company. See London Company.
Voting, secret ballot inaugurated, 283.
Voyage of first colonists, account of, 16-19

Wallis, S Teackle, 361
War of 1812, chapter XVII
Ward, Rev. J T, president Western Maryland College, 409.
Ware, Francis, 135
Warfield, Edwin, elected governor, 420
Warren, Lieutenant, commands Clairborne's vessel, 29
Warren, Thomas, 152
Washington, George, aid-de-camp to Braddock, 105; elected President, 276, sent on embassy to France, 102; resigns commission of colonel, 104; portrait of, placed in House of Delegates, 267; given command of army against French Directory by President Adams, 281, monument erected to, 329.

INDEX. 437

Washington City, taken by British, 297-9.
Washington College, 406
Washington County, erected 1776, 177.
Watson, Col. W. H , 334.
Western lands, Virginia's claims denounced, 179, Maryland protests against claims of Virginia, 202, ceded to the U S , 219
Western Maryland College, 409.
White, Father Andrew, accompanies colonists, 15; sent in chains to England, 46, dies in London, Dec 27th, 1656, 47.
White Plains, battle of, 169.

Whyte, Wm Pinckney, U S. senator, 400.
Wildey, Thomas, 309
Williams, Otho H , 152; prisoner, 172, given command Maryland line, 229, 256; collector Port of Baltimore, 277.
Wilmer, Col L. Allison, 415
Winder, Col William, 288.
Wintour, Edward, 42.
Wiseman, Henry, 42.
Woman's College, of Baltimore, 410.
Worcester County, erected, 91
Wright, Solomon. judge Court of Appeals, 201
Yellow Fever epidemic, 309

H. E. HOUCK & Co.,
PRINTERS,
BALTIMORE, MD.

CPSIA information can be obtained at www.ICGtesting.com
Printed in the USA
LVOW09*1013120616

492274LV00012B/142/P